# NADIA BOULANGER AND HER WORLD

THE BARD MUSIC FESTIVAL

LEON BOTSTEIN AND CHRISTOPHER H. GIBBS,
SERIES EDITORS

# NADIA BOULANGER
## AND HER WORLD

### EDITED BY JEANICE BROOKS

THE UNIVERSITY OF CHICAGO PRESS
CHICAGO AND LONDON

The University of Chicago Press, Chicago 60637
The University of Chicago Press, Ltd., London
© 2020 The Bard Music Festival
Published 2020
Printed in the United States of America

29 28 27 26 25 24 23 22 21 20   1 2 3 4 5

Cloth ISBN-13: 978-0-226-75068-2
Paper ISBN-13: 978-0-226-75071-2
E-book ISBN-13: 978-0-226-75085-9
DOI: https://doi.org/10.7208/chicago/9780226750859.001.0001

This publication has been produced by the Bard College Publications Office:
Irene Zedlacher, project director
Karen Spencer, design
Text edited by Paul De Angelis and Erin Clermont
Music typeset by Christopher Deschene
Indexed by Scott Smiley

This publication has been underwritten in part by grants from
Roger and Helen Alcaly and Kathleen Vuillet Augustine.

Library of Congress Cataloging-in-Publication Data

Names: Brooks, Jeanice, editor. | Boulanger, Nadia.
Title: Nadia Boulanger and her world / edited by Jeanice Brooks.
Other titles: Bard Music Festival series.
Description: Chicago; London: The University of Chicago Press, 2020. | Series:
The Bard Music Festival | Several contributions translated from French. | Includes
bibliographical references and index.
Identifiers: LCCN 2020022876 | ISBN 9780226750682 (cloth) | ISBN 9780226750712
(paperback) | ISBN 9780226750859 (ebook)
Subjects: LCSH: Boulanger, Nadia—Criticism and interpretation. | Music—
France—20th century—History and criticism. | Women musicians—France. | Women
music teachers—France. | Women composers—France. | Women conductors
(Music)—France.
Classification: LCC ML423.B52 N34 2020 | DDC 780.92 [B]—dc23
LC record available at https://lccn.loc.gov/2020022876

♾ This paper meets the requirements of ANSI/NISO Z39.48-1992
(Permanence of Paper).

# Contents

# Preface: The Only Woman in the Picture

When leafing through the metaphorical photo album of Nadia Boulanger's career—the many pictures taken to commemorate particular moments in her long professional life in music—it is hard not to be struck by her singularity. Very frequently, she is the only woman in the image. In the highly posed photograph of the contestants for the 1908 Prix de Rome, in which her male counterparts self-consciously smoke, read newspapers, and adopt elaborately casual attitudes, Boulanger occupies a central position sitting upright and looking directly at the camera (Figure 1). Her light-colored blouse stands out from her colleagues' dark coats like a spotlight calling attention to the anomaly of her presence. Nearly thirty years later, a formal picture of the French committee of the International Society for Contemporary Music, taken in spring 1937 during deliberations over the French nominations for that year's ISCM festival, shows Boulanger with her male colleagues Arthur Honegger, Arthur Hoérée, Albert Roussel, Henry Prunières, and Darius Milhaud (Figure 2). This image of her as the lone female member of a group with decisive power in new music circles can also stand for the role she had held as the only woman on the program committees of the Société nationale (from 1919) and the Société musicale indépendante (from 1921), whose concerts were similarly a significant factor in shaping reputations and careers in contemporary music.

Photos of Boulanger as conductor not only highlight her position alone on the podium, but also often make clear how few female players were employed by the major symphony orchestras—such as the London Philharmonic Society and the Boston Symphony Orchestra—that she was the first woman to conduct. Even pictures of Boulanger in the more conventionally feminine role as teacher can produce the same impression of exceptionality: for example, the 1923 image of Boulanger and her students posed in front of the organ in her home (Figure 3).

Nadia Boulanger occupies a similar position in the history of the Bard Music Festival. Founded in 1990 with a celebration of Johannes Brahms, the festival has since then explored the work of thirty composers, from Schubert to Schoenberg, Chopin to Chávez, and a host of figures in

Figure 1. Contestants for the Prix de Rome, 1908. The winner of the *Premier Grand Prix* was André Gailhard (seated, extreme right); Boulanger received the *Second Grand Prix*.

between. Both the festival and its companion book series have explored the work of each year's selected figure in broadly conceived historical and musical contexts, and both take their titles from this central aim, highlighting the interaction of the topic figure with his surroundings through the formulation "X and His World." In this anniversary year of 2020, Boulanger is the first woman to become a festival subject, and the first festival subject not principally known for achievements as a composer.

This choice has major implications: changing not only the subject but also a single word of the title—the possessive—opens up a series of challenges. The formulation "X and His World," while providing room for social and contextual histories that are sensitive to recent changes in musicological methods and focus, is nevertheless built upon similar premises to older forms of musical scholarship such as the "life and works" genre of composer biography. The figure at the center of the endeavor is assumed to merit attention for his achievements as a creator of musical works. But the historiography of music and musical works has traditionally depended so heavily on masculine concepts of genius—especially in dealing with composition, but to some degree in representing all aspects of professional musical life, with the possible exception, tellingly, of pedagogy—that the representation of a female subject within such a model immediately calls the historiography itself into question. Thus our

Figure 2. Meeting of the French committee of the
International Society for Contemporary Music, March 1937.

title *Nadia Boulanger and Her World* demands not just that we explore the
world in which Boulanger lived and worked, but also that we interrogate
the opportunities and constraints that marked her ability to move within
it, and the extent to which it was—or was not—hers to occupy or possess.

Boulanger's world was made up of many different and overlapping
"worlds" that embrace both physical places and conceptual domains
ranging from national and global geopolitics to philosophy, aesthetics,
and areas of musical activity such as composition, performance, analysis,
and pedagogy. In taking up the challenge of exploring our title, contributors to this volume have aimed to map Boulanger's movement in one

Figure 3. Nadia Boulanger and her students at 36 rue Ballu in 1923. From left to right,
Eyvind Hesselberg; unidentified; Robert Delaney; unidentified; Nadia Boulanger;
Aaron Copland; Mario Braggioti; Melville Smith; unidentified; Armand Marquiset.

or more of these terrains. In addition to contributors' chapters, editions
and translations of primary documents provide further texture to our
account. Boulanger was a committed internationalist and her professional success was based to a large extent upon her reputation beyond
French national borders. Her career was marked by increasing geo-
graphical reach, as witnessed by the influx of international students from
around the world to her classes. Marie Duchêne-Thégarid shows how
the foundation of new institutions for foreign students in interwar Paris
provided opportunities for Boulanger to develop a distinctive pedagogy
that both drew upon and expanded the forms of her own education as
a student of the Paris Conservatoire. As Duchêne-Thégarid points out,
these institutions were the offspring of war: while they created both stable
musical employment and unprecedented opportunities for Boulanger to
encounter musicians from far-flung origins, they are also a reminder of
how her career unfolded against a backdrop of international conflicts
that disrupted her musical life and transformed the physical, political,
and social geographies she navigated.

Alexandra Laederich's chapter shows how the dashing of Boulanger's
hopes for the 1914 premiere of her co-authored opera *La ville morte*,

whose performance could have changed the course of her career as a composer, resulted from the disastrous combination of the death of her collaborator Raoul Pugno with the outbreak of World War I. Further effects of the war, not only on Boulanger's life but on those of her Conservatoire classmates, are forcefully brought home by the responses to her questionnaire in the trench newspaper, the *Gazette des classes du Conservatoire*, published by Boulanger and her sister Lili. Here selected and introduced by Annegret Fauser, the soldier-musicians' reflections on music in wartime, and particularly on musical nationalism, provide a vivid image of the new realities that marked musicians' careers. In a chapter dealing with Boulanger's later career, Andrea F. Bohlman and J. Mackenzie Pierce show how strong musical and personal links formed within the international atmosphere of interwar Paris were challenged and transformed by the devastation of World War II and the imposition of Cold War barriers between Boulanger and the large and important group of her friends and students in Eastern Europe.

As Bohlman and Pierce's contribution makes clear, Boulanger's own voyages—for example, her postwar visits to Poland—were often exercises in official or unofficial cultural diplomacy. Her stays in the United States, initially as a visiting performer and speaker during the interwar period, and subsequently as wartime exile between 1940 and 1946, provided her with opportunities to advocate for French music in general and in particular to promote the work of Lili Boulanger and of her former teacher, Gabriel Fauré. My own chapter explores her efforts to present Fauré as a modern composer working within a specifically French aesthetic whose architectural qualities nevertheless transcend national boundaries. The American poet May Sarton's verses, addressed to Boulanger after concerts of Lili's works and published here for the first time, provide a poignant testimony to some of the meanings Boulanger's audiences heard in her work; while selections from Boulanger's epistolary journal written during her first tour of the United States in 1925 explore her own understanding of her journey to a place she had until then experienced only second-hand through her American students. Gayle Murchison's reflections on what this tour did not include expose how the country Boulanger encountered was structured by segregation and how her understanding of it was filtered through race.

In contrast to these texts on Boulanger's engagement with the wider world, Cédric Segond-Genovesi's chapter focuses on the space in which she received her students in her Parisian apartment at 36 rue Ballu. Attentively deconstructing the deployment of spatial and iconographical vocabularies of archetypes including the classroom, the salon, and the

church, he shows how Boulanger's home became a microcosm that pro-
jected her vision of the musical world and her own place within it.

In counterpoint to physical and geopolitical contexts for Boulanger's
activities, several of our contributions engage with her navigation of
professional and conceptual "worlds" ranging from composition and performance to music analysis, music history, and musical pedagogy. Kimberly
Francis and I have made a collaborative exploration of Boulanger's work
in collaborative composition; we take advantage of newly released documents that provide unprecedented insights into Boulanger's musical and
personal relationship with Raoul Pugno, reading these against the music
of their opera *La ville morte* to illuminate both her creative aspirations and
personal and societal obstacles to achieving them. In a separate contribution, Francis interrogates Boulanger's efforts to come to terms with the
musical languages of atonality, showing how she deployed an analytical
toolkit conceived for very different musical logics in an effort to expand her
own and her students' horizons. In his introduction to Boulanger's analyses of Beethoven's string quartets, prepared for the Longy School (today
the Longy School of Bard College) during World War II, Cédric Segond-
Genovesi shows how this toolkit was itself a multifaceted instrument whose
sources range from the French treatises employed at Boulanger's beloved
Conservatoire to a series of international texts whose variety provides further evidence of her intellect and curiosity. Leon Botstein's consideration
of how Boulanger's thought drew upon and intersected with wider currents in philosophy and aesthetics provides a compelling portrait of her
navigation of the world of ideas.

In each of these domains, stories emerge not only of singularity but of
connectedness, as networks and links emerge that can be obscured by an
emphasis on Boulanger's status as "first" or "only." Such stories notably
feature the appearance of many other women whose images are often
absent from the photo album of Boulanger's career, but whose work was
essential to her musical world and her ability to function within it. These
include the female assistants, patrons, and new music activists who enabled
her activities, as well as the female students who worked for and with
Boulanger, and who went on to become composers, performers, and pedagogues themselves. Emotional connections, including the depth of her
relationship with her mother, become newly apparent; intellectual links
with female thinkers emerge. And our contributions highlight how professional milieus, cultural institutions, and personal networks otherwise
populated almost exclusively by men nevertheless enabled aspects of her
career, from the support of her earliest mentors and the skills instilled
by her education, to the frameworks supplied by the institutions and

organizations that provided—sometimes freely, sometimes grudgingly or partially—a place for her ideas and her work.

When Boulanger toured the United States in 1925, she was billed as France's foremost *woman* musician (emphasis mine). A few years before, a testimonial from one of her most enthusiastic supporters, the American conductor Walter Damrosch, similarly praised her by saying that she was the best *female* musician he had met. Even her lover and collaborator Raoul Pugno, whose support was crucial to her early success as a composer, expressed his doubts about women's capacity for musical genius in print. Boulanger's contemporaries saw and understood her through a perceived anomaly, between her gender and the work she aimed to do as a professional musician. This historical situation needs to be accounted for in our work today; the woman in the picture is inescapable, even when she is not the only one. In exploring how Boulanger lived and worked in a world deeply shaped by gender, however, we have also aimed to explore some of the other discourses of power, inclusion, and exclusion that shaped her world, and how concepts of national, cosmopolitan, and international identities intersected with both musical ideas and professional possibilities. This collection helps explain how Boulanger became the woman in the picture, tracing her life from a time when to be female and a composer, conductor, or critic was almost an oxymoron, toward the more inclusive world that could be glimpsed, at least, by the end of her century, and for which we must still strive today.

# Acknowledgments

My grateful thanks are due to the contributors to this volume not only for their thoughtful scholarship, but for their patience and good humor as the work on this book carried on through increasingly challenging times. Thank you to Anna Lehmann, Charlotte Mandell, and Miranda Stewart for their sensitive translations of contributions in French, and to Erin Clermont for her attentive editing. I am especially grateful to Paul De Angelis, whose work on shaping and producing the book from its inception has been vital and who has made the entire process a pleasure. The artistic directors and staff of the Bard summer festival, particularly Christopher Gibbs, Byron Adams, and Irene Zedlacher, have been invaluable interlocutors; and for documents and images, information and advice, the support of Alexandra Laederich and the Centre international Nadia et Lili Boulanger has been especially precious. I am grateful to all for their help.

When studying the life of Nadia Boulanger, one is continually reminded of the importance of mothers and sisters. So I would like to devote this book to mine: to Lisa, Heather, and Eleana Brooks, and the memory of Eileen Everist, who passed away as this volume neared completion.

# Permissions and Credits

The following copyright holders, institutions, and individuals have graciously granted permission to reprint or reproduce the following materials:

**Centre international Nadia et Lili Boulanger** for Figure 1 and Figure 2 (photo by Boris Lipnitzki) in Brooks, "Preface: The Only Woman in the Picture"; for Figures 1–4 in Laederich, "The Strange Fate of Boulanger and Pugno's *La ville morte*"; for Figures 2, 3, 4, and 6 in Brooks and Francis, "Serious Ambitions"; for Figure 2 in Duchêne-Thégarid, "From Technique to *Musique*"; for Figure 4 (bottom) and Figure 6 in Segond-Genovesi, "36 rue Ballu"; for Figures 1 and 3 in Brooks/Boulanger, "What an Arrival!"; for Figure 1 in Brooks, "Modern French Music"; and for Figures 1, 3, 4, and 5, and the four analyses on pages 270–73 in Segond-Genovesi, "The Beethoven Lectures for the Longy School."

**Library of Congress, Music Division**, for Figure 3 in Brooks, "Preface: The Only Woman in the Picture"; for Figure 2 (photo by Bain News Service) in Brooks/Boulanger, "What an Arrival!"; and for Figure 4 (photo by Victor Kraft) in Brooks, "Modern French Music."

**Hal Leonard Europe** for the music examples 1–3 in Brooks and Francis, "Serious Ambitions"; composed by Nadia Boulanger and Raoul Pugno, © 1914 by Heugel. Rights transferred to Éditions musicales Alphonse Leduc, Paris. Used by Permission of Hal Leonard Europe Limited.

**Bibliothèque nationale de France** for Figure 1 in Duchêne-Thégarid, "From Technique to *Musique*"; for Figure 1 in "Nadia Boulanger's 1935 *Carte du Tendre*"; for Figure 3 in Brooks, "Modern French Music"; and for Figure 1 in Mycielski, "What Awaits Them Now?"

**Bibliothèque et Archives nationales du Québec** for Figure 3 in Duchêne-Thégarid, "From Technique to *Musique*."

**Conservatoire américain de Fontainebleau** for Figure 4 in Duchêne-Thégarid, "From Technique to *Musique*."

**Cédric Segond-Genovesi** for Figures 1 and 3 (after Pierre Abondance) as well as Figure 7A in Segond-Genovesi, "36 rue Ballu."

**Musée de la Musique, Paris** for Figures 2, 4 (top), 5 (top, bottom, and continuation; photos by Pierre Abondance) and 7b (photo by Pierre Abondance) in Segond-Genovesi, "36 rue Ballu."

**Conservatoire national superieur de musique et de danse de Paris** for Figures 4 and 5 in Segond-Genovesi, "36 rue Ballu."

**Staatsbibliothek zu Berlin, Preussischer Kulturbesitz** for Figure 2 in Brooks, "Modern French Music."

**Russell & Volkening** for the poems of May Sarton. Reprinted by the permission of Russell & Volkening as agents for May Sarton, copyright ©1939, 1945 May Sarton.

**Polska Agencja Prasowa** for Figure 1 in Bohlman and Pierce, "Friend and Force."

**Andrzej Zborski** for photograph, Figure 2, in Bohlman and Pierce, "Friend and Force."

**Polskie Wydawnictwo Muzyczne** for permission to reproduce Examples 1 and 2 in Bohlman and Pierce, "Friend and Force."

**Mediathèque Nadia Boulanger, Conservatoire national superieur de musique et de danse de Lyon** for Figures 1–5 in Francis, "Boulanger and Atonality."

**Boosey** for Violin Concerto No. 2 by Béla Bartók as reproduced in Figure 3 in Francis, "Boulanger and Atonality." Copyright © 1941 by Hawkes & Son (London) Ltd. All rights reserved. Used with permission.

**Universal Edition** for the Webern String Quartet, reproduced in Figures 4a/4b/4c in Francis, "Boulanger and Atonality." Copyright © 1939 Universal Edition Vienna. Copyright © renewed. All rights reserved. Used by permission of European American Music Distributors Company, U.S. and Canadian agent for Universal Edition Vienna.

# NADIA BOULANGER AND HER WORLD

# The Strange Fate of Boulanger and Pugno's *La ville morte*

ALEXANDRA LAEDERICH
TRANSLATED BY CHARLOTTE MANDELL

On 31 May 1910, Nadia Boulanger, Raoul Pugno, and Gabriele D'Annunzio gathered at the Heugel publishing house in Paris to sign the publication contract for *La ville morte*, an opera in five acts, which they would write in collaboration.[1] These well-known personalities were the creators of a magnificent project, undertaken confidently and enthusiastically, that led D'Annunzio to transform his tragedy into an opera libretto, which Raoul Pugno and Nadia Boulanger would set to music. The three artists respected and valued one another, and Henri Heugel, who was already the publisher of the two musicians, was engaged to market and promote the work.

After examining the circumstances of *La ville morte*'s genesis and studying the close relationship linking the two composers, I will analyze the obstacles that prevented any performance of the opera, victim of a strange fate. Finally, I will present the various musical sources that are available today.[2]

## A Close Artistic Partnership

In 1904 Nadia Boulanger finished her studies at the Paris Conservatoire, where she won diplomas in organ, piano accompaniment, counterpoint, and fugue. At the age of seventeen, she was destined for a musical career, but did not yet know which path she would follow: Organist? Pianist? Composer? In 1904 the Boulanger family moved to 36 rue Ballu, the Paris apartment where Nadia Boulanger would live for the rest of her life. She had a Cavaillé-Coll house organ installed there, which would be useful for organizing private concerts. At once promotional and social, these home concerts gave Boulanger the opportunity to invite performers, composers, Conservatory professors, and friends. The organ's inauguration took place on 4 February 1905, and already Raoul Pugno's name figured on the guest list.

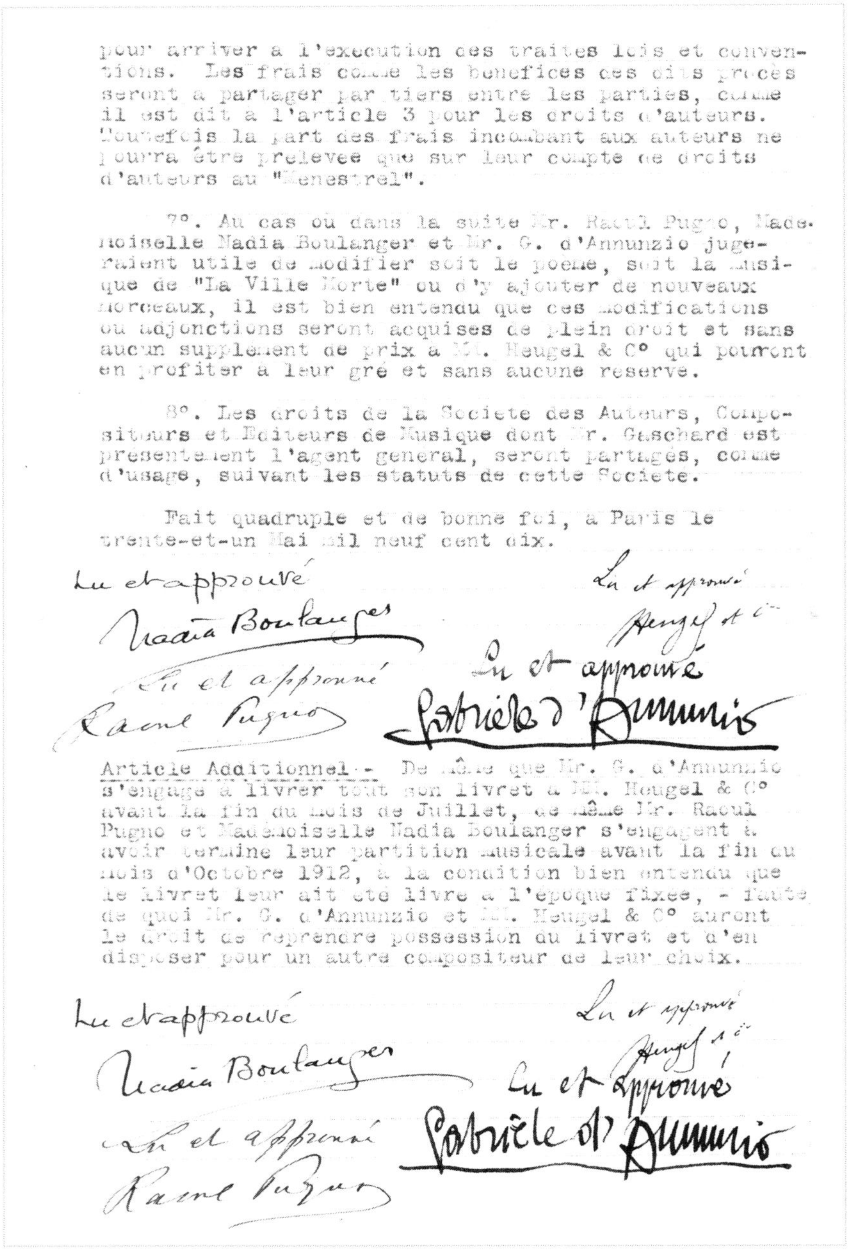

pour arriver a l'execution des traites lois et conventions. Les frais comme les benefices des dits proces
seront a partager par tiers entre les parties, comme
il est dit a l'article 3 pour les droits d'auteurs.
Toutefois la part des frais incombant aux auteurs ne
pourra être prelevee que sur leur compte de droits
d'auteurs au "Menestrel".

7°. Au cas où dans la suite Mr. Raoul Pugno, Mademoiselle Nadia Boulanger et Mr. G. d'Annunzio juge-
raient utile de modifier soit le poeme, soit la musique de "La Ville Morte" ou d'y ajouter de nouveaux
morceaux, il est bien entendu que ces modifications
ou adjonctions seront acquises de plein droit et sans
aucun supplement de prix a MM. Heugel & C° qui pourront
en profiter a leur gré et sans aucune reserve.

8°. Les droits de la Societe des Auteurs, Compositeurs et Editeurs de Musique dont Mr. Gaschard est
presentement l'agent general, seront partagés, comme
d'usage, suivant les statuts de cette Societe.

Fait quadruple et de bonne foi, a Paris le
trente-et-un Mai mil neuf cent dix.

Lu et approuvé

*Nadia Boulanger*

Lu et approuvé

*Heugel et C°*

Lu et approuvé

*Raoul Pugno*

Lu et approuvé

*Gabriele d'Annunzio*

Article Additionnel.- De même que Mr. G. d'Annunzio
s'engage a livrer tout son livret a MM. Heugel & C°
avant la fin du mois de Juillet, de même Mr. Raoul
Pugno et Mademoiselle Nadia Boulanger s'engagent a
avoir terminé leur partition musicale avant la fin du
mois d'Octobre 1912, a la condition bien entendu que
le livret leur ait été livre a l'epoque fixee, - faute
de quoi Mr. G. d'Annunzio et MM. Heugel & C° auront
le droit de reprendre possession du livret et d'en
disposer pour un autre compositeur de leur choix.

Lu et approuvé

*Nadia Boulanger*

Lu et approuvé

*Heugel et C°*

Lu et approuvé

*Raoul Pugno*

Lu et approuvé

*Gabriele d'Annunzio*

Figure 1. Signature page of the publishing contract for *La ville morte*,
between Nadia Boulanger, Raoul Pugno, Gabriele D'Annunzio, and the firm of
Heugel and Company, executed 31 May 1910.

Raoul Pugno was a virtuoso pianist who began as a student at the Ecole musicale religieuse Niedermeyer, where he was introduced to liturgical music and trained in the organ while very young. He entered the Paris Conservatory in 1866, at the age of fourteen, where he won first prize for piano. He went on to obtain the same diplomas—and at about the same age—as Nadia Boulanger did a generation later: organ, accompaniment, counterpoint, and fugue. The precocious talents of Raoul Pugno and Nadia Boulanger, their similar training and shared musical tastes, inspired a recip-rocal admiration and a real artistic complicity between them. The nature of their relationship evolved between 1905 and 1914, passing from friendship to love. Pugno gradually became the masculine figure absent from the trio formed by Nadia Boulanger, her mother, Raïssa, and her younger sister Lili. Their many occasions for coming together were facilitated by the geo-graphical proximity of their apartments in the 9th arrondissement of Paris as well as their neighboring country homes in Gargenville.[3]

Raoul Pugno's own renown would prove helpful to Nadia Boulanger, and serve to promote the young woman's first public recital, on 5 December 1906. Pugno's celebrity was an excellent vector, and other concerts would soon follow: sometimes Boulanger played solo on the organ, at other times they played together on two pianos or piano four-hand, first in Paris, later in the provinces and abroad. Their artistic partnership was intensified when, from April to August 1909, the two collaborated in composing the song cycle *Les heures claires,* on poems by Émile Verhaeren. Boulanger was not a begin-ner, since she had already composed a dozen songs, choruses, and several works for orchestra, especially for the Prix de Rome competition for musical composition.[4] As for Pugno, he was a prolific author of comic operas, songs, and pieces for piano—all works published by Heugel Editions.

Pugno maintained many literary relationships, and there is evidence for Emile Verhaeren's presence at Pugno's house. In February 1913, the poet presented *Les heures claires* as his "tenderest book" in his introduction to the concert given by Nadia Boulanger and Raoul Pugno. He added:

> In the first five songs . . . love presents itself first in its simple, calm, peaceful poetic setting. Little by little, its flame grows and intensifies; we follow it like a beautiful, rising light. . . . Nadia Boulanger and Raoul Pugno . . . have stayed faithful to the sovereign passion. . . . The last three songs continue to celebrate love's force and fervor.[5]

The work shared in composing this cycle brought the two musicians closer together; love soon slipped in as counterpoint to their artistic lives,

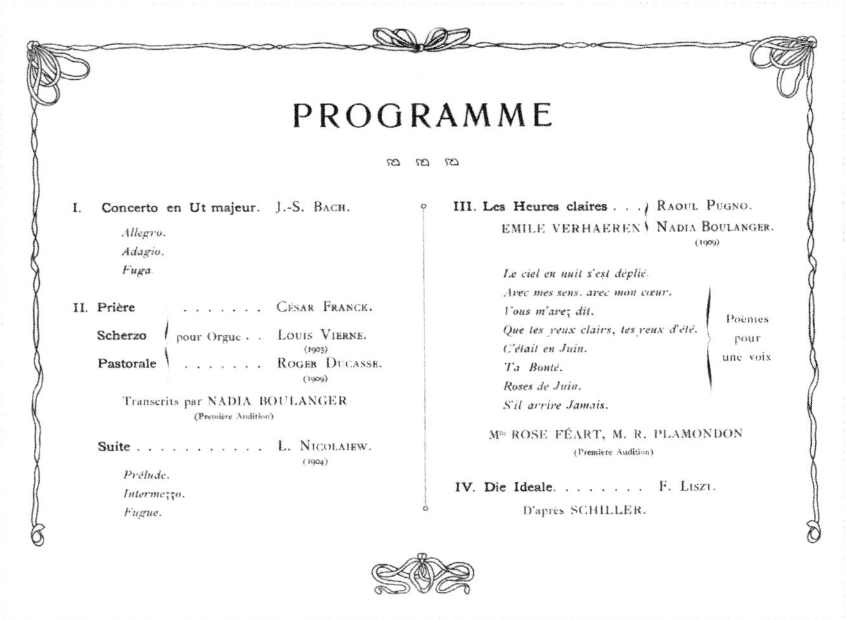

# PROGRAMME

ဃ ဃ ဃ

I. Concerto en Ut majeur. J.-S. BACH.
   *Allegro.*
   *Adagio.*
   *Fuga*

II. Prière . . . . . . . CÉSAR FRANCK.
    Scherzo } pour Orgue . . LOUIS VIERNE.
                          (1903)
    Pastorale } . . . . . . ROGER DUCASSE.
                          (1909)
    Transcrits par NADIA BOULANGER
              (Première Audition)

    Suite . . . . . . . . . . L. NICOLAIEW.
                          (1904)
    *Prélude.*
    *Intermezzo.*
    *Fugue.*

III. Les Heures claires . . . } RAOUL PUGNO.
     EMILE VERHAEREN } NADIA BOULANGER.
                          (1909)
     *Le ciel en nuit s'est déplié.*
     *Avec mes sens, avec mon cœur.*
     *Vous m'avez dit.*                    } Poèmes
     *Que les yeux clairs, les yeux d'été.*  } pour
     *C'était en Juin.*                      } une voix
     *Ta Bonté.*
     *Roses de Juin.*
     *S'il arrive Jamais.*

     Mⁿᵉ ROSE FÉART, M. R. PLAMONDON
              (Première Audition)

IV. Die Ideale. . . . . . . F. LISZT.
     *D'après SCHILLER.*

Figure 2. Concert program for Boulanger and Pugno's
*Les heures claires*, Salle Pleyel, 30 April 1910.

despite the thirty-five-years' age difference between them. Loving but adulterous feelings are the very subject of D'Annunzio's *La ville morte*, which echoed their liaison. *Les heures claires* was published right away by Heugel. Coincidence would have it that the first performance, at the Salle Pleyel on 30 April 1910, with Nadia Boulanger and Raoul Pugno on the piano accompanying two singers from the Opéra de Paris, Rose Féart and Rodolphe Plamondon, was the very day that Nadia Boulanger first met Gabriele D'Annunzio.[6]

## The Project of *La ville morte*

The first mention of *La ville morte* can be found in Nadia Boulanger's daybook on 8 January 1910.[7] Could the idea of setting D'Annunzio's play to music have occurred before then? As early as August 1909, the composer Jean Roger-Ducasse had begun work on the text of *La ville morte*.[8] A student of Gabriel Fauré at the same time as Boulanger, Roger-Ducasse, fourteen years older than she, would become one of her most loyal friends. On Boulanger's recommendation, D'Annunzio would later contact Roger-Ducasse to suggest he compose the music for the poet's *Martyre de Saint Sébastien*.

D'Annunzio's first letter to Nadia Boulanger is dated 28 April 1910, soon after the Italian poet's arrival in France, where he joined his companion, Nathalie Goloubeff, who was staying at the Hotel Meurice.[9] He wrote to Boulanger on the advice of the organist Louis Vierne, "who spoke to me about you with the noblest fervor." A meeting was set up at the hotel on the rue de Rivoli for the next day. Everything then happened very quickly, since on 22 May 1910, barely a month later, we can read in Boulanger's daybook: "We wrote the first notes of *La ville morte.*"[10] This was even before the contract with Heugel was signed.

D'Annunzio's difficult financial situation might explain this haste: according to the terms of the contract, he agreed to produce the libretto, to be extracted from his play *La ville morte*, by the end of July 1910. He would immediately receive a sum of 3,000 francs as well as an advance of 5,000 francs for the Paris performances of the work. From a pecuniary perspective, D'Annunzio emerged very much a winner in this agreement.[11] As we can infer, Henri Heugel believed in the project and agreed to take the financial risk: he knew the poet's fame and the composers' talent guaranteed its success. In addition, he organized a publicity campaign to be published in *Le Ménestrel*, a music journal that had been Heugel's mouthpiece since the nineteenth century.

### Two Years of Enthusiastic Work

The publisher's contract set the composers a deadline at the end of October 1912, two years from signing. This deadline was respected, and all the music was written between 22 May 1910 and 27 August 1912. Since both musicians had very full professional lives, the moments devoted to the opera's composition were usually taken during summer vacations when they would meet in Gargenville, Saint-Jean-Cap-Ferrat, or in Paris. August 1910 was mainly devoted to preparing the libretto. In June 1911, Acts 1 and 2 were composed, and the work continued the following August on scenes 5 and 6. Between August and September 1911, Act 3 was completed. Finally, in July and August 1912, Act 4 was brought to fruition. Dates of composition figure in the manuscript piano-vocal score. After the final measures of Act IV (p. 37), in Boulanger's hand, is the inscription "Alleluia!!!!/ 19 August 1912/ N.B. R.P." (see Figure 4).[12] At the end of July 1912 the composers found themselves awaiting D'Annunzio's corrections, since he wanted to add some final touches to Act 3.[13] They became impatient:

> We're missing the third act with its edits; . . . but the fever of writing, which possesses us so wholly, needs to experience no interruption. . . . Let us receive the third act quickly—*so we can finish!*[14]

Figure 3. Nadia Boulanger working on *La ville morte*, Saint-Jean-Cap-Ferrat, 1911.

A few days later, Nadia Boulanger insisted, "You alone are preventing us from finishing *La ville morte*."[15] It was not until 18 August 1912 that D'Annunzio wrote to excuse himself for the delay: "As you'll see, my task

Figure 4. Final page of piano-vocal score for *La ville morte* punctuated by "Alleluia!!!!"

was very easy. I just had to make one transposition and one condensation of the scene between Léonard and his sister. . . . Please reread a few pages of Aeschylus, before confronting so many old ghosts."[16]

A reading of the correspondence exchanged between the artists highlights a fair number of comments having to do with enthusiasm and work. The development of the opera was carried out in periods of happiness, but required obvious effort. A few extracts from their correspondence attest to this: "If you knew with what ardor, with what devotion and joy we work," Boulanger wrote, adding, "Since you left, we have worked furiously. . . . The weeks that have just passed were for us full of enthusiasm, joy, emotion."[17]

And from Pugno came this avowal, addressed to D'Annunzio: "We're eager to tell you that for two years and two months, we have experienced, thanks to you, hours of unforgettable joy."[18]

D'Annunzio outlined his idea for their roles in another letter to Boulanger:

> The male element belongs to Raoul—I recommend to you the song of the blind woman and the lament of the virgin. I thought of your fresh inspiration when creating them.[19]

One wonders which of the two, Boulanger or Pugno, composed what. The first manuscript of the piano-vocal score is a precious source in which one can clearly distinguish two types of handwriting, always overlapping and complementary.[20] The lively, sure script of Pugno predominates, and over two-thirds of the work would have to be attributed to him on that basis. Apparently, however, the musicians did not divide the scenes or roles between them; rather, they worked together in close collaboration.

Similarly, the libretto was the result of a veritable three-person effort. In a letter dated 3 September 1910, D'Annunzio announced to Heugel that he had completed his work and that the libretto was already in the hands of the composers:

> I radically edited and completely rewrote the third and fourth acts. . . . I introduced an invisible chorus, "the song of thirst," sung by the (invisible) procession climbing up to the chapel of the prophet Elijah. In this way, this act rivals the first in *musical* richness. So I expect from this Boaz and this Ruth— in the idealism of poetry—a wonderful child.[21]

After receiving the libretto, in which D'Annunzio reduced five acts to four, the musicians decided to visit him in Arcachon to offer their own version. During the summer of 1910, they had prepared a complete libretto on their own, in five acts, and they hoped to convince D'Annunzio to accept their ideas. With much circumspection, Pugno explained their side in a long letter to D'Annunzio, with the main question revolving around the shape of the acts.[22]

D'Annunzio, however, was already occupied with another project, *The Martyrdom of St. Sebastian*. In a postscript to his letter to Heugel of 3 September, he had asked Nadia Boulanger for Roger-Ducasse's address.

This had aroused in her the mad hope of composing the score for the *Martyrdom* herself. On 8 November she wrote to the poet: "This note has no other purpose than to confess to you the redoubled impatience in which I will henceforth live."[23] She waited until Roger-Ducasse, hesitant to accept D'Annunzio's offer, desisted, and then she counted on D'Annunzio choosing her as composer for his new work. But he did not follow up on her suggestion, and instead contacted Claude Debussy a few days later.

### Promoting the Work

As soon as the first two acts were completed, Pugno and Boulanger played them for Heugel and D'Annunzio, who were "very happy with them."[24] Then, in March 1912, the violinist Eugène Ysaÿe, who with Pugno was part of a celebrated duo, had the privilege of a performance by Pugno himself:

> Of this very private performance, . . . I keep the most profound and happiest impression; . . . at the same time I understood both the music and the motives, which make it so beautiful, so sound, so poignant.[25]

On 25 June 1912 D'Annunzio attended a private performance of the work at Pugno's home.[26] On December 9 another performance was organized at the home of Nadia Boulanger, and D'Annunzio confirmed he would come, "delighted to be able to hear once again the 'robust' work."[27] Later he would remind Nadia Boulanger of that "holy emotion with which certain cries of our Hébé filled me, when you stood singing, next to our big breathless friend."[28]

Promoting the work was the task of the publisher, who undertook to bring out the piano-vocal reduction. According to Pugno, it took the composers from August 1912 until November to produce the reduction for publication: "We are working tirelessly on the piano-vocal reduction of the score, an arduous, meticulous task which is now reaching its end."[29]

In January 1913, Heugel began negotiations with the director of the Opéra, André Messager.[30] "It is understood that as soon as Pugno gets in touch with him, Messager will listen to the end of the work, with which he is quite satisfied so far."[31] Then Heugel had the piano-vocal score printed: between June and July 1913, the first proofs of Acts 1 and 2 were corrected by the two composers. Act 3 was not printed and corrected until October and November. On 15 November 1913, Pugno asked for a second set of proofs, since there were many corrections to be made.

Just before that, in September 1913, Boulanger and Pugno went to see Albert Carré, the director of the Opéra-Comique, to play their opera for him. Nadia Boulanger describes the performance to Heugel:

> Both he and Mme Carré were tirelessly attentive. . . . I should add that we gave a very poor performance! Pugno had a bad cold and couldn't sing—as for me, my throat is in such a state that I'm forced to leave Paris so I can take at least a month of complete rest, without saying a word.[32]

Although several approaches were made, no engagement was signed with either of the great Parisian lyric stages.

According to Pugno, it was not until August 1913 that the orchestration was undertaken: "We've begun to orchestrate and we're not stopping."[33] At this time, Pugno composed a *Prelude* to *La ville morte* for orchestra, for which Nadia Boulanger would fashion, in November 1913, a two-piano reduction, probably to be played with Pugno. They promoted the work using this reduction of the prelude, of which the manuscript preserved by the publisher shows marks for a printed edition that was planned but not realized.[34] The important thing was to finish the second set of proofs of the piano-vocal score of Act 4, which was printed on 11 December 1913, just before the departure of the two composers for Moscow, where Pugno was about to start a concert tour. But Nadia Boulanger would be correcting them alone, four months later.

### Nadia Boulanger, Acting Alone

The brutal and unexpected death of Raoul Pugno on 3 January 1914 was the first catastrophe, and probably the most decisive tragedy that impeded the realization of *La ville morte*. The pair were on a concert tour together when Pugno fell seriously ill and died in Moscow.[35] Although Nadia Boulanger was surrounded by friends, although she received many testimonies of support and affection, she was devastated, her heart broken. A letter from Ysaÿe offers sad testimony:

> I have seen in the very gentleness of your tears . . . that your mind and heart . . . were going toward him . . . that mingled with the profundity of your sorrow was the bitterness of a love wounded by a . . . sudden, unexpected rending asunder, a fatal separation whose sufferings are all the more cruel to you . . . for being endured in the shadows where your first love expires in tears.[36]

Nevertheless, *La ville morte* continued to have its supporters, especially the new manager of the Opéra-Comique, where in January 1914 a change of directors led to the naming of Pierre-Barthélemy Gheusi to the post. A trial performance was organized in his office in April 1914, and on that date the commitment was made to add the work to the fall season's program.[37] Gheusi would remember this in 1938 in a speech he gave on the occasion of D'Annunzio's death:

> The score . . . vibrant with love and tragic destiny, was going to be premiered on the admirable Favart stage of those days, where the whole House, radiating with lyric faith, devotion and friendly fervor, devoted itself in advance to its success.[38]

What is more, *Le Ménestrel* continued its support, as did the non-musical press, which in July announced the performance of *La ville morte* in November 1914, and also reported the casting.[39]

### A Strange Fate

Fate, however, seemed set against the project: a chain of difficulties and a succession of tragedies followed. First of all, the director of the Opéra, André Messager, who had fully supported the work, was replaced by Jacques Rouché, who seemed to show no interest in the project and was having difficult relations with Pierre-Barthélemy Gheusi. Then the summer of 1914 arrived, along with the season closing of the Opéra-Comique on 20 June, with a new season planned for September. Then, on 2 August came the general mobilization and on the next day the declaration of war. Long, terrible months passed before the opera houses reopened, rather timidly, with the Opéra-Comique promising a shortened season beginning in February 1915, and the Opéra beginning only in December of the same year.

Despite difficulties due to the war, Gheusi continued to believe firmly that a performance at the Opéra-Comique was possible. His relationship with D'Annunzio was warm and marked by mutual respect; it was soldierly as well, since Gheusi was mobilized and D'Annunzio signed on to serve. However, no decision could be made without D'Annunzio, and the poet had other things on his mind. As he wrote to Gheusi, one had to devote oneself "not to *La ville morte*, but to the *Ville vivante* [Living city]," alluding to the defense of Paris, a city threatened.[40] He added:

> The *Ville morte* that you were going to put on should be put back into your cupboard. We'll find it there after the victory.

> The music of this Nadia Boulanger exalts and astounds me. Her collaborator, Raoul Pugno, is a magician of the keyboard; but the soul of the score is Nadia.[41]

D'Annunzio, called by duty, left for Italy in May 1915 with great military plans and no decision of any kind about production for the opera.

A year later, in May 1916, Nadia Boulanger wrote anxiously to him: "Can we still think about *La ville morte*? . . . Can you just tell me if you'll be able to visit in October? . . . Tell me what I should do."[42] She was obviously at a loss. Then, a few days later Henri Heugel, the work's most effective last supporter, died.

Nadia Boulanger's dismay was understandable: What could she do on her own? She was already caught up in the Conservatoire's Franco-American Committee, which she created with her younger sister Lili to provide aid for musicians in the military.[43] She also had accompanied the ailing Lili on her return to Rome to complete the stay at the Villa Médicis to which Lili was entitled as the grand prize winner of the Prix de Rome, and in the hope that the good Italian air would help the young woman recover from the illness that would never leave her. Lili's death, on 15 March 1918, came to darken forever the life of Nadia Boulanger: "She was the light of my life, and it is one more huge veil that has been cast over the Past," she wrote to D'Annunzio.[44]

What happened after the First World War? Gheusi, criticized, was no longer directing the Opéra-Comique. But Nadia Boulanger still believed in the project, since in 1923 she worked on the orchestration, completing Act 1, the manuscript of which can be found today at the Heugel-Leduc publishing house.[45]

It was not until fifteen years later, on the occasion of D'Annunzio's death in 1938, that people talked again in Paris about *La ville morte*. Gheusi gave a speech on the radio, and Gustave Samazeuilh, composer and pianist, friend of Nadia Boulanger, thought about programming the work. With this in mind, he organized a private performance.[46] Four years later, in the midst of the Second World War, Samazeuilh wrote an article published 10 July 1942 in *Information musicale*, one of the few musical periodicals left in Paris during the German Occupation. One of the goals of this weekly journal was to support French composers through reviews, which were featured on the cover. Samazeuilh's review, titled "*La ville morte* en musique", illustrated with a photo of the conductor Charles Munch, praised the work, which for him ranked as highly as Fauré's *Prometheus*, Debussy's *Pelléas et Mélisande*, and Dukas's *Ariane et Barbe-Bleue*. He mentions the absence of Nadia Boulanger, who had gone

to the United States, where, he writes, "she usefully serves French music."
Did politics at that point perhaps slip into the opera's destiny? Is it possible that this work was lost sight of during the rebuilding process after
the Second World War? Whatever the reason, *La ville morte* was no longer
spoken of.[47]

## Conclusion

Thus, despite the unanimous enthusiasm that was shown for *La ville
morte*, despite the support, despite the relationships of all sorts, despite
the positive opinions published in the press, a series of tragic events
overwhelmed the solid opportunities the opera deserved. The archives
hold some mysteries, but do reveal that when Pugno was alive, everything seemed easy. Once Nadia Boulanger was promoting *La ville morte*
alone, did the fact that she was a woman prevent her from making herself
heard? After 1923, she obviously lost interest in the work, as she did with
all her compositions, preferring the role of ardent defender of the music
of Lili Boulanger, and deliberately letting her own music languish in the
shadows for the rest of her life.

It has taken nearly forty years since her death for Nadia Boulanger's
works to become more widely known.[48] Boulanger's international reputation, the memories retained by her numerous and often prestigious
pupils, and performers' curiosity about her work have been joined to
the interest today in rediscovering the work of women composers. The
edition and performance of Nadia Boulanger's works has now become
possible, and *La ville morte*'s day has perhaps finally come.

# APPENDIX:
## THE MUSICAL SOURCES AND THE LIBRETTO

The autograph manuscripts of the libretto and the music, as well as the corrected proofs of *La ville morte*, are preserved in Paris in four different collections: the Music Department of the Bibliothèque nationale de France; the Musée de la musique; the publishing house Leduc; and the Centre international Nadia et Lili Boulanger.[49]

### Orchestral Score
*Bibliothèque nationale de France, Département de la Musique*
—Prelude to Act 1, autograph manuscript in the hand of Raoul Pugno, 19 pp. + 29 pp. of outlines, Ms. 19676
—Act 3, autograph manuscript in the hand of Nadia Boulanger except for the vocal lines in the hand of a copyist, preprinted nomenclature, 137 pp. (missing p. 98), Ms. 19675

*Archives Heugel-Leduc*
—Act 1, autograph manuscript in the hand of Nadia Boulanger except the vocal lines and the nomenclature in the hand of a copyist, 214 pp., dated 6 September 1923

### Libretto
*Bibliothèque nationale de France, Département de la Musique*
—Libretto for Acts 1, 3, 4, and 5, one small notebook, 61 pp., in the hand of a copyist in black ink, Th. B. 4929 (1)
—Libretto for Act 2, one small notebook, 32 pp., in an unidentified hand; the plot is summarized, Th. B. 4929 (2)
—Libretto for Act 4, one notebook, 7 pp., title in the hand of D'Annunzio, printed pages, Th. B. 4929 (3)

*Musée de la musique, Fonds Nadia Boulanger*
—Libretto for Acts 2, 3, and 4, autograph manuscript in the hands of Nadia Boulanger and Raoul Pugno, 23 pp., 15 pp., 14 pp.
—Libretto for Act 3, autograph manuscript in the hand of D'Annunzio, 33 pp. (sent in August 1912)

### Piano-Vocal Reduction
*Centre international Nadia et Lili Boulanger*
—Acts 1, 3, and 4, autograph manuscript in the hands of Nadia Boulanger and Raoul Pugno, 37 pp., 86 pp., 65 pp.

*Bibliothèque nationale de France, Département de la Musique*
—Acts 1, 2. 3, and 4, autograph manuscript in the hands of Nadia
Boulanger and Raoul Pugno, 42 pp., 97 pp., 78 pp., 77 pp., prepared
for printing, Ms. 19674 (1–4)

## Two-Piano Reduction

*Archives Heugel-Leduc*
—Prelude [to Act 1], autograph manuscript in the hand of Nadia
Boulanger, 6 pp., dated November 1913

## Corrected proofs for the Piano-Vocal Score
## (Heugel, H. & Cie 26095)

*Musée de la musique, Fonds Nadia Boulanger*
—Acts 1, 2, and 3, first proof corrected by Nadia Boulanger and Raoul
Pugno, June–November 1913
*Bibliothèque nationale de France, Département de la Musique:*
—Acts 1, 2, 3, and 4, second proof corrected by Nadia Boulanger and
Raoul Pugno, August–December 1913, Vma. 3994
—Act 4, third proof corrected by Nadia Boulanger, also contained in
Vma. 3994

# NOTES

1. The contract specified five acts, in keeping with the tragedy by D'Annunzio, but in the end the opera's libretto featured only four acts.

2. An earlier version of this chapter was published in French as "L'étrange destin de *La Ville morte* de Nadia Boulanger et Raoul Pugno," in *D'Annunzio musico magnifico*, ed. Adriana Guarnieri, Fiamma Nicolodi, and Cesare Orselli (Florence: Olschki, 2008), 183–99. Since that time new sources have become available in the Nadia Boulanger archive held at the Bibliothèque nationale de France. At the time of the deposit in 1981, the executrix of Boulanger's will placed some personal documents in reserve because of their confidential nature, with an interdiction on their consultation for thirty years. In 2011, members of the Centre international Nadia et Lili Boulanger examined the documents and authorized their release. See Alexandra Laederich and Rémy Stricker, "Les trois vies de Nadia Boulanger," *Revue de la Bibliothèque nationale de France* 46 (2014): 77–83. Significantly, these documents confirm the intuitions that Boulanger's previous biographers have had about the nature of her relationship with Pugno.

3. The closeness of the connection has even been attributed to a possible family relationship, with Pugno imagined as Lili Boulanger's biological father; see Jérôme Spycket, *À la recherche de Lili Boulanger: Essai biographique* (Paris: Fayard, 2004), 82. There is no evidence to discount or confirm this hypothesis.

4. See Alexandra Laederich, "Catalogue de l'oeuvre de Nadia Boulanger et de l'oeuvre de Lili Boulanger," in *Nadia Boulanger et Lili Boulanger: Témoignages et études*, ed. Alexandra Laederich (Lyon: Symétrie, 2007), 309–402. On Boulanger's participation in the Prix de Rome competition, see Annegret Fauser, "'La guerre en dentelles': Women and the Prix de Rome in French Cultural Politics," *Journal of the American Musicological Society* 51 (1998): 83–129.

5. Emile Verhaeren, "*Les heures claires*," lecture, 13 February 1913; published in the *Journal de l'Université des Annales* 2/19 (15 September 1913): 338–49.

6. On 22 May 1911, soprano Rose Féart would sing in the production of Claude Debussy's setting of D'Annunzio's *Martyrdom of St. Sebastian* at the Théâtre du Châtelet in Paris.

7. Nadia Boulanger's daybooks are preserved in the Music Department of the Bibliothèque nationale de France (F–Pn), Rés. Vmf. ms. 85 (1). The collection has been augmented by the documents released in 2011 but there remain gaps for some periods.

8. Jean Roger-Ducasse, *Lettres à Nadia Boulanger*, introduced and annotated by Jacques Depaulis (Sprimont: Mardaga, 1999), 33.

9. F–Pn, N.L.a 294 (47–54).

10. F–Pn, Rés. Vmf. ms. 85 (2).

11. According to a quick calculation made in 2004 by Michel Crichton, artistic director at Heugel Editions, this sum would be about 24,000 euros, that is, around 30,000 euros in 2020.

12. The score can be found in the archives of the Centre international Nadia et Lili Boulanger.

13. After hearing the work at Pugno's house on 25 June 1912, D'Annunzio wanted to change scene 4 of Act 3, but it was not corrected until the following August.

14. Nadia Boulanger to Gabriele D'Annunzio, 28 July 1912, Fondazione Il Vittoriale degli Italiani (I–GARvi), XCII, 2.

15. Boulanger to D'Annunzio, 11 August 1912, I–GARvi, XCII, 2.

16. D'Annunzio to Boulanger, 18 August 1912, F–Pn, N.L.a. 294 (47–54). D'Annunzio wishes for the composers to reimmerse themselves in reading classic Greek tragedy in order to capture the atmosphere of classical drama that pervades *La ville morte*.

17. Boulanger to D'Annunzio, 28 July 1912, I–GARvi, XCII, 2.

18. Raoul Pugno to D'Annunzio, 16 November 1912, I–GARvi, XCII, 4.

19. D'Annunzio to Boulanger, 3 September 1910, F–Pn, N.L.a. 294 (47–54).

20. Manuscript held in the archives of the Centre international Nadia et Lili Boulanger.

21. D'Annunzio to Henri Heugel, 3 September 1910, Paris, Heugel-Leduc Archives. D'Annunzio refers to the Book of Ruth to establish a dramatic and provocative parallel between the young and combative Ruth/Nadia and the aging Boaz/Pugno, an improbable couple who, contrary to all expectations, engendered a glorious son—just as the Boulanger-Pugno couple will give birth to a great work.

22. Pugno to D'Annunzio, 7 September 1910, I–GARvi, XCII, 4.

23. Boulanger to D'Annunzio, 8 November 1910, I–GARvi, XCII, 2.

24. Pugno to Pierre-Barthélemy Gheusi, 28 June 1911, quoted in Spycket, *À la recherche de Lili Boulanger,* 142.

25. Eugène Ysaÿe to Nadia Boulanger, 30 March 1912, F–Pn, N.L.a. 118 (334–36). Written after Pugno's death, Ysaÿe's letter suggests that he was the discreet witness of the love that joined the two artists.

26. Daybook of Lili Boulanger, 25 June 1912, "Dinner with the Pugnos with D'Annunzio and Muratore / after, *Ville morte* until 3 AM," F–Pn, Rés. Vmf. ms 113.

27. D'Annunzio to Nadia Boulanger, 8 December 1912, F–Pn, N.L.a. 294 (47–54).

28. "Our big breathless friend" alludes to Raoul Pugno's imposing physique, a result of his character as a *bon vivant.* Images from that time show him as corpulent and portly. On the day in question he had sung for D'Annunzio and one can imagine him being out of breath, given his lack of vocal technique. D'Annunzio to Nadia Boulanger, 1914, F–Pn, N.L.a. 65 (147–149), [1914]. See facsimile in Jérôme Spycket, *Nadia Boulanger* (Lausanne: Lattès-Payot, 1987), 48–49.

29. Pugno to D'Annunzio, 16 November 1912, I–GARvi, XCII, 4.

30. André Messager, born the same year as Pugno, 1852, was, like Pugno, a student at the Ecole Niedermeyer and an organist before he became a composer. Their friendship led Messager to conduct Fauré's Requiem for Pugno's funeral.

31. Henri Heugel to Nadia Boulanger, 31 January 1913, F–Pn, N.L.a. 75 (155)

32. Nadia Boulanger to Henri Heugel, [September 1913].

33. Raoul Pugno to Henri Heugel, 5 September 1913.

34. The manuscript bears a 1917 copyright, but was never published. See Laederich, "Catalogue de l'oeuvre," 338.

35. Raoul Pugno had been invited to give a concert in Moscow on 23 December 1913. The sixty-one-year-old pianist fell sick during the long, midwinter trip from Paris. Despite the loving presence of Nadia Boulanger and the prodigious efforts of doctors in Berlin and later Moscow, he died suddenly on 3 January from the after-effects of an acute bronchitis.

36. Eugène Ysaÿe to Nadia Boulanger, 19 March 1915, F–Pn, N.L.a. 118 (340–41).

37. "Monday, in M. Gheusi's office, there took place, in the presence of the directors, of Mlle. Croiza and M. Paul Vidal, the performance of *La ville morte.* . . . It was Mlle. Nadia Boulanger who, at the piano, played and sang the score." *Le Ménestrel* 80/14 (4 April 1914): 111.

38. Pierre-Barthélemy Gheusi, radio speech, 6 May 1938, upon the death of Gabriele D'Annunzio, Gheusi Collection, Bibliothèque musée de l'Opéra, Paris, 5 f.

39. "*La ville morte* by Nadia Boulanger and Raoul Pugno will be performed during the month of November, with this fine cast: Mlles [Marthe] Chenal, [Claire] Croiza, [Suzanne] Brohly and MM. [Jean] Altchewsky, [Hector] Dufranne." *La Liberté,* 8 July 1914.

40. Letter of 12 September 1914 published in Gheusi, *Guerre et théâtre, 1914–1918: Mémoires d'un officier du general Galliéni et journal parisien du théâtre national de l'Opéra–Comique pendant la guerre* (Nancy-Paris-Strasbourg: Berger-Levrault. 1919), 77. This letter came up for sale in Paris at Salle Drouot on 4 July 2005 (specialist Thierry Bodin).

41. Pierre-Barthélemy Gheusi, *Cinquante ans de Paris: Leurs femmes, mémoires d'un témoin* (Paris, Plon, 1940), 148.

42. Boulanger to D'Annunzio, 2 May 1916, I–GARvi, XCII, 2.

43. See Alexandra Laederich, "Nadia Boulanger et le Comité franco-américain du Conservatoire (1915–1919)," in *La Grande Guerre des musiciens*, ed. Esteban Buch, Myriam Chimènes, and Georgie Durosoir (Lyon: Symétrie, 2009), 161–73.

44. Boulanger to D'Annunzio, 28 June 1919, I–GARvi, XCII, 2.

45. There survives today only the orchestration of Acts 1 and 3, by Nadia Boulanger. Act 1 is dated 6 September 1923; Act 3 is not dated. An indication in Nadia Boulanger's daybook, 15 September 1923, "2nd Act will soon be finished," leads us to suppose that she had made progress on the orchestration of Act 2. But neither this act, nor Act 4, nor any orchestral parts have been found at the Heugel-Leduc publishing house or in the archives.

46. Gustave Samazeuilh to Nadia Boulanger, 19 September 1938, F–Pn, N.L.a. 103 (208).

47. After Nadia Boulanger's death, Leonard Bernstein, who had a profound admiration for her—calling her "La grande Mademoiselle"—thought of having the work performed in the United States. But nothing came of this, and the publisher Leduc possesses only the letter accompanying the return of the score, dated 1988.

48. The Centre international Nadia et Lili Boulanger is the copyright holder for Boulanger's compositions, including *La ville morte,* and has promoted editions and performances of her work as part of its mission. It is to be hoped that increasing interest in Boulanger's work as a composer will lead to performances of *La ville morte* with the Centre's authorization.

49. See also Caroline Potter, "Nadia Boulanger's and Raoul Pugno's *La ville morte*," *The Opera Quarterly* 16/3 (Summer 2000): 402.

# Serious Ambitions:
# Nadia Boulanger and the Composition
## of *La ville morte*

JEANICE BROOKS AND KIMBERLY FRANCIS

In a portrait of Nadia Boulanger published in 1960, at a time when her fame as a pedagogue had long been established, Aaron Copland reminisced about his lessons in Paris nearly forty years before. He prefaced his enthusiastic description of Boulanger's abilities with remarks about the two principal disadvantages she faced as a teacher of composition: that she was not herself an active practitioner, and that no woman had ever been ranked among the world's most famous composers. After wondering whether this absence was because women's minds were essentially ill adapted for musical creativity, Copland cast doubt on Boulanger's own compositional output, completed largely before he met her in 1921:

> To what extent Mademoiselle Boulanger had serious ambitions as a composer has never been entirely established. She has published a few short pieces, and once told me that she aided the pianist and composer Raoul Pugno in the orchestration of an opera of his.[1]

Sixty years on from Copland's statement, we know much more about Boulanger and Pugno's opera *La ville morte*. Her role in the work's creation was far greater than that of a simple orchestrator, and her collaboration with Pugno was more extensive than this single work.[2] Yet there remain many questions about their creative partnership and Boulanger's role within it. The musical evidence is difficult to evaluate; the hands of the two composers appear in a complex mix in the manuscripts of their collaborative compositions, and responsibility for writing out a passage is not necessarily an indication of authorship. Attempts to attribute music to one or the other partner on the basis of musical style are also fraught.[3]

That there are no clear markers of individual contribution is perhaps a sign of the success of the collaboration, but this also impedes attempts to understand how the partnership worked.

Although not every question can be answered, newly released documents shed considerable light on Boulanger's compositional ambitions, her relationship with Pugno, and the process of composing *La ville morte*. At the time her archives were donated to the Bibliothèque nationale de France in 1981, Boulanger's executors placed material that they considered to be particularly sensitive or personal under seal for thirty years. These documents, which have only recently been made available to scholars, include many of her daybooks from the time of her liaison with Pugno. The daybooks are daily agendas, published as twelve small booklets representing each month of the year and intended for keeping track of appointments and events. Boulanger used them to note times for lessons and social engagements, but also frequently employed margins and blank pages to record retrospective impressions of events and people and to write confessional prose in the manner of a diary. Though several daybooks from crucial periods and most of Pugno's letters to her were destroyed, the remaining documents can contribute to a new reading of *La ville morte* and what it meant to Boulanger both personally and professionally.[4] Here, we draw on this new evidence to reconsider *La ville morte*'s genesis and content, and to explore how gender discourses affected Boulanger's development and output as a woman composer in early twentieth-century France.

## Boulanger and Pugno

Boulanger's relationship with Raoul Pugno (1852–1914) was cause for speculation among early biographers.[5] Pugno was thirty-five years older than Boulanger (1887–1979) and a celebrated figure on the international concert circuit as a soloist and chamber musician, particularly in collaboration with the violinist Eugène Ysaÿe and cellist Pablo Casals. Revered as a concert artist, he was also a prolific and successful composer of piano and vocal music as well as works for the stage. He was sought after as a teacher, particularly by private piano pupils, and was a professor of harmony, and then piano, at the Paris Conservatoire between 1892 and 1901. Viewed through present-day eyes, Boulanger's relationship with this much older married man seems disturbing, considering the power imbalance between an internationally respected professional and an emerging artist as well as the asymmetries linked to gender and age. Relationships between older men (whether married or not) and much younger women were not exceptional in the Belle Epoque; Boulanger herself was the daughter of a father some forty years older than her mother, a factor that may have contributed to normalizing the relationship between her and Pugno in her immediate circle.[6] Teacher-student musical partnerships of various kinds—such as that between Boulanger's teacher Gabriel Fauré and his pupil and musical right-hand man, Jean Roger-Ducasse—regularly served as professional apprenticeships. Compositional partnerships, if not especially common, were also far from unprecedented in French stage culture of this time. Pugno wrote two ballets in collaboration with other artists: *Viviane* with André Messager in 1886 and *Le chevalier aux fleurs* with Clément Lippacher in 1899. Collaboration, then, was normal for Pugno and not exceptional during the Belle Epoque in general. It is the combination of the romantic liaison and the collaborative musical process between Boulanger and Pugno that was unique, and a part of what made their relationship so unusual during their time and so difficult to interpret today.

Pugno was a family friend: as a professor at the Conservatoire he had known Nadia's father, Ernest Boulanger, and the pianist was an increasingly prominent member of her mother Raïssa's social network after Ernest's death in 1900.[7] Pugno's importance was such that the inauguration of the Boulanger family's new Cavaillé-Coll organ, purchased at the end of Nadia's studies at the Conservatoire, was arranged around Pugno's availability. The program for the event on 4 February 1905 shows the pianist among the musical luminaries, including Nadia's teachers Alexandre Guilmant and Louis Vierne, who performed at what might be read as the symbolic launch of seventeen-year-old Nadia's career.[8]

A closer relationship with Nadia began later that year, in the summer of 1905. Boulanger's daybooks record two months largely spent in Gargenville, where Pugno had a country house. From mid-July until near the end of September, Nadia spent most of her time with Pugno and his family, including his wife, Marie, and daughter Renée, while Raïssa and Lili Boulanger were away. Pugno encouraged Nadia's development as a pianist, giving her lessons and allowing her to sit in on his own practice and rehearsals, an experience she found exhilarating. The combination of musical and personal attraction proved powerful. By 21 September, Boulanger noted, "When He isn't there, there's nothing," and a week later, recorded her "immense joy" at being asked to be Pugno's rehearsal partner for concerto preparation.[9] At the end of her September diary, her happiness overflowed:

> What a person, and how generously great, is my great, my dear friend Pugno. Truly, every day there are new revelations,

new surprises, and certainly the immense impression that I bring back from Gargenville was produced not only by the artist, because the man is just as fascinating. What an extraordinary union of strength, of nobility, of greatness and of charm. Blessed be fate to have permitted me to grow so close to him, because I will never again in my life find a person who comes near him. I am happy to observe all these things and completely happy: everything is beautiful for me and without clouds today. Since Mother comes back from Geneva day after tomorrow, what emptiness I will have in not seeing him anymore, he holds such a huge place in everything and for everyone. But after all, I know that he has a real affection for me and that I love him with all my heart.[10]

Over the following year, Pugno became increasingly central to Boulanger's life. Her daybooks from 1906 show them frequently together —the Pugno and Boulanger apartments in Paris were minutes away from each other in the 9th arrondissement—and she recorded his activities alongside her own, noting details of his engagements and concert repertory even when he was away. By the summer, the Boulanger family was involved in buying their own property in Gargenville near Pugno's country house. Boulanger and Pugno played together, both in four-hand and piano duet repertoire and in concerto rehearsal for Pugno, and she continued to work with him on her solo piano technique. Annotations in the daybooks reveal her profound admiration for Pugno's playing as well as the thrill of her own progress with his support: comments such as "transformation—illumination," added to her note of a solo lesson, evoke the musical revelations she experienced with him.[11] She frequently commented on her happiness when she was with Pugno, noting his efforts to boost her confidence and her excitement about the future. The library of his country house in Gargenville, where they met in private and worked together, became a site charged with meaning for her (see Figure 1).[12]

The daybooks also trace tensions caused by Pugno's frequent absences and heavy touring schedule. In September 1906, after summer holidays of near-daily contact, Pugno told Boulanger he was fearful of the separation that winter would inevitably bring; he talked of cutting dates from his concert calendar to shorten his absences.

We go into the library, we talk, he tells me that he fears the winter very much, and the separation that it will entail. He wants to cancel certain concerts in order to shorten it

Figure 1. Raoul Pugno in his library at La Maison Blanche, Gargenville, 1905.

as much as possible. He is kinder every day—he even talks
again about the concert which we will give—when I tell him
I won't come tomorrow, he says, you will let me come to you
instead—we walk for a little while.[13]

A few days later, when Boulanger raised the possibility of leaving to study
in Russia, he was deeply hurt:

I say that I plan to leave for Russia. P says brusquely that the
Conservatoire won't reopen then he says: Ah I want to have
a word with you . . . we go into the library and there, with
tears in his eyes, [he says] it makes me very sad to hear you
always talking of leaving, [if you did] then I would go myself
to America—far from separating us, I have projects so that
we can be more together than ever.[14]

Pugno did tour for several weeks in October–November, plunging
Boulanger into emotional turmoil. On 8 November, she wrote: "I tell
myself it is stupid to expect something from life, it brings you nothing

**SALLE BERLIOZ**
55, Rue de Clichy

*Le Mercredi 5 Décembre 1906, à 9 heures précises*

# CONCERT D'ORGUE

DONNÉ PAR Mlle

# NADIA BOULANGER

AVEC LE CONCOURS DE Mme

## JEANNE RAUNAY

ET DE M.

## RAOUL PUGNO

**PRIX DES PLACES**

**Fauteuils d'Orchestre, 10 fr. — Fauteuils de Balcon, 5 fr. — Fauteuils de Galerie, 3 fr.**

*On trouve des Billets : à la Salle **BERLIOZ**; chez MM. **A. DURAND** et Fils, 4, Place de la Madeleine ; **HAMELLE**, 22, Boulevard Malesherbes, et **AU MÉNESTREL**, 2 bis, Rue Vivienne.*

**Direction de Concerts R. STRAKOSCH, 56, Rue La Bruyère.**

Figure 2. Program for Boulanger's solo organ concert,
Salle Berlioz, Paris, 5 December 1906.

but disillusion. I am not working anymore, I am good for nothing, what atrophy I create." And on the following day she continued, "Today the gloom and discouragement reach their maximum. I can hardly live."[15] But a few weeks later, after Pugno's return, they gave their first public concert together. The recital on 5 December 1906, at the Salle Berlioz on rue de Clichy, was designed to put Boulanger in the spotlight, providing her with top billing and presenting her as a concerto soloist at the organ while Pugno provided the orchestral reduction at the piano (see Figure 2). Boulanger's daybook records her satisfaction with her playing but also the emotional charge of performing with Pugno: "What makes me happiest of all is to have given this very first concert with him—it is a union that is dear to me."[16] Throughout the 1906 daybooks, the complex intersection of feelings about love and work underlines how the pair's increasingly active professional collaboration over the subsequent years took at least some of its impetus from their emotional relationship, just as that relationship drew on their admiration for each other as musicians. This combination was decisive for Boulanger's career in a way that it was not, however, for the well-established older man.

Although the daybooks show Boulanger's immense admiration for Pugno's musicianship and a strong tendency to orient her life around his, they also demonstrate that she exercised creative agency from early in their relationship. In a 1906 daybook entry she describes a lunch at the Pugno apartment followed by a session during which Pugno played four newly completed piano compositions for Boulanger and Antonin Marmontel, who was himself a much-published composer and professor of piano at the Paris Conservatoire. Boulanger's note records how she advised a change to one piece, which is an index of how important the act of expressing a musical opinion to two senior male artists was to her.[17]

Capturing the details of the subsequent years in which Boulanger and Pugno's relationship deepened is more complicated. The daybooks for most of 1907 are missing, as are the love letters from Pugno that Boulanger refers to in later diaries. It is likely that the missing materials were even more personal than the daybooks from 1905 and 1906, and that these documents were destroyed by Boulanger herself or by her executors. Although she continued to employ her daybooks sporadically to reflect on major events in her life, from 1909 to 1913 Boulanger principally used daybooks for appointments; in comparison to the heavily annotated daybooks of 1905 and 1906, she rarely recorded feelings and impressions. But if her emotional reactions in these years are less clear, the importance of the relationship with Pugno remains obvious. It is also at this time that Boulanger began to invest her efforts seriously into becoming known as a composer.

Boulanger's solo-authored, non-student works already date from 1905, and by the time she began collaborating compositionally with Pugno, she had produced a cantata, *Les sirènes*; at least one orchestral work; and several *mélodies*.[18] The songs in particular suggest Boulanger was already thinking in terms of larger forces and forms. She orchestrated some of her early *mélodies*, including *Ecoutez la chanson bien douce* and *Soleils couchants*, both 1905, to texts by Paul Verlaine; and *Elégie*, 1906, orchestrated 1907, on a text by Albert Samain. These can be viewed as likely preparatory exercises for the Prix de Rome competition and its requirement for the composition of a cantata employing vocal soloists and orchestra. Boulanger's compositional aspirations indeed spilled into the public sphere in 1906 in the beginning of a four-year campaign to win the Prix de Rome. Entering the competition was a clear indicator of her ambition, since winning the prize, with its paid residency at the Villa Médicis in Rome and guaranteed performance and publication opportunities, was an important first step in many French composers' careers (including that of her father Ernest). Her efforts culminated with a scandalous round in 1908 for which she was begrudgingly awarded the Deuxième Grand Prix. The following year, in 1909, tradition dictated that Boulanger could be reasonably confident of winning the Premier Grand Prix; but she advanced to the final round only to receive nothing from the jury, which decided not to award a first prize in that year's competition, perhaps to avoid the unprecedented step of giving the award to a woman.[19]

Although she failed to win the prize many believed she deserved, Boulanger's achievements in the Prix de Rome brought praise and attention for her music.[20] She had many powerful supporters for her compositional work during her transition from student to professional, most notably from Gabriel Fauré, Charles-Marie Widor, Paul Vidal, and Louis Vierne.[21] Her familial connections with the Parisian musical and theatrical world and her ties to the Conservatoire, where she had been a star pupil, also aided in her early professional pursuits. Boulanger's works began to receive performances in prestigious venues: several of her *mélodies* featured on programs at the Salle Pleyel in 1907 and 1908, and in January 1909, orchestrated versions of two of her songs were performed by the Lamoureux orchestra at the Salle Gaveau. Leading artists such as the French-Canadian tenor Rodolphe Plamondon were enthusiastic about her work, and in 1909 the Hamelle publishing house began to issue her music.[22] These activities testify to Boulanger's determination and ambition at this moment in her career.[23]

Yet there is no doubt that Pugno was her principal mentor, and this became increasingly visible in public musical culture. As a keyboard duo, they collaborated on events designed to promote Boulanger's work, for example, at the Salle Pleyel on 11 January 1908 and 27 January 1909 (Figure 3). Their concerts increasingly included Boulanger's compositions and were designed to promote her as a composer as much as to showcase her talents as a pianist and organist. And then, from April to August 1909, the pair began to collaborate as composers, producing their first joint work: the song cycle *Les heures claires*, a setting of texts by the Belgian Symbolist poet Emile Verhaeren.[24] The cycle was published in 1910, the same year that Pugno served as one of the two members to sponsor Boulanger's admission to the Société des Auteurs, Compositeurs, et Editeurs de Musique (SACEM), the professional organization responsible for the collection and payment of artists' rights. The application from February of that year lists Boulanger's occupation as "compositeur de musique" and provides a list of published and unpublished works in support of her application, including songs, ensemble vocal music, and works for voice and orchestra.[25] By 1910, Boulanger's career—now increasingly dedicated to musical composition—was thriving. She was well respected within Parisian musical circles, although her professional security became increasingly intertwined with Pugno's presence. How much Pugno still functioned as Boulanger's champion and how much they moved toward being peers remains unclear, although the reality likely fluctuated situationally and sat uneasily between the two. Their emotional relationship added extra tensions to the mix, both in the public's reception of Boulanger and in her working partnership with Pugno. It was at this time that the pair took on their most ambitious project to date: writing an opera.

### La ville morte

Boulanger's close friend Jean Roger-Ducasse began to consider writing an opera on Gabriele D'Annunzio's first drama, *La ville morte*, in 1909, but by the spring of 1910 he had given it up and Boulanger and Pugno manifested interest in the work.[26] At the age of twenty-two, on 30 April 1910, Boulanger met D'Annunzio at the Salle Pleyel premiere of *Les heures claires*. A month later, on 31 May, she and Pugno signed the contract with the publisher Henri Heugel to write an opera on D'Annunzio's play. Completed in 1896 as *La città morta*, the drama had premiered in Paris in French translation in 1898, with the celebrated Sarah Bernhardt in the role of Anne. An equally famous actress, Eleonora Duse, D'Annunzio's lover and collaborator, starred in the Italian premiere in Milan three years

# PROGRAMME

🙢 🙢 🙢

1. **Variations et Fugue** sur un Thème
   de Beethoven, pour deux Pianos . . . . . . . **MAX REGER.**

   M. Raoul PUGNO.
   Mⁱˡᵉ Nadia BOULANGER.

2. **Trois Mélodies** . . . . . . . . . . . . . . . . . . **NADIA BOULANGER.**
   (1ʳᵉ AUDITION)

   M. R. PLAMONDON.

3. **Petite Suite** . . . . . . . . . . . . . . . . . . . . **CLAUDE DEBUSSY.**
   A) *En bateau.*
   B) *Cortège.*
   C) *Menuet.*
   D) *Ballet.*

   **Danses.**
   A) *Danse sacrée.*
   B) *Danse profane.*

   M. Raoul PUGNO.
   Mⁱˡᵉ Nadia BOULANGER.

4. **Trois Mélodies** . . . . . . . . . . . . . . . . . . **NADIA BOULANGER.**
   (2ᵉ AUDITION)

   M. R. PLAMONDON.

5. A) **Variations** . . . . . . . . . . . . . . . . . . . . **L. NICOLAIEW.**
   B) **Pelléas et Mélisande** . . . . . . . . . **G. FAURÉ.**
   1. *Prélude.*
   2. *Fileuse.*
   3. *Molto adagio.*

   C) **Variations** . . . . . . . . . . . . . . . . . . . . **R. FISCHHOFF.**

   M. Raoul PUGNO.
   Mⁱˡᵉ Nadia BOULANGER.

Figure 3. Program for Pugno-Boulanger piano and organ collaborative
performance, Salle Pleyel, Paris, 27 January 1909.

• 28 •

later in 1901. The writing of the play informed the plot of D'Annunzio's novel *Il fuoco* (*The Flame*, 1900), in which D'Annunzio's alter ego, Stelio Effrena, writes his first tragedy with his muse, Foscarina, representing Duse. *La ville morte* thus figured centrally in D'Annunzio's efforts to revitalize classical tragedy within modernity—a project heavily influenced by the theories of Friedrich Nietzsche—but it also includes strong connections to Symbolism as well as elements of the *verismo* and bourgeois drama that D'Annunzio self-consciously rejected.[27]

Boulanger's interest in Symbolist texts was already clear in her choice of poems by Paul Verlaine, Albert Samain, and Maurice Maeterlinck for the texts of her *mélodies*, as well as from the decision to set Verhaeren's *Les heures claires* in collaboration with Pugno. This interest was part of the wider musical trend that included Fauré's incidental music for Maeterlinck's *Pelléas et Mélisande* (1898) and Claude Debussy's opera on the same play (1902), to name only two prominent examples. Following her sister's lead, Lili Boulanger began setting texts by Maeterlinck among her earliest melodies (*Attente* and *Reflets* from 1910 and 1911), at about the same time Nadia began work on *La ville morte*. A few years later, Lili too would embark upon a Symbolist opera based on Maeterlinck's play *La Princesse Maleine*, while D'Annunzio would seek to place his subsequent play, *Le martyre de Saint Sébastien*, written in French, with Roger-Ducasse before agreeing on an operatic collaboration with Debussy. These musico-literary currents, D'Annunzio's notoriety in France, the celebrity of the actresses associated with the play, and the many similarities in structure and theme to the much admired *Pelléas* must have seemed to augur well for the choice of *La ville morte* and its successful adaptation.[28]

At the same time, the play's oppressive gender dynamics can be read as posing an existential challenge to female creativity. Unlike many other contemporary dramas set by French musicians, it was at least nominally set in the present. Taking inspiration from Heinrich Schliemann's discovery of the supposed ruins of Mycenae (which D'Annunzio visited in 1896) the main characters are European contemporaries involved in the excavation of the classical past, providing the mythical elements of the text. Leonardo/ Léonard, an archaeologist, has been excavating the ruins of Mycenae for two years, attempting to discover the tombs of the Atrides, the family of Agamemnon. Léonard lives in a villa near the ruins with his sister Bianca Maria, whose name in Italian—White (Pure) Mary—overdetermines her virginity. In the French version of the play, the character's name was translated as Blanchemarie, but in D'Annunzio's opera libretto for Pugno and Boulanger she is called Hébé, named after the Greek goddess of youth. Living with the siblings are Léonard's friend, the poet Alessandro/

Alexandre, who aims for a literary recovery of classical antiquity in parallel to Léonard's rediscovery of its physical remains, and Alexandre's middle-aged wife, Anna/Anne, who has lost her sight and become estranged from her husband but retains a visionary ability to understand the unfolding tragedy of the other characters' relations. The final character is an unnamed Nurse who looks after Anne.[29] Both men (and in some readings, Anne herself) are consumed with passion for Hébé. Hébé herself feels affection for Alexandre but resists what she considers to be illicit feelings about her friend Anne's husband. Anne laments her isolation but encourages Hébé to live her life fully and plans to remove herself to allow Alexandre and Hébé to consummate their love. Léonard confesses his incestuous desire for Hébé to Alexandre; then, when Anne reveals that Hébé loves Alexandre, Léonard becomes obsessed with preserving his sister's "purity" and kills her by drowning her in the Fountain of Perseia. (See Figure 4.) The final act takes place around Hébé's corpse, where Léonard explains to Alexandre that in preserving his sister's virginity he has purified himself. Anne appears, accidentally brushes against Hébé's body, and at once exclaims that she can see again, drawing the drama to a close.

D'Annunzio's plays consistently work to represent masculinity as will to power in the mold of the Nietszchean *Übermensch*, expressed through the domination or destruction of weaker elements marked by gender and race. In her analysis of D'Annunzio's "masterful men," Maggie Günsberg describes how suppression or possession of the female body and "fear of oneness" with a devalued femininity is an essential component of this vision.[30] In *La ville morte*, Anne's body is figured as a site of sterility and decay: like her blindness, her age and inability to have children are presented as forms of disability, even punishment, and mark her as incapable of sharing the male characters' quest for glory. Alexandre believes sexual possession of Hébé is essential to his creative work and insists upon her capitulation to his desire as necessary to the fulfillment of his artistic potential. Léonard's own quest furnishes D'Annunzio's central tragic device: the attempt to unearth traces of the ancient tragedy of the Atrides brings their curse to bear on modern lives. The corpses of Cassandra, Clytemnestra, and Agamemnon disintegrate on contact with air when Léonard discovers them; and the discovery of the horror within himself requires the annihilation of the body of his sister, destroyed for the "fault" of female sexuality.[31] As Günsberg observes, Hébé's body, preserved in its virgin state, becomes a site for the containment of femininity: "Leonardo places the sister he has drowned among the artefacts he has excavated, where she will lie 'in glory' as one of his treasures. She is now idealized, objectified, commodified—and dead."[32]

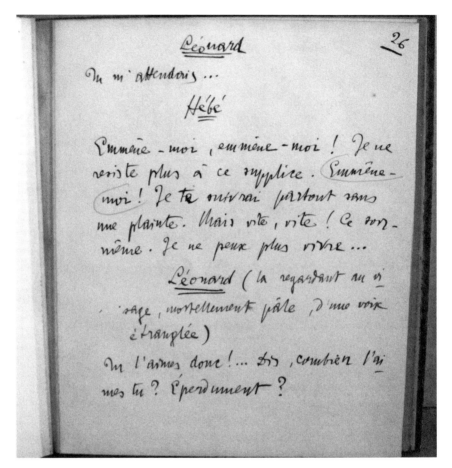

Figure 4. Page from Gabriele D'Annunzio's manuscript libretto for *La ville morte*, show-
ing the passage from the play's Act 4, scene 2 that became Act 3, scene 4 of the opera.
Translation: Léonard: You were waiting for me . . . Hébé: Take me away, take me away!
I cannot resist this torture any more. Take me away! I will follow you anywhere with-
out complaining. But quickly, quickly! This very evening. I cannot live any longer . . .
Léonard (looking into her face, deathly pale, in a strangled voice): You love him then! . . .
Tell me, how much do you love him? Madly?

Thus any composer who chose to set *La ville morte* had to decide how
to handle D'Annunzio's representation of artistic expression as predicated on the creation and destruction of an essentialized femininity. For
Boulanger specifically, the play may have raised other issues, particularly
surrounding the adulterous relationship at the center of the drama and
the sacrificial murder of the character most like herself in age and gender.

Moreover, D'Annunzio seems to have considered Boulanger as a Duse-like embodiment of the understanding of the feminine that underpinned his creative work on the libretto, as well as the eventual musical translator of the creative work she inspired. Shortly after beginning the libretto for Boulanger and Pugno, D'Annunzio expressed the view that their compositional work should be divided by gender: in a letter to Boulanger he asserted, "The male element belongs to Raoul—I recommend to you the song of the blind woman and the lament of the virgin. I thought of your fresh inspiration when creating them."[33] However, there is little evidence that D'Annunzio understood the composers' creative process, and as our exploration of the daybooks shows, there is no evidence at all to suggest that they apportioned work on the piece in this way.

In exploring how the collaboration functioned in practice, we ask how setting *La ville morte* furnished Boulanger with opportunities to imagine and inhabit both masculine and feminine roles musically. The transition from play to opera involved a number of changes, including cuts and additions, such as the "lament of the virgin" that D'Annunzio wrote especially for the opera. In some cases, these changes significantly affect representation of female characters and their agency. And a reading of the play and libretto texts alone leaves the aspect of performance unaccounted for: consideration of stage representation can furnish different perspectives. James Nikopolous, for example, sees Anne as the central character in the drama—in contrast to readings that focus on Léonard as tragic hero—partly in light of critical reactions to the performances of Bernhardt and Duse in the role. Nikopolous interprets Anne as D'Annunzio's Greek chorus, "the conduit through which the characters are presented to a modern audience," whose incorporation into the drama "looked to the *diva* and what she could accomplish onstage."[34] How did Boulanger's own performance of the female characters' roles—a responsibility she regularly took in presenting the score to potential supporters—inflect her understanding of her position during the composition of the work? To engage with these questions, we first consider what primary sources tell us about Boulanger and Pugno's compositional process before turning to a reading of Hébé's lament, with an eye to a feminist reading of the score and its performative potential.

According to Boulanger's daybooks, the opera's first notes were written on 22 May 1910. News of the collaboration spread quickly, and promotional articles for the project appeared in periodicals already supportive of Boulanger and Pugno, including *Le Ménestrel* (which was owned by Heugel) and *Femina* (the journal of the Conservatoire Femina-Musica, where both Boulanger and Pugno taught).[35] If D'Annunzio's conflation of Boulanger with his characters collapsed her work into concepts of the essentialized Other and creative muse, the article in *Femina*, "Mademoiselle Nadia Boulanger and Monsieur Raoul Pugno Collaborate," shows another way in which Boulanger's contribution to the compositional partnership could be problematically feminized. In the Figure 5 photograph, Pugno occupies the active position at the piano with the score, while Boulanger leans gracefully against the instrument in a way that displays her dress, suggesting that her role is decorative or ornamental rather than substantial. Her pose evokes the fashionable elegance characteristic of women's magazines, and resonates with similar images of female composers in contemporary newspapers.[36] Pugno's professional reputation further dominates the photograph through the duplication of his representation in action at the keyboard, an image which also appears in the large portrait hanging over the piano as if overlooking the work of the pair. This image contrasts with the photograph of Boulanger working alone on *La ville morte* in 1911 (see Alexandra Laederich's essay in this volume) in which she pores over the score with pencil in hand, posed as if in the act of composing. Boulanger seems to have aimed for a public persona more in keeping with images such as this, which presented her work in the guise of the early twentieth-century *femme nouvelle*—a capable, confident, and successful professional woman—rather than evoking concepts of bourgeois propriety, amateurism, and the salon.[37] Both images, however, underline how Boulanger's contribution to *La ville morte* was viewed through the lens of socially constructed femininities that she herself had to negotiate in her interactions with potential supporters of the work as well as with her creative collaborators.

Much of the summer of 1911 was spent reviewing the libretto, and D'Annunzio delivered rewrites to the composers in September. Work began in earnest during the winter of 1910–11. From February to March 1911, Pugno was largely absent, performing concerts in Hungary, Austria, Germany, Belgium, England, and the French provinces; thus work progressed slowly and sporadically. Yet Boulanger noted in her daybook of 19 March that "the duet from Act II is almost finished," showing that she continued to work on the opera even in Pugno's absence. Indeed, throughout the opera's composition, she appears to have drafted work independently.[38] The publisher Heugel maintained his readers' interest by providing news on the work's progress, announcing in mid-March that the libretto was complete and the reviewer from *Le Ménestrel* had heard portions of the first act.[39] April saw the end of Pugno's travels, allowing time for work during the Easter break and in between teaching commitments. On 4 April, Boulanger recorded the joy she found in creativity, declaring that it was worth any difficulty or sacrifice, and on 17 April she noted that the

Figure 5. "Mlle Nadia Boulanger et M. Raoul Pugno Collaborent,"
published in *Femina*, July 1910.

beginning of Act 1, scene 4 was complete.[40] The pair began to seek reactions among their colleagues, playing the first act for Louis Vierne on 3 April 1911.[41] By 5 June, they played two acts for the conductor Maurice Kufferath, director of the Théâtre de la Monnaie in Brussels, which they may have envisioned as a home for the opera's premiere. A month later, on 6 July, they played the initial version of the second act for Heugel.[42]

But during the summer of 1911 Pugno and Boulanger disputed where the work was headed. According to their contract, they had to finish the opera by September 1912, so the summer of 1911 was crucial; yet despite Boulanger's earlier enthusiasm, by the middle of the summer the project was near to breaking down. Boulanger's daybooks record signs that her relationship with Pugno was already under strain in the early months of summer. They made up after a quarrel in mid-June, Boulanger writing, "We both remain a little defensive—but he is kind, good, and a little shy—once we arrived [in Gargenville] we talked it over and all is well because our affection can and will bear much greater tests than this."[43] Only a week later, however, she comments: "The situation is really nebulous as far as concerns me."[44] Other entries suggest that differences over *La ville morte* and the collaborative working process were a significant source of tension.

Boulanger records several days in July when she went to work with Pugno but felt ignored. She was reluctant to express her dissatisfaction, and a letter to D'Annunzio suggests that the risk of being patronized was among the reasons for her silence. On 2 July 1911, Boulanger wrote to D'Annunzio to update him about their progress, only to confess:

> I know well that all manifestation of enthusiasm in a woman, toward a man, has a slightly ridiculous, irrational side and that she always risks producing a smile of male vanity, and indulgence for those excessive and imponderable beings who are too numerous to pay attention to. Knowing this has frequently made it difficult to express my feelings, because I would be upset, sad, and a little ashamed, that the expression and summation of the best of me might be taken for one of those temporary or enduring, but nevertheless superficial, passions that in any case are very foreign to my way of being or feeling.[45]

Boulanger's comments here reference her desire to speak candidly about her admiration for D'Annunzio's writing rather than describing her working relationship with Pugno, but they clearly show that in summer of 1911, gender inequity and frustrations at not being taken seriously were foremost in her mind. On 10 July, after a composition session with Pugno, she noted in her daybook: "We worked a little or rather . . . he worked!"; and the following day continued: "The tension mounts and the situation keeps on being difficult, because he does everything alone—while I read!"[46] Two days later, she wrote more explicitly about the problem:

> And yet another afternoon passes without anything serious but in an uneasiness that increases my partial silence—I amass regrets, resentment and . . . it's no good—he works, writes lovely music, remains very tender and very attached— without guessing anything and I continue to suffer, at times to cry, without accusing anyone but in the cruel disappointment of realizing that we will each have our own child in *La ville morte* [and] with the certainty that this is not the one that our two minds would have created if they had been able to continue uniting.[47]

This entry provides the first explicit mention of Boulanger connecting collaborative creativity and procreation. The layers of her relationship with Pugno easily lent themselves to mapping sexual relations onto the act of composition, and the notion of the work as offspring was a metaphor Boulanger used when discussing the character of Princesse Maleine with her sister.[48] Later in life, Boulanger would become known as someone who emphasized the importance of a women's role as wife and mother. Possibly, she thought of compositional creation as a chance to bring new life into the world, when actual childbirth with Pugno was not achievable. That this is something she desired, at least in some moments, is suggested by the draft poem, "A mon enfant," which she entered in her daybook in 1913, with musical annotations indicating that she may have planned to set the words as a *mélodie*. The verses specifically concern her wish to see the eyes of her beloved reflected in the gaze of an as yet unborn child.[49]

In the summer of 1911, Boulanger finally decided that she could no longer remain silent about her unhappiness with the collaboration. She shared her feelings with Pugno, describing explicitly the conflict between her admiration and love for him and her creative ideals:

> Went to Pugno's—a little sadness and explanations—confession of the complex emotion made up of my pride as a woman, as a lover, and my sorrow as an artist—but this gratefully, tenderly and not decisively enough for things to get worse, then those rare and unforgettable hours—of sincerity, of emotion, of giving—what immense affection unites us—it is unbelievable.[50]

The discussion continued the following day, when Boulanger announced that she was withdrawing from the project. After over a year of work on *La ville morte*, this was a dramatic move. In Boulanger's account of the incident, the break with the opera was a premonition of a definitive end to the relationship with Pugno as well, and it was the threat of that loss that moved both partners to attempt to repair the broken working relationship:

> The most serious and sad day of all, for after my clearly expressed decision to abandon the work which is no longer *ours*, but his or mine in turn, we end up, without anger and on the contrary, after a *clear* and noble refusal from him to continue without me, in such incomprehension that I have for a moment the impression of a definitive farewell, or at least of its premature, but precise, appearance. A word, a gesture from him erases it all, I see him so sad, so worried, so profoundly distressed by my pain and to see that something threatened to disappear between us, that a look brings us together and we forget everything in the immense and indestructible tenderness that we find in it. We promise each other to resume our work together, one mind with the other, and we are closer to each other than ever.[51]

The renewed collaborative process seems to have begun immediately, as later on the same page Boulanger recorded, "The 2nd act is finished."[52] The following day, she reflected on the entire incident, taking a perhaps overly generous view of Pugno's suppression of her compositional input in the preceding weeks: "I reread the preceding pages and I feel guilty that I did not force myself to write that he had no ulterior motives and that never did he intend either to hurt me or prevent me from working."[53] Boulanger's striking commitment to forgive Pugno contrasts greatly with her preceding frustrations and mounting threats. One can read in her words the process by which she internalizes traditional gender roles, assuming the blame for the tensions between her and Pugno. Herein lies a central difficulty in the power dynamic shared between Pugno and Boulanger: the conflict between Boulanger's desire to subvert gender norms and be a driving part of the creative process with a man significantly more experienced than she was, and her desire to be part of a loving relationship with a much older, married man, a desire that almost certainly required her to play the subservient role. As she puts it, she struggled to reconcile her "pride as a woman . . . a lover . . . and her sorrow as an artist." The complexities of maneuvering within these lopsided power dynamics clearly preoccupied much of Boulanger's mental and emotional energies throughout the compositional process, informing her professional and personal development.

The near breakdown of the project in July 1911 seems to have sparked determination in both partners. They immediately began to rewrite portions of the first act, perhaps to eliminate the sense of alternating rather than joint composition. Pugno and Boulanger were ready to play the revised Acts 1 and 2 for Paul Vidal on 21 August and by 6 September they had completed the beginning of Act 3. This act, the climax of the opera, continued to occupy them for the rest of the month and represents the main new compositional work completed after the restarting of their compositional partnership. Boulanger first notes work on this section in her daybook on 12 September; on 7 October she writes: "We are working frenetically as we want to perform up to the end of the stanzas tomorrow."[54] "Stanzas" is a reference to the character Hébé's strophic aria "Vous me voyez, mes soeurs" (You see me, my sisters), which makes up the entirety of Act 3, scene 5, and which is her last music before her death offstage at the hands of her brother. In a letter to D'Annunzio from 28 July 1912, Boulanger called Act 3 the "capstone [*pierre d'achèvement*] of the opera."[55] We will return to the musical content of this aria below. Thanks to their redoubled efforts, Boulanger and Pugno managed to complete the draft on time and on 8 October played through all three acts for Albert Carré, director of the Opéra-Comique.[56]

This was the last compositional activity for the year. At the end of the summer, doctors ordered Boulanger to Nice to recover from throat problems that had plagued her for months, and Pugno began his concertizing season. While alone in Nice, Boulanger worked on a piece of her own and from 14 October to the end of November worked steadily on a composition which, the daybooks note, was for Pugno. Likely, this is a reference to the *Fantaisie* for piano and orchestra that Boulanger finished the following year.[57] It was not until the following spring that *La ville morte* is mentioned again, when the collaborators turned to the task of the piece's staging and performance. On 11 April 1912, they performed the first act and passages of the others for the soprano Claire Croiza, who was "crazily moved" (*follement émue*).[58] Croiza would later be cast in the role of Hébé. By the end of the month, Pugno and Boulanger turned their attention to the piano-vocal reduction of the first act.

At this point, Lili Boulanger's failing health and needs as a budding composer began to complicate her older sister's own professional progress. Determined now to enter the Prix de Rome competition herself, Lili Boulanger began composing in earnest, sending pieces to Nadia regularly and requesting feedback and advice. Lili also frequently fell ill while Nadia entered this hectic time in *La ville morte*'s development. These heavy demands splintered Nadia's time and energies. In 1912, she had to miss one of Pugno's performances at the Trocadéro to respond immediately to a letter from Lili, written in the loge at Compiègne where Lili was competing for the first time in the Prix de Rome. Pugno was annoyed by the conflict. Difficulties of this sort continued to be a major factor throughout Nadia's personal-professional activities from 1912 to 1913, as Pugno also suffered from various illnesses. In a rare moment of blunt analysis on 24 July 1913, after Lili won the *premier grand prix* in the Prix de Rome (see Figure 6) and it became clear she would need help to take up the prize in Italy, Nadia wrote in her daybook: "I try to reconcile what I can do for Lili and for Pugno—it's complicated because she is too young to fully understand and he is not young enough to give me up."[59] The slow progress made on the opera during 1912 was often a byproduct of factors outside of Nadia Boulanger's control, as her own professional aspirations had to adapt to the needs of two people whom she loved dearly.

In May and June of 1912, D'Annunzio returned to Paris, and as was typical throughout the opera's creation, Boulanger served as the primary correspondent with the poet. The artists were in continual contact, working to finish the fourth and final act of *La ville morte*. On 8 June, work on this final portion began and continued steadily for the remainder of the summer. By 3 August, the first draft of Act 4 was nearly complete.[60] On 6 August, Boulanger's daybooks again contain her reflection on the gender disparity between herself and her collaborator. She writes: "He tells me things about his childhood, and later ... I realize the sadness of women, for in stirring up his past, *he* still has a present, while a woman of his age has long since finished life—*we speak of us* and work, very well."[61] It is difficult to say how she viewed herself in this equation; one wonders what Boulanger imagined her life would be like when she reached the same age as Pugno. Driven by youthful ambition and emotional devotion, she seems to drop the subject, focussing instead on their current hard work and productivity. At the same time, her response to an investigation by *Femina*, published in the journal later in 1912, suggests that her struggle to reconcile a successful compositional career with gendered expectations had convinced her that the combination was impossible. Boulanger was among a suite of female celebrities asked to reflect on the theme "What do young girls dream of" and to provide advice to young women on their aspirations. The journal stated that Boulanger believed "Artists dream only of their art and consider it absolutely incompatible with the joys of familial existence," and quoted her as saying:

> The moment a woman wishes to carry out her true role as wife
> and mother, it is impossible for her to carry out her role as

Figure 6. Nadia and Lili Boulanger together in 1913, after Lili became the first woman to win the *premier grand prix* of the Prix de Rome. This photograph is one of several produced to celebrate Lili's achievement.

artist, writer or musician. Therefore, before deciding to take one or the other route, before making her way, it is indispensable for her to ponder her decision for a long time, and to weigh up familial joys and artistic ones.[62]

This quote serves as another glimpse of how often Boulanger reflected on the realities of gender disparity when it came to professional aspirations and how much she invested in the emotional bonds between her and Pugno.

On 27 August, Boulanger notes "We finish Act 3—what joy," most likely meaning they had at that time completed the long postlude to Hébé's aria. Boulanger expressed her immense satisfaction at the end of summer 1912 in a letter to her student Marcelle de Manziarly. Excusing herself for epistolary silence, Boulanger confided:

> Every day since I left you, the hours have multiplied so to say, and never has a summer been so productive—you know, or perhaps you don't, that I had to finish a work in collaboration with Pugno—in fact, since the end of August, *La ville morte* is finished, and now it is necessary to orchestrate, reduce, copy. All this, not to complain (I have just lived through months of very profound joy) but to make you admit that, after all, human powers have their limits—this to such an extent, that I haven't written a single line [of a letter] for quite a long time.[63]

The all-encompassing nature of their work on the opera eclipsed other professional activities. The letter testifies to the centrality of the act of composition to Boulanger at this time, and how determined she was to see the project complete. Later in the month, Pugno and Boulanger performed the third and fourth acts: first both acts for Vidal on 19 September, and then, on the 22nd, they performed Act 3 for the Chapelots, acquaintances from the Paris music world.[64] As in previous performances, the partners sang the roles themselves, with Boulanger performing the role of Hébé. On this occasion she noted, "Performance Act III for the Chapelots—[I am] very moved, sing it really well—they are *very impressed*."[65] Two days later the partners went to Heugel to announce that their opera was finished.

### "Le lamento de la vierge" and the Role of Hébé

As Pugno and Boulanger performed excerpts of their work for others, she generally took all the women's roles; her admission that she sang Hébé well for the Chapelots because she was moved suggests she was particularly highly invested in Act 3 and its music. In a much later letter, D'Annunzio recalled her performance as Hébé as a central memory of their work together on the piece. It is not difficult to imagine Boulanger associating herself with the young character of Hébé who sees the injustice in her gender and situation only to eventually submit to its realities. There is evidence, too, that the character of Hébé was the source of some of the differences between Boulanger and Pugno that led to the project's near breakdown in the summer of 1911.

Manuscript notebooks containing working copies of *La ville morte*'s libretto that Pugno and Boulanger employed during the compositional process are preserved in the Bibliothèque nationale de France.[66] Portions of the libretto are heavily annotated, containing multiple sections of extensive comments in both partners' hands and certain places where ideas have been forcefully crossed out. Though our reading remains speculation, these particular primary documents may well correspond with the daybook descriptions of rifts in the Pugno-Boulanger collaboration. We hypothesize that the second daybook contains Boulanger's musings while Pugno was away on tour, with the subsequent layer of annotations and cross-outs indicating his responses after he returned. For example, Boulanger writes about Hébé's lines: "It would be nice to lengthen [her] responses a little. Her role in this scene is far too passive, especially after her behavior in the first act." In the margin, a new layer of writing simply states "impossible," suggesting the issue had been raised and then dismissed outright.[67] This example of a change in interpretation may represent a moment when Pugno rejected Boulanger's input, causing her to threaten to leave the collaboration. At issue here was Hébé's representation on stage and an assertion of her own agency, which in D'Annunzio's original play is virtually nonexistent. Turning now to the musical score provides further fuel for reading strength and agency into the character of Hébé as she appears in the completed opera.

The text for Hébé's Act 3 aria—the "Lament of the Virgin"—was not a part of the original play; D'Annunzio wrote this section expressly for the Pugno-Boulanger adaptation. This addition mirrors the opening of the opera, where Hébé reads out loud the scene from Sophocles's *Antigone* in which Antigone goes to her death, and which Hébé understands as a premonition of her own fate. Having Hébé assume her own voice in response to Antigone and Cassandra, the figurative sisters she addresses in the new stanzas in Act 3, already makes her an actor in her own right rather than a transmitter of others' words, the role she occupied at the beginning of the play. It also changes the dramaturgy and the sense of the tragedy. For Patrizia Piredda, one reason that *La città morta* fails as a classical tragedy is that Bianca Maria/Hébé is essentially passive; she does nothing for herself but submits to her brother's will without knowing why he murders her.[68] In the play, her death is not a free choice, unlike Antigone's decision to disobey Creon's immoral law and risk condemnation for burying her own brother. Indeed, in the play, the audience is made aware of Léonard's murderous intentions as he speaks openly of his plans to kill Hébé before she enters; but Hébé remains oblivious to Léonard's plan and follows him innocently to the fountain.

Although throughout both the play and the opera libretto Hébé has fears and premonitions that predict her inevitable demise, the placement and content of Hébé's aria "Vous me voyez"—the longest set piece of *La ville morte*—depict her with greater understanding and choice in relation to her fate. In this aria, Hébé calls to Antigone and Cassandra, asking them to accompany her to death.[69] Hébé unequivocally knows she has chosen to share the tragic fate of her classical "sisters." In the rewrite, Hébé gains self-awareness and agency over her own life, and she shifts roles from the innocent victim seen in the play to that of a martyr. The change, and the solo aria that results, mean that Hébé occupies the stage for a great deal more time than in the play. Her solo takes place near the end of the piece in the usual structural position of the prima donna's *preghiera* in nineteenth-century opera, causing her to occupy the realm of the operatic diva; her character becomes more like the Anne interpreted by Duse or Bernhardt—the center of audience attention—than the Bianca Maria of the play, who is gradually crushed by the other characters and whose voice becomes less articulate and powerful as the play goes on.

The music mirrors Hébé's emotional tumult and eventual determination. The prelude to the aria at the opening of Act 3, scene 5 is tonally ambiguous, containing a musical texture saturated with enharmonically spelled, nonfunctional French augmented-sixth chords (see Example 1). This instability is further heightened by the exploitation of partial and complete whole-tone scales below a C tremolo. The downbeat of measure 15 first hints at the aria's eventual tonality of G-sharp minor, with the fleeting appearance of the dominant minor chord enharmonically spelled as an E-flat major/minor seventh sonority. Moments later, first in measure 19 and then more explicitly in measures 21–26, the composers insert an A-♭/C-augmented chord, exploiting the symmetry of this sonority to loosely gesture toward the eventual home of G-sharp minor. The choir reinforces this by singing a final sonority of A-flat in octaves at measure 26. In measures 27–29 the texture thins, and just as the music repeats bass octaves of A♮, the Neapolitan of G-sharp minor, the music hints at Hébé's resolve. Following a series of shifting suspensions from measures 32–34, the aria proper begins with a cadence on G-sharp minor.[70] The

Example 1. Opening of Hébé's aria "Vous me voyez," Act 3, scene 5, mm. 1–5.

central aria is in ABA[1] form. The large architectural portions of the piece follow the poetic prosody for the most part. Hébé's constrained vocal line spans only an octave and an augmented second, F to G♯. Of her ascents to G♯, only one is maintained for any length of time. This piece is not virtuosic, then, because of an expansive tessitura, though it does call for a depth of acting ability for which Claire Croiza, whom the composers had in mind for the role, would have been particularly suited.[71] The lack of vocal freedom mimics the suffocating situation in which Hébé finds herself.

Within those constraints, Hébé achieves strength and arguably expresses a feminist stance. For example, both of the aria's agogic accents mark moments when Hébé expresses empathy for the suffering of her mythological sisters. She links her own death with the injustice that leads Antigone and Cassandra to their fatal ends, situating herself as morally superior to her attacker, as both Antigone and Cassandra did. (See Examples 2a and 2b.) Similarly, the ending of the aria allows Hébé strength through resignation. At a dynamic marking that begins *mezzo forte* and gradually softens to *pianissimo*, Hébé begs for the night to fall quickly and for her sisters to come and collect her. The aria ends with almost acerbic arpeggiated major chords ascending through several octaves, only for each in their turn to be suppressed by the insistent and crushing G-sharp minor tonality. Twice, major chords seem to attempt to inject a sense of hope or peace into Hébé's predicament, and twice hope is denied by the overall minor mode and the thick bass sonorities

x

with which the chords are orchestrated. Thus, the aria begins with uncertainty and ends in resignation. Hébé has made her choice; she will let her brother kill her and thereby bring an end to the collective suffering of her small community. In so doing, Hébé, the youngest, most dependent, and least sexually aware character of the entire opera becomes a stronger figure whose choices precipitate real change.

The oscillation between modality and tonality employed by Boulanger and Pugno bears much in common with the music of Debussy's *Pelléas et Mélisande*, which Elliott Antokoletz argues uses musical syntax to indicate gender politics. According to Antokoletz, Debussy's music connects women with fate and the unconscious in a way inaccessible to men. Debussy draws upon a musical palette of modal and symmetrical structures to depict these associations. Conversely, tonality represents the mundane, the real, and the masculine.[72] Considering Boulanger's familiarity with Debussyan techniques, it is intriguing to see "Vous me voyez" as structured around

Example 2a. Agogic accents in Hébé's Act 3, scene 5 aria, sung as she's invoking Antigone and Cassandra, mm. 43–45.

Example 2b. Agogic accents in Hébé's Act 3, scene 5 aria, sung as she invokes Antigone and Cassandra, mm. 74–79.

Example 3. Chromatic interjections followed by assertion of tonality in
Hébé's Act 3, scene 5 aria, mm. 60–63.

a similar tension between tonal and symmetrical structures: French augmented sixth chords and whole-tone sets in dialogue with G-sharp minor.
Moreover, where Debussy links unstable modal sounds with femininity,
"Vous me voyez" allows Hébé to shed these elements when transitioning
to a state of decisiveness. In Boulanger and Pugno's hands, tonality represents agency. Consider, for example, when chromatic instability begins
to infiltrate Hébé's aria in measures 61 and 62 of the aria. At this highly
emotional point, as Hébé drifts away from tonality and is in danger of
losing her self-control, the accompaniment performs harmonically identi-
fiable sonorities that dissolve into the whole-tone collection E♭/D♯, F, G, A,
B, C♯. Further exacerbating this sense of instability is the hemiola pattern
employed. In emphasizing her strength, resolve, and denial of those forces
outside of her control, the final pitch of measure 62 assumes a dominant
function, decisively returning the music to G-sharp minor on the downbeat

of measure 63. (See Example 3.) Similarly at, the ending of the aria, interjections of whole-tone collection fragments are overcome by the definitive,
ultimate G-sharp sonority. In this way, Boulanger and Pugno played with
Debussyan techniques to infuse their lead woman role with depth and
complexity, giving her access to both fear and strength and landing her in
a place controlled by her self-determination.

To imagine Boulanger performing the role of Hébé, then, is to imagine the exceptional possibility of a modernist woman composer bringing
to life her own work while also enacting women's resistance and agency.
Boulanger's performance, even if private, resonates with Carolyn Abbate's
claim that "the unique phenomenal realities of musical performance
demand their own tribute."[73] Emily Wilbourne extends this idea, arguing
for the complex relationship between the body of the performer and how
they engage in the "authorial creativity" of performance.[74] Boulanger's
embodiment of Hébé shares features with the creation of other women
characters on Parisian stages in the first decade of the twentieth century. Linda and Michael Hutcheon argue that similar transgressive acts
occurred during performances of Salome in Richard Strauss's epony-
mous text, writing "our gaze . . . empowers this woman . . . To look upon
[Salome] . . . is to feel her power."[75] Similarly, Anya Suschitzky and Laura
Watson argue that Georgette Leblanc, in creating the role of the *nouvelle femme* Ariane in Paul Dukas's *Ariane et Barbe-Bleue* (1907), was able
to advocate for powerful women both on and offstage, promoting a character with deep autobiographical connections to herself.[76] Boulanger's
performances of Hébé offered the opportunity to perform womanhood
in a way impossible in her day-to-day existence but that her daybooks
and letters imply she longed to experience. Knowing that singing the
part of Hébé brought Boulanger joy suggests that the various elements of
expressivity, drama, self-determination, and martyrdom spoke to her. By
embodying this work, Boulanger performed her own agency.

## Postlude: Surviving Pugno

Ultimately, audiences never had the chance to meet Boulanger and
Pugno's Hébé. Pugno died during an ill-advised concert tour to Moscow
with Boulanger in January 1914; already ailing in Germany en route to
Russia, he rapidly declined on reaching Moscow. Despite his illness, his
death at age 61 was unexpected. World War I soon followed, and the
composers' engagement with the Opéra-Comique was cancelled. During
her residency in Rome with her sister in 1916, Boulanger nevertheless
returned to work on the opera with great determination, consulting
with Eleonora Duse on several occasions and drawing strength from

the musical exchange she enjoyed with Lili, then at work on *La Princesse Maleine*.[77] Lili's death in 1918, the loss of other key supporters during and after the war, and her own doubts proved powerful discouragement for Nadia's work alone, and *La ville morte* was never publicly performed during her lifetime. Later in life, Boulanger would disparage her early works as *inutile* (useless), easily lending her compositional career to interpretations such as Copland's dismissive statement cited at the beginning of this chapter.

But the newly accessible material in Boulanger's daybooks contributes to our understanding of the depth and seriousness of her ambitions as a composer, the pleasure and joy she derived from creative work, and the opportunities that musical composition and performance offered for her imagination and identity. The daybooks also reveal her heavy investment in ideals of collaboration and mutual support. Such concepts were not traditionally valued in the training or practice of modernist composers and they rarely figure in musicological accounts of composition today; the notion of a single creative vision remains deeply embedded in classical music culture, already posing stumbling blocks to a nuanced understanding of the partnership between Boulanger and Pugno.[78] And their collaborative work took place within a heterosexual relationship, functioning within the gendered and heterosexist norms of early twentieth-century France. The partnership was marked by extreme differences in age and experience as well as by power differences generated by gender discourses, making the working relationship highly asymmetric and problematic.

On the one hand, Boulanger benefited from her interactions with Pugno. Through his practical and emotional support, and reinforced by her immense talent, Boulanger derived confidence and enthusiasm from her work with Pugno and gained access to opportunities that far exceeded those of other women—and men. On the other hand, the new material makes it clear that she was obliged to do a great deal of emotional work to modify her vision of her place within a truly collaborative compositional process and to reconcile her ambitions with societal norms. These obligations and pressures clearly bent and shaped her compositional efforts in profound ways and affected both realities and perceptions (including self-perception) of her creative efforts. Eventually, Boulanger was unable to overcome the personal, institutional, and cultural barriers she faced as she attempted to make her way as a woman artist alone. And so this early chapter of her life was closed, and she moved forward in different directions.

# NOTES

1. Aaron Copland, *Copland on Music* (New York: Doubleday, 1960), 85.

2. For more on their collaboration, see Alexandra Laederich's essay in this volume, which is an updated translation of Alexandra Laederich, "L'étrange destin de *La Ville morte* de Nadia Boulanger et Raoul Pugno," in *D'Annunzio musico magnifico: Atti del convegno internazionale di studi, Siena, 14–16 luglio 2005*, ed. Adriana Guarnieri, Fiamma Nicolodi, and Cesare Orselli (Florence: Olschki, 2008), 183–99. See also Caroline Potter, "Nadia Boulanger's and Raoul Pugno's *La Ville morte*," *The Opera Quarterly* 16 (2000): 397–406; and Caroline Potter, *Nadia and Lili Boulanger* (Aldershot: Ashgate, 2006), 79–87.

3. On the problems of attribution, see Potter, *Nadia and Lili Boulanger*, 82–85; and Laederich's description of the extant sources in her essay in this volume.

4. On the sealed materials, see Alexandra Laederich and Rémy Stricker, "Les trois vies de Nadia Boulanger: Extraits inédits de la valise protégée," *Revue de la Bibliothèque nationale* 46 (2014): 77–83; and Fiorella Sassanelli, *Lili Boulanger: Frammenti ritrovati di una vita interrotta* (Barletta: Cafagna, 2018), 13–22.

5. Léonie Rosenstiel, *Nadia Boulanger: A Life in Music* (New York: W. W. Norton, 1982), 62–64 and 73–76; Jérôme Spycket, *Nadia Boulanger* (Lausanne: Payot, 1987), 22–49.

6. Raïssa Boulanger's birthdate appears as 1854, 1856, or 1858 in different sources. Nadia believed that her mother was born in 1858, the date she had placed on her mother's tomb following Raïssa's death in 1935; this would make her mother forty-three years younger than her husband. See Jérôme Spycket, *A la recherche de Lili Boulanger* (Paris: Fayard, 2004), 62–63.

7. Sassanelli, *Lili Boulanger*, 41–45.

8. Boulanger daybook, 4 February 1905, Bibliothèque nationale de France (F-Pn), Rés. Vmf. ms. 145. This entry suggests Boulanger was in charge of the musical arrangements, and specifies that fifty people came to dinner and 139 attended the concert afterward. See Spycket, *Nadia Boulanger*, 22–24, for reproductions of the invitation and concert program; Rosenstiel, *Nadia Boulanger*, 54–55, translates the correspondence with Pugno about the date.

9. Boulanger daybook entries for 21 and 30 September 1905, F-Pn, Rés. Vmf. ms. 145. Boulanger noted the date "14-7-1905 – 1er soir" with Pugno in a daybook entry written after Pugno's death, on a day when she was at Gargenville and reminded of the beginning of their partnership (F-Pn, Rés. Vmf. ms. 153, entry for 11 April 1915).

10. Note inserted at the end of the Boulanger booklet for September, F-Pn, Rés. Vmf. ms. 145 (1905).

11. Boulanger daybook, entry for 11 June 1906, F-Pn, Rés. Vmf. ms. 146.

12. Daybook entries make it clear that this space was often the site of their most intense musical and emotional encounters. By the autumn of 1907, Pugno had also taken a studio at 60 rue de Clichy, called the "atelier" or workshop in Boulanger's daybooks, less than fifty meters from the Boulanger apartment, where the pair could meet in private and work on their projects together while in Paris (Spycket, *A la recherche*, 108).

13. Boulanger daybook entry for 15 September 1906, F-Pn, Rés. Vmf. ms. 146.

14. Boulanger daybook entry for 18 September 1906, F-Pn, Rés. Vmf. ms. 146.

15. Boulanger daybook entries for 8 and 9 November 1906, F-Pn, Rés. Vmf. ms. 146. Boulanger uses the French *spleen* to describe her state of mind on 9 November: "Aujourd'hui le spleen et le découragement atteignent leur maximum j'ai peine à vivre."

16. Boulanger daybook entry for 6 December 1906, F-Pn Rés. Vmf. ms. 146.

17. Boulanger daybook entry for 15 July 1906: "Pugno joue ses 4 pièces à Marmontel et à moi. Je lui conseille un changement." F-Pn Rés. Vmf ms. 146.

18. For details of these and later compositions, see Alexandra Laederich, "Catalogue de l'oeuvre de Nadia Boulanger," in *Nadia Boulanger et Lili Boulanger: Témoignages et études*, ed. Alexandra Laederich (Lyon: Symétrie, 2007), 315–54.

19. In 1908, Boulanger caused a scandal by setting the vocal fugue subject proposed by Camille Saint-Saëns as an instrumental fugue; there were calls for her to be disqualified. She was allowed to remain in the competition but did not win, and this incident may also have affected the result the following year. On both years, see Annegret Fauser, "*La Guerre en dentelles*: Women and the Prix de Rome in French Cultural Politics," *Journal of the American Musicological Society* 51 (1998): 83–129.

20. Kimberly Francis, "Nadia Boulanger and Louise Cruppi: Triumphs and Tragedy in the Shadow of the First World War," in *Creative Women at the End of the First World War*, ed. Kimberly Francis and Margot Irvine, forthcoming.

21. In 1905, for example, Fauré performed Boulanger's Allegro for Orchestra at the Conservatoire, and Widor served as a reliable champion for Boulanger during the Prix de Rome competitions.

22. For a complete list of Boulanger's published scores see Laederich, "Catalogue de l'œuvre."

23. For further discussion, see Kimberly Francis, "Nadia Boulanger and *La Ville morte*: En'gendering' a Woman's Role in the Making of an Opera" (Master's thesis, University of Ottawa, 2005), 58.

24. Laederich, "Catalogue de l'œuvre," 332–33. Verhaeren was a friend of Pugno's as well as a friend and model for his younger colleague Maurice Maeterlinck.

25. The application, dated 2 February 1910 and approved the following month, is held at the Musée SACEM; it has been digitized and is available at https://musee.sacem.fr/index.php/Detail/objects/10770.

26. In her daybook from early 1910, Boulanger noted that she and Pugno were already discussing the *La ville morte* project. Entry for 8 January 1910, F-Pn, Rés. Vmf. ms. 86,

27. Patrizia Piredda, "Impossibilità del tragico ne *La città morta* di D'Annunzio," in *Laboratorio di Nuova Ricerca: Investigating Gender, Translation and Culture in Italian Studies*, ed. Monica Boria and Linda Risso (Leicester: Troubador, 2007), 59–72. For the complete text of the Italian original see D'Annunzio, *La città morta* (Milan: Treves, 1900), available at https://archive.org/details/lacittmortatrag00dangoog/page/n11.

28. On the many parallels, see Potter, *Nadia and Lili Boulanger*, 80–82. On the striking similarities between the character of Bianca Maria (Hébé in *La ville morte*) and Mélisande, see Mary Anne Frese Witt, *The Search for Modern Tragedy: Aesthetic Fascism in Italy and France* (Ithaca, NY: Cornell University Press, 2001), 44–45.

29. There is no chorus in the play, though D'Annunzio added one to the libretto he devised for Boulanger and Pugno.

30. Maggie Günsberg, *Gender and the Italian Stage: From the Renaissance to the Present Day* (Cambridge: Cambridge University Press, 1997), 139–40.

31. Witt, *The Search for Modern Tragedy*, 45. See also Mary Anne Frese Witt, "D'Annunzio's Dionysian Women: The Rebirth of Tragedy in Italy," in *Nietzsche and the Rebirth of the Tragic*, ed. Mary Anne Frese Witt (Madison, NJ: Fairleigh Dickinson University Press, 2007), 72–103.

32. Günsberg, *Gender and the Italian Stage*, 158–59.

33. D'Annunzio to Boulanger, 3 September 1910, F-Pn, N.L.a. 294 (47–54).

34. James Nikopolous, "The Spirit of the Chorus in D'Annunzio's *La città morta*," *Comparative Drama* 44/2 (2010): 155.

35. *Le Ménestrel*, 11 June 1910, 191; "Mlle Nadia Boulanger et M. Raoul Pugno Collaborent," *Femina*, 228 (15 July 1910): 377.

36. Fauser, "*La Guerre en dentelles*," 100–103. The image of the composer Juliette Toutain, Boulanger's predecessor in the Prix de Rome competition, published in *Musica* in 1903 ( 101) has much in common with the illustration of Boulanger and Pugno's partnership in *Femina*.

37. Fauser, "*La Guerre en dentelles*," 119.

38. Boulanger noted in her daybook entry for 19 March 1911: "Le Duo du 2nd acte est presque fini," F-Pn, Rés. Vmf. ms.. 149.

39. *Le Ménestrel*, 11 March 1911, 79.

40. Boulanger daybook entries for 4 and 17 April 1911, F-Pn, Rés. Vmf. ms. 149. On the 4th, she wrote, "Aujourd'hui la joie de produire vaut toutes les peines et toutes les sacrifices."

41. Boulanger daybook entry for 3 April 1911, F-Pn, Rés. Vmf. ms. 149.

42. Boulanger daybook entries for 5 June and 6 July 1911, F-Pn, Rés. Vmf. ms. 149.

43. Boulanger daybook entry for 16 June 1911, F-Pn, Rés. Vmf. ms. 149.

44. Boulanger daybook entry for 23 June 1911: "La situation est vraiment nébuleuse quant à moi." F-Pn, Rés. Vmf. ms. 149.

45. Boulanger to D'Annunzio, 2 July 1911, F-Pn, N.L.a. 297 (15). The letter is preserved in Boulanger's archive, rather than D'Annunzio's, and it is unclear whether it was sent.

46. Boulanger daybook entry for 11 July 1911: "L'après midi travail—la tension augmente et la situation ne laisse pas que d'être difficile, car il fait tout seul—moi, je lis!!" F-Pn, Rés. Vmf. ms. 149.

47. Boulanger daybook entry for 13 July 1911, F-Pn, Rés. Vmf. ms. 149.

48. For example, in 1917 Nadia Boulanger wrote to her sister of "their princess," whom she and her sister had brought into being. The plea was an effort on Nadia's part to urge her sister to fight against her failing health. Nadia Boulanger to Lili Boulanger, 17 March 1917, edited in Sassanelli, *Frammenti ritrovati*, 344.

49. The poem begins: "I seek in my memory / your eyes that I do not know," and a later line reads: "I imagine your sweet, clear face / you who will come one day." The poem is incomplete and the musical sketch consists of only two chords, suggesting that the project did not progress further. Boulanger daybook entry for 26 July 1913, F-Pn Rés. Vmf. ms. 151.

50. Boulanger daybook entry for 17 July 1911, F-Pn, Rés. Vmf. ms. 149.

51. Boulanger daybook entry for 18 July 1911, F-Pn, Rés. Vmf. ms. 149.

52. Ibid. As they had already played drafts of this act for Kufferath and Heugel in June and early July, this suggests the act was nearly complete and that the process of reconciliation involved revisions, perhaps the solicitation of input on passages composed alone by one or the other partner or resolution of points of difference.

53. Boulanger daybook entry for 19 July 1911, F-Pn, Rés. Vmf. ms. 149.

54. Boulanger daybook entry for 7 October 1911, F-Pn, Rés. Vmf. ms. 149.

55. "It is for that reason that I write ardently to beg you to send us without delay [the text] that will allow us to put the capstone on *La ville morte*." Boulanger to D'Annunzio, 28 July 1912, F-Pn, N. L.a. 297 (18).

56. Boulanger daybook entry for 8 October 1911, F-Pn, Rés. Vmf. ms. 149.

57. Laederich, "Catalogue de l'œuvre," 340.

58. Boulanger daybook entry for 11 April 1912, F-Pn, Rés. Vmf. ms. 150.

59. Boulanger daybook entry for 24 July 1912, F-Pn, Rés. Vmf. ms. 151.

60. Boulanger daybook entries for 8 June and 3 August 1912, F-Pn, Rés. Vmf. ms. 150.

61. Boulanger daybook entry for 6 August 1912.

62. "A quoi rêvent les jeunes filles," *Femina* 284 (15 November 1912): 647.

63. Nadia Boulanger to Marcelle de Manziarly, 6 September 1912, F-Pn, N.L.a. 289 (1–2).

64. It is unclear who this couple was. Five letters from a Marie–Louise Chapelot, all dated 1947, appear in Boulanger's archive, F-Pn N.L.a. 294 (17–21). Their content suggests she was a pianist, and the letters show that she knew both Lili Boulanger and Pugno before 1914.

65. Boulanger daybook entry for 22 September 1912, F-Pn Rés. Vmf. ms. 150.

66. For source details on the libretto, F-Pn ThB 4929 (1–3), see the appendix to Alexandra Laederich's essay, this volume.

67. *La ville morte*, manuscript libretto, F-Pn ThB 4929 (2), folio 15.

68. Piredda, "Impossibilità del tragico," 63.

69. This aria was originally placed at the end of Act 3 of five, as revealed by the first booklet of the manuscript libretto, F-Pn ThB 4929 (1), 41. This means that the aria was originally meant to be a reaction to Anne's pain, rather than a soliloquy.

70. G-sharp minor may play a larger significance in the opera as a whole, as the dominant of the opera's concluding sonority, C-sharp minor. Coincidentally, C-sharp minor is also the final sonority in *Pelléas et Mélisande*. The larger-scale, dominant-tonic signification here resonates with similar relationships sought out by Boulanger when analyzing the formal characteristics of other composers such as Stravinsky.

71. For more on Croiza's career, see Jean-Michel Nectoux, "Hommage à Claire Croiza" (Exhibition, Paris, Bibliothèque nationale [15 June–1 September 1984], 3ark:/12148/bpt6k65328278); and Megan Sarno, "Claire Croiza: Mother and Muse," in Francis and Irvine, *Creative Women and the First World War: Endings and New Beginnings*, forthcoming.

72. Elliott Antokoletz, *Musical Symbolism in the Operas of Debussy and Bartok: Trauma, Gender, and the Unfolding of the Subconscious*, with Juana Canabal Antokoletz (New York: Oxford University Press, 2004), 27, 31, and 56.

73. Carolyn Abbate, *Unsung Voices: Opera and Musical Narrative in the Nineteenth Century* (Princeton: Princeton University Press, 1991). See also Mary Ann Smart, "Ulterior Motives: Verdi's Recurring Themes Revisited," in *Siren Songs: Representations of Gender and Sexuality in Opera*, ed. Mary Ann Smart (Princeton: Princeton University Press, 2000), 139.

74. Emily Wilbourne, "*Lo Schiavetto 1612:* Travestied Sound, Ethnic Performance, and the Eloquence of the Body," *Journal of the American Musicological Society* 63/1 (2010): esp. 5–6.

75. Linda and Michael Hutcheon, "Staging the Female Body: Richard Strauss's *Salome*," in Smart, *Siren Songs*, 204.

76. Laura Watson, "Fifty Shades of Bluebeard? Dukas's *Ariane et Barbe-Bleue* in the Twenty-First Century," *Twentieth-Century Music* 15/1 (2018): 404; and Anna Suschitzky, "*Ariane et Barbe-Bleue*: Dukas, the Light and the Well," *Cambridge Opera Journal* 9/2 (1997): 133–61.

77. Kimberly Francis, "The Valise Correspondence: A Reconsideration of Nadia and Lili Boulanger, Composers," forthcoming.

78. Sam Hayden and Luke Windsor, "Collaboration and the Composer: Case Studies from the End of the 20th Century," *Tempo* 61 (2007): 28–39. For a review of how ideals of collaboration conflict with modernist understandings of authorship more generally, see Lisa Ede and Andra A. Lunsford, "Collaboration and Concepts of Authorship," *PMLA* 116 (2001): 354–69.

# From the Trenches:
# Extracts from the Final Issue of the
# Paris Conservatory *Gazette*

EDITED BY NADIA AND LILI BOULANGER
SELECTED, INTRODUCED, AND ANNOTATED
BY ANNEGRET FAUSER
TRANSLATED BY ANNA LEHMANN

It might seem extraordinary—if not extraordinarily thoughtless—to send out an inquiry to young French musicians at the front in spring 1918 to ask which works should be performed on Parisian concert stages and whether one should play at home the compositions of the very enemy they were fighting in the trenches:

> 1. What should the orientation of concerts be this winter? Should the classics be played, or should space be predominantly given to modern music?
> 2. Should German musicians keep their place? Brahms and Wagner?
> 3. Which artists should be sent on propaganda tours (concerts, theater, musical theater)? Those who are no longer of an age to be mobilized, those in the auxiliaries, or even the mobilized, who already have an influence because of their celebrity?[1]

As the detailed and engaged responses to these questions reveal, however, Nadia Boulanger knew what she was doing when she requested the opinions of deployed musicians about what they thought should be performed in Paris. Henry Vasseur, for instance, answered that it was a valid exercise because the inquiry addressed the future of music in France as well as the future for those musicians who would return from battle. To be consulted, even when stationed far from the musical world of the French capital, gave the deployed musicians a sense of involvement with, and a say in, a way of life from which the war had cut them off.

Inquiries about burning issues of the day were a familiar form of journalism in French culture, often presented on the front pages of daily newspapers such as *Le Figaro*. In music, some famous examples addressed the future of French music, the influence of Wagner, or the genre of French song.[2] To be asked one's opinion was a mark of distinction, and even in the case of so special-interest a publication as a homegrown newsletter, a request for information was nonetheless a sign that the responses would matter both to the editors and the readers with whom they would be shared. Such inquiries represented a form of written debate to which each writer could contribute an opinion. How significant this particular inquiry was to the deployed musicians can be seen in the sheer volume of responses—the issue ran to eighty-one pages, faithfully transcribed on a typewriter by the editorial team.

It is remarkable that this particular issue of the *Gazette des classes de composition du Conservatoire* was ever put together. Dated 1 June 1918, it was sent out less than three months after the death of Lili Boulanger on 15 March 1918. Devastated by grief and survivor guilt, Nadia had pushed herself to continue her work with the Comité franco-américain du Conservatoire national, a war-relief foundation that the two sisters had established after the outbreak of the war. With the help of Renée de Marquein—who exchanged secretarial duties for weekly composition lessons with Nadia—the two sisters set out to send material and moral support to their deployed fellow students. In 1915, they realized that sharing information about one another helped the musician-soldiers maintain a sense of belonging, and thus the Boulangers created a kind of "message board" in the form of a typewritten newsletter, with illustrations by Jacques Debat-Ponsan. Its first issue, sent out in January 1916, consisted of 300 mimeographed copies, and its distribution grew over the following three years.[3]

Nadia's first two questions addressed issues connected to French musical life in general, and the third spoke to the actual experience of music in the war theaters. By starting out inquiring about ideal concert programming for the upcoming winter season—including the best ratio of contemporary music compared to standard concert repertoire—Boulanger got to the core of the deployed composers' concerns: their place and their future in music. It is not surprising that the majority of the answers came down emphatically in favor of an increased proportion of contemporary music. Yet the responses reveal a wide range of opinions that speak to the diverse aesthetic positions of French musicians at the beginning of the twentieth century. Few were as radical as Charles Koechlin, who answered twice: first with a short letter and then with a long "article," as he called it, in which he pointed out that the dichotomy between classic and contemporary music was a false one. Great contemporary French music, he declared, was classical by its very nature and needed to dominate French concert life. Most musicians envisaged a balance between the old and the new, though they hoped that it might be skewed in favor of the latter. Jacques Ibert's eloquent response made the point that new music kept the soul of France alive, even though the classics also had their place—just as exquisite old furniture provided comfort. Several musicians resorted to specific proportions: in Marcel Boyer's opinion, it should be three modern works for one old one; René Doire opted for two-thirds of new music, half of which should be French. The general opinion, however, was that the classics had a role to play on concert programs, whether to educate audiences and fellow musicians, preserve France's cultural heritage, or bring in audiences for new works sandwiched between old favorites. If Koechlin was an outlier in favor of new music, Martial Jacques and Henri Bouillard were the exceptions where older music was concerned. For Bouillard it was a question of public health: programming such classics as Bach and Beethoven would soothe the strained nerves of a war-scarred population.

By 1918, the question of whether to perform German music in France during the war had already generated a long-lasting debate. In fall 1914, Camille Saint-Saëns had published a manifesto titled "Germanophilie" in the right-wing newspaper *Echo de Paris*, demanding the removal from French musical practice of recent and contemporary German works. The article garnered intense discussion in 1915, both in the press and in musical circles.[4] Boulanger herself took part in this debate, for instance, in February 1915 during a private evening recorded in the diary of Marguerite de Saint-Marceaux.[5] Given the connection of the *Gazette* to the Comité franco-américain, the return to that particular issue might have been triggered by the entry into the war by the United States in 1917, when the influx of new forces and intensification of the conflict contributed to a heightening of anti-German sentiment for the remainder of the year. Two matters of concern are particularly noticeable in the responses. One is that the distinction between classics and moderns that was introduced in Nadia's first question—as well as its specific reference to Brahms and Wagner—allowed for differentiating, in the second, between a cosmopolitan and canonic repertoire of concert staples and recent and contemporary German output. The musicians generally did not write about earlier Austro-German music but focused on more contemporary works, emphasizing that the likes of Mozart and Beethoven were to remain untouched.

The second noticeable aspect is the diversity of responses, running the gamut from complete exclusion to a balanced if not wholehearted inclusion. Some respondents engaged with the musical value of Austro-German music, evoking Felix von Weingartner and Richard Strauss, for example.[6] More than one respondent referred to the adage that art had no fatherland, and thus cosmopolitanism and universalism often warred with nationalism, sometimes in the same answer. Some sought to restrict or to stop the performance of modern German music, not for musical reasons but for political ones; others warned of false patriotism. Here, too, Nadia's first question had created the ideological framework: if the performance of contemporary music needed to be strengthened, then—so the answers maintained—it should not be in favor of enemy music. Certainly Jacques Ibert pushed against the performance of music with a pronounced Teutonic (*boche*) accent that evoked, in his ears, the cannon noise of Big Bertha ("tintamarre de leur batterie de 420"). Emile Nerini mentioned specifically those musicians who had signed the "Manifesto of the 93" (*An die Kulturwelt*) in 1914, a declaration defending Germany's entry into war; the signatories included Engelbert Humperdinck, Siegfried Wagner, and Weingartner. Overall, however, the deployed musicians considered Wagner and Brahms as well as other German music an integral part of their musical world: if their presence on Parisian concert programs needed to be regulated, it was not for musical reasons *per se* but practical ones, such as making more space for French moderns.

The cagiest responses were to the third question about music as a means of cultural diplomacy. Propaganda and raising morale were seen as ways in which to further the recognition of French music and artists. Many answered simply that it would be most advantageous to send the best artists representing French music and art abroad, independent of whether they were of draft age or whether they were already in uniform. Very few responses named particular musicians, although Marcel Welsch suggested sending out the most important French composers, from Claude Debussy and Gabriel Fauré to Vincent d'Indy and Maurice Ravel. Quite a number tackled issues that were more controversial, such as the use of musicians in uniform, especially in propaganda missions abroad. Whereas the answers to the first two questions generally remained on the level of aesthetic or political engagement, the answers to the third were often personal, addressing the situation of musicians whose careers were being derailed by military service. Some were bitter: Jacques Pessard accused those who were not deployed of selfishness and lack of engagement with the realities of war; and Charles Quef made it clear that propaganda missions should not allow a musician to escape military service and further his own career. More than one response addressed the effect of deployment and military service in personal professional terms, often expressed as having lost a connection to the world of music or mourning a vanished musical future.

The collection of answers that Boulanger's three questions elicited offer a unique window on the musical ideas and realities of musician-soldiers in World War I. Because the inquiry took place almost four years into the war, any hurrah patriotism had disappeared under the hardship of military experiences. The responses reveal men who used this opportunity to engage with an art they might not ever use again professionally if and when the war ended. They also bear witness to how important it was for the musicians to share musical and cultural ideas rather than simply describing their activities in the war theater, as they had in previous issues of the *Gazette*. Welsch pointed out that it helped the newsletter become a uniquely musical enterprise; in Maurice Faure's view, these questions brought their mimeographed exchanges to life. Perhaps it was fitting that this was the last issue of the *Gazette*. Some who had given their opinions about the future of musical life in Paris while under enemy fire could, in effect, experience the realities of postwar concerts in the 1918–19 winter season. As for Nadia Boulanger, she continued her work with the Comité franco-américain to build a transatlantic network of musical exchange that would shape the rest of her professional life.

*Gazette des classes du conservatoire*
No. 10, 1 June 1918
Extracts translated by Anna Lehmann

**ELLIS Roger** (Lavignac) Music at 101st Infantry, SP, 15 May

*Here, and throughout the excerpts that follow, the name in parentheses indicates the professor for the most advanced class a respondent would have attended.[7] Ellipses indicating the* Gazette's *cutting of personal greetings and news from the beginning or end of responses have been omitted; otherwise the use of ellipses/ suspension points follows the original French text. "SP" stands for "secteur postal militaire" and indicates that the musician was deployed at the time when he posted his response. Because of wartime censorship rules, the* Gazette *could not identify where any individual (and their respective regiments) were posted.*
*Roger Ellis was a composition student of Albert Lavignac (1846–1916).*

I hasten to answer the questionnaire you were kind enough to send me and which is of such great interest, now and for the future development of our art form and its influence abroad; especially opportune given the extraordinary timeliness of the matter for neutral countries. I even think we have been slow at home to use music as a propaganda tool, and to notice that it is in fact a powerful one. I will answer your questions one at a time:

1 – I am giving you my opinion, I have to say, while thinking about our great Sunday concerts and which programmatic direction they should take: at every concert, play one or two classics (including the Romantics who have become classics, such as Schumann and Schubert) but place the emphasis on modern music, in any style, and, in particular, present *young people* every time. That is, as I see it, the ideal direction for concerts to benefit and popularize our art form in the coming season.

2 – German musicians should retain the place they occupied, but it is to be hoped that Wagner, for example, does not take up most of a program, as was the case before the war, when one could search in vain for a single French name in the same program!

In the absence of special, but frequent, recitals devoted to our own glory as well, the infatuation for music from "the outside" that we tend to favor should be especially avoided.

On the other hand, unfortunately, we have tried since the war began to react to the enemy threat and present a strictly national character by limiting ourselves to our own composers or those of our friends, and as a result we have excluded Brahms, Wagner, Strauss, Mahler, etc. . . . to which our enemies have been responding for a long time by brilliantly staging *Faust* and *Werther*, to mention only those two works! . . . That gives me a second reason (the first being artistic value outside of any other consideration) to ask that everything that was formerly on our programs be restored.

3 – As to which artists to send on a propaganda tour, in my opinion send first the best, the most prestigious, those who would be heralded by the greatest reputations; of course, if possible, begin with those who are not mobilized, then choose from among the ranks of the auxiliaries, and even from among the armed services, whoever can usefully serve this artistic and national cause.

I am taking the liberty of adding a paragraph that is nevertheless about the topic that occupies us, summarizing a few impressions from my furloughs:

Do we not have, in France, the perfect grounds for such propaganda? Isn't our country full of foreigners who attend our shows and become more familiar with our masterpieces? But, to mention only Paris, the quality of performances has been neglected, we have become much less demanding of performers; for example, what male singers do we have right now who are worthy figures? . . .

We are only just beginning to pay attention to this, even though the topic has serious consequences for our national art! I had occasion to attend a substandard performance that was a painful surprise to me—I mention only this one example, so as not to make this letter any longer, but such an immortal masterpiece always deserves that great care is lavished on its interpretation!!

The symphony orchestras in Paris have been unable to maintain the perfection that used to characterize them and made them the best in the world, having had to fill the gaps created by the turmoil of war expediency—but which could have ceased to be an issue several years ago if these questions had not been deemed secondary.

It seems to me that the best propaganda should begin at home, where the entire population can benefit from it immediately and expand it.

I hope my thoughts are in line with those of many of my colleagues.

## DELMAS BOUSSAGOL Joseph (Charpentier),
### Brigadier 43rd Artillery, SP, 15 May

*Alphonse Joseph Delmas Boussagol (1891–1958) studied double bass with Hyppolyte Lejolivet-Charpentier (1844–1917). His distinguished career would later include positions with Concerts Lamoureux, the New York Philharmonic Orchestra, and the Orchestre national de France. In 1939, he became professor of double bass at the Conservatoire.*

I think everyone will be happy to answer your questionnaire for it is painful to see this sad and long period of war remain sterile as far as the growth of the arts.

As for me, I will try to answer, and I ask that you receive my humble opinions, which I try to give with as much impartiality as possible, even if I do not succeed in doing so.

I believe our concerts in the coming winter season should give prominence to modern music; it is still too little known, but it should be known, and its critics, who have obstructed it until now, proven wrong.

Nevertheless, the classics should not be ruled out completely from programming; they form a heritage that is in our care and also the foundation of music education.

As for the question of Brahms and Wagner, the answer is more difficult and, as concerns the latter in particular, it caused a conflict among some leading musicians. My intention is not to convert others to my opinion but, nonetheless and in all sincerity, here it is—I strongly oppose *l'esprit de guerre* that does not deign to recognize the genius and beauty that were glorified only yesterday, and I find that, in matters of art, one cannot push back too strongly any thought where resentment and personal grudges begin to emerge.

Wagner and Brahms should keep their place, but it is up to us to fight the ridiculous infatuation of a few "snobs" who, through the stupidity inherent in their ignorance, became the accessories to so many art "profiteers."

As for the third question about which artists to choose for successful propaganda, their military position should not be of concern for we have, in each of the given categories, artists worthy of the task, which itself must not be thought of as an opportunity but, quite to the contrary, as a duty.

To defend one's country in its ambitions, its artistic ideals, is also a combat position . . .

## TIERSOT Julien (Savard, Massenet, Frank),
### Captain with the Infantry Territorial Regiment, 15 May

*Julien Tiersot (1857–1936) was a distinguished French musicologist and folksong collector. Between 1909 and 1921, he was head of the Conservatoire library, the most significant French music collection of the time. He also served as president of the Société française de musicologie.*

As an old Wagnerian from the beginning, from the "heroic times of Wagnerism" as it has been called, I have not renounced any part of the admiration I once felt for his art. But the question of Wagner has always been very complicated. It has never been an exclusively musical question, and it is more and more clear to me that the non-musical elements are increasingly important, perhaps of the greatest importance. I cannot, in this letter, go into a question that would require a long study. May I simply mention that, in four years' experience, it has now been shown that one can do quite well in France without the music of Wagner. As for Brahms, I have always done quite well without his music. . . .

Concerts have always been programmed around an appropriate balance of classics and modern music; it seems to me they need only to continue in this manner, but I would add that the moderns should be performed with the idea that they will become classics in due course.

The question of propaganda tours seems to me to be more of a professional question than a purely artistic one.

There is no doubt that, as we wait for what comes next, these four years at war are a disaster for those who had planned on careers as musicians, and it is natural as well as admirable that they should try hard to continue in their chosen profession. But for now these efforts can only be temporary; this moment can only be one in which we prepare for the future. Allow me simply to express the wish that the art of tomorrow stop being too exclusively preoccupied with form, virtuosity, dilettantism; may those entrusted with it not forget that being a musician does not prevent one from being a citizen; that it matters if their ideals spring from essentially national sources; finally, that the hardship our country faces today must have repercussions, and profound ones at that, on the art that is yet to come—the true art of the future.

## IBERT Jacques (Vidal) Ensign, Dunkirk, 16 May

*The well-known French composer Jacques Ibert (1890–1962) studied with Paul Vidal (1863–1931) who was also Lili Boulanger's teacher. Ibert's contemporaries in Vidal's composition class included Arthur Honegger and Darius Milhaud.*

I answer the questionnaire enclosed with your letter hurriedly, and I ask that you please forgive my scribblings.

1 – It would be a shame to separate classical music and modern music at concerts. The former is like a nice piece of furniture, an old paunchy oak trunk with a nice patina, an old armchair upholstered in slate-blue Utrecht velvet, and it would listen to the latter's irreverent and marvelous adventures with a surprised and shocked ear. . . . It is a real delight. . . . It must be preserved. Music is the soul of a country, its living history. Like a country's philosophy, it expresses its feelings and its ambitions; it is the reflection of its thinking. Therefore, to my mind, modern music must be presented as much as possible, its production encouraged by making it better known, making it loved, and giving to classical music only the respectful and admiring share it deserves.

2 – No. Modern German musicians cannot and must not keep the place that a backwards snobbishness too generously "unleashed" to them before the war; that would be nonsense, a lack of tact and restraint. Oscar Wilde said somewhere, "Whatever music sounds like, I am glad to say it does not sound like German"; that is not accurate.[8] There is music that speaks "Kraut" and wherein one finds—and I don't mean to sound like the literature dear to Mr. Romain Rolland—the pitiful tone of these false apostles of mysticism, the heavy and sickening arguments of their barren culture, and the din of their 420-mm artillery battery.[9]

Doing away with the Germans on our programs would be an innocent joke, insignificant in fact, a laughable and fake patriotism, but let us seriously limit the amount of space we give them and perform mostly French music, which, after all, is at least as good as theirs.

3 – I feel completely unqualified to answer your last question. However, it seems to me that many artists would be more useful to their country in front of an orchestra than behind a greasy government desk, or even a stack of hospital "mandolins."[10]

**JACQUES Martial** (Diémer) Musician, 51st Infantry, SP, 16 May

*Martial Jacques (1895–?) completed his studies at the Concervatoire in 1914 with a first prize in piano. Louis Diémer (1843–1919) was professor of piano at the Conservatoire. Diémer is known also for his role in the French early-music revival.*

Forgive me for giving so little detail in my response, but I am in a sector where I have little time.

1 – Yes, more than ever, we must play the classics, the *foundation of musical art*. Without completely pushing aside modern music, it would be a great mistake to give it a prominent place.

2 – Yes, German musicians should retain their place. The war is not a reason to declare that something is bad today when we found it admirable yesterday. Only individuals, for personal reasons, can dismiss Brahms and Wagner.

3 – If one wants to *truly engage in propaganda* (something barely organized up to now), one must send musicians, *whether or not they are mobilized*, who are capable of having an influence and not limit ourselves to one group either mobilized or not.

That is my thinking, in all honesty.

**PESSARD Jacques** (Brémond), H.Q. Colonial Corps, SP, 16 May

*Jacques André Pessard (1888–?) was the son of the composer Emile Pessard (1843–1917) who taught Harmony at the Conservatoire. François Brémond (1844–1925) taught horn at the Conservatoire.*

New idea to ask our opinion, to give the right to vote to us mobilized troops. We thank the Committee for treating us like intelligent beings. I believe each of us, proud to reclaim our personality for this occasion, will share our thoughts without hesitation.

1st Question – I think we overuse the classics a bit in our concerts and, although the audience is often attracted to that repertoire (e.g. ticket sales at theaters for *Faust*, *Carmen*, *Mignon*, etc.), they would readily accept a greater number of modern works.

2nd Question – Even if it means angering those who are fighting the Krauts—from their armchairs—I assert that *Art Has No Homeland*.

Through analysis, one can recognize the influence of such and such a country in a masterpiece, or such and such a school, but what was beautiful, what moved us before the war still moves us—maybe even more so since we have suffered; and I find very amusing all these people who swooned behind the baton of a Weingartner and others—these people, sincere—who felt joy and delight in hearing, playing the works of Wagner, Beethoven, and Brahms and who—to punish them—deny themselves this immense pleasure, unless they feel at least a little of it by throwing their scores into their stoves to heat themselves with!

Others cleverly do genealogy searches and manage to conclude that the author of *The Merry Widow* or *Ein Walzertraum* is the distant cousin of a French woman, or that their great great great great great grandfather on their mother's side was from an allied nation and that . . . he remained a good Frenchman by whistling every morning "L'heure exquise qui nous grise" . . . [11]

Nonetheless, before the war, those composers were the ones who filled all the programs! It would be good now to reserve part of it for ourselves.

French music must not fear foreign music; instead, let it have its place so that the public can judge for itself. If it can find genius in a foreigner, it will be even more likely to find genius among our French composers, who will speak to their soul even more and make them appreciate the charm and beauty of our music.

As for the 3rd question, it is a little tricky, I imagine myself a politician voting myself into the budget! To be impartial, I have to imagine myself peacefully at home!

Those who have not been called up, in general, seem to me to have passed the age of enthusiasm. Oh! Sorry! They are full of enthusiasm when it is others who make the effort! It is hard for me to imagine them embarking on rough seas with their shawls, blankets, and little basins around them, worried that they are going to be torpedoed and sleeping little because of the life-jackets cinching their bodies. Being held up and carried in triumph by the strong arms of Americans must make a person dizzy, and then they would also be haunted by the fear of returning by sea. . . . No, they would not be as full of that goodwill and that energy along with the absolute joy of being temporarily returned to who they were before as would be mobilized men chosen to make France loved and to leave in neutral or friendly hearts emotions and memories that would forever tie them to us, to France.

I can feel it already; many of the non-mobilized staring at each other, saying: "But we are here, we can do it!"

To them we would propose, quite kindly, that they come, out of curiosity, to spend a little time, not in the trenches, but simply at a military camp, far from the Krauts, 5 or 6 kilometers away, one shelled no more than three times a week; whereas we, having done our duty here from the start, would continue doing so with all our soul—but from far away. And if an artist returning from the front has lost a little of his ability during his years away, he would on the other hand possess, in the eyes of all, beyond his talent, the undeniable prestige of having *held up* at the front; he would be truly qualified to present to friendly nations a little of our intellectual heritage, that ever growing richness from which the homeland is formed.

**KOECHLIN Charles** (Massenet), 30 Villa Molitor, Paris, 16 May

*The prolific and well-known composer and writer Charles Koechlin (1867–1950) studied, from 1892, in the class of Jules Massenet (1842–1912).*

I received your letter and the questionnaire attached to it. I will send you a *detailed* response (actually an article) because the question of the future of our music is of particular interest to me, and I have thought about it often these past few years, especially as I wrote my second series of lectures. The article I am sending you is a kind of summary or paraphrase of part of these talks.

We cannot do anything about the direction of great concerts nor about the orchestra musicians, but we can, and we must, defend the right ideas and shout from the rooftops that the modern French school is the greatest *classical* school right now in Europe (even if I belong to this very school). Classic and ultra-modern—they go together well, whatever officials may think; and this school is unknown, or at least little known by the public (except for a small elite).

**BINEAUX Henri** (Turban & Rougnon), Adjutant, 115th Infantry, SP,
Croix de Guerre two citations, 17 May

*Henri Bineaux (1883–1918) studied clarinet with Charles-Paul Turban (1845–1905) and solfège with Paul-Louis Rougnon (1846–1934). A clarinetist in the Concerts Lamoureux before the war, he was killed in action at Chatillon sur Marne on 15 July 1918 and was commemorated in the monument erected for the students of the Conservatoire killed in World War I.*[12]

1 – Continue to develop people's musical education by performing the "Great Classics" but give preference at major concerts to young musicians, especially French musicians.

2 – Keep "German musicians" but completely and energetically exclude all barkers, obvious builders of sub-*musik* by "intellectuals," who saw in the opportunity we gave them only a chance to promote themselves, enabling them to do well in our concert halls and take hold in France. I think Brahms & Wagner should be kept, but the latter should not appear as much as he once did on the programs of our great symphony orchestras.

3 – Make use of artists in a well thought-out and organized international propaganda: non-mobilized servicemen, auxiliaries, and, if necessary, a few *mobilized men from the front*, whose presence at some concerts (in America for example) could only increase the audience's enthusiasm—an audience only too eager to admire French soldiers. It is obvious that if one of the "Diables Bleus" currently in America were one of our great masters or virtuosos or singing actors, it would be wild to see him in concert, where he would combine fame and talent with the glory of having been "at Verdun or at the Battle of the Somme"; the deferment granted him could only benefit our great French cause.[13]

The best means of propaganda: *performances of French music*, symphonic music with our great orchestras and chamber music with our great virtuosos—instrumentalists as well as singers—under the patronage of the French government.

**MENU Pierre** (Widor), 63rd Artillery, Rueil, 17 May

*Pierre Albert Menu (1896–1919) studied composition with Charles-Marie Widor (1844–1937). He died of injuries sustained during the war.*[14]

I approve unreservedly your decision concerning the *Gazette* as well as the idea of a questionnaire about musical culture. As you say, a useful and desirable movement might come of it, especially at this dreadful time.

Here are my answers to the 1st questionnaire:

1 – We know the classical masterpieces by heart. We understand their undeniable beauty, but it is a mistake to constantly program the same things, as was done the past few years at major Parisian concerts.

Programs should include works that we don't know or that we don't know well; there are many that are admirable and unknown to the majority of people, like Liszt's symphonic poems, which are never performed. And the largest part of programs should be devoted to works by young people. It is indeed the only way to encourage new production and to help new works bloom that might reveal future geniuses, who risk being forever unknown if we refuse to play them.

2 – Art, they say, has no Homeland; and, really, the work of Wagner no longer belongs to a single nation but to the Universe. Those who contemplate removing from concert programs these monuments of musical literature by invoking so-called patriotic principles can hardly be considered musicians. *Parsifal* cannot die, and a true musician cannot live without *Parsifal*.

3 – Art exists above all else. It seems to me that for our musical propaganda to succeed, it would be preferable to send artists, regardless of military status, who by their renown have the best chance of success and of seeing the struggle for our artistic cause triumph.

To summarize, 1st – Play modern composers; 2nd – Play Wagner and Brahms; 3rd – Send artists in consideration first and foremost of our goals.

**GROVLEZ Gabriel** (Fauré), 9 rue de Moscou, Paris, 17 May

*Gabriel Grovlez (1879–1944) studied composition with Gabriel Fauré (1845–1924) and was the director of the Opéra de Paris from 1914. Between 1899 and 1909, he taught piano at the Schola Cantorum, an institution founded by Charles Bordes and Vincent d'Indy.*

I hasten to respond to the questionnaire you were kind enough to address to me.

1 – The direction of concerts? It must in my view be inspired by only one goal: to play good music. It goes without saying that it should be predominantly modern music and that when choosing from the classical repertoire, a special effort should be made to let us hear works that are little known, rather than repeat the same symphonies over and over. There are beautiful pages of Bach, Handel, Mozart, and Haydn that we never hear!

2 – Wagner? It seems to me that to any artist worth that title, to any clear mind, there is no *question*! Mr. Vincent d'Indy, whose patriotism is above suspicion, has clearly given his opinion on the matter, and that opinion can only be shared by anyone who loves music.[15]

3 – A propaganda tour can only be of use if the musicians are first class and the programs perfect. A concert in which an artist from the Opéra-Comique sang an aria from *Carmen* or *Manon* in between a Debussy quartet and one by Ravel, would only make us a laughing stock, and that is what happened at a certain event abroad! I hasten to add that it was a private tour, the planning of which had nothing to do with the admirable Beaux Arts Office of Propaganda led by our friend Alfred Cortot.[16]

As for selecting which artists to send, consider only the impact of these artists' fame and talent on defending the cause of French Art, irrespective of their military situation.

**MIGOT Georges** (Widor), 6 rue Sedaine, Paris, discharged following very serious injuries, 17 May

*Georges Elbert Migot (1891–1976) studied composition with Charles-Marie Widor (1844–1937). He was severely injured in 1914. Both in his prolific work and his writings he took a position against neoclassicism; in his own works, he adopted a notably polyphonic style. Between 1949 and 1961, he directed the Museum of Instruments at the Conservatoire.*

1 – It is important to hear principally modern and French music because the focus of musicians from Europe and elsewhere will center on the desire to discover the new France through its artistic creations.

We do not wish to exclude classics from our programs, but magnificent performances have been given daily for so long, to every kind of audience, that it seems to me natural for them to yield to the moderns.

Indeed, the musical education of the public tends toward the classics, so much so that we should not fear directing all our resources at modern and unknown music, which there is too little opportunity to discover.

2 – German musicians like Wagner and Brahms can keep their place— indeed, their works have been performed and popularized for so long that they are already classics.

As for young or unknown German musicians, it is not necessary to reserve space for them in our programs. Let us leave it to Germany.

Without any bias on my part, it is fair to say that France leads the modern musical movement. We should not allow an exaggerated and, at the moment, misplaced modesty to let us fail to recognize our role or to surrender to foreign music.

Even the allied nations will not take offense at this momentary semi-exclusion; they know what an important place we have always given them in our concerts and what a warm welcome they have always received from us.

A large group of little-known, or even unknown artists, led by celebrities, should be sent to perform these works. It makes sense to select them from among the auxiliaries, the injured, the discharged. Above all, it is important for the new France to be known, in its thinking and through its performers. To that end, the most brilliant and gifted stars are a great help. Concert programs should bring together the names of modern and classical musicians, unknown artists as well as stars, so as to make the most room for modern thinking and interpretation.

**VASSEUR Henry** (Widor), Musician of the 154th Infantry, SP,
Croix de Guerre two citations, 18 May

*Henry Vasseur, a composition student of Charles-Marie Widor (1844–1937), published a war song titled "Les pointus! Chanson du front" in 1917.* [17] *Like many military musicians, he was employed as a stretcher bearer.*

We are at the moment in a very busy sector, and I am sorry that the little time and peace I have prevent me from answering as fully as I would like the quite interesting questions you submitted to me.

Alas! How distant music is to those of us who are in the line of fire. Will we ever again know the joy of writing and hearing music?

Despite our distress, we cannot remain indifferent to questions that are the future of music, the future of those who will return.

And right away, the predominant place we could give to modern music becomes obvious, even as we reserve for the classics a place to which they have an indisputable right; we owe everything to the classics, and the works of Bach, Mozart, and Beethoven are monuments in music that no one, at least, would think to attack.

One must love music for what it is and not because it was written by X or Y, or by a Frenchman or a German. Despite the hate for the German race that may have taken root in our hearts because of the war, we cannot judge things in that way. We would then fall into the "snobbery" that sadly ruled before the war, and we would be like those people who applaud not a work of art but rather a name.

It would be madness on the part of some people to want to exclude Wagner's oeuvre. Our only mistake was to give him such a large share in our concerts and at the theater, especially to the detriment of our greatest contemporary masters. What punishment it would be for us musicians to no longer hear the sublime pages of *Tristan and Isolde*. For that to be possible, we would have had to have never heard them.

I spoke as a musician and not as a soldier because, having been on the front for four years, first as a combatant and then as a stretcher-bearer, I am not inclined to forgive our enemies. Let us welcome music in France—music that is beautiful, music that moves us (that is the only point of Art) whatever its origin; I would be almost tempted to say, with Musset, that "Never mind the bottle, as long as it gets you drunk." [18]

Men pass, true works of art remain, and time will tell.

**TAILHARDAT Félix** (Melchissédec), Radio Department C.A. [Corps d'Armée] SP, Croix de Guerre one citation, [no date]

*Félix Tailhardat (1891–?) received a first prize in the opera class of Pierre-Léon Melchissédec (1843–1925) in 1914.*

In your last letter there are three questions of great interest to me although I do not feel qualified to answer the first. I have been away too long from the atmosphere at symphony concerts to still have many ideas concerning the direction they should take—and, what's more, my limited musical knowledge forbids me from having too definite a point of view on the matter. I can only call on common sense for this question, and it seems to me that, in this case, it would be sufficient to find a more or less "happy medium" and generally keep to it. . . . If we moved away from it from time to time, I think it would be best to favor modern composers and young musicians.

Should German musicians keep their place? "And how!"—I can't imagine anything more stupid than ostracizing the work of Wagner, as it has been up to now. What does it have to do with the theories of Bernhardi or with *Weltpolitik*?[19] And will all the Big Berthas in the world be able to drown out the rich and divine harmonies of *Parsifal, Tristan,* and the rest?

Will they keep us from being delighted by them? Why should artists give in to the whims of snobs who swooned over the works of Wagner before the war, and whose fake patriotism leads them to burn what they had pretended to love? Should we take their judgment into account? Do they even possess judgment? In that case, long live the work of the great musician! To my mind it is indisputable. Personally, I can assure you that after being shelled by Ludendorff and Von Arnim and their ilk, I was often delighted at rest time to find a piano and, with my friend Fourestier as accompanist, to go through *Tristan* from one end to the other or to hear *Siegfried's Funeral March* from *Gotterdämmerung*—and wish for an orchestra![20] As for Brahms, I do not know him well—but that would be the very reason to wish to hear him. Everyone in my situation will likely say what I do.

Which artists should be sent on a propaganda tour? Why, everyone capable of spreading the prestige of French Art! Whether they are fifty years old or twenty, gouty, one-eyed, or on the contrary have the profile of heroes, what importance does that have? What matters is to find a way to judge their merit without bias.

Forgive me for this interminable letter. I jumped on a familiar "hobby horse"! If I have been tactless, do not hold it against me—six years of military service, three and a half of them at war, have led me to forget my manners . . .

I am still in good health, and I convey to all my friendly regards.

**BOUILLARD Henri** (Widor), Secretary, Automobile
Regulating Commission, Dunkirk, 18 May

*Little is known about Henri Bouillard (1882–after 1931) other than that he stud-*
*ied flute with Paul Taffanel, that he was a composition student of Charles-Marie*
*Widor, and that he was active as a flutist in Lille, between 1905 and 1914.*[21]

To answer your questionnaire: in my opinion, this winter's concerts
should tend to performances of the great classics, which are much more
calming than modern music given the trying events of the times. I am not
naturally opposed to making modern music, but I would leave most of it
to classics such as Bach, Beethoven, etc. . . .

I think we could play some of the best works by Brahms and Wagner
from time to time, without, of course, giving them the importance they
had before the war.

As for propaganda tours, I think every artist who has influence could
do concerts of exclusively French music, and that would be the time to
play the moderns. Non-mobilized soldiers and auxiliaries could be sent; as
for mobilized troops, in my view, they should also be included in the tour
because artistic propaganda is also necessary to boost morale at the rear.

**KOECHLIN Charles** (Massenet), 30 Villa Molitor, Paris, 18 May

Here is the article I mentioned; I fear it is excessively long for your journal,
even though I condensed it as much as possible. Nevertheless, I hope you
will be able to publish it in its entirety because I believe everything holds
together, and it would be difficult to cut parts of the argument. As you
see, the primary idea is that we must play more modern French music—
and also older music—and also foreigners—in order to cure the public
(and instrumentalists) of this *Kraut* intoxication, which spread a long time
ago to the musical sphere (with the exception of young composers who,
for their part, now write works that are rather too short—one always
goes from one extreme to the other). You know me well enough to know
that there is no attempt at a narrow protectionism in my thoughts, and that
what I say is not at all out of hatred for the enemy, however odious he
might be in his excessive militarism. But I have studied the question
extensively, and I believe I am not mistaken, especially regarding the
dangers of the "traditional" form of the first theme in a symphony—
the repeat of the exposition, even with a change in key in the second
theme, is difficult to achieve without boredom; and the most fearsome
dead point is the repeat of the second theme. There are many examples

of this, even in the work of Beethoven; see, for example, the finale of the Symphony in C Minor, the beginning of which is admirable and striking, but with the repeat of the two themes (especially this one)

there is a terrible cold spot, and Beethoven only gets away with it by heating up the movement until the end; although I cannot conclude that he really gets away with it.[22]

"Don't you find that the unintentional musical truce has lasted long enough?" Those were the words M. F. Delgrange addressed in earnest to the public when he tried bravely (in these troubled times) to stage concerts *"in defense of music."*[23] Ah! The absurd injustice suffered by classical music has lasted long enough while film and music hall, which naturally are more popular, have flourished. There is only one reason for that: the lack of understanding, the heavy hostility of the masses toward true music. Ordinary people (and the bourgeoisie just as much as the lower classes share in this) see in it nothing more than a kind of noisy festivity, a blatant "tactlessness" in the face of the grief of so many families… Do we need to defend the Goddess, the *"musique adorable!"* celebrated by our dear and great Chabrier?[24] Will these narrow-minded and vulgar people ever grasp the superior, infinite beauty of the art of sound? There is no chance they will admit it, and yet this is certain: to play a Bach chorale is a way to pray, and not the least Christian nor the least sincere way to do so. To immerse oneself completely in the feeling of "Dans la forêt de Septembre" or "Le parfum impérissable," to be moved by the eternal humanity of Golaud, of Pelléas, of Arkel is to elevate oneself, to gain in nobility.[25] But why insist? I know that real musicians are already convinced; and as for the others, will they not always be resistant?

No, indeed. I am mistaken. Amid that great crowd that forms an Audience, there are many who hesitate, semi-knowledgeable, ignorant of admirable modern music; and grace can touch them. Yes, let us not lose courage in the face of difficulties: these very obstacles should invigorate us. Let us fight. No concert that is truly beautiful is useless, the sound waves it propagates reach noble souls, move truly sensitive hearts; some still exist, even many.

But, you say, *what should we play?*

That is indeed the fundamental question. First, let us state in principle that the nationality of the musician should not be taken into account. Do we deny the beauty of paintings by Holbein or Albrecht Dürer? Should we forbid Bach or Mozart because they were born on the other side of the Rhine? Has anyone ever taken seriously the joke by a member of the French Academy, who knew nothing about music, that *Meistersinger* is nothing but a "miserable rhapsody"?[26]

However, while I remain resolutely opposed to any protectionism *in principle*, and to any boycott that would reduce art to a commodity, let me be clear: the influence and the faults of the Krauts do exist. We did not have to wait for the war to find that out. German music, the truly great German classics, revealed the supreme splendor of symphonies long ago; they introduced us to the meaning of large free-flowing phrases, and they express feelings that are universally human; in France, it revived the technique of an art based in the multiple melodies of harmonic counterpoint. But, since then, art has continued to evolve. In contrast to our modern French music where, although it is essentially new, one finds the qualities of pure classical music, Germanic musicians have erected sound monuments that are more and more Kraut and which sometimes give off real poisons. While most of our composers have overcome the virus, our audiences and sometimes our instrumentalists have become dangerously intoxicated. What is curious is that in the fine arts, we did not make the same mistake. It is a recognized fact that Poussin, Claude Lorrain, Watteau, Chardin, La Tour are great painters. But it appears that, in music, German thought and German form are too often preferred (and for exactly what is flawed and needing improvement) to subtle nobility, to independence, to the French imagination. What then are these Kraut flaws? My colleagues undoubtedly know them, especially since they tasted the delicious and surefire antidotes, *Pelléas* and *Pénélope*.[27] I would not like to appear writing a lesson at this point for colleagues who are as "well-informed" as I am. And yet, the desire to be clear forces me to be detailed. The arrogant and obsessive fear of the *Kolossal* has been stigmatized: remember all those "punches" delivered in brutal rhythms to the listener's ears; so much interminable emphasis and inflated noise—all of that wrongly taken for *force*.[28] The never-ending repetitions, the atrophied sense of proportion, and this first rule of music forgotten: interest must increase or be renewed.

Convenient but boring development sections that are already set, as if machine-made and mass-produced to fit exactly within *predetermined* frames;—a rigid, lifeless architecture: that is too often what becomes of the "primo tempo" of symphonies with their inevitable re-exposition. It is a form that, in theory, seems perfect but that is nonetheless questionable—even Beethoven cannot always avoid its boring character. (Mozart's exquisite and brilliant and *instinctive* skill is required: see the opening Allegro in Symphony in G minor.) If we continue with a narrow, conventional, lazy, and deadly observance of this useless tradition, we risk often making the same mistakes as our eighteenth-century playwrights, poor imitators of Racine and Corneille. Let us not forget either (not just because the Germans are our current enemies, but because the criticism seems warranted) the kind of expression that seems both vapid and clumsy, a mawkishness that is especially regrettable in some appoggiaturas in which the third is lowered by a half step. (In the prelude to *Tristan*, I admit, these appoggiaturas are profoundly beautiful: but they are an exception.) Finally, shall I cite the "correct" monotony of the harmonic language, which is often flat and vulgar, the ignorance of, or disdain for, the Greek modes, the poverty and absence of harmony in a counterpoint that has no memory of Bach?

Alas! Perhaps you find me fiercely nationalist, sectarian, unfair, envious, careerist, who knows? Do I need to add that my criticism is not directed *as a whole* to Beethoven's German contemporaries or successors—and even less so to himself and his precursors? I am only looking for beauty, wherever it may come from. But the more I think about it, the more I am convinced that these flaws do exist, here and there, in German music, sometimes even in works by the most famous masters. And the influence of these flaws has distorted, to a great extent, the taste of French audiences: not the elite, who are discerning and forward thinking, but a large portion of the listeners at our orchestra concerts.

Their appetite is enormous and undiscriminating and does not require good ideas so much as length and noise. It is an appalling preconception that one should write page after page, expand at length, and excessively draw out little bourgeois ideas, or inflate them without care, fabricating something grandiose and aiming at the sublime in the whir of squadrons of woodwinds and the roar of batteries of brass. Have no fear: the serene, intimate beauty of a canon in *Pénélope* is only more precious for it and will last . . .

What cravings, which can only be satisfied by being copiously "bombed" (forgive the slang!). What thick and overflowing soups in which the spoon stands upright on its own, as Gounod said! (Yet how many absurdities have been written about Gounod! How often was he stupidly trounced by critics! He remains nonetheless a very great musician.) Our young composers view these tastes as those of an already distant past; but not the public. People used to complain that Pélléas was not long enough (In fact, J. P. [Jean Paul] Richter said the same thing about *Candide*); and remember the disdainful air some fake music lovers felt they had to take on hearing modest songs by Fauré or Debussy (greater, in truth, than a gigantic pile of boring symphonies).[29] I admit that significant length and amplitude are sometimes necessary; thirty measures and an orchestra of ten musicians cannot interpret some expression of feelings or a complex and grand vision. But that is not the question. What matters is finally to accept the complete freedom and legitimacy of all sorts of artistic expression, even if it is commonplace or comical (as long as the author brings out its beauty); what is essential is to understand that *absolute dimensions* need not enter into it: it is only about sincere feeling expressed in a language free of impurities, with the right features and harmonious proportions. Everyone knows that the *Parthenon* is a greater monument than the *Maison Carrée*, which in turn is better than the *Madeleine*.[30] One can agree that a small Christian object carved out of ivory in the fourteenth century or a simple Japanese "inro" may possess more real beauty and grandeur than many of the colossal history-paintings exhibited at our art salons. In music, it is the same thing, but that seems to have been forgotten.

Thus we begin to understand the importance of the work to come: the reeducation of our national taste. Only concerts can get us there. None better than modern French music (including the most daring, the newest, the most spontaneously free) would contribute to this huge task: rich, simple, refined, strong, and concise, a balance between fantasy and reason, it possesses all the characteristics of a pure classical art. This music is a whole world. Yet, its place (especially in major concerts) is much too small; we must urgently change that. Once the public gets to know it, by hearing it often, they will love it.

There is no reason that there should not be an audience for it. As a true expression of today's sensibilities, it represents our times; it is alive, intensely alive. It will live a long time. And, future generations will understand what an important place it deserves in the history of art.

It is evident now how wrong and duplicitous it is to criticize "music in dribs and drabs." If we wish to search our own past for quintessentially French works that are both complex and sweeping, we might remember more often that Berlioz did not write only the *Damnation of Faust*. Besides, is the idea to ban German musicians we call "classical"? (In my humble opinion, that adjective is not very accurate as applied to Beethoven and his successors; but let's move on . . .) And, why should we leave aside Brahms and Wagner, since we play so much Beethoven? Any refusal of a beautiful work would have to come from a narrow mind. But, first, we should know how to choose. In the meantime, the public is satisfied to hear the *Eroica* and the C-minor Symphony.[31] It is left to us to introduce them to almost all the other great musicians! And why would they not love them? I realize that J. S. Bach, as he wrote his cantatas, had not planned for our orchestras' distinct preference for works without choral parts (with the exception of their performances at the Schola Cantorum and the lovely experiment by the Pasdeloup Orchestra). But, why do we never hear at least any of the great Cantor's admirable pieces for organ, which are perhaps the most beautiful in all of music? And what would you say of a curator at the Louvre who obstinately kept closed every room containing a Rembrandt? And, then, it seems to me that we are forgetting Mozart. He composed many symphonies; one would not guess so at the Salle Gaveau. Haydn too, I think. As for H. Schütz, Buxtehude, and the admirable Purcell, they have no place there. Nor Rameau. And, I assume that Rameau is not our only eighteenth-century composer—but the others are neglected even more. And those from the seventeenth and sixteenth centuries: the same. As for the works of Frescobaldi, I regret that they are only known to us through the treatise by Cherubini. What about Cavalli's operas? Or Luigi Rossi's *Orfeo*? Monteverdi? And Mussorgsky, and his predecessors? Further in the past, don't we know there exist beautiful Gregorian Chants and profoundly beautiful Breton melodies? To say nothing of Russian, Hebrew, Armenian, Peruvian folklore . . . Closer to the future, the strange but very interesting works by Schoenberg, Kodály, Bartók. . . .

I mention all these names quickly as I write this; they represent only a few of all the ones we should be thinking about. However, this incomplete presentation reveals the vastness of past *classical* music, and our concert programming committees only draw on a tiny bit of it. As beautiful as it is, it is not enough.

I hasten to add that, abroad, governments support instrumentalists with an intelligent generosity (see the subsidies to the Augusteo in Rome, or symphonic concerts in Berlin).[32] It is in painful contrast to our democracy's indifference, alas so "un-Athenian." Indifference? What am I saying? Worse, I am told that in some provincial towns, they collect taxes on concerts—taxes that are exorbitant and an absolute *crime* against music. How can we stop this scandal?

As for Paris, I cannot believe that a well-organized and methodical effort—with consistent and logical programs that respect the "unity of time" preferred by the listener (because it is absurd to try to squeeze in a modern work, chosen on purpose to be very short so that it takes less time to rehearse, between the *Eroica* and the overture of *Die Meistersinger*)—I cannot believe, as I was saying, that such an endeavor would not succeed. The success of the new Concerts Pasdeloup and (before the war, but let us hope they will resume later) the performances led by Monteux of various works by Stravinsky, Casella, and Ravel are clear proof of it.

Forgive me for this overly long essay. Certain ideas, however, have to be presented in detail, supported with names and without being afraid of exploring the meaning of things, or we risk being obscure and not thorough. A lot could be said about the possible partnership between the state and musicians (composers, music-history professors, instrumentalists). Reopen for the nation the lost path to real music that was planted with so many bad seeds! Education in elementary school, in high school, at popular concerts, at choral societies. . . That is a topic for another time.

Meanwhile, I am certain that art lives on; and all our colleagues resume their work with profound joy as soon as they are given the opportunity to do so. Our school of modern French music will not die: that would be nothing less than a disaster for it is our century's greatest school of classical music. That is what needs to be known, that is what needs to be repeated, and that is why I hope I will be forgiven for discussing at length questions that are of interest to every one of us. On that note, I close, with affectionate admiration for my young colleagues.

**WELSCH Marcel** (Lafleurance), 131st Artillery Regiment
T.S.F., SP, 19 May

*Maurice Marcel Welsch (1893–1931) studied flute with Léopold Baptiste Lafleurance (1865–1953). He became a member of the Orchestre de la Suisse Romande. T.S.F. is an abbreviation for télégraphie sans fil (wireless telegraph).*

The *Gazette* is becoming more and more interesting, and its purely musical nature, where any discussion is possible, will by this very fact be of great help to the evolution of our art.

To answer the memo included with your letter, there is much to say about this first question, although in my view the classics and the moderns are one. How many historic works are still unknown to us! Take the programs of any season—you will see Handel, a little Haydn, and Rameau will show himself furtively, but the great Palestrina . . . no news of him. Should such an oversight not be rectified? As we know the classics, we should know the moderns; we must at the very least be capable of judging our times soundly by giving easier access to our concerts to young people. May Fanelli's fate no longer be feared.[33]

Let us pay homage to the old masters and encourage the discovery of our young people.

I have never understood this misguided patriotism that makes it so that all of a sudden we completely eliminate a genius who was too highly praised, too celebrated as recently as 1914.

What does he have to do with a time he does not know nor ever will? He is already a distant figure to us; the same goes for Brahms, even though he does not have the same talent or stature.

Does that change the order of things? . . . Alas!

Do you believe that musicians who own high-quality scores or even manuscripts of Wagner would want to burn them for fear of an evil spell and out of patriotism? That would be ridiculous.

Let us not fear the Kraut, let him take up his place once more, and let us include him wisely without repeating the mistakes of the past. Can one do without Goethe, Mozart, Beethoven?

To the third question, I would answer that we should send on propaganda tours those musicians who are representative of our beautiful school, the people who put it at the top in our time; I mean: Debussy, P. Dukas, Fauré, d'Indy, and all those to whom they gave rise, Florent Schmitt, Ravel, etc.

**QUEF Charles** (Dubois), 11 rue des Potagers, Bellevue, 20 May

*The composer and organist Charles Paul Florimond Quef (1873–1931) studied composition with Théodore Dubois (1837–1924), the director of the Conservatoire, between 1896 and 1905. In 1901, Quef became the titular organist of the Eglise de la Sainte Trinité in Paris.*[34]

The questions you have seen fit to ask us are rather delicate and awkward as they touch on personal feeling and preference. These subjects could be explored in so many ways! Certainly interesting, but their length might scare the reader away! Should we play the classics or give a prominent place to modern music? At first sight, it seems the second part of this question should be answered in the affirmative. . . . One should consider the progress of art, encourage it, stimulate it, and bring it to life by playing French composers, who are generally sacrificed. . . . At the same time, one must think of the younger generations, who need classical music, who must hear it, know it, and become immersed in it.

As for Brahms and Wagner, after the war they should continue to have their place—and just their place, nothing more; I can hardly insist on it considering that, for me personally, Wagner is a genius of music and Brahms an unrefined and pompous expression of German thought.

Which artists to send on tour? Those who will not see in it an opportunity to avoid military duty, or an opportunity for personal gain and success, but whose sole interest is French musical art. In the end, for that matter it is this last point that should inspire the answers to the questions you were kind enough to address to us: the great interest of French music! And French musicians: they have been so often criticized and opposed by the French people themselves, whose xenomania is as well known as it is regrettable. . . . Montaigne cited it while deploring it. . . .

And, if one has traveled even a little bit abroad, one realizes that it is (and for many reasons) an error on the part of our compatriots as great and as stupid as it is prejudicial to France, whose artistic productions, authors, and performers will always be superior (something some people do not recognize or do so with difficulty) and will always be one of the glories of our country.

**FAURE (Maurice)** (Diémer), pilot trainer,
Sancheville, Croix de Guerre one citation, 20 May

*Maurice Faure (1891–1991) studied piano with Louis Diémer (1843–1919). In 1930, he became professor of piano at the Conservatoire, a position from which he retired in 1961.*

I am quite late answering your letter and also the questions for the *Gazette*; this delay is only due to an increase in work because of the beautiful weather.

But of course! Our *Gazette* must "live"! This interesting work, whose principal goal is to bring together artists who will get to know one another better, and thus like one another more, must develop freely. . . .

I will now briefly answer the questions for the *Gazette*. As for the first, there is no doubt: without neglecting the classics, our French modern musicians must be given a prominent place! I insist particularly on French because, in France, we have always favored foreign musicians and their works, which are often mediocre, to the detriment of our own. Now or never is the time to put an end to this anomaly.

And why not play the music of Brahms or Wagner? Do they not play French music in Germany? But I do not dare expand freely on the subject with all the defeatism lately! I would quickly become a client of Capitaine Bouchardon![35] . . .

As for the last question, I have no hesitation! Did you read the newspapers about the success of the Blue Devils in America? What a shame there are (or were) no famous artists among the Blue Devils, the Zouaves, the Fantassins, in a word, among those who fought the war![36] . . . If you know of anyone, use all your influence to send them on a propaganda tour. They will do more for France than all the others taken together. Otherwise, the choice does not matter; whether it is a musician who was not mobilized because of his age, a staff officer at headquarters, or a soldier attached to a hospital, etc. . . . They will represent French music, but not really the French people, and the propaganda will not achieve its goal.

**DEBRUN J. H.** (Gédalge), Medical Orderly, Fort, SP, May

*J. H. Debrun studied counterpoint and fugue with André Gédalge (1856–1925) after 1905.*

If the three questions from the Committee had been addressed to us with a response requested within two weeks, I could have given more suitable answers. As it is, invoking current circumstances and mitigating factors—and how!—my answers will be just a summary of notes hastily thrown together. If they were about artistic preference, my answers would be very brief. But here the point, at least as I see it, is for each of us to defend our point of view.

1 – Symphony concerts, with or without choir, with or without a soloist, should have as their mission to present music, simply music (classical and modern). If, at one concert performance, the classical portion is greater and the modern portion less so, they should alternate at the next one.

Present "music" over any other consideration, that's the goal.

Of course, one must nurture young musicians, but neither the insane nor the ignorant.

In the same way that I find there is a divide between Wagner and Debussy, there is an even greater one between Debussy and Stravinsky.

This is all going too fast.

Too rare are musicians like Fauré and H. Rabaud (listen to *Mârouf*) who take into account the aesthetic that preceded them, while at the same time creating something new and preserving their personality.[37]

2 – The oeuvre of Wagner is the oeuvre of a genius. It is inadmissible for any musician to have any thought of rejecting such a body of work.

And if that musician, that artist existed, I would not hesitate to tell him that he does not know or understand the work of Wagner, or even that he has lost his memory. And then, quite sincerely, I would pity him.

Wagner's music is not, as suggested by a certain critic (Louis Laloy) "only expressive"—imagery and color are reflected and revel in it just as intensely as emotions. It is not Debussy's impressionism—it is something else.

Although to a lesser degree, the same could be said of the music of Brahms.

But as concerns these two musicians, especially the first, will politics and blind chauvinism quarantine these two authors for an indeterminate time . . . ??

And a new question! What weight will be given to the opinion of musicians??—I am referring in particular to those who will have seen, who will have suffered on the front lines. . . .

3 – A propaganda tour is certainly a good idea. If it is organized in a serious way, musicians of all ages would gladly participate. Those on the "front" would certainly not refuse to lend their support! As for the performers, people more qualified than I should choose.

But the only solid basis for an effective propaganda campaign directed at the masses begins with musical instruction and education on a wholly different level than what is happening today.

This subject alone would be a most interesting question to address. Let us hope it is presented for our consideration. At the very least, it would be a powerful distraction from our worries, which are as disturbing as they are ill-defined. . . .

On the subject of this third question, I would like to bring to your attention, if you organize tours of quartets or quintets, etc., the cellist Challet (from the Opéra) whom I met at Verdun, and my brother (first violin at the Concert Séchiari), who are both fine instrumentalists . . .

# NOTES

1. *Gazette des classes de composition du Conservatoire* 10 (June 1918). For a digital copy of the *Gazette*, see https://gallica.bnf.fr/ark:/12148/bpt6k911403q. Nadia Boulanger preserved the original responses; see Bibliothèque nationale de France (F-Pn), Rés. Vm. dos. 88 (4).

2. See, for example, "L'orientation musicale," *Musica* 1/1 (October 1902): 5–6.

3. Jérôme Spycket, *A la recherche de Lili Boulanger* (Paris : Fayard, 2004), 274–75. On the *Gazette*, see also Alexandra Laederich, "Nadia Boulanger et le Comité franco-américain du Conservatoire (1915–1919)" (161–73), and Charlotte Segond-Genovesi, "De l'Union sacrée au *Journal des débats:* Lecture de la *Gazette des classes du Conservatoire* (1914–1918)" (175–90), in *La Grande Guerre des musiciens*, ed. Stéphane Audoin-Rouzeau et al. (Lyon: Symétrie, 2009).

4. See Rachel Moore, *Performing Propaganda: Musical Life and Culture in Paris, 1914–1918* (Woodbridge, UK: Boydell, 2018), 65–96. One of the better-known outgrowths of wartime nationalism is the Ligue pour la defense de la musique française which was founded in 1916 by Charles Tenroc. As Moore points out, it had far less influence than musicological literature has attributed to it (11). This notoriety was due, in part, to Maurice Ravel's resolute refusal to join its cause.

5. Marguerite de Saint-Marceaux, *Journal 1894–1927*, ed. Myriam Chimènes (Paris: Fayard, 2007), 847.

6. Felix von Weingartner (1863–1942) was an Austrian conductor, composer, and pianist who, among other positions, held those of conductor of the Vienna Philharmonic Orchestra and director of the Royal Opera House in Vienna. He was the first conductor to record the complete Beethoven symphonies and had a prominent international career on both sides of the Atlantic, especially during the interwar years.

7. Two publications are particularly helpful to establish the background of lesser-known musicians and were used to annotate this selection: Constant Pierre, *Le Conservatoire national de musique et de déclamation: Documents historiques et administratifs* (Paris: Imprimerie nationale, 1900) ; and Anne Bongrain, *Le Conservatoire national de musique et de déclamation, 1900–1930: Documents historiques et administratifs* (Paris: Vrin, 2012).

8. Ibert cites Oscar Wilde from memory. The quotation reads: "Now, whatever music sounds like, I am glad to say it does not sound in the smallest degree like German." Oscar Wilde, "The Critic as Artist," in *The Complete Works of Oscar Wilde*, vol. 4: *Criticism*, ed. Josephine M. Guy (Oxford and New York: Oxford University Press, 2007), 127.

9. The writer, poet, and music scholar Romain Rolland (1866–1944) published, between 1902 and 1912, *Jean Christophe*, a 10-volume sequence of novels that draws on the German composer Ludwig van Beethoven as the inspiration for its hero.

10. Pretty much forgotten during most of the nineteenth century, the mandolin was revived in the 1880s and became a wildly popular instrument, leading the formation of mandolin orchestras across the Western world and Japan. It was used for music making both in the trenches and in hospitals during World War I. It declined in popularity again after the end of World War I. See J. Paul Sparks, *The Classical Mandolin* (New York and Oxford: Oxford University Press, 2005).

11. The Austrian composer Franz Léhar wrote the music for *The Merry Widow* (1905) and the Austrian Oscar Straus, *Ein Walzertraum* (1907). "L'heure exquise qui nous grise" is the French translation of the duet "Lippen schweigen" from *The Merry Widow*.

12. See "Au Conservatoire," *Le Ménestrel* 85/24 (15 June 1923): 275.

13. *Diables bleus*, or Blue Devils, is the nickname of the Chasseurs Alpins, the elite mountain infantry of the French Army.

14. For details on Menu's death in service, see https://www.memoiredeshommes.sga. defense.gouv.fr/fr/arkotheque/client/mdh/base_morts_pour_la_france_premiere_guerre/ index.php.

15. D'Indy, whose nationalist agenda was widely known in France, was among the musicians who supported Wagner publicly against Saint-Saëns's charge in "Germanophilie." See Moore, *Performing Propaganda*, 75.

16. In 1915, the French government began to centralize propaganda efforts under the umbrella of the ministry of Foreign Affairs. Musical propaganda was institutionalized in May 1916 as the Service de propaganda artistique, which was headed by Alfred Cortot (1877–1962). See Moore, *Performing Propaganda*, 50–52.

17. Paris: Comptoir général de la musique.

18. This widely cited *bon mot* comes from Alfred de Musset, *La Coupe et les lèvres* (1832). See Fred R. Shapiro, *The Yale Book of Citations* (New Haven: Yale University Press, 2006), 543.

19. Friedrich von Bernhardi (1849–1930) was a German general and military historian. In 1912, he published *Deutschland und der nächste Krieg* (Germany and the Next War), an analysis of the contemporary military and geopolitical situation. It was translated the following year into both English and French and was widely understood as a manifesto of German military aggression.

20. Louis Fourestier (1892–1976) was a French composer, pianist, and conductor. In 1928, he cofounded the Orchestre symphonique de Paris.

21. See Guy Gosselin, *La symphonie dans la cité: Lille au XIXe siècle* (Paris: Vrin, 2011), 417.

22. Ludwig van Beethoven, Symphony no. 5 in C minor, Op. 67, m. 275. The theme first appears at the end of the exposition at m. 64 in G.

23. Félix Delgrange was a French conductor, cellist, and concert organizer. In 1917, he organized a series of concerts that he called "Pour la musique" in Montparnasse, where he programmed new works by such composers as Georges Auric, Francis Poulenc, and Erik Satie. See Robert Orledge, *Charles Koechlin (1867–1950): His Life and Works* (Chur, SWI, and New York: Harwood Academic Publishers, 1989), 27.

24. Koechlin refers to the "Ode à la musique" (1890) for soprano, female choir, and orchestra, by Emmanuel Chabrier (1841–94), with a text by Edmond Rostand, which opens with the line, "Musique adorable, ô Déesse."

25. Koechlin refers to two songs by Gabriel Fauré: "Dans la forêt de Septembre" (Op. 85, no. 1), with words by Catulle Mendès, and "Le parfum impérissable" (Op. 76, No. 1), with words by Leconte de Lisle. Golaud, Pelléas, and Arkel are the three male characters of Claude Debussy's *Pelléas et Mélisande* (1902).

26. Koechlin refers to a trope in the French reception of *Meistersinger*. By the outbreak of World War I, critics had used the term "misérable rhapsodie" for decades to describe Wagner's work. Frédéric Masson used the term again in his response to Camille Saint-Saëns's "Germanophilie." See Jacques-Gabriel Prod'homme, *Richard Wagner et la France* (Paris: Senart, 1921), 34.

27. In addition to Debussy's *Pelléas et Mélisande*, Koechlin cites Gabriel Fauré's opera *Pénélope* (1913), evoking two works whose reception emphasized their respective roles in a possible pantheon of quintessentially French operatic masterpieces. This nationalist reception history forms part of the later developments of French Wagnerism.

28. Koechlin summarizes here the most frequently leveled criticism against Wagnerian and (more broadly) compositional techniques labeled German—monumentality, monotony, repetition, lack of proportion, and noise—and contrasts them with the bedrock of French aesthetics, which often is summarized as classic elegance, simplicity, and variety. These tropes of reception were in place from the middle of the nineteenth century. See Annegret Fauser, "'Cette musique sans tradition': Wagner's *Tannhäuser* and its French Critics," in *Music, Theater, and Cultural Transfer: Paris, 1830–1914*, ed. Annegret Fauser and Mark Everist (Chicago: University of Chicago Press, 2009), 228–55. As Jean Mongrédien has pointed out, these dichotomies were already in play when Mozart's *Die Zauberflöte* was given in Paris in 1801. See Jean Mongrédien, *La Musique en France des Lumières au romantisme* (Paris: Flammarion, 1992).

29. Koechlin deliberately uses the German last name of the Romantic poet Jean Paul, who—as a German—would criticize Voltaire's *Candide* as being too concise. In 1925, Koechlin expands this point by contrasting French song with symphonic and operatic composition. See Charles Koechlin, "La Mélodie," in *Cinquante ans de musique française de 1874 à 1925*, ed Ladislas Rohozinski, 2 vols (Paris: Librairie de France, 1925), 2:1–62.

30. Koechlin here uses three classical monuments to reference the concept of *translatio studii*, the notion that over the centuries culture had moved from Greece (Parthenon in Athens) through the Roman Empire (Maison Carrée in Nîmes) to France (Madeleine). The claim that France was the heir to Greek culture was first established in the sixteenth century. See Jeanice Brooks, "Italy, the Ancient World, and the French Musical Inheritance in the Sixteenth Century: Arcadelt and Clereau in the Service of the Guises," *Journal of the Royal Musical Association* 121/2 (1996): 147–90. This claim became particularly powerful in the late nineteenth century when Hellenism could serve as an antidote to Wagnerism. See Annegret Fauser, "Gendering the Nations: Ideologies of French Discourse on Music (1870–1914)," in *The Politics of Musical Identity: Selected Essays* (Surrey: Ashgate, 2015), 71–102.

31. Before World War I, these two symphonies—Beethoven's Symphony No. 3 in E-flat Major ("Eroica"), Op. 55 and Symphony No. 5 in C Minor, Op. 67—were his best known and most frequently performed orchestral works not only in France but globally.

32. Koechlin refers to the subventions received by both Italian and German concert houses (passing under silence the substantive subventions that the French state offered, for instance, to the Concerts Lamoureux and Concerts Colonne). The Augusteo was a Roman concert hall incorporating the Augustus Mausoleum that was torn down, in 1937, by Mussolini to make space for Istituto Nazionale Fascista Previdenza. It was home to the Academia Nazionale di Santa Cecilia.

33. After completing his studies at the Conservatoire, the French composer Ernest Fanelli (1860–1917) made his living as a copyist and music engraver. His compositions were discovered after he submitted them to Gabriel Pierné as samples for his handwriting. Pierné was so impressed with the quality of Fanelli's music that he conducted two of his works—the symphonic poem *Thebes* (1883) and the *Impressions pastorales* (1890)—at the Concerts Colonne in 1912. His compositional style was celebrated for its innovative qualities, but Fanelli did not return to composition. See William Rosar, "Fanelli, Ernest," *Grove Online*. As M.-D. Calvocoressi captured the sense of discovery when he wrote in 1912 about Pierné's discovery of "a totally unknown composer of genius . . . who, about thirty years ago, had begun writing symphonic works of the highest originality and interest, in which the most advanced tendencies of the modern French school were wonderfully forestalled, but had never succeeded in getting his music produced." M.-D. Calvocoressi, "An Unknown Composer of Today," *The Musical Times* 56 (1912): 225–26, at 225.

34. For more on Quef, see Steven Young, "Introducing Charles Quef: Forgotten Master of La Trinité in Paris," *The Diapason*, September 18, 2006, https://www.thediapason.com/introducing-charles-quef-forgotten-master-la-trinité-paris.

35. Captain Pierre Bouchardon (1870–1950) was well known as a vocal opponent of the pacifist press and "Defeatism," a campaign in French newspapers to encourage capitulation. It was financed by German funds via the intercession of Bolo Pasha (Paul Bolo) who was convicted of espionage and executed in 1918. Bouchardon is also known for being on the military prosecution team that convicted Mata Hari as a German spy.

36. *Zouaves* is the name for a class of highly decorated, light-infantry regiments, often stationed in and recruited from French North Africa, between 1830 and 1962. They were disbanded after the Algerian war. *Fantassin* is a term used more generally for infantry soldiers.

37. Henri Rabaud (1873–1949) was a French composer who retained a traditional musical idiom. His opera *Mârouf, savetier du Caire* (1914) was popular, and he served as director of the Conservatoire between 1922 and 1944.

# From Technique to *Musique*:
# The Institutional Pedagogy of
# Nadia Boulanger

MARIE DUCHÊNE-THÉGARID
TRANSLATED BY MIRANDA STEWART

Nadia Boulanger played a central role in the music education landscape of the twentieth century. Very few teachers leave an impression so strong that students identify as a community like that of the "Boulangerie." Jeanice Brooks, reflecting on the reasons for this fascination, refers to numerous tributes and musician biographies and mentions Boulanger's "extraordinary charisma and inspirational effect on her students."[1] There is abundant evidence of her teaching activities and several studies have been devoted to her unique teaching approach.[2] However, less is known about the debt owed by "Mademoiselle" to the institutions at which she taught in the period immediately after the First World War.[3]

In the early 1920s, two innovative musical institutions came into being: the Ecole Normale de Musique de Paris and the Conservatoire américain de Fontainebleau (American Conservatory), which opened in 1919 and 1921, respectively. These schools, which emerged in the aftermath of conflict, were specifically geared toward foreign students and shared the same, indissolubly intertwined political and aesthetic goals: to fight against the allegedly pernicious influence of German conservatories by channeling, in the direction of France, all the foreign students who had attended them prior to the war.

Auguste Mangeot, the prime mover behind the creation of the Ecole Normale de Musique, sought to attract to France "students of music from all over the world" who, prior to the war, had trained on the other side of the Rhine and were on their way to being "propagandists for German music."[4] In Mangeot's view, it was through these students that "we will strengthen our influence abroad and make our works and our artists known."[5] He was not the only one to marshal this argument on a regular basis in his dealings with the authorities—the founders of the Conservatoire américain deployed the same approach. At the beginning of the 1920s, they too wanted to promote the "expansion of French art" by "holding on to American students when they passed through Europe and preventing them from going on to study music in other countries."[6]

Nadia Boulanger's interest in issues of cultural diplomacy and her personal ties to a number of musicians involved meant that she learned of these projects early on. Her professional relationship with Auguste Mangeot predated the First World War. The son of a piano manufacturer from Nancy, Mangeot quickly became involved in education. Initially, he used his columns in *Le Monde musical*, of which he had been editor since 1898, to explore essential reforms before founding the Société des Musiciens de France, an organization that started to award music teaching certificates in 1910. Nadia Boulanger joined his team of examiners at the outset. In 1918, he built on their close professional relationship and employed her at the Ecole Normale de Musique before the institution even officially opened.[7] The school was distinctive in its innovative pedagogical approach. The new institution built on Mangeot's work at the Société des Musiciens de France, and its diplomas certified that its graduates were competent to teach music.

Thus in the early 1920s Nadia Boulanger occupied a tenured post at a school whose teaching approach and openness to foreign students had allowed it to expand rapidly. Two years later, her association with the Conservatoire américain would allow her to extend her institutional teaching activity into the summer.

The Conservatoire américain inherited a structure that was set up during the First World War in Chaumont, the General Headquarters of the American troops in Europe. At the request of General John Joseph Pershing, Walter Damrosch, the American conductor who had arrived in France in June 1918 to conduct symphonic concerts for the benefit of U.S. soldiers, assessed the quality of the American military bands; he found that their main problems were due to hasty assembly and a lack of experienced conductors.[8] He saw a distinct need for a school to train conductors, oboists, bassoonists, and horn players, and, assisted by Francis Casadesus, rapidly created one in Chaumont. The end of the war and demobilization led to the closure of the school on 1 June 1919. Casadesus and Damrosch were keen to pursue this productive endeavor and extend their friendship, born of combat, to the realm of art. The founding of the Conservatoire américain met this need and marched to the tune of the anti-German rhetoric favored by Mangeot.

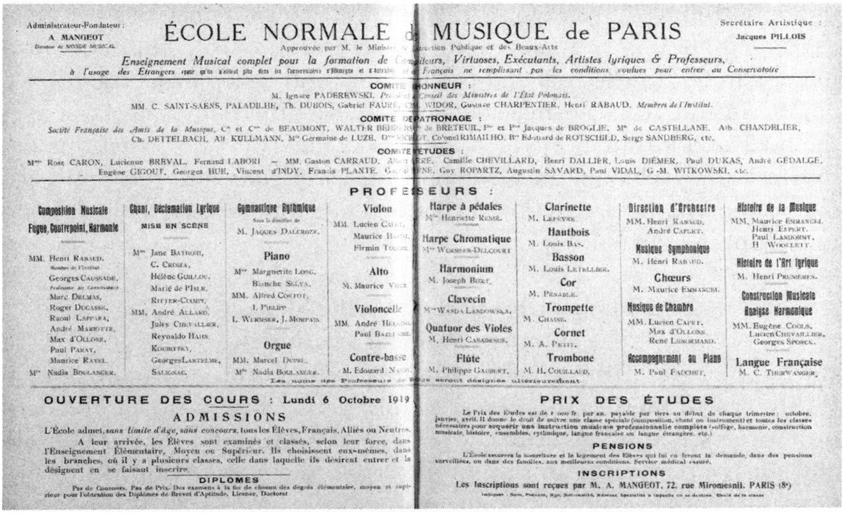
Administrateur-Fondateur :
A. MANGEOT
Secrétaire Artistique :
Jacques PILLOIS

ÉCOLE NORMALE d MUSIQUE de PARIS

Approuvée par M. le Minis ruction Publique et des Beaux-Arts

Enseignement Musical complet pour la formation de Co ileurs, Virtuoses, Exécutants, Artistes lyriques & Professeurs, à l'usage des Étrangers … Français ne remplissant pas les conditions voulues pour entrer au Conservatoire

COMITE ONNEUR :
M. Ignace PADEREWSKI, … Conseil des Ministres de l'État Polonais.
MM. C. SAINT-SAENS, PALADILHE, Th. DUBOIS, Gabriel FAURE, … WIDOR, Gustave CHARPENTIER, Henri RABAUD, Membres de l'Institut.

COMITE DE PATRONAGE :
Société Française des Amis de la Musique, C^e et C^{sse} de BEAUMONT, WALTER BEHR… de BRETEUIL, P^ce et P^sse Jacques de BROGLIE, M^is de CASTELLANE, Alb. CHANDELIER, Ch. DETTELBACH, Alf KULLMANN, M^lle Germaine de LUZE, … Colonel RIMAILHO, B^on Edouard de ROTSCHILD, Serge SANDBERG, etc.

COMITE ETUDES :
M^mes Rose CARON, Lucienne BREVAL, Fernand LABORI — MM. Gaston CARRAUD, … Camille CHEVILLARD, Henri DALLIER, Louis DIÉMER, Paul DUKAS, André GÉDALGE, Eugène GIGOUT, Georges HUE, Vincent d'INDY, Francis PLANTE, … Guy ROPARTZ, Augustin SAVARD, Paul VIDAL, G.-M. WITKOWSKI, etc.

PROFESSEURS :

Composition Musicale
Fugue, Contrepoint, Harmonie
MM. Henri Rabaud, Membre de l'Institut
Georges Caussade, Professeur au Conservatoire
Marc Delmas,
Roger Ducasse,
Raoul Laparra,
André Mariotte,
Max d'Ollone,
Paul Paray,
Maurice Ravel,
M^lle Nadia Boulanger.

Chant, Déclamation Lyrique
Mise en scène
M^mes Jane Bathori,
C. Croiza,
Hélène Guillou,
Marié de l'Isle,
Ritter-Ciampi,
MM. André Allard,
Jules Chevallier,
Reynaldo Hahn,
Koubitzky,
Georges Lanthelme,
Salignac.

Gymnastique Rythmique
Sous la direction de
M. Jaques Dalcroze,

Piano
M^mes Marguerite Long,
Blanche Selva,
MM. Alfred Cortot,
I. Philipp
L. Wurmser, J. Morpain

Orgue
MM. Marcel Dupré,
M^lle Nadia Boulanger.

Violon
MM. Lucien Ca…,
Maurice H…,
Firmin To…

Alto
M. Maurice V…

Violoncelle
MM. André He…,
Paul Baz…

Contre-basse
M. Edouard N…

Harpe à pédales
M^lle Henriette Renié.

Harpe Chromatique
M^me Wurmser-Delcourt

Harmonium
M. Joseph Bizet.

Clavecin
M^me Wanda Landowska.

Quatuor des Violes
M. Henri Casadesus.

Flûte
M. Philippe Gaubert.

Clarinette
M. Lefèvre.

Hautbois
M. Louis Bas.

Basson
M. Louis Letellier.

Cor
M. Pénable.

Trompette
M. Chaine.

Cornet
M. A. Petit.

Trombone
M. H. Couillaud.

Direction d'Orchestre
MM. Henri Rabaud,
André Caplet.

Musique Symphonique
M. Henri Rabaud.

Chœurs
M. Maurice Emmanuel.

Musique de Chambre
MM. Lucien Capet,
Max d'Ollone,
René Lenormand.

Accompagnement au Piano
M. Paul Fauchet.

Histoire de la Musique
MM. Maurice Emmanuel,
Henri Expert,
Paul Landormy,
H. Woollett.

Histoire de l'Art lyrique
M. Henri Prunières.

Construction Musicale
Analyse Harmonique
MM. Eugène Cools,
Lucien Chevaillier,
Georges Sporck.

Langue Française
M. C. Thirwanger.

Les noms des Professeurs … seront désignés ultérieurement

OUVERTURE DES COURS : Lundi 6 Octobre 1919

ADMISSIONS
L'École admet, *sans limite d'âge, sans concours,* tous les Élèves, Français, Alliés ou Neutres.
A leur arrivée, les Élèves sont examinés et classés, selon leur force, dans l'Enseignement Élémentaire, Moyen ou Supérieur. Ils choisissent eux-mêmes, dans les branches, où il y a plusieurs classes, celle dans laquelle ils désirent entrer et la désignent en se faisant inscrire.

DIPLOMES
Pas de Concours. Pas de Prix. Des examens à la fin de chacun des degrés élémentaire, moyen et supérieur pour l'obtention des Diplômes de Brevet d'Aptitude, Licence, Doctorat

PRIX DES ÉTUDES
Le Prix des Études est de 1 000 fr. par an, payable par tiers au début de chaque trimestre : octobre, janvier, avril. Il donne le droit de suivre une classe spéciale (composition, chant ou instrument) et toutes les classes nécessaires pour acquérir une instruction musicale professionnelle complète (solfège, harmonie, construction musicale, histoire, ensembles, rythmique, langue française ou langue étrangère, etc.)

PENSIONS
L'École assurera la nourriture et le logement des Élèves qui lui en feront la demande, dans des pensions surveillées, ou dans des familles, aux meilleures conditions. Service médical assuré.

INSCRIPTIONS
Les Inscriptions sont reçues par M. A. MANGEOT, 72, rue Miromesnil, PARIS (8^e)

Figure 1. Announcement of the opening of the Ecole Normale de Musique, 1919. The purpose of drawing students away from German and Austrian institutions and toward France is clearly stated at the top. Boulanger's name appears on the chart of teachers at the bottom left, in the section devoted to composition, fugue, counterpoint, and harmony.

Nadia Boulanger, among the conservatory's first teachers, did not actually initiate this project; she did, however, rapidly become associated with its development. As early as 13 August 1919, Robert Brussel, who worked for the Service d'Etudes artistiques—the unit that succeeded the Service de Propagande artistique where Auguste Mangeot had conceived the Ecole Normale de Musique—sought to ascertain from her the progress of the proposed American music school.[9] Boulanger's prior relationships with people from the United States were the main reason why, in Robert Brussel's eyes, she was potentially a key player in an emerging French cultural diplomacy, and an ideal interlocutor. In autumn 1915, the Boulanger sisters created the Franco-American Committee of the Conservatoire, which raised material assistance for mobilized students and published a *Gazette* designed to foster links between the students, scattered widely by the war.[10] This committee, supported by donations from American sponsors, also received help from Walter Damrosch. Her growing friendship with the conductor led to her being "taken on board" at the Conservatoire américain.[11]

Nadia Boulanger's commitment to these two young institutions opened up a new world to her first in the literal sense, by affording her the opportunity to teach foreign students.[12] Her interaction with them expanded not only her geographical horizons, however, but also, metaphorically, her intellectual and professional universe. The Conservatoire américain and Ecole Normale de Musique, with their innovative teaching methods and artistic projects, offered Boulanger the ideal environment in which to develop an unconventional teaching method. Her approach had its roots in the practices of the Paris Conservatoire but would develop in unexpected directions.

### The Heiress of the "Vieille Maison": A Selective National Institution

Biographies of artists attach considerable importance to the period during which they acquire their technical skills and start to forge their own careers.[13] Budding artists, when they consort with future colleagues and recognized artists and sponsors, create their own networks, which very often prove crucial to their professional success. Often this is also the time when musicians espouse individual aesthetic and interpretative approaches and develop their own personalities.

Although Nadia Boulanger is known primarily for her role as a teacher, her career owed much to the artistic training she received at the Conservatoire. It allowed her to shape her conception of musical language and, after graduation, gave her the professional status that befitted a graduate of a selective national institution.

The Conservatoire national de musique et de déclamation was founded in 1795 to train professional musicians and guarantee France's musical independence.[14] It was from the outset national in scope; an iconic public, state-funded, and nationally controlled organization, attracting students from all over France. Consequently, it was incumbent upon its successive administrators to set a maximum number of available places and to recruit students abiding by the principle of "equality" as embodied in the Republican motto. This governed its decision to hold both general and entrance examinations and earned the Conservatoire a growing reputation. It was known for the quality of its teaching and later for the severity of its entrance examination boards. A new student was permitted to join a class only when another young musician had left. The small number of places meant that the establishment recruited only the most talented and promising future artists, who were mainly French.

From 1886 on, the Conservatoire's regulations effectively limited the number of foreign musicians admitted to its classes. The institution's director Ambroise Thomas argued, in 1886, that due to the small number of student vacancies each year and the Conservatoire's mission to "ensure recruitment to our subsidized theater and concert orchestras, which should ideally give preference to French artists," and given that this education was free, the institution should limit the number of foreign students.[15] Marcellin Berthelot, the Minister of Public Instruction, set a limit of two foreign students per class.

Thus when Nadia Boulanger entered the Conservatoire in 1896, she joined a public institution delivering advanced education to selected students, the great majority of whom were of French nationality.[16] She chose to enroll in compositional studies, a demanding pathway and one that was very unusual for a young woman.[17] After two years learning solfège, or sight-singing and ear training, under Marie Antoinette Roy, she became the youngest student in Auguste Chapuis's harmony class, from which she graduated top of the class in 1903. Following the school's regulations, after having been second runner-up (*deuxième accessit*) in harmony in June 1900, she was allowed to register for Paul Vidal's piano accompaniment class for the next academic year. These classes were soon supplemented by Alexandre Guilmant's organ classes (begun in November 1902) and Gabriel Fauré's composition classes (begun in January 1904).[18] Indeed, 1904 proved to be a particularly successful year: Nadia was awarded three first prizes (piano accompaniment, organ, composition), which crowned a glittering career as a student.

The first unusual feature of her curriculum was related to Nadia Boulanger herself. She joined a series of women who were keen to learn a trade that was still considered to be the preserve of men—that of composer.[19] During the Conservatoire's first century, classes in writing music were exclusively for men. But from 1878, both men and women attended the same classes. With the exception of the harmony class, classes in writing music were mixed, and Nadia was never the only woman.[20] Like most of the women apprentice composers who attended classes at the Conservatoire during the nineteenth and early twentieth centuries, she was born in Paris, entered the school at a young age, and studied there for a period of ten years.[21]

A woman in a man's world, Nadia Boulanger's precociousness further set her apart from her classmates, both male and female. She was only eleven when she joined the harmony class, and was the youngest student at all points in her studies. In June 1904 when, at the age of sixteen and a half she received her first composition prize, the average age of the rest of the class was twenty-four and a half.

Her success demonstrates her unusual ambitions: unlike the other girls who were admitted to solfège classes at the Conservatoire at a very young age, Boulanger registered for the harmony class directly, without ever studying an instrument—with the exception of the organ, which was included in the courses in writing music because of the practice of improvisation. In contrast to the usual trajectory, she gave her performing aspirations a lower priority, contriving to study piano only after she had finished her compositional studies. She was admitted to Victor Alphonse Duvernoy's piano class in November 1905, but she withdrew one year later, not without causing a degree of disappointment: "Exceptional student. Charming musician. What a shame she didn't think of studying the piano ten years earlier!"[22]

As Duvernoy's words suggest, Nadia Boulanger was an exceptional student. As a precocious young woman enrolled in studies demanding a certain level of maturity and mainly chosen by men, she became intimately acquainted with the intricacies of the French academic musical world in which she was trying to carve out a place for herself. This training also developed the intellectual toolkit that later underpinned her teaching approach.

## A Rational Apprenticeship in Musical Techniques

Throughout her career, Nadia Boulanger grounded part of her teaching in the education she had received at the Conservatoire, an education largely based on the acquisition of musical techniques.[23] There are various reasons for the importance of technique in musical education in France. The rise of the virtuoso performer, along with the increasing number of improved instruments, helped to dissociate musical intelligence from mechanics—a term that permeates nineteenth-century pedagogical literature. Reflecting the increasing importance given to virtuoso finger performance in learning music, musical literature started to abound in examples of the etude genre, and method books pinpointing precise technical difficulties began to emerge.[24] This move in music pedagogy toward breaking down musical language into different units, each requiring specific training and exercises, affected not only the instrumental disciplines but also theoretical subjects.

Boulanger, like all other students at the school, was first trained in the practice of solfège, a discipline that was "so familiar to the teachers at the Conservatoire, that it [was] pointless to produce a syllabus for them on this subject."[25] A syllabus of 1871, reproduced by Constant Pierre, does, however, detail its components: "The teaching of solfège for instrumentalists should include: 1) the principles of music; 2) separate study of intonation and rhythm; 3) musical dictation; 4) solfège in all keys; 5) transposition."[26] This approach contributed to the training of genuine virtuosos in the art of sight reading and gave rise to the reputation of French solfège, the technical difficulties of which seemed formidably challenging to foreign musicians unfamiliar with the method.

The teaching of composition was not immune to this development. The Conservatoire, and, consequently, a number of the composers and teachers trained by it, divided the teaching of writing music into different subjects and created a strict hierarchy governing progression from one level to the next. The regulations of 1878, which applied when Boulanger first entered the Conservatoire, ensured that students followed a strict pathway, starting with solfège: "No student may follow classes in solfège and harmony at the same time, nor classes in harmony and composition."[27]

This provision integrated the courses in writing music to advanced-level teaching and made harmony an essential prerequisite. Budding composers were required to win a prize in harmony if they wished to be admitted to courses in counterpoint and fugue—disciplines practiced in the "composition" class—so they had to acquire advanced technical skills before they could hope to be admitted to that class. The piano accompaniment class was poised between these two extremes and open only to students "eligible to take the examination in written harmony," a requirement that made this additional class complementary to, or even at a more advanced level than harmony.[28] It included "accompaniment from figured bass, *cantus firmus*, open score, full score and transposition at sight," and enabled accompanists to develop a range of skills.[29] As seasoned keyboard players, they could combine their instrumental talents with a sufficient knowledge of harmony to accompany singers and musicians by creating polyphony that adhered to the rules of harmony from a variety of different media: figured bass, melodic line, piano or orchestral score.

The course description reveals a new subdivision in musical knowledge. The teaching of composition was delivered not only through separate classes with students progressing along a predetermined pathway, but through a number of components that followed the order commonly found in textbooks today. Each individual feature of musical language was subject to specific, in-depth study. For example, counterpoint was studied by means of progressive learning exercises: "Successive study of five kinds of counterpoint of two to eight voices, of double choir, then . . . the study of double counterpoint . . . and the study of imitations and canons."[30] This technical baggage was apparently indispensable for composers who "have always known that a solid technical education, whatever differences there may be in content, is crucial to any high-level creative activity."[31]

## From Specialization to Versatility

The French approach to the learning of composition helped shape the musical profession. The Conservatoire recruited to each discipline teachers with advanced technical skills who were prepared to specialize in a specific domain. No teacher was permitted to cover two areas.[32] This restriction applied to the Conservatoire alone, yet its status as a national institution led it to be regarded as a benchmark. Many music schools strived to model their curricula and teaching approach on those of this public institution in a bid to attract students seeking quality teaching.

Nadia Boulanger's first institutional position after graduation partially followed this logic. The Conservatoire des amateurs, also known as the Conservatoire Femina-Musica, which opened in autumn 1907 in the premises occupied by the publishers, Pierre Lafitte, at 90 Avenue Champs-Elysées, targeted a wealthy aristocratic public. This establishment did not conceal its inspiration—borrowing its terminology and part of its teaching staff from the Conservatoire, it also limited its student intake, dividing students between "advanced" and "preparatory" classes, and planned to hold annual competitions judged by prestigious jurors.

Boulanger was introduced to this establishment by Raoul Pugno, who taught the advanced piano class and was billed as "the most famous virtuoso in the entire world and a direct descendant of the Rubinsteins and the Liszts."[33] Her name appears from autumn 1908, when she was listed as teaching accompaniment;[34] in the following year she extended her course to cover "ensemble music."[35] As her career developed within the institution, she was asked to deliver a class in "preparatory piano."[36]

This gives a foretaste of the type of versatile teacher Nadia Boulanger ultimately became. She took a path diametrically opposed to the specialization inherent in the Conservatoire's recruitment process and constantly took on new teaching duties, enabling her to offer her students an extremely wide range of techniques. After she graduated from the Conservatoire, she supplemented her income from performance by giving "private lessons in piano, organ, harmony, fugue and accompaniment" to which she added sight reading.[37] She also accommodated "pianists who [were] not following her courses, but who want to make ensemble music."[38] Group lessons quickly complemented these private lessons and allowed her to diversify.

Boulanger's inclusion among the inner circle of Conservatoire award winners thus was a determining factor in her career progression. Her extremely comprehensive educational background gave her the intellectual footing for most of the principles she strove to impart throughout her career. It also provided her with a living. An extremely versatile teacher, she always had something to offer a wide range of students with differing needs. The prestige associated with this academic world also led her to be employed by new institutions for which the recruitment of teachers or former students from the Conservatoire was seen as a major asset.

In 1919, in a bid for funding, Auguste Mangeot and Alfred Cortot, the architects of the Ecole Normale de Musique, presented their future shareholders with a list of musicians on whose support they could count; the name of Nadia Boulanger appeared under "Grands Prix de Rome."[39] Her educational background also explained why she was employed by the Conservatoire américain. In December 1921, Francis Casadesus decided to recruit solely "French teachers who belonged or had belonged to the Conservatoire or former award-winning students from this establishment."[40] His justification was:

> Only the French education delivered by the Conservatoire was truly of interest abroad, on account of its status. The Conservatoire, as its name suggests, has the "Mission to Conserve" our musical traditions, to add to them as they develop over time and to pass them on. We must draw on this source to find the men that we want.[41]

Casadesus's proposal, seconded by Isidore Philipp, was adopted unanimously. When the school opened, Paul Vidal (composition, chamber music and orchestra), Isidore Philipp (piano), Lucien Capet (violin), André Hekking (cello), Amédée Hettich (singing), and Charles-Marie Widor (organ) represented the Conservatoire. An ex-student of the institution and a prizewinner in the Prix de Rome, Nadia Boulanger was also entitled to join the teaching staff.

The opportunity to teach in these two schools immediately after the First World War opened up new prospects for Boulanger. First, she gained a stable institutional position that allowed her to actively create a new teaching environment. These institutions maintained an intricate relationship with the Conservatoire, wanting to differentiate themselves from it and at the same time exploit the prestige of French education to boost their own appeal. This meant that they adopted those teaching approaches and innovative methods that the "heiress of the *vieille maison*" found to be fertile territory.

**The Conservatoire Américain: Winning over American Students**
The Conservatoire américain introduced Boulanger to a type of student who, until that time, she had had little occasion to teach. According to its statutes, the Conservatoire américain only admitted students who were "Americans from the United States."[42] Between 1921 and 1939, the summer school was attended by 1,596 students.[43] Designed as a replica of the famous French national conservatory, it offered similar teaching. In

1921, the Conservatoire américain reproduced the division between the disciplines of musical notation in harmony, counterpoint and fugue, and musical composition. It offered classes in piano, violin, cello, organ and harp, reflecting the instruments mainly played by American students; it also accepted singers and students of conducting, a discipline central to its history.

The number of piano classes, as at the Conservatoire, was significantly greater than those for other instruments. In 1926, for example, six assistants prepared students for their weekly private lessons with Isidore Philipp; violinists were taught by two different teachers. The Conservatoire américain, however, had only one teacher for each of the remaining instrumental disciplines. That very year, Francis Rogers put forward an explanation for the overrepresentation of pianists at the school:

> As ever, there is a preponderance of piano students and I don't see how that can be changed in any way. In this country, the piano is a popular instrument and there are more young people who study it than all the other instruments put together.[44]

Although the Conservatoire américain is today inseparable from the name of Nadia Boulanger, most students who registered in the interwar years were taught by others. Throughout this period, Boulanger taught harmony or keyboard harmony to 195 students, 12 percent of the student body.[45] We have several reasons to believe that this is an underestimate, however. In 1926, for example, Conservatoire américain archives record three students registered in Nadia Boulanger's classes, but a photograph of her class shows around thirty.[46] The essentially random information included on the registration forms partially explains this mismatch. Some students may have followed her classes on an informal basis. For instance, Boulanger may have added some students she met during the classes she gave on music history. Some of her students pursued several disciplines; for example, in 1921, Ellsworth MacLeod, a student of harmony, studied piano, organ, and conducting at the same time. Boulanger, who taught numerous pianists, also taught non-keyboard instrumentalists, including harpist Djina Ostrowska and singer Margaret Ackroyd.

The quality of the teaching delivered by Nadia Boulanger and her growing reputation explain the emergence, in 1930, of an unusual phenomenon. Until that date, Boulanger had taught completely new groups each year. At the beginning of this new decade, some students would come back year after year, as can be seen in the mismatch between the two curves in Table 1.

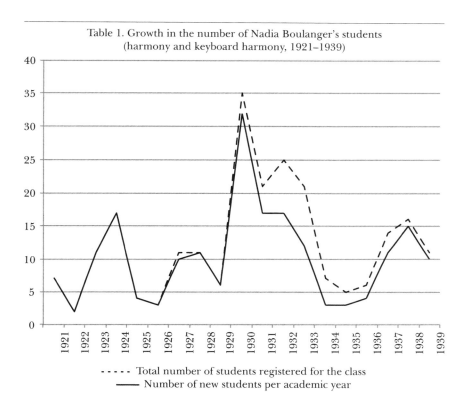

Table 1. Growth in the number of Nadia Boulanger's students
(harmony and keyboard harmony, 1921–1939)

- - - - - Total number of students registered for the class
——— Number of new students per academic year

In 1933, for example, 12 of her 21 students had previously studied
at the Conservatoire américain. Some had registered on more than one
occasion, such as Louise Talma who, between 1930 and 1936, followed
Boulanger's classes continually before becoming a member of the teaching staff at the Conservatoire américain. Others prolonged their summer
visit and, to complete the education they had received at Fontainebleau,
studied at the Ecole Normale de Musique, and added the finishing
touches to their apprenticeship at rue Ballu. The Conservatoire américain was responsible for Boulanger's growing reputation among budding
American composers, and her commitment to this institution led her to
adapt her teaching approach to varied groups of students.

### "A Whole New World"

For Nadia Boulanger, teaching at the Conservatoire américain was akin
to entering a whole new world. Her career up to that point had clearly
sensitized her to some typically American cultural traits. For example,
in 1919 she drew Robert Brussel's attention, when designing the school,

to the need to adapt to American social mores, both conceptually and practically, and advised him to "keep a very close eye on" the choice of teachers, and preferably choose people "of universally recognized moral and artistic superiority."[47] She went on:

> Here, I must insist—moral superiority. Foreign families (and, as more detailed information suggests, American families) are, in fact, very concerned about the environment in which their children are going to live.[48]

Yet in spite of this familiarity, Boulanger discovered musical practices and notions among the students of the Conservatoire américain that were far from familiar (leaving aside the problem that she had not fully mastered English). The comments she left on the reverse of her students' registration forms reveal not only the difficulties they had in understanding musical concepts they considered typically French, but also the strategies she deployed to help them address these gaps in their knowledge.

The strict organization of the specifically French syllabus in music writing proved problematic to the American students.[49] In 1921, Francis Casadesus, the director of the Conservatoire américain, recorded the impressions of Paul Vidal, the composition teacher:

> Students in this class confused harmony and counterpoint; no order in the classification of chords; no purity in writing; they wrote for the piano anything that their fingers dabbling on the keyboard might bring to their imaginations; generally they would aim only at bizarre or baroque effects and so were unable to express themselves. The fugue, in their eyes, was something just about good enough to try the patience of a few curious souls. They felt that they could do without it because, as they said themselves, they wrote "free music"![50]

What most astonished Boulanger were the working methods of her American apprentice composers. While the French teachers insisted on the intellectual rigor derived from the gradual mastery of the rules of harmony, counterpoint, and fugue, the American students adopted an empirical approach. Boulanger, responsible for the harmony class, made this observation:

> Students, who followed this class had not studied solfège, dictation or analysis, or if so, not sufficiently. They started

from the principle that it was no use cluttering up your mind with so many things because all you have to do is sit at the piano and you'll find the right chords.[51]

She mentions three disciplines that she considered vital to the learning of musical writing: solfège, dictation, and analysis. She was not alone in deploring this lack of mastery of what everybody agreed to be the basics. Shocked by the American students' poor command of solfège, the school's administrators made it a compulsory subject in the second year, in 1922.

Yet Nadia Boulanger, like other teachers, believed that the solfège practiced by the Conservatoire did not train the student's ear sufficiently: it was a "very compartmentalized, a very specific and highly technical" teaching approach; it led teachers to "separate out rhythm, singing and reading notes," which "in the classroom, leads to the loss of any sense of unity or purpose."[52] However, expressions like "develop one's ear," "training the ear," and "auditory technique" recur frequently in the comments she wrote about her students at the Conservatoire américain, showing the importance she attached to the need for effective auditory training.[53]

From 1937, the administrators charged one of her students, Louise Talma, with delivering the compulsory aural or "ear training" class, described as follows: "Study of the production of sound, its transmission by air, its perception by the ear, its successive or simultaneous combinations, scales, intervals, chords, consonances, dissonances. Solfeggio. Musical Dictation (rhythmic, melodic, harmonic)."[54] This approach, which combines academic study and harmony, is reminiscent of the challenging exercises set by Boulanger during her cantata sessions. She would play, for example, an eight-part counterpoint and expect her students to sing one of its voices once they had heard it.[55] Christiane Montandon remembers her asking them to identify the intervals played, on the piano, by an instrumentalist interpreting a polyphonic work.[56] This approach bore fruit, as we can see in the gratitude expressed in a letter to Boulanger by the Mexican composer Juan Tercero, on his way home:

> Before I leave Europe, I would just like to write a few lines to you. To tell you these three, to my mind crucial, things that I owe you—the knowledge that we have an ear and how to use it; the knowledge that there is admirable early music; and finally, you taught me a better understanding of music and the high quality of artistic performance that comes to you so naturally.[57]

Although Boulanger herself did not offer aural training to the American students at the institution, her comments suggest that she firmly favored a practice that she found to be insufficiently developed, particularly among the students, "because, in America, people do not work on solfège."[58] When asked by Bruno Monsaingeon about the value of the Conservatoire américain, Boulanger replied: "They have very talented people, but . . . in many cases they have not mastered the basics, as they have not developed their ear."[59]

Solfège and aural training thus became prerequisites for compositional study. In this area, Nadia Boulanger met the disorderly empiricism of the American composers with a rigorous and progressive learning of the techniques of composition, modeled on the teachings of the Conservatoire. The young people started by acquiring the basics of harmony: "Very serious minded, gifted, hardworking, has now finished the perfect chords."[60] Boulanger regularly mentions, in her comments, a harmony treatise identified by Cédric Segond-Genovesi as by Théodore Dubois.[61] "Remarkable musician, cultured, highly intelligent, managed to fully review the harmony treatise in two-and-a-half months, to be followed with the greatest interest."[62] Studies of counterpoint and fugue then followed: "A born composer—exceptionally gifted in every way—no encouragement is too much—should study certain areas further: harmony, counterpoint, fugue."[63]

Whether teaching solfège, harmony, counterpoint, fugue or, more generally, composition, Nadia Boulanger appears to have been particularly keen on "technique." This term appears in 35 of the 119 comments she wrote on this subject about her students at Fontainebleau. As used in these assessments, it serves two functions. On the one hand, the acquisition of solid technique acts to discipline inspiration, as in the case of Andrew Imbrie: "Has the most indisputable gifts: born a musician—must now acquire the technic [*sic*] which will permit his striking gifts to develop—fail in this direction would be an unforgivable mistake, for well prepared, has certainly a great future."[64] Technique is also seen as the sine qua non of musical expression. She refers to Margaret Hopkins Leonard as a "conscientious student" and advises her to use the techniques she teaches her more systematically:

> Technic must always be operative as well as intellectual—it must include the automatic employ of [what] one could try to call "formulas of commonplace language." These words would be easily misunderstood; would it [be more] precise to say: the composer the scholar must have in his head in his fingers, what scales and technical independence are to the performer. The lack of what is the only way of getting freedom is the reason for so many tragic problems.[65]

Like performers, composers should, in Boulanger's eyes, have automatic reflexes to help them develop their musical thought and communicate works to the public.

Contact with students at the Conservatoire américain de Fontainebleau led to the development of a rigorous intellectual process that Nadia Boulanger would impress on all her students. When asked by Bruno Monsaingeon about her students' curriculum, she explained: "I have them work on solfège with Mademoiselle Dieudonné, while I teach harmony and counterpoint." When Monsaingeon said, "So you teach technique, then?" she replied, "The strictest of techniques!"[66] Thus Boulanger developed a multidisciplinary teaching approach that the Conservatoire américain allowed her to develop further.

### A Growing Pedagogical Engagement

Recruited as a teacher of harmony in 1921, Nadia Boulanger became involved, from 1930 onward, in a variety of disciplines, to such an extent that she would teach up to six subjects simultaneously. This ensured her preeminent role within the teaching staff at the Conservatoire américain. Her mastery of different areas, unthinkable at the Paris Conservatoire where all teachers specialized in a single subject, allowed her to cover the entire musical education of those students who chose to follow all her classes.

This growing involvement was due to several factors. First, Boulanger would replace colleagues who delivered existing courses. She took over the history of music class from Jacques Pillois in 1930 and then, two years later, the "general pedagogy" class previously delivered by Paul Fauchet. In 1936, she assisted André Bloch, who taught composition, before taking over the class from him in 1937. She now headed this department and taught counterpoint, fugue, and "the principal forms of musical structure"—"with the possibility of a collaboration with M. Igor Strawinsky."[67]

Second, she took the initiative and developed new courses. This led, in 1932, to a class in "keyboard harmony," described as follows: "In this class will be studied the working out of figured basses and the harmonization of melodies at the piano, transposition, and the reduction at sight of orchestral scores."[68] Five years later, she separated one of the activities covered under her harmony syllabus and offered a class in "musicology" in which students "will be free to choose their own fields of study."[69]

This subject arose out of Boulanger's propensity to cover increasing numbers of subject areas in each of her courses and, consequently, to increase the amount of time devoted to each one. In 1930, for example, her harmony students also received a weekly group class in addition to their private lessons; in 1932, Boulanger taught her students as a whole group three times a week. That year, she supplemented her "lectures on past and present music, with musical illustrations," with time spent on contemporary music: "At the end of each Lecture, Mlle Boulanger will hold a conference for all students interested in discussing new works."[70]

The multiplicity of subjects Boulanger taught meant that she was replicating, at the Conservatoire américain, the teaching practices she used in her Paris apartment, which served as the headquarters of what Rémy Campos called her "home school" for five years.[71] The cantata classes she held there resembled "a lecture and a concert at the same time, or even more, a rehearsal, an analysis class and a master class in performance," types of teaching that she tested out within the institutional framework offered by the Fontainebleau school.[72]

As suggested by the description of her history of music class, the Conservatoire américain's aesthetic orientation further allowed her to introduce her students to her favorite repertories. In 1925, her harmony class acquired a subtitle: "Appreciation and Philosophy of Modern Music." Successive brochures specified its contents. She combined three "points of view: 1. Practical, 2. Historical, 3. Pedagogical."[73] The syllabus of works that she studied and analyzed from a historical perspective included, in addition to early works, several pieces by such composers as Fauré, Debussy, Paul Dukas, and Hindemith.[74]

The philosophy of the Conservatoire américain, as laid down by its founders, gave Boulanger considerable scope to explore little known repertories. As she explained to Robert Brussel in 1919, institutions of this nature should, in her view, represent the different schools of French music, involving "where possible, those individuals most representative of the spirit of French art, the most all-encompassing and eclectic personalities, those of universally recognized moral and artistic superiority."[75] Francis Casadesus, the main architect of the Conservatoire américain, planned to invite "all those who, in France, enjoy a magnificent reputation as composers, conductors, teachers, singers, virtuosos, teachers of Music History, observers of the laws of acoustics."[76] Though this ambition was never realized, his desire to present different French artistic elements to American students was reflected in the curriculum according to the choices made by individual teachers at the school.

Nadia Boulanger's encyclopedic teaching at Fontainebleau was a natural fit for an institution that openly welcomed a range of repertories and teaching methods considered representative of the "French school" of music. It may be that this meeting of minds explains not only her increasing involvement in the Conservatoire américain during the summer period, but also her commitment to the Ecole Normale de Musique during the academic year.

### Ecole Normale de Musique: A "Teaching Laboratory"

Boulanger's teaching career at the Ecole Normale de Musique followed, to some extent, a similar path. She was recruited as a teacher of harmony, but also taught counterpoint and fugue as well as organ; Max d'Ollone held the chair in composition and orchestration.[77] In 1928, the "table of teachers" mentioned her name under the same heading, with two slight differences: Paul Dukas, who succeeded Max d'Ollone, took over the teaching of fugue, leaving her in charge of harmony and counterpoint, two disciplines that she merged into a single class. Nadia Boulanger's name also appeared in the list of teachers (Maurice Emmanuel, Henry Expert, Jeanne Thieffry, Louis Vuillemin, Marc Pincherle, and H. Woollett) jointly responsible for the course in music history.[78] In 1935, she followed Paul Dukas, and added a course in composition to her duties, in which she involved Igor Stravinsky, who was invited to "inspect" her classes.

Her employment at the Ecole Normale de Musique afforded her not only considerable professional stability, but also the ideal environment in which to devise innovative tools to further the teaching approach that governed the development of a school designed to be particularly welcoming to foreign musicians. Auguste Mangeot saw his establishment as "a kind of teaching laboratory where all teachers enjoy the opportunity to show their results to others, demonstrate the effectiveness of their methods, have them discussed, amended and offered to all those prepared to adopt them."[79]

In response to this invitation, Nadia Boulanger developed, within the Ecole Normale de Musique, specific teaching tools that reflected her approach to the history of music. Her students proved responsive to this repertory. Spanish pianist Sofía Novoa, a student at the Ecole Normale in the late 1920s, mentions in her letters the role played by early music in Boulanger's teaching of history; she was delighted, for example, to learn to discern the harmonic evolution of musical language and cites, in evidence, the names of Dufay, Dunstable, Josquin des Prés, Palestrina, and Monteverdi.[80] The second area that Boulanger focused on concerned the development of the sonata as a form, from its origins to Beethoven.[81] The questions in the music history examination taken by Sofía Novoa provide evidence for the importance of the early repertory: they cover Palestrina and his contemporaries and the most important musicians of the second half of the sixteenth century and all of the eighteenth century.[82]

Novoa's enthusiasm for Boulanger's teaching is motivated less by her repertory than by her working methods. She appreciates her teacher's constant comparisons with other artistic fields, in all the classes she taught, giving her students an overview of each period.[83] Boulanger's

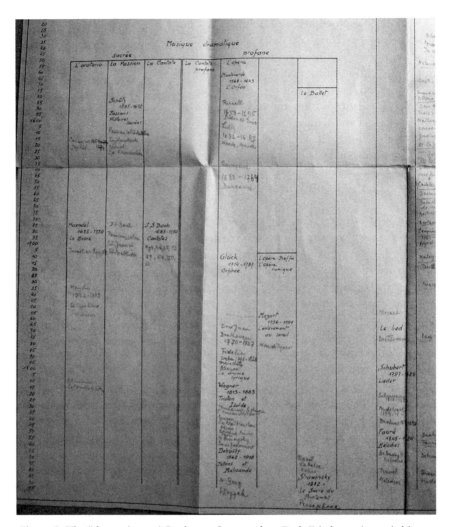

Figure 2. The "dramatic music" columns from student Ruth Friedenson's music history chart. Religious music is on the left, secular music on the right of the double line.

students, taking the music history examination at the same time as the young Spaniard, were not only asked to cite composers but also artists from the centuries studied in the class. Novoa's answers reveal the sheer diversity of the artists covered in class: when invited to name the most important musicians of the eighteenth century and their contemporaries, she listed "Rousseau, Voltaire, Goethe, Schiller, Kant, Reynolds, Goya, Napoleon, the French Revolution, etc., etc."[84]

Novoa also described to her family the teaching tools designed by Nadia Boulanger. Students were encouraged to complete, in the course of the year, a large chart listing all the works mentioned in the class. The chart was divided into three columns—for dramatic music, vocal music, and instrumental music--and showed chronological reference points. The students would then enter the titles of works discussed in class (see Figure 2).[85]

Boulanger also asked the students to memorize musical themes from the works they studied. In the mid-1930s, when she submitted her music history syllabus to Auguste Mangeot and Alfred Cortot, she said that it was essential to "make the students sing." She went on:

> We know nothing about music before Bach, we never play or sing it, people are scarcely aware of the names of any of the musicians, and yet it is extremely beautiful and meaningful and perhaps the most vocal of all (I'm not talking about virtuosity).
>
> There are countless reasons why we should make an effort in this direction as it is the only way to open up unknown horizons to our students which, without us, would remain unknown.[86]

Boulanger was keen for her students to learn not so much "dates, names and facts" as "*style* . . . which only auditory intelligence can discern":

> By making students familiar with works representative of each period, and having them sing them as a choir, we will encourage them to read music and understand in such a way that they are able to match a word or a name immediately to a particular type of music; it will no longer be a meaningless label, but will have an inner resonance for them through the very sound of which [the label] is only ever a symbol.[87]

### Studying "Musical Humanities"

By promoting the acquisition of a broad general culture on the part of her students, Nadia Boulanger breathed life into one of the Ecole Normale's founding principles, whereby "all students should study what are, in a sense, 'musical humanities.'"[88] This goal, reminiscent of the humanist ideal of training the *honnête homme* or cultivated gentleman, was met by an approach to teaching entirely new to France in that it emphasized the acquisition of a solid general culture.[89] This is described in the final version of Auguste Mangeot's report:

There should be no singer, pianist, violinist, etc., who is not above all an excellent musician, who cannot sight-read fluently, who has no knowledge of the general history of music, of how one period leads to another, of the most significant works that they have produced and their musical construction. The History of Music should be studied along with instrumental ensemble and vocal music, performance always following a lecture as closely as possible. Study of the piano should not be limited exclusively to students of the piano classes; all students of the vocal, string, and wind classes should be able to play the piano sufficiently well to be able to accompany a melody, a song or concerto. Similarly, all instrumentalists should participate in the choir class.[90]

This ambitious project was first summed up by a specific terminology. The founders of the Ecole Normale de Musique saw their theoretical classes, generally thought of as supplementary classes, as part of a "general education." A short text in the school's brochure notes that: "General education is compulsory for all students intending to graduate [and] it is not supplementary, but rather the essential basis for any specialized teaching, and a *prerequisite* rather than an add-on."[91]

Furthermore, various documents describing the school devoted a page to what their authors referred to as "the spirit of the education" in which they outlined the teaching approaches taken by the establishment. Mangeot and Cortot strove to introduce "rational pedagogy" based on "the physiological principle that muscle action is controlled by the brain, and muscles can only perform properly if they are properly controlled. Consequently, good finger or larynx technique depends on good 'intellectual technique,' namely the spontaneous perception of music."[92] This technique, albeit innate in "musical geniuses and prodigies," is acquired by musicians through "the study of solfège, harmonic analysis, musical arrangement, etc."[93] All these precepts should contribute to the quality of education offered by the Ecole Normale de Musique, which should be "comprehensive insofar as it leaves nothing out and is born of a perfect match between various fields of general education and different specialized classes."[94]

Boulanger's classes, which fell under the heading of "general" education, fulfilled these recommendations to the letter. By inviting her students to assimilate the masterworks of the history of music through choral practice, she trained "excellent musicians" of the kind described by Mangeot. Despite the meeting of minds between Boulanger and the editor of *Le Monde musical*, she was nonetheless bound by the constraints imposed by the type of student attending the Ecole Normale de Musique. In 1936, for example, Mangeot wrote to Boulanger about her course in the history of music. At the same time, he reminded her of his guiding principles:

> I think I should point out to you again my unalterable wish to forge links between the history class and our other areas of teaching, and ensure, that when authors are introduced by you in the history class, their works are also covered, insofar as is possible, in the instrumental, chamber music, singing, sight-reading, etc. classes.
>
> I would also like the class to be followed by a concert in which these masterworks, of which only fragments have been covered in the history class, are played.
>
> This modus operandi would have, to my mind, the advantage of forging links between the different classes offered by the School and be of the greatest benefit to students.[95]

In the same letter, Mangeot recognized the presence of numerous foreign students in the school and suggested that Boulanger should "concentrate on the French masters as they will probably not have the opportunity to study them when they return to their home country."[96] Cortot, in a letter to Mangeot, went on to add that, as Boulanger's colleague, he found her course "of too high a quality . . . to respond to the modest needs of our young aspiring teachers" and considered asking her "to start her course at around the period of Couperin and Rameau—so that it could immediately be applied to the works in the instrumental keyboard repertory."[97] The two men feared that Nadia Boulanger's music history course might prove inappropriate for the school's students. It might be pitched at too high a level and detract from efforts to introduce a national repertory to foreign students who were considered at that time by the main actors in musical education as future ambassadors of French music.

**Opening Up to an International Audience**

Unlike the Conservatoire, which admitted very few foreign students, and the Conservatoire américain, bound by its statutes only to accept U. S. nationals, the Ecole Normale de Musique imposed no restrictions on the nationalities it accepted.[98] Consequently, the proportion of foreign students attending the young school rose rapidly, particularly in the music writing classes. In 1928, Nadia Boulanger taught 30 foreign students out of a class of 46; 3 of the 5 students in Marcel Dupré's class were foreign; and Paul Dukas's class contained only one French student out of 20 registered.[99] These classes had very different profiles. The foreign musicians, who hailed from 17 different countries, mainly came from North America. Fifteen of them, 30 percent of the total cohort, were from Canada or the United States. French-speaking students came second: 10 Swiss and 2 Belgians took these courses. Then, in descending order, Eastern Europe 6, Central and Latin America 5, Asia Minor, Mediterranean Europe, and Russia 3 each, and finally England and Austria, one each. Of all these trainee composers, only three registered in both Boulanger's and Dukas's classes: Romeo Alessandresco (Romanian); Gabriel Cusson (Canadian); and Felix Labunski (Polish). The remainder chose between the two classes. Almost all the Americans in this particular year group took Nadia Boulanger's classes: she taught 30 foreign students, including 9 Americans, 6 Swiss, 2 Canadians, 2 Romanians, 2 Turks, and one student from each of these countries: England, Armenia, Austria, Belgium, Spain, Mexico, Poland, Russia, and Uruguay. Dukas's class was a little more cosmopolitan with 4 students from Switzerland and 2 each from Poland, Romania, Russia, and Mexico. Their classmates also came from Belgium (1), Bulgaria (1), Canada (1), Chile (1), Spain (1), Greece (1), and the United States (1). These numbers reflect the attractiveness of the Ecole Normale de Musique's classes to foreign students and the appeal of Boulanger's classes to American and French-speaking apprentice composers, particularly the Swiss.

The numbers also highlight the cosmopolitan nature of the "Boulangerie" which met every Wednesday at rue Ballu for "cantata classes," which were thus named because of the preponderance of Bach's work.[100] This "music" course, in the wider sense of the word, offered students at the Ecole Normale de Musique a natural complement to the institutional curriculum.[101] In November 1930, Jean Lévy brought Gabriel Cusson "news from the Boulangerie": "Things continue as normal, just like last year—counterpoint at the school and cantatas at rue Ballu."[102] There they met musicians of all kinds from all disciplines. Around the same time, Nadia Boulanger sent a greeting card to Cusson signed not just by her but also sending greetings from her students, most probably from the Ecole Normale de Musique, "whom you might or might not know."[103] The card's listing of Boulanger's students indicates in most cases their country of origin, and provides ample evidence of their diversity (see Figure 3).[104]

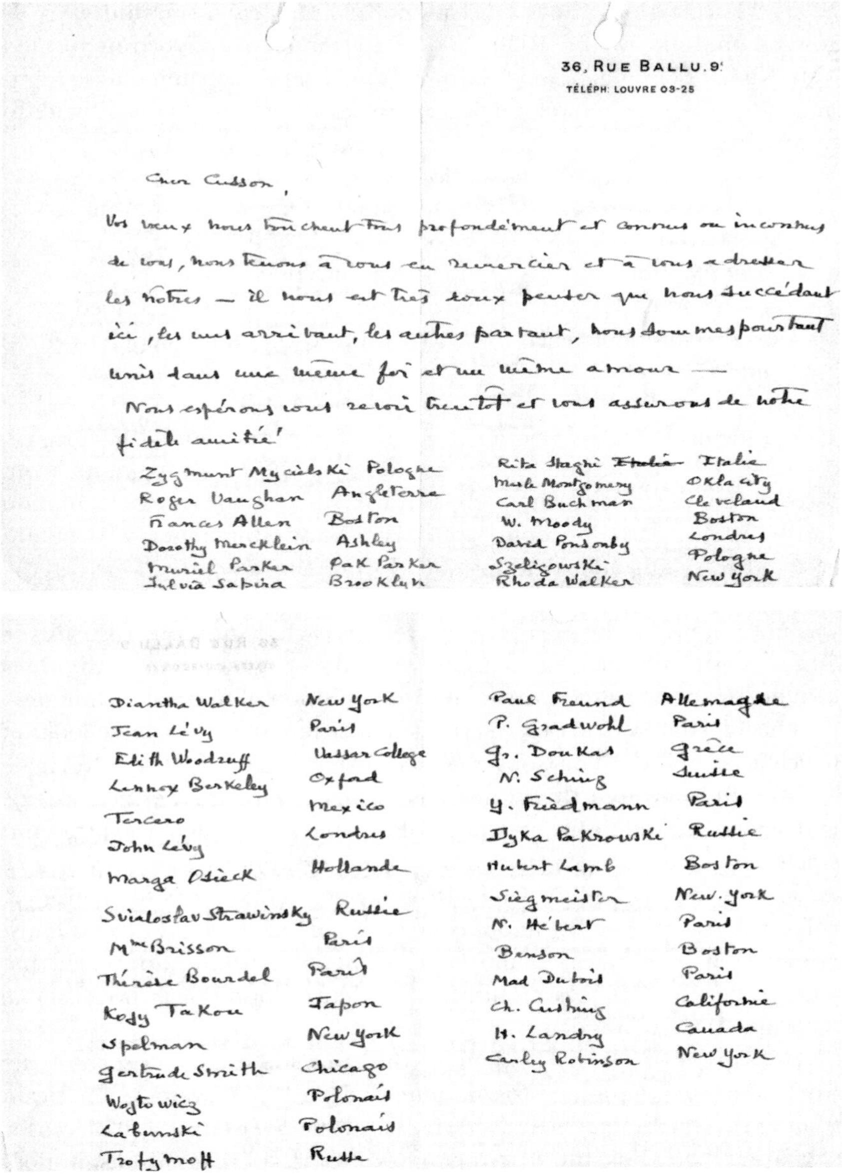

36, RUE BALLU. 9e

TÉLÉPH: LOUVRE 03-25

Cher Cusson,

Vos voeux nous touchent tous profondément et connus ou inconnus de vous, nous tenons à vous en remercier et à vous adresser les nôtres — il nous est très doux penser que nous succédant ici, les uns arrivant, les autres partant, nous sommes pourtant unis dans une même foi et un même amour —

Nous espérons vous revoir bientôt et vous assurons de notre fidèle amitié!

Zygmunt Mycielski Pologne
Roger Vaughan Angleterre
Frances Allen Boston
Dorothy Merckleim Ashley
Muriel Parker Pak Parker
Julvia Sapira Brooklyn
Rita Staghi Italie
Merle Montgomery Okla city
Carl Buchman Cleveland
W. Moody Boston
David Ponsonby Londres
Szeligowski Pologne
Rhoda Walker New York

Diantha Walker New York
Jean Lévy Paris
Edith Woodruff Vassar College
Lennox Berkeley Oxford
Tercero Mexico
John Lévy Londres
Marga Osieck Hollande
Svialoslav Strawinsky Russie
Mme Brisson Paris
Thérèse Bourdel Paris
Kody Takou Japon
Spelman New York
Gertrude Smith Chicago
Wojtowicz Polonais
Labunski Polonais
Trofymoff Russe
Paul Freund Allemagne
P. Gradwohl Paris
Gr. Doukas Grèce
N. Sching Suisse
Y. Friedmann Paris
Dyka Pakrowski Russie
Hubert Lamb Boston
Siegmeister New. York
N. Hébert Paris
Benson Boston
Mad Dubois Paris
Ch. Cushing Californie
H. Landry Canada
Carley Robinson New York

Figure 3. Nadia Boulanger to Gabriel Cusson, November 1930. The handwritten text at the top reads: "Dear Cusson, Your good wishes touched us all deeply, and whether acquainted with you or not, we all want to thank you for them and send you ours in return. It is very sweet to think that we follow each other here, some arriving, others leaving, yet all united in a single faith and a single love. We hope to see you again soon and assure you of our faithful friendship."

**The "Boulangerie": A Cosmopolitan Musical Community**

Toward the end of the 1930s, a veritable musical microcosm formed with Nadia Boulanger as its center. Composers, instrumentalists, and singers followed an encyclopedic approach to teaching that is difficult to summarize:

> What did she actually teach? Solfège, harmony, counter-point and fugue, the history of music, musical analysis, piano accompaniment. . . All these disciplines piled up one on top of the other, yet this approach could not merely be described as the sum of its parts as it went further than music alone to effectively embrace life.[105]

This difficulty is in part because her teaching transcended geographical, institutional, and intellectual boundaries. She taught students from throughout the world who were attracted by her growing reputation and by her original conception of music. Nadia Boulanger, who taught at the Ecole Normale de Musique during the academic year, at the Conservatoire américain over the summer, and at rue Ballu at all times, was not bound by the curricula offered by each institution. Instead she forged a path of her own that encouraged her students to shape their own artistic personalities, through the acquisition of musical techniques.

The blossoming of this microcosm was indebted to the schools in which it was rooted. The Conservatoire américain and the Ecole Normale de Musique, through their innovative teaching approaches and artistic endeavors, offered fertile ground for Boulanger to develop the ideas and teaching tools that made her name. These institutions, which were now on a stable footing and proving extremely popular, offered her considerable professional stability and a constantly replenished pool of students. However, it was the originality of Boulanger's teaching approach that allowed her to create a community of students around her who all spoke the same musical language.

Her advice is clearly evident in the common characteristics of the works that the young artists who attended the Conservatoire américain frequently sent to her.[106] Alongside pieces of chamber music and pieces for solo instrumentalists, there are many vocal works of religious inspiration. In using choral writing these composers demonstrated their mastery of the harmonic and contrapuntal techniques that Nadia Boulanger had taught them. Preserved among the works she was sent is an unpublished play by her former student Marcelle de Manziarly, who had studied privately with Boulanger in the 1920s and by the 1930s was a member of her inner

```
TOUS.- Allo , allo,.

UN RUSSE.- Alo ( accent russe ) niet pojalowska, tridsat ohest
    dvatzat I... Boyé moI !...

UN ALLEMAND.- Allo, allo fraülein , Ich habe doch gefagt zbei
    hundred und vier und viertzig .

L'AUTRE ALLEMAND.- Es ist strecklich , mit diesem téléphone can
man vahusinig wersen .

UN AMERICAIN.- Allo, allo what do you say ? President Roosevelt
    not at home ? when can I ring again ? no ... it is a pleasure .
    ( il repose l'appareil ) Damn it all .

L'AUTRE.- That is what I call luck, we have waited three hours ,
    and at last when we got the right number it was too late !...

LA TELEPHONISTE.- Stand , three , three four two , ( avec une
    voix monotone ) Yes . ( accent anglais très fort ) , ne coupez
    pas , parlez monsieur , vous avez votre correspondant . Rhine-
    lander one , 0, six four - New-York , allo, allo . ( Sonnerie )
    - en français -: 36-48 ? , on vous cause de New-York : ne quit-
    tez pas . ( Sonneries ) Allo , l'Elysée ? , mici, la Société des
    Nations - on demande le Président de la part de son Altesse le
    Prince de Madagascar , ne quittez pas , ne quittez pas - allo ,
    allo ... allo , raccrochez je vous prie , le correspondant n'
    est plus au bout du fil . Je rappellerai .

    Pendant ce temps , les groupes continuent à parler , on entend
    des " Allo " , des sonneries .

    La porte s'ouvre , Annette , Marcelle , Armand ,-en costumes de
    voyages , des valises à la main , entrent .

ARMAND, s'approchant d'un polonais .- Pardon, Monsieur , pourriez-
    vous me dire à qui l'on peut s'adresser pour avoir une communica-
    tion téléphonique ?

LE POLONAIS - réponse en polonais , voulant dire " Excusez-moi Mon-
    sieur , je ne parle pas le français " .
```

Figure 4. A phone call to the League of Nations, scene from a
1932 playscript by Marcelle de Manziarly.

circle. Titled "Les préparatifs du 19 décembre: Opérette" (Preparations
for 19 December: Operetta), the work humorously reflects the geographical and artistic world of the "Boulangerie." In this "spoken and sung
entertainment in 3 acts and 4 scenes," Marcelle de Manziarly, Annette
Dieudonné, and Armand Marquiset, the main actors, play themselves.
The script depicts the "Boulangerie" getting ready for the birthday of
Nadia's mother, Raïssa Boulanger, on 19 December, and pokes fun at the
cosmopolitan nature of this community. Marcelle and Annette, according
to the document, are taking a few days of well-deserved rest in Geneva.
Armand interrupts their peace and quiet and asks them to return to
Paris to "discuss, compose, rehearse, produce, that kind of thing."[107] The
telephone becomes both an essential tool and a source of misunderstanding. Armand must "alert Smith, Copland, Cobleigh, Hesseberg, Tercero,

Posada, Labunski, etc.... in time for them to catch their respective boats and trains."[108] The three young people intend to make their presentations the following day at the League of Nations.

Figure 4 shows a scene from the playscript in which there is widespread misunderstanding by the phone operator at the League of Nations due to the use of several languages in the call. In the margin, Boulanger's pencil notes indicate which student speaks each role.

ALL: Hello, hello.

A RUSSIAN: (Russian accent) Alo, nyet poyalowska, tridsat chest dvatzat! . . . Boyé moî! . . .

A GERMAN: Allo, allo Fräulein, ich habe doch gefragt bei hundert und vier und vierzig.

THE OTHER GERMAN: Es ist shrecklich, mit diesem Telefon kann man wahnsinnig werden.

AN AMERICAN: Hello, hello what do you say? President Roosevelt not at home? When can I ring again? No . . . It is a pleasure (puts down phone). Damn it all.

THE OTHER: That is what I call luck, we have waited three hours, and at last when we got the right number it was too late!

OPERATOR: (In a monotone) Stand, three, three four two . . . Yes. (Strong English accent) Don't hang up, talk sir, you have your party on the line. Rhinelander one, zero, six four —New York, hello, hello. (Ringing) En français—36-48? On vous cause de New York—ne quittez pas (Ringing) Allo, l'Elysée? Ici, la Société des Nations—On demande le Président de la part de son Altesse le Prince de Madagascar, ne quittez pas, ne quittez pas—allo, allo . . . allo, raccrochez je vous prie, le correspondant n'est plus au bout du fil. Je rappellerai.

*During this time, the groups continue to talk, one hears many "hellos," and much ringing. The door opens, Annette, Marcelle, Armand enter—in travel outfits, suitcases in hand.*

ARMAND: (Approaching a Pole) Pardon, Monsieur, pourriez-vous me dire à qui l'on peut s'adresser pour avoir une communication téléphonique?

Mycielski [~~THE POLE~~]: (Responding in Polish, trying to say) Excusez-moi Monsieur, je ne parle pas le français.

A score for an a cappella choir with three voices, signed by Marcelle de Manziarly, accompanies the scene. Another extract, which is set in the apartment of one of the students, introduces a misunderstanding: the young people try to talk—in French, in Russian, in German, in Polish, and then in English with the "son of the Shah of Persia," to whom Marcelle says that she "once opened the door, at rue Ballu." This character, who can only grunt, turns out to be the Prince of Madagasco [*sic*] and his departure puts an end to this musical project of Nadia Boulanger's students. A "cantata" by Jean Françaix saves the show from the disaster that its characters are struggling to prevent and brings the entertainment to a close.[109]

The play is a witty take on the Nadia Boulanger microcosm. Both cosmopolitan in nature and faithful to the teachings of "Mademoiselle," the "Boulangerie" delighted in expressing itself using contrapuntal techniques and the language of choral works, the common language of these students from all over the world.

# NOTES

1. Jeanice Brooks, *The Musical Work of Nadia Boulanger: Performing Past and Future Between the Wars* (Cambridge: Cambridge University Press, 2013), 7.

2. See, for example, Caroline Potter, *Nadia and Lili Boulanger* (Aldershot: Ashgate, 2006); Doda Conrad, *Grandeur et mystère d'un mythe: Souvenirs de quarante quatre ans d'amitié avec Nadia Boulanger* (Paris: Buchet-Chastel, 1995); Bruno Monsaingeon, *Mademoiselle: Entretiens avec Nadia Boulanger* (Luynes: Van De Velde, 1981); Alexandra Laederich, ed., *Nadia et Lili Boulanger: Témoignages et études* (Lyon: Symétrie, 2007).

3. This article draws on research completed for Marie Duchêne-Thégarid, "'Les plus utiles propagateurs de la culture française?': Les élèves musiciens étrangers à Paris pendant l'entre-deux-guerres" (PhD diss., Université François-Rabelais de Tours, 2015).

4. Auguste Mangeot, "Rapport sur la fondation à Paris d'une École Normale de Musique 1° Pour les Étrangers; 2° Pour les Français ne remplissant pas les conditions voulues pour entrer au Conservatoire," 1 October 1918, Archives nationales, Paris (hereafter F-Pan), Collection Beaux-Arts, F²¹ 4625, 1.

5. Ibid., 2.

6. Minutes of the meeting of 20 May 1921, "Registre des procès-verbaux des réunions du conseil d'administration des écoles d'art américaines (1921–1933)," Archives of the Conservatoire américain de Fontainebleau (hereafter ACA), held by Catherine Delloye, Fontainebleau, 21–22; Camille Saint-Saëns to Francis Casadesus, 6 December 1920, in the guestbook for the foundation of the institution, donation J.-R. Casadesus (1971), Fontainebleau Municipal Library, CAM 0. For a general history of the institution, see Kendra Preston Leonard, *The Conservatoire Américain: A History* (Lanham, MD: Scarecrow Press, 2007).

7. With a view to garnering financial support from future shareholders, Auguste Mangeot attached to his standard letter a list of musicians who had already been recruited to his project; Nadia Boulanger's name appears as a teacher. Standard letter, n.d. (late 1918) Archives of the Ecole Normale de Musique, black folder.

8. See Walter Damrosch, "The Musical Aftermath of the Great War," *The Etude*, March 1920, http://www.wgpark.com/page.asp-pid=19.html.

9. Nadia Boulanger to Robert Brussel, n.d., Bibliothèque nationale de France (F-Pn), Rés. Vm. dos. 121 (1–4).

10. See François Anselmini, "Vers une biographie d'Alfred Cortot (1877–1962): Un pianiste dans la Grande Guerre (1914–1918)" (M.A. thesis, Université de Caen-Basse Normandie, 2010), 111–13; and Alexandra Laederich, "Nadia Boulanger et le Comité franco-américain du Conservatoire (1915–1919)," in *La Grande guerre des musiciens*, ed. Stéphane Audoin-Rouzeau, Esteban Buch, Myriam Chimènes, and Georgie Durosoir (Lyon: Symétrie, 2009), 161–73.

11. Monsaingeon, *Mademoiselle*, 25.

12. This article adopts the approach of recent research on spatial logics, following the example of the Artl@s project, which "aims to highlight not only the link between a work of art and its space (both social space as well as material place), but also its underlying political, social, aesthetic or economic issues." Béatrice Joyeux-Prunel, "ARTL@S: A Spatial and Transnational Art History. Origins and Position of a Research Program," *Artl@s Bulletin* 1 (2012): 10, https://docs.lib.purdue.edu/artlas/vol1/iss1/1.

13. The expression "vieille maison" (old house) comes from an undated letter in F-Pn, cited (without shelfmark) in Potter, *Nadia and Lili Boulanger,* 129–30. Boulanger was applying for a position to teach harmony at the Paris Conservatoire in 1919, and in her cover letter wrote: "Furthermore, all those I have loved lived at the Conservatoire to a certain extent and the ties which bind me to the old house are as ancient as they are deep.

My father and my grandfather were teachers there, my grandmother started her glorious career there, my mother was a student there and my poor little sister studied there."

14. The establishment was known by various names at different times over the nineteenth century. I shall use the term "Conservatoire" to refer to this institution.

15. "Demande de limitation du nombre des étrangers dans les classes," Ambroise Thomas, 14 May 1886, in Constant Pierre, *Le Conservatoire national de musique et de déclamation: Documents historiques et administratifs* (Paris: Imprimerie nationale, 1900), 273.

16. Teachers' reports about their students' progress allow a list of Nadia Boulanger's classmates to be constructed; very few were foreign, yet, as these lists do not explicitly mark them as such, it is difficult to identify them precisely. See "Registres de rapports des professeurs sur leurs élèves pour les examens, 1842–1925," F-Pan, AJ³⁷ 260–303.

17. I will use the anachronistic expression "compositional studies" to cover the broad range of classes that involved writing music and contributed to the teaching of composition, whose course titles varied over time. I will also use the titles that appeared most frequently: harmony, piano accompaniment, organ, counterpoint and fugue or composition.

18. This is the date of her official admission as a student, though she was probably taught by Gabriel Fauré as early as 1901, as an auditor in his class. See Jean-Michel Nectoux, "Nadia Boulanger: La rencontre avec Gabriel Fauré," in Laederich, ed., *Nadia et Lili Boulanger*, 35.

19. See various works by Florence Launay, particularly *Les Compositrices en France au XIXᵉ siècle* (Paris: Fayard, 2006); "Les musiciennes: De la pionnière adulée à la concurrente redoutée—Bref historique d'une longue professionnalisation," *Travail, genre et sociétés* 19/1 (2008): 41–63; "L'éducation musicale des femmes au XIXᵉ siècle en France: Entre art d'agrément, accès officiel à un enseignement supérieur et professionnalisation," in *Genre et éducation: Former, se former et être formée au féminin*, ed. Paul Pasteur, Marie-Françoise Lemonnier-Delpy, Martine Gest, and Bernard Bodinier (Mont-Saint-Aignan: Presses Universitaires de Rouen et du Havre, 2009), 203–10.

20. The regulations nonetheless specified that "mothers of women students are permitted to attend lessons." Internal regulations (1878), article 33, cited in Pierre, *Le Conservatoire national*, 262.

21. This information is taken from the Conservatoire de Paris student database, produced as part of the research project *Histoire de l'enseignement public de la musique en France au XIXᵉ siècle (1795–1914)*, funded by the Agence Nationale de la Recherche and supervised by Cécile Reynaud. This tool currently identifies 13,986 students registered at the institution between 1822 and 1906 inclusive. Of these, 59 women were admitted to organ or composition classes at the end of their studies, 37 of them were born in Paris, half were admitted to the Conservatory between ages 9 and 13, and the average duration of their studies was 10.5 years.

22. See Victor Alphonse Duvernoy, "Registres de rapports des professeurs sur leurs élèves pour les examens, 1842–1925," (piano), June 1906, F-Pan, AJ³⁷ 300.

23. Potter, *Nadia and Lili Boulanger*, 137–40.

24. Blanche Selva, for example, dedicated an entire method book to practicing octaves. See *Le Travail technique du piano: Choix d'exercices et d'études avec la manière de les travailler et les doigtés par Blanche Selva, L'Étude des octaves d'après Th. Kullak* (Paris: Editions B. Roudanez, 1915).

25. Syllabus (1871), cited in Pierre, *Le Conservatoire national*, 281.

26. Ibid., 280.

27. Regulations (1878), article 45, cited in Pierre, *Le Conservatoire national*, 263.

28. Regulations (1878), article 5, cited in ibid., 261.

29. Ibid. Various reports by members of the examination board provide evidence of a fifth examination; it bears a variety of titles and was probably designed to assess the candidates' instrumental technique.

30. Coralie Fayolle, "Les traités de contrepoint en France aux xıxᵉ et xxᵉ siècles," *Le Conservatoire de Paris, 1795–1995, Deux cents ans de pédagogie*, ed. Anne Bongrain and Alain Poirier (Paris: Buchet-Chastel, 1999), 271.

31. Anthony Bergerault, "L'enseignement du contrepoint et de la fugue au Conservatoire de Paris (1858–1905)," *Transposition* 1, 2011, https://journals.openedition.org/transposition/418, para. 65.

32. When, in 1910, Nadia Boulanger first applied for a post at the Conservatoire, she was specifically after the position of professor of piano accompaniment.

33. Anon., "Un Conservatoire des amateurs," *Je Sais tout*, 15 October 1907, 338.

34. Anon., "On forme de véritables artistes au Conservatoire Femina-Musica," *Comoedia* (31 October 1908): 3.

35. Hélène Avryl, "La réouverture des cours au 'Conservatoire Femina–Musica' (Saison 1909–1910)," *Femina* (15 September 1909): 208.

36. Anon., "Concours du Conservatoire 'Femina-Musica,'" *Comoedia* (1 July 1910): 2.

37. Prospectus announcing the resumption of the classes of Mademoiselle Nadia Boulanger, reproduced in Jérôme Spycket, *Nadia Boulanger* (Paris: Lattès; Lausanne: Payot, 1987), 26.

38. Ibid.

39. Promotional mailer, n.d. (late 1918), Archives of the Ecole Normale de Musique, black folder.

40. Proposal by Francis Casadesus, "Minutes of the meeting of 20 December 1921," in Register of the minutes of the meetings of the boards of directors of Ecoles d'Art Américaines, 1921–1933, 52, ACA.

41. Ibid., 53. In this context, the use of the collective noun "men" suggests a military lexicon: for Francis Casadesus, it is a matter of finding individuals capable of accomplishing an important mission. Nevertheless, this means excluding the women who had actually taught at the Conservatoire américain the summer before. According to the 1921 brochure, three other women were on the staff in addition to Nadia Boulanger: Mrs. M. L. Henri Casadesus (Chromatic Harp and Lute-Harp), Ritter Ciampi (Singing), Regina Patorni (Harpsichord).

42. "Règlement intérieur des Écoles d'Art Américaines de Fontainebleau," Art. 1 (1926), in the dossier "Conservatoire de musique 1927," ACA, Hôtel Barassy, Fontainebleau, 1.

43. This comes from a database listing information taken from individual student registration forms. Its quality depends on the state of preservation of the archives. For 1929, for example, the forms for students whose names begin with the letters D to L have been lost; or an individual may appear under various names, given that the administrative services may spell the name differently or a woman might start to use her husband's surname.

44. Francis Rogers to Maurice Fragnaud, 18 March 1926, ACA, file 1926.

45. I have excluded the composition classes that she started to give at this institution in 1939.

46. Photograph reproduced in Spycket, *Nadia Boulanger*, 61.

47. Nadia Boulanger to Robert Brussel, n.d., F-Pn, Res. Vm dos. 121 (1–4).

48. Ibid.

49. In his article on musical teaching abroad, Théodore Dubois notes, for example, that in Germany "there is a deliberate mingling of counterpoint and harmony" and that classes in harmony are compulsory for everyone, as is the case at the Geneva Conservatory. Théodore Dubois et al., "L'Enseignement musical à l'étranger," in *Encyclopédie de la musique et dictionnaire du Conservatoire*, ed. Albert Lavignac, vol. 2 (Paris: Delagrave, 1925), 6.

50. Report by Francis Casadesus, "Minutes of the meeting of 20 December 1921," 32, ACA.

51. Ibid.

52. Odette Gartenlaub, "Le solfège dans la formation musicale," in Bongrain and Poirier, *Le Conservatoire de Paris, 1795–1995: Deux cents ans de pédagogie*, 310.

53. Comments by Nadia Boulanger written on students' individual forms: "Develop one's ear" comment on Mildred Bickett's form, 1931; "training the ear" comment on Helen Brown's form, 1938; "auditory technique" comment on Cleveland Jauch's form, 1937. Student forms, Archives of the Conservatoire américain, Hôtel Barassy, Fontainebleau. Boulanger wrote commentary on student reports in both French and English, largely writing in English from 1937 onward. Here reports written in French are translated without comment, while reports originally in English quote Boulanger's words exactly, including any linguistic errors or anomalies.

54. "Fontainebleau School of Music," promotional brochure, 1937, ACA.

55. See Igor Markevitch, *Point d'orgue: Entretiens avec Claude Rostand* (Paris: Julliard), 58–59.

56. Interview by the author with Christiane Montandon, 19 April 2010.

57. Juan Tercero to Nadia Boulanger, 28 December 1935, F-Pn. N.L.a. 69 (326–27).

58. Interview with Ruth Friedenson by Alexandra Laederich, Cédric Segond-Genovesi, and Marie Duchêne-Thégarid, Paris, 6 February 2010.

59. Monsaingeon, *Mademoiselle*, 26.

60. Comment by Nadia Boulanger written on John Benson's student form, 1931, ACA. Note that her comments are often written in telegraphese.

61. Cédric Segond-Genovesi, "Fin de règne? L'enseignement de Nadia Boulanger après la Seconde Guerre mondiale," in *De la Libération au Domaine musical: Dix ans de musique en France (1944–1954)*, ed. Laurent Feneyrou and Alain Poirier (Paris: Vrin, 2018), 199–214, esp. 204.

62. Comment by Boulanger written on Louise Talma's student form, 1931, ACA.

63. Comment by Boulanger written on Livingston Gearhart's student form, 1938, ACA.

64. Comment by Boulanger, in English, written on Andrew Imbrie's student form, 1937 ACA.

65. Comment by Boulanger, in English, written on Margaret Hopkins Leonard's student form, 1937, ACA. What Boulanger meant here, clearly, was that the mastery of technique was the only means of achieving freedom. It is interesting to see the kind of syntax that her American students sometimes had to fight their way through to figure out what she was driving at.

66. Monsaingeon, *Mademoiselle*, 55.

67. "Fontainebleau School of Music," promotional brochure, 1937, ACA.

68. "Fontainebleau School of Music," promotional brochure, 1932, 24, ACA.

69. "Fontainebleau School of Music," promotional brochure, 1937.

70. "Fontainebleau School of Music," promotional brochure, 1932, 25.

71. Rémy Campos, "L'analyse musicale en France au xxᵉ siècle: Discours, techniques et usages," in *L'Analyse musicale: Une pratique et son histoire*, ed. Rémy Campos and Nicolas Donin (Geneva : Droz, 2009), 384.

72. Segond-Genovesi, "Fin de règne?," 200; see also Campos, "L'analyse musicale en France," 385.

73. "Fontainebleau School of Music," promotional brochure, 1936, 12, ACA.

74. "The second category will comprise the study and analysis of works by G. de Machaut and his time, G. du Fay, the masters of the Renaissance, Monteverdi, Schutz, Lulli, Rameau, and some other classic, romantic and modern works, including parts of: *St John's Passion*, J. S. Bach, *Cosi fan tutte*, Mozart, *Quartets*, Beethoven, *Freyschütz*, Weber,

*Songs*, Schubert, *Mazurkas*, Chopin, *Faust*, Schumann, *Damnation of Faust*, Berlioz, *Boris Godounov*, Moussorgsky, *Requiem*, Fauré, *Pelléas et Mélisande*, Cl. Debussy, *L'Apprenti Sorcier*, Paul Dukas, *Psaume*, Schmitt, *Gaspard de la Nuit*, Ravel, *Padmavâti*, Roussel, *Marienleben*, Hindemith, *Symphony of psalms*, Stravinsky." Ibid., 200.

75. Ibid.

76. Report by Francis Casadesus, "Minutes of the meeting of 29 November 1920." 17, ACA.

77. Ecole Normale de Musique de Paris, undated promotional brochure (before 1928), F-Pan, F²¹ 4625, 4.

78. École Normale de Musique de Paris, promotional brochure, 1928, Archives of the Ecole normale de musique, Paris.

79. Auguste Mangeot to Alfred Cortot, 2 September 1923, Archives of Ecole Normale de Musique, black folder.

80. See Sofía Novoa's letter to her family, 23 December 1929, cited in Carmen Losada, "Mujeres pianistas en Vigo: Del salón aristocrático a la Edad de Plata (1857–1936), Sofía Novoa" (PhD diss., Universidad de Santiago, Chile, 2015), 403.

81. Ibid. 403–4.

82. See Sofía Novoa's letter to her family, 23 December 1929, cited in Losada, "Mujeres pianistas en Vigo," 403.

83. Ibid., 403.

84. Ibid., 403–4.

85. See the example donated by Ruth Friedenson to the Centre International Nadia et Lili Boulanger (gift of 6 February 2010).

86. Nadia Boulanger to Auguste Mangeot, ca. 1935, F-Pn, Res. Vm dos. 127 (9).

87. Nadia Boulanger, talk presented to a group from the Université des Annales, 1933, cited in Zygmunt Mycielski, "La visite de l'Ecole Normale de Musique de Paris," *Conferencia: Jounal de l'Université des Annales* 24 (1933): 642.

88. Anon., "Minutes of a meeting held with the Marquis de Castellane, 24 May [1919], to set up the Ecole Normale de Musique de Paris," 3, Ecole Normale de Musique Archives, Varia.

89. This approach is, however, similar to the one adopted in Germany. In many respects, the Ecole Normale de Musique fulfills some of Théodore Dubois's ambitions for the "ideal Conservatory" described at the end of his "L'Enseignement musical à l'étranger" in the *Encyclopédie de la musique et dictionnaire du Conservatoire*, 3454–71.

90. Auguste Mangeot, "Rapport sur la fondation à Paris d'une École Normale de Musique," 1 October 1918, F-Pan, F²¹ 4625, 2–3.

91. Ecole Normale de Musique, promotional brochure for 1928–1929, 11, Ecole Normale de Musique Archives.

92. Ibid., 9.

93. Ibid.

94. Ibid., 18.

95. Auguste Mangeot to Nadia Boulanger, 3 October 1936, F-Pn, Res. Vm. dos. 127.

96. Ibid.

97. Alfred Cortot to Auguste Mangeot, 16 October 1937, F-Pn, Res. Vm. dos. 127.

98. From 1886 onward, the Conservatoire set a limit of two foreign students per class. In response to competition from the Ecole Normale de Musique de Paris and the Conservatoire américain, this number was raised to three in 1932.

99. A single register for the Ecole Normale de Musique de Paris for the 1928–29 academic year provides a reliable list of registered students and distinguishes French from foreign nationals.

100. Segond-Genovesi, "Fin de règne?" 200–201.

101. See ibid.; Campos, "L'analyse musicale en France," 385; and the report by Don Campbell cited by Barrett Ashley Johnson, "A Comparative Study Between the Pedagogical Methodologies of Arnold Schoenberg and Nadia Boulanger Regarding Training the Composer" (PhD diss., Louisiana State University, 2007), 204.

102. Jean Lévy to Gabriel Cusson, November 1930, Bibliothèque et Archive nationales du Québec, Collection Gabriel Cusson, annex, 006, Correspondence.

103. Nadia Boulanger to Gabriel Cusson, November 1930, Bibliothèque et Archive nationales du Québec, Collection Gabriel Cusson, annex, 006, Correspondence.

104. Ibid., Bibliothèque et Archive nationales du Québec, Collection Gabriel Cusson, annex, 006, Correspondence.

105. Alexandra Laederich, "Introduction," in Laederich, *Nadia et Lili Boulanger: Témoignages et études*, 8.

106. These works were previously stored in the music library of the Conservatoire américain.

107. Marcelle de Manziarly, "Les préparatifs du 19 décembre," 1932, 3. Conservatoire américain Music Library, beige box 12 A.

108. Ibid.

109. Ibid.

# Nadia Boulanger's 1935 *Carte du Tendre*

INTRODUCED BY MARIE DUCHÊNE-THÉGARID
INTRODUCTION TRANSLATED BY ANNA LEHMANN

In 1935, the death of Paul Dukas left vacant the composition chair at the École Normale de Musique. Nadia Boulanger, who had taught harmony and counterpoint at the school since its founding, succeeded him. For the first time in her career, she was officially named to the prestigious position of professor of composition. In contrast to her predecessor, who was a renowned composer, Boulanger could not point to the qualities of her own compositions in order to attract new students; so she placed her teaching under the aegis of Stravinsky, who was called on to "inspect" her composition class. This unusual situation seems to have worried Auguste Mangeot, the director of the Ecole Normale de Musique, who wrote to her: "I will advertise as much as possible with the very limited resources at my disposal, but I fear that, at the beginning, student enrollment will be quite low."[1] This concern was friendly but far from disinterested; the financial resources of the school depended in part on student tuition. In Nadia Boulanger's case, the school agreed to take only a percentage of student fees once the annual total of fees received exceeded a baseline of 15,000 francs.

Determined to ensure the success that the composition course of his colleague and friend deserved, Auguste Mangeot, who was also the publisher of *Le Monde musical*, began putting together the next issue of the journal in early September. In it, he wished to announce her nomination and "note the names of the most prominent students [she] taught, like Markevitch, Français [*sic*] and other American students, Polish students, etc. . . whose names you will be kind enough to send."[2] Nadia Boulanger immediately responded to the request, and wrote these few names in the margin of Mangeot's letter: "Lennox Berkeley, Marcelle de Manziarly, Aaron Copland, (Roy Harris), R. R. Bennett, Piston, B. Wojtovicz, Felix Labunski, T. Szeligowski, Z. Mycielski."

This initial selection did not seem to satisfy Boulanger, however, and she subsequently put together a long list of former students. Her litany of 229 names appears to have necessitated quite a bit more work: her disciples are grouped by nationality listed alphabetically, and the process was repeated within each group, sorted by last name. Arrows pointed to changes to be made in a later version. In choosing to group these musicians by geographic area, the teacher in effect made a map of an existing microcosm: the "Boulangerie." Despite appearances, the inventory she made was not rigorous, and it reveals a geography that is more emotional than objective.[3]

The first characteristic of this topography of her affections, her *carte du Tendre*, is that it breaks down barriers between musical institutions.[4] While Auguste Mangeot's request might have led her to give preference to composers who had been trained at the Ecole Normale, those cited in Boulanger's list did not all attend the school. The Americans Howard Abell, David Dushkin, Edgar Groth, Virginia Mackie, Arthur Oglesbee, Louise Talma, and Edith Woodruff, among others, were chosen from among those who studied with her mainly at the Conservatoire américain de Fontainebleau. Following the summer sessions, some of these students likely continued their studies at the Ecole Normale or at rue Ballu; but the absence of readily available records makes it difficult to verify this hypothesis. A comparison of this list with the roster of students enrolled at the Conservatoire américain reveals a second peculiarity. Although it is extraordinarily long (143 names), the list of American names is incomplete: Nadia Boulanger left out some of the musicians who took her summer classes. The same is true of her students at the Ecole Normale, who did not all seem to have caught her attention. No objective criteria explain the choices she made; perhaps she only kept the composers she felt were the best known or the most promising.

Indeed, the group was a mix of newcomers and veteran composers. In 1935, Aaron Copland was already famous; Elliott Carter, in contrast, was at the start of his musical career. The list is also striking for what it leaves out. Dinu Lipatti, for example, until then a student of Paul Dukas, was not yet a student of Nadia Boulanger. Written at a precise moment, this inventory does not look anything like a class photo for the year 1935: musicians who had been trained for many years and current new students appear in it pell-mell.

The Boulangerie, at that time, thus seemed like a community founded on the professor's selection of artists of all age, who shared a certain talent. If it did away with borders between musical institutions, this microcosm remained subject to geopolitical borders: the teacher was careful to categorize her students according to nationality. While it answered the question asked by Auguste Mangeot, this choice appears to have been dictated by practical considerations (making legible a list that was unwieldy) as well as rhetorical ones: the diversity of the twenty-two nationalities it represented underlined Boulanger's appeal and at the same time validated the quality of her teaching.

The Boulangerie's cosmopolitanism was not unique at the time. Paris was the *ville-lumière*, and it attracted artists from all over the world; in the field of music education, the teacher also benefitted from the warm welcome the Ecole Normale de Musique gave to foreign students. Yet the way in which the various nationalities were distributed within Nadia Boulanger's "world" is nevertheless surprising, beginning with the complete dominance of North American students, who comprised nearly 64 percent of those on the list.[5] The preponderance of American students was a reflection of the teacher's fame across the Atlantic, which led her to welcome at Boulevard Malesherbes almost every composer in training who came from America.[6]

Conversely, Boulanger's list featured relatively few francophone musicians—except for French people—and no Belgians. The small number of Russian artists also seems surprising, given how many Russians lived in Paris at that time and Nadia Boulanger's own family origins. Finally, she attracted a large number of Finnish and Norwegian composers, nationalities that were rarely represented at Parisian music schools. The map of the world of the Boulangerie thus only partly overlapped with the physical world: it revealed a particular balance of international musical relations that was largely dependent on Nadia Boulanger's own personality and her decision to include in it—or not—the names of her students.

In the end, it may be difficult to determine Nadia Boulanger's intent when she conceived this list. Its length certainly underlined the undeniable experience of a teacher who was already well-known on the international scene, but it made it more difficult to identify the most famous names, and precluded publishing it in its entirety, something Auguste Mangeot implied, when he wrote: "I received the long list of your former students, and I will make a selection that I will submit to you for your review."[7] Publicity or *carte du Tendre*? Today, this document is valuable evidence of the character of the Boulangerie in 1935.

Draft list of students by nationality, prepared for Nadia Boulanger in 1935.

# NOTES

1. Auguste Mangeot to Nadia Boulanger, 18 September 1935, Biblothèque nationale de France (F-Pn), Rés. Vm. dos. 127 (7).

2. Auguste Mangeot to Nadia Boulanger, 4 September 1935, Rés. Vm. dos. 127 (5), BnF, Paris.

3. The list is held today with a letter from Auguste Mangeot requesting information about her students, in Paris, F-Pn, Rés. Vm. dos. 127.

4. *Carte du Tendre* was the name given to the map of an imaginary country called *Tendre* (Tenderness) created by a group of women intellectuals in the seventeenth century. The engraving by François Chauvau was published in 1654 in Madeleine de Scudéry's novel *Clélie*. It maps the path to love through a geography of emotions, navigating routes through mutual affection, esteem, and faithfulness and warning of pitfalls such as the "lake of indifference."

5. It differs from the overall distribution of foreign music students in Paris between the wars. See on this topic Marie Duchêne-Thégarid, "Les plus utiles propagateurs de la culture française? Les élèves musiciens étrangers à Paris pendant l'entre-deux-guerres" (PhD diss, Université François-Rabelais de Tours, 2015).

6. See my chapter in this book.

7. Auguste Mangeot to Nadia Boulanger, 18 September 1935. Auguste Mangeot in fact reduced this list to 47 names, originating from eleven countries. He also added information, mentioning for example the titles and current posts of certain American pupils. See Mangeot, "Mlle Nadia Boulanger et M. Igor Strawinsky vont enseigner la Composition à l'Ecole Normale de Musique, " *Le Monde musical* 46, nos. 8-9 (30 septembre 1935): 252.

# 36 rue Ballu: A Multifaceted Place

CÉDRIC SEGOND-GENOVESI
TRANSLATED BY ANNA LEHMANN

> When people talk about "rue Ballu," they mean the center
> of a web woven by Nadia Boulanger over seventy-five years,
> in which she held generations of musicians spell-bound by
> her charisma.
>
> —Doda Conrad

In October 1904, the Boulanger family moved from 30 rue La Bruyère
to the fourth floor of 36 rue Ballu, a short distance away (today the
address is 3 Place Lili-Boulanger, at the corner of rue de Vintimille, in
the Saint-Georges neighborhood of the 9th arrondissement, in Paris).[1]
Nadia, who was the oldest of two daughters, had just won five First
Prizes at the Conservatoire, and she began giving private lessons in the
apartment where she would live until her death in October 1979.[2] For
nearly seventy-five years, she taught four to nine students a day, every
day except Sunday. In addition to these private lessons, there were the
famous group classes, *cours de cantate*, rehearsals of her vocal and instrumental ensembles, parties with friends and famous people, and many
other musical events.[3] In short, Nadia Boulanger made 36 rue Ballu into
a seat of intense social and artistic activity, and the center of gravity of a
well-known international career as a musician and pedagogue.[4]

Nadia Boulanger used her apartment as a public space, one could
even say an exhibition space, for students, colleagues and fellow musicians, journalists, and potential benefactors and patrons. Distinct from a
private museum—or a simple living space—it was a calling card used in
her professional career to publicize her name as well as her teaching and
her aesthetics. This powerful "means of communication" resulted from
the coexistence of several archetypal places within a single space.[5] Indeed,
beyond its function as a private space, the apartment at 36 rue Ballu was
equal parts classroom, society salon, and place of worship. Before examining these three features, a quick tour is in order.

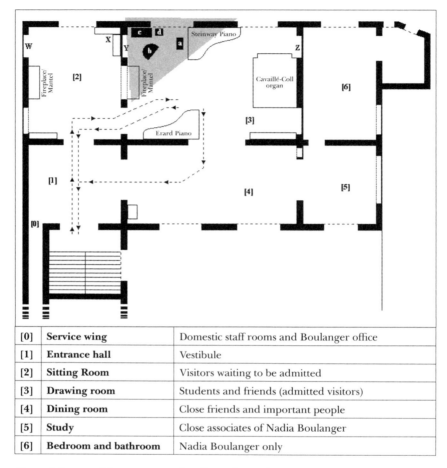

| [0] | Service wing | Domestic staff rooms and Boulanger office |
|-----|--------------|-------------------------------------------|
| [1] | **Entrance hall** | Vestibule |
| [2] | **Sitting Room** | Visitors waiting to be admitted |
| [3] | **Drawing room** | Students and friends (admitted visitors) |
| [4] | **Dining room** | Close friends and important people |
| [5] | **Study** | Close associates of Nadia Boulanger |
| [6] | **Bedroom and bathroom** | Nadia Boulanger only |

Figure 1. Layout of the apartment of Nadia Boulanger based on plans by Pierre Abondance. The dotted arrows indicate the path followed by students through the apartment, from the door to the drawing room, with two possible return paths. According to one-time student Narcis Bonet, students again crossed the sitting room at the end of their lesson; the singer Doda Conrad, on the other hand, stated that "a student who had just had their lesson was spirited away through another exit," which meant that the student had to cross the dining room. Not reproduced here is the service wing, which consisted of a small room, a bathroom, an office, used mostly to store the thousands of pages of music that made up Nadia Boulanger's working library, and a kitchen, at the end of which a service staircase led to a small room under the attic, on the sixth floor.

At rue Ballu, Nadia Boulanger lived in a comfortable Haussmannian apartment typical of its kind, with rooms organized according to their function, from the most public to the totally private.[6] Was Boulanger particularly attached to a certain object and how was it acquired or received? What about the identities of the individuals in the portraits? The visitor or student who saw the place for the first time inevitably missed all or part of such details that would allow for a subtle understanding of the quintessentially French décor (composed of furniture, curios, paintings and portraits, books and music in the bookcases) as both personal museum and autobiographical statement. The issue of *readability* was connected to *visibility*: some tiny objects high up, or very low, were easily overlooked—more so because the apartment was frequently plunged in semi-darkness. The seating arrangement of students in the drawing room, where Nadia Boulanger gave her lessons, was also crucial.[7] During the *cours de cantate*, folding chairs were arranged in a semicircle from the end of the Steinway baby grand piano to the door of the drawing room. Nadia Boulanger's *cours de cantate* have been described many times:

> These Wednesday classes always followed the same ritual: the secretary brought out the sheet music of the pieces to be studied, placing one on Nadia's piano, another on the students' piano, and one each on folding chairs arranged around the four vocal parts: soprano, alto, tenor, bass.[8]

> The students shared the same passion and were under the same powerful influence that reduced them all to total submission; they filled the drawing room at rue Ballu, where chairs were stacked between the organ and two grand pianos cluttered with photographs, icons, azalea and cyclamen, various objects that attested to the touching devotion that all the faithful of "la Boulangerie" had for Nadia.[9]

Nadia Boulanger sat next to her desk, either at the piano or in her armchair (see Figure 1, c, a, and b). Since a telephone was also within reach (d), the teacher almost never left that corner of the room:

> When sitting at the piano, Nadia Boulanger had within reach a small automatic telephone exchange, which she used dexterously with her left hand. . . . She continued to play the piano with her right hand and did not interrupt her lesson or her practice. . . . At lunchtime, a table on wheels appeared on her right, and her left hand took over playing the piano.[10]

In this manner the students' attention was focused onto a zone shown in Figure 1 as a gray triangle. To analyze the layout and the decor of 36

Figure 2. Bust
of Lili Boulanger.

rue Ballu as a communication tool one must take into account these different elements while prioritizing the ones that were visible to and readable by each student.

According to several witnesses, the white marble bust of Lili Boulanger displayed on the drawing room's fireplace mantel (Figure 2) was especially eye-catching.[11] Imposing, immediately readable, and situated within the students' field of vision, this key element played different symbolic roles depending on the archetypal space it evoked (classroom/society salon/place of worship)—roles I will now identify and whose functioning calls for analysis.

### The "Conservatoire" at Rue Ballu

The layout of the sitting room and drawing room met the need for a teaching space within which students found elements that were familiar and expected—but also "personalized" by and for Nadia Boulanger (Figure 3). As a waiting room and a place for students to prepare before lessons, the sitting room emphasized the teacher's musical authority, her credentials, and her prestige, but also her pedagogical and aesthetic imperatives. Notably, the space revealed the genealogy of an artistic and teaching lineage that went back to the eighteenth century and whose last direct descendant was Nadia Boulanger. Upon entering the room, informed visitors discovered on their left a portrait of the imposing figure of Ernest Boulanger ("eb" in Figure 2) and then a large portrait of his mother, the singer Marie-Julie Halligner ("mjh" in Figure 2) above two photographs of Lili.[12] The collection was completed with a portrait of Élisabeth Vigée-Lebrun ("vl") on which is clearly inscribed: "First woman admitted to the Académie Royale de peinture"—the parallel with Lili needs no explanation.[13] The entire Boulanger musical dynasty thus unfolds before the student's eye in its symbolic light: in bookcase "X" in Figure 1, autograph musical manuscripts by Lili and by Ernest Boulanger, and Marie-Julie Halligner's annotated scores were written proof of this lineage.

Likewise one found in the sitting room the figures of an exclusively French professorial heritage, of which Nadia Boulanger then seemed to be the indisputable repository. In bookcase "W" in Figure 1, one could see Théodore Dubois alongside Vincent d'Indy, Paul Vidal, Camille Saint-Saëns, and Georges Caussade; the bust of Gabriel Fauré ("gf" in Figure 2); and, of course, the various portraits of Ernest Boulanger that also appear in this gallery.[14] The dedications, which were often to Lili, once again attested to a close and direct affiliation with the masters; these tributes thus confirmed

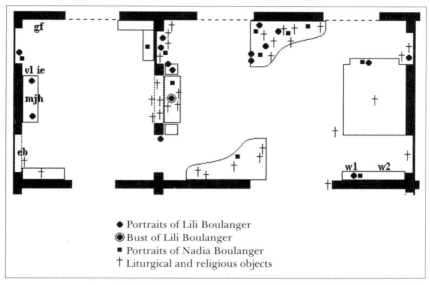

● Portraits of Lili Boulanger
◉ Bust of Lili Boulanger
■ Portraits of Nadia Boulanger
† Liturgical and religious objects

Figure 3. Detail of the sitting and drawing rooms of Nadia Boulanger.

Nadia Boulanger's position as a direct heir and uncontested ambassador of French culture and, especially, of the teaching of the Conservatoire de Paris, two essential components of the musician's career.[15] On this topic, it should be noted that Nadia Boulanger taught at the Conservatoire as an unofficial assistant to Henri Dallier in 1909 (women's harmony class) and that she twice applied unsuccessfully, in 1910 as professor of accompaniment and again in 1919 as harmony professor, before being given much later the accompaniment class (1945–57). During World War I, she devoted her time and energy to editing a *Gazette des classes du Conservatoire* (1915–18). She also taught at numerous institutions and "satellite" schools of the Conservatoire, ranging from the Conservatoire Femina-Musica to the Conservatoire américain de Fontainebleau.[16] Nadia Boulanger's attachment to the codes and methods of the Conservatoire de Paris, and the value she placed on this attachment, thus seem inseparable from her career path.

The drawing room, unlike the sitting room, did not include any representatives of music pedagogy except Nadia herself. As was traditional, the classroom was reserved for busts and statues of the "great men" in the history of music; in this case, Beethoven, Chopin, Debussy, Bartók, and Stravinsky, cornerstones in the corpus of canonical works studied at rue Ballu.[17] Beyond that detail, there are many other markers of music teaching in the room.

Figure 4. Top, a solfège class at the Conservatoire de Paris in the 1920s; bottom, *cours de cantate* class at rue Ballu in 1960.

The photo on top in Figure 4 was taken in a classroom at the Conservatoire de Paris (rue de Madrid). The piano—indispensable for teaching—is the only piece of furniture. At the edge of the image one can make out the door to the vestibule where students await their lessons. The most significant element is without doubt a bust overlooking the scene, a kind of role model for students—representing a composer and thus having aesthetic as well as musical value.[18] The choice was frequently a French master, a (former) professor at the school (and usually a former student), or an artist belonging to the pantheon of musical history.[19]

The photo at bottom in Figure 4 was taken in 1960 during a cantata class, and shows that all these types of elements were integrated and personalized in the drawing room at rue Ballu. Nadia Boulanger's teaching, organized around the piano, took place under the stony gaze of an aesthetic authority, a French master, who was also a former student, and clearly the most brilliant and validating student, namely, Lili Boulanger.

Lili's presence in the field of vision of students was not limited to the bust on the mantel.[20] Indeed, Figure 5 shows that students with their back to the organ could see no fewer than six portraits of the musician—and those facing the Steinway piano could see three.[21] Similarly, when a student was called to the piano by Nadia Boulanger, two more photographs of Lili awaited them to the right of the music rest. The pedagogical imperative of "la Boulangerie" was clear, well defined, and could be summarized in a simple formula: Beethoven, Chopin, Debussy, Bartók, Stravinsky—and Lili Boulanger.

The apartment at 36 rue Ballu thus incorporated all the distinguishing features of a music classroom in order to stage and inscribe them at the heart of an artistic and professional heritage of which Lili was all at once the first success, the first exhibit, and the first aesthetic symbol.

A quick glance at a few of the photographs in this essay is nevertheless enough to ascertain that Nadia Boulanger's apartment had more in common with the salons of Parisian high society than with the empty (or at least quite basic) classrooms at the Conservatoire. Although one saw all the characteristic elements of a site of musical study at rue Ballu, here they took place under the light of a crystal chandelier surrounded by a multitude of paintings, antique clocks, a golden candelabra, fruit bowls and candy boxes, exotic curios, draperies and oriental rugs.[22]

## "La Boulangerie" and Society Life

The career of Elisabeth Vigée-Lebrun, whose portrait graced the front room, could only have been possible in aristocratic circles and with the sustained support of the Polignac family.[23] As Jeanice Brooks has shown, the same was true for Nadia Boulanger, and evidence of the Polignac

Figure 5. Images of Lili Boulanger in the field of vision of students:
Top, from the end of the Steinway piano; bottom, from the drawing room door.

Figure 5 (continued). Image of Lili Boulanger in the field of vision
of students: on the piano.

patronage can be found in the drawing room at rue Ballu.[24] This evidence was obviously intended for a very few people who were able to identify and decipher such clues, such as the two large paintings signed "Winaretta" ("w 1" and "w 2" in Figure 2).[25] Indeed, the Princesse de Polignac (Winaretta Singer) was an amateur painter who signed her work with her maiden name—being privy to this information at the time implied that one was familiar with the social milieu.

Nadia Boulanger thus exhibited the paintings of her most important patron at rue Ballu—but in a way that was largely invisible to her students. There were other signs of the musician's high-society and aristocratic friendships; for example, several photographs of her with the Monaco family were prominently displayed on the Steinway piano, next to a signed portrait of Queen Marie-José of Italy. Herself the daughter of a Russian princess (she liked to remind one of that fact), Nadia moved in high society circles, and she let it be known.[26]

These objects were, however, late additions to the drawing room and are therefore a result rather than a cause of the musician's social activity. The question therefore is to understand how (and if possible when) the

Figure 6. Nadia Boulanger in her drawing room, around 1925.

apartment at rue Ballu began to incorporate the visual codes and social rituals of the upper-class salons of Paris.

Anne Martin-Fugier notes that a salon is "first and foremost a woman . . . and preferably a witty woman."[27] The second *sine qua non* condition is that a salon must be frequented by regulars who know each other and meet there regularly (which distinguishes it from a society evening). At rue Ballu, the cantata group lessons on Wednesdays met both criteria, and Nadia Boulanger strengthened those with a distinctive social practice that further asserted her identity: receiving day. She explained:

> Maman had "her days" when she entertained her personal friends on Wednesdays after 5 pm. . . . As soon as I finished the Conservatoire in 1904, I began teaching a class and decided: it will be on Wednesdays. It was then every Wednesday, as it still is after all these years, on Wednesdays at 3 pm. After lessons, Maman entertained my students . . . she treated them to tea, good pastries. . . . And so, I too kept it on Wednesdays.[28]

Indeed, the weekly group lessons were held on Wednesdays from 3 pm to 5 pm starting in 1921: before then, they were held on Fridays from 1 pm to 3 pm.[29] Far from insignificant, this detail is, on the contrary, fundamental from a sociocultural standpoint. While there can be differences on some points between the "handbooks on good manners" and other "codes of elegance and *bon ton*," they all agree on the proper hour for receiving. On one's "day," it was indeed not only unthinkable but "supremely bourgeois" for a high-society lady to entertain anyone before 4 pm or 5 pm.[30]

Thus it was, not starting in 1904, but in  the 1920s, that Nadia Boulanger altered her schedule to conform to aristocratic sociocultural customs, which were probably borrowed from her mother or learned from Marguerite de Saint-Marceaux (whose salon Nadia and Lili had frequented).[31] Were her fruitless attempts at securing a position at the Conservatoire (in 1910 and 1919) factors in the musician's decision, immediately after the war, to change the focus of her work and direct it toward a more high-society clientele and possible patrons? In addition to giving her financial security, this would have allowed her, as a woman, to contemplate having a career as a pedagogue and orchestra conductor, something that at the time remained difficult to imagine within the framework of public and official institutions. This theory is supported by the photographic archive of the Centre international Nadia et Lili Boulanger (CNLB) which shows that the decor at rue Ballu was "set" from around 1925–30 onward. With the exception of a few portraits that seem to have been moved to suit the mood and, of course, a few objects acquired over the years, the place remained unchanged for more than half a century. However, two photographs from the 1910s show the drawing room in quite a different state: fewer paintings and curios, books and sheet music stacked on chairs, and, in front of the organ, a large table and a desk, all of which attest to the functionality required by both Boulanger sisters' musical activity.[32] In the 1910s, the drawing room was still a private space primarily intended for the day-to-day work of the two composers.

The reconfiguring of the "conservatoire" at rue Ballu around the standards and décors of Parisian high society built upon Nadia Boulanger's pre–World War I experience as a salon performer and her work with affluent American and French patrons in charity initiatives during the war. As well, it appears to coincide in particular with the beginning of the friendship between Nadia Boulanger and the Princesse de Polignac in the mid-1920s.[33] Though the "receiving day" custom can be dated precisely, the transformation of the apartment into a "salon" can only be approximated, which leaves unanswered the question of which came first—the evolution of the decor or the drawing of a high-society audience to rue Ballu.

As a "salon object," the legitimacy of the bust of Lili Boulanger is twofold. First of all, it is an *art piece* among the essential paintings and other elements

Figure 7a. Chapel of the Virgin at Sainte-Trinité in Paris.

that make up a high-society salon.[34] In that regard, it is not dissimilar to the bust of Isabelle d'Este that previously sat on the fireplace mantel and was then relegated to the sitting room ("ie" in Figure 2) at the beginning of the 1920s. This further validation of Lili Boulanger in a space dedicated to teaching thus coincides with the higher social status of the space.[35]

To the society audience who frequented "La Boulangerie," the legitimacy of Lili's bust was also tied to the idea of heritage. As noted by Anne Martin-Fugier, "A salon ensures continuity. Even historical continuity, if the hostess has famous ancestors."[36] In other words, an aristocratic salon is part private museum whose seemingly eclectic "collections" are embodied by the master of the house (or the lady of the house), who acts as a guide and the keystone of the salon/museum.[37] It is likely that many of the aristocrats at rue Ballu were less eager to learn how to avoid parallel fifths than to meet a living monument to the history of music, sister of Lili, friend of Stravinsky, and student of Gabriel Fauré. Like the signed photographs of d'Indy, Saint-Saëns, and Debussy, the bust of Lili was an object that represented professorial authority and aesthetic credo, and it was also a relic of an aristocratic devotion to musical history. This idea is explored in the next section.

Figure 7b. The drawing room at rue Ballu.

## Place of Worship: The "Boulangiste Religion" and Its Chapel

On 15 March 1918, young Lili Boulanger passed away before the eyes of her older sister, ending a brilliant and promising career as a composer. The effects of this tragedy on the professional and private life of Nadia

Boulanger are well known, and we also know the musician's untiring devotion to preserving her sister's memory and to spreading and promoting her work.[38] Jeanice Brooks and Jean Boivin have elsewhere shown the importance of Nadia Boulanger's relationship to the divine and religious feeling in the construction of her socio-professional image.[39]

A particularly effective mise-en-scène within the walls of rue Ballu led to the inevitable concurrence of devotion to Lili's memory, the mystical aura attached to her, and Nadia's Catholic fervor.[40] The drawing room literally overflowed with objects directly or indirectly belonging to Catholic worship ("+" in Figure 2) and resembled a chapel. Indeed, a magnificent chasuble hung to the right of the organ, the archetypal liturgical instrument. Visitors were thus warned that a "high priestess" indeed officiated between these walls. These religious objects combined with the large collection of musical iconography (most importantly the portraits of Lili) to form the essential basis of a distinctive religion.

The space represented in Figure 7a was well known to Nadia Boulanger: it is the church of Sainte-Trinité, the church of her own parish, the church that accompanied her through life from her first communion in May 1899 to her funeral in 1979.[41] More precisely, the photograph shows the Chapel of the Virgin behind the main altar, in the continuation of the nave of Sainte-Trinité. The focal point was a large statue of the Virgin with Child at the center of the altar, crowned by stained-glass windows forming a large arch that symbolized the canopy of heaven. Two candelabra decorated the sides (electric sconces have replaced them today). At the foot of the statue, on the left, a red light signaled the Holy Sacrament. A large cross and a pulpit from which the gospel was read and commented upon circumscribe the space.

The photo in Figure 7b shows the background into which the bust of Lili was incorporated in Nadia Boulanger's apartment, and displays an obvious analogy between Sainte Trinité's Chapel of the Virgin and the drawing room at rue Ballu.[42] The customary "candelabra" on either side adorns the arch provided by the architecture of the space.[43] By making a direct association between iconographies, one can substitute the statue of the Virgin with the statue of Lili at the center of the fireplace mantel "altar." A large icon of the Virgin and Child surrounded by two archangels is prominently displayed above the bust.[44] The small triptych sitting beneath the bust shows, from left to right, the Virgin, Christ, and Saint John the Baptist.[45]

As can be inferred from an examination of these elements, the religious service officiated at rue Ballu involved the worship of a Trinity. To the left and to the right of Lili one sees the other two fundamental figures of the "Boulangiste religion": Igor Stravinsky and Nadia herself—indeed, this triptych occurs elsewhere in the room.[46]

The symbolism was not limited to the mantel-altar. The drawing room scrupulously followed the layout of a church: with their backs to the organ, turned toward the altar, the congregation (the students) listened reverently to the Word of God uttered by the church celebrant (Nadia) from the ambo or lectern—that is, the Steinway piano, which was later decorated with a large silver crucifix.[47] As for the sitting room, it performed the liturgical function of a narthex, an interstitial space between the church and the outside world used, as it were, to prepare the faithful for the ceremony.[48] One can additionally observe other more specific indications that this was a place of worship, which were probably meant to be understood only by Nadia Boulanger and her immediate circle:

- **Saints** celebrated in the iconography: Where bookcase "Y" and the desk of Nadia Boulanger met (Figure 1), there was, for example, a portrait of Miki Piré, one of Lili's closest friends, lit by a red icon lamp.[49]
- A **treasure.** We know that the Boulanger family's musical manuscripts were stored in bookcase "X" in the sitting room (Figure 1). One work, however, did not follow that rule: the manuscript of *Faust et Hélène*, the cantata for which Lili Boulanger won the Premier Grand Prix de Rome, was kept apart, in bookcase "Z" in the drawing room (Figure 1).

Because of the plurality of its symbolic elements, the apartment of Nadia Boulanger becomes the multifaceted *apartments* of Nadia Boulanger, whose uses and meanings are layered and melded: the professor's chair is also the preacher's chair, the classroom piano merges with the piano of the bourgeois salon, and admiration for art becomes a cult of artistic personality and history inspired by Catholicism. The compartmentalization into conservatory/salon/church is obviously only a formal constraint: the point is to fuse these three porous spaces by playing on the homonymy and ambiguity of their respective markers. Inherited from the salons of the nineteenth century, this practice shows certain continuities that go well beyond the traditional boundaries contained in the chapters of our music history books.[50]

It is inevitable that the coexistence at rue Ballu of three archetypal spaces was not possible without a diminishing of each of these spaces. The classroom is not very practical: students crowded together on folding chairs in a room cluttered with objects, and the bookcases held no practice parts but instead art books for bibliophiles. The society salon was not officially recognized: Nadia Boulanger's address was never listed in the *Livre d'or des salons* (Paris: E. Bender), the official directory of high-society addresses.[51] And the church occupied a diffuse symbolic space. It should be pointed out that the multivalent nature of the spaces noted at rue Ballu is only one example of a more general trend that characterized the long nineteenth century— indeed, Sainte-Trinité would have been considered a "church-salon."[52] In the same fashion, the key spaces of Nadia Boulanger's teaching career connect the appearance of aristocratic luxury with the austerity of the classroom. The Ecole Normale de Musique was formerly the *hôtel particulier* of the Marquise de Maleissye and the Conservatoire américain was located in the Louis XV wing of the Château de Fontainebleau. Along these same lines, Jean-Pierre Babelon and André Chastel have shown the prominent role played by religion in our understanding of heritage, which is central to Nadia Boulanger and her legacy.[53] Is the museum itself not a space devoted to the cult of art or history?

The rooms at rue Ballu thus did not impose any single reading on visitors: from the simple student to the rich aristocrat, each person could find meaning according to the reason for the visit. The bust of Lili Boulanger, which legitimately belonged in the classroom and the salon, and which was a legitimate element in the church as a "substitute," served as the cornerstone that focused any reading of the space. Whether students, patrons, or pilgrims, Boulanger's visitors (who were often a little of all three), would always encounter the figure of Lili as an artistic, pedagogical, patrimonial, and spiritual reference.

Several points in the systematic and formalist approach in this analysis must now be considered:

- The layout and furnishing of her rooms by Nadia Boulanger was also shaped to a significant extent by questions of privacy, feeling, and personal taste. In addition to the autograph score for Lili Boulanger's *Faust et Hélène*, the manuscripts by Raoul Pugno that were kept by Boulanger represent another departure from the principle of an artistic *curriculum vitae* greeting visitors. Too personal to be exhibited in the sitting room, these scores were instead kept close to Nadia, in bookcase "Y" in the drawing room (Figure 1), alongside one of the rare portraits of Pugno.[54]
- Was Nadia Boulanger fully aware of the organization of the apartment into the three interdependent and overlapping archetypal spaces: conservatory/salon/place of worship? These archetypes seem too obvious for her to have missed

them. For the "official" photographs that she sometimes posed for in the apartment, she understood quite well how to differentiate and stage the drawing room into different symbolic functions: *Lili's sister,* to honor her sister's memory, posed in the formal attire of a vestal, in front of the mantel-altar, whereas the *musician and pedagogue* appeared in a less solemn gray suit, in front of shelves of music or in front of her organ, carefully pushing out of the frame any liturgical and high-society elements.[55] One more significant clue: Nadia Boulanger never went anywhere without her "décor"; for example, she reconstructed the drawing room at rue Ballu (or at least its main features) for each new season of the Conservatoire américain de Fontainebleau.[56]

- Contrary to other artists' residences, the apartment at 36 rue Ballu was not designed specifically for Nadia Boulanger's artistic and professional activity. The preexisting architecture thus imposed certain constraints and interior choices on typical conservatory, salon, and religious spaces. For example, the narthex usually leads the faithful to enter the church from the back, from the side of the organ. At rue Ballu to the contrary, the location of the fireplace with its arched alcove between the two rooms made such a configuration impossible: the faithful had to enter from the side of the altar.

Beyond the picturesque decor found in biographies of Nadia Boulanger, the apartment at 36 rue Ballu is an excellent archive that should be examined as such. As a complex functional and symbolic space, it played an active role in the construction and, later, in the preservation and expansion of the "Boulangiste religion" (and, incidentally, the musician's professional career), as much as it contributed to the fashioning of an aesthetic built around composition and musical interpretation. In this regard, it is an important component of the famous "web of magnetism" evoked in Doda Conrad's epigraph for this essay, and an essential lens through which to examine Boulanger's exceptional charisma.

# NOTES

This essay is an expanded and updated version of an article originally published in French in Jean Gribenski, Véronique Meyer, and Solange Vernois, eds., *La maison de l'artiste: Construction d'un espace de représentations entre réalité et imaginaire (XVIIe–XXe siècles)* (Rennes: Presses universitaires de Rennes, 2007), 203–15.

1. Doda Conrad was a singer who worked with Boulanger regularly from the mid-1930s. Her epigraph is from *Grandeur et mystère d'un mythe: Souvenirs de quarante-quatre ans d'amitié avec Nadia Boulanger* (Paris: Buchet/Chastel, 1995), 67.

2. Nadia Boulanger's first prizes at the Conservatory were solfège in 1898 (class taught by Marie-Antoinette Roy), harmony in 1903 (taught by Auguste Chapuis), organ (taught by Alexandre Guilmant), piano accompaniment (taught by Paul Vidal), counterpoint and fugue (taught by Gabriel Fauré) in 1904.

3. The expression *cours de cantate* was used to describe Nadia Boulanger's weekly group lesson in "choral song and analysis"; it was renamed "analysis and interpretation" in 1962. It was open to all (up to fifty students would attend in the 1930s), and the Bach cantatas occupied a privileged place. See Cédric Segond-Genovesi, "Fin de règne? L'enseignement de Nadia Boulanger après la Seconde Guerre mondiale," in *De la Libération au Domaine Musical: Dix ans de musique en France (1944–1954)* eds. Laurent Feneyrou and Alain Poirier (Paris: Vrin, 2018), 199–216.

4. Nadia Boulanger's activities in Paris were concentrated, for the most part, in a small area bordered to the southeast by the former building of the Conservatoire at rue Bergère, to the southwest by the Opéra Garnier, to the northwest by the Ecole Normale de Musique (where she began teaching in 1919), and to the northeast by rue du Faubourg Poissonnière. In this regard, Boulanger's artistic and professional career continued a musical geography inherited from the nineteenth century. See, in particular, Christophe Charle, *Paris, fin de siècle: Culture et politique* (Paris: Seuil, 1998); Nigel Simeone, *Paris: A Musical Gazetteer* (New Haven: Yale University Press, 2000); and Hugh Macdonald, "De L'Opéra au Conservatoire: La géographie musicale de Paris sous la Monarchie de Juillet et le Second Empire," in Gribenski, Meyer, and Vernois, *La maison de l'artiste*, 164–69.

5. The idea of an *archetype* (an "invariant ideal model" in biology) in this context refers to spaces with strong identities that are immediately recognizable.

6. Such apartments, constructed in large numbers during the Second Empire development of Paris led by Baron Haussman, are discussed in François Loyer, *Paris xixᵉ siècle: L'immeuble et la rue* (Paris: Hazan, 1994). Descriptions and plans were widely circulated in "handbooks for the hostess" at the turn of the twentieth century; for example, the *Nouveau manuel complet de la maîtresse de maison*, by Mᵐᵉˢ Pariset et Celnart (Celnart is a pseudonym for Elisabeth-Félicie Bayle-Mouillard) (Paris: Mulo, 1913), 64–66.

7. Annette Dieudonné, Nadia Boulanger's sole heir, gave the entire contents of the drawing and sitting rooms to the Musée Instrumental du Conservatoire de Paris on 11 March 1981, with the plan, unfortunately not completed, to re-create the space at the future Musée de la Musique. The museum opened in 1997, but had been in the process of being planned at La Villette since 1979–80. See Josiane Bran-Ricci, "Du musée instrumental au Musée de la Musique," in *Musée de la Musique: Guide*, ed. Philippe Blay (Paris: Cité de la Musique/Réunion des musées nationaux, 1997), 10–13. Before the transfer, a detailed inventory of this furniture collection (spanning items E.981.3.1 to E.981.3.8) was thus drawn up at rue Ballu by Florence Gétreau (Abondance), who was then curator at the Musée Instrumental, between April 1980 and March 1981. Along with approximately seventy photographs, the architect Pierre Abondance also produced plans and topographical layouts. On this topic, see esp. Florence Abondance, "Nadia Boulanger au futur Musée de la Musique," *La Revue musicale* 353–354 (1982): 93–94; and Alexandra

Laederich, "Les fonds Nadia Boulanger: Un héritage musical complexe," *Bulletin hors série du Groupe français de l'AIBM*, (2005): 39–48.

8. Christiane Trieu-Colleney, "Nadia Boulanger," *La Revue musicale* 353–354 (1982): 77. The Boulanger family owned a Pleyel grand piano which appears in some photos of the salon of the rue Ballu taken before 1920. By 1925 Nadia had added a second piano for her students, likely the Erard given to Boulanger by her friends the Sachs family (both the Pleyel and the Erard appear in the photo c. 1925 in Figure 6). The Pleyel that Nadia reserved for her own use during classes (see Figure 6) was replaced by the Steinway c. 1953.

9. Agathe Rouart-Valéry," Évocation de Nadia Boulanger," *La Revue musicale* 353–54 (1982): 60.

10. Conrad, *Grandeur et mystère d'un mythe*, 69.

11. The bust (Paris, Musée de la Musique [hereafter MM], inventory no. E.981.3.8.178) was sculpted in Rome around 1915–16 by Lucienne Heuvelmans (Premier Grand Prix de Rome, sculpture section, in 1911), who was then a friend, the only female friend, of Lili Boulanger at Villa Medicis. See Jérôme Spycket, *À la recherche de Lili Boulanger* (Paris: Fayard, 2004), n.p. (image gallery between pages 180–81). This collection of images includes a photograph of Lucienne Heuvelmans in front of her bust of Lili, Rome, 1916. See also Conrad, *Grandeur et mystère d'un mythe*, 68; Alan Kendall, *The Tender Tyrant: Nadia Boulanger* (Wilton, Conn.: Lyceum Books), 2–4; Christiane Trieu-Colleney, "Nadia Boulanger," *Jeunesse et orgue* 46 (1980): 36–50; and Narcis Bonet, unpublished interview by the author, 2 November 2005.

12. The oil on canvas portrait of Ernest Boulanger is attributed to Thomas Couture, c. 1835 (MM E.981.3.8.2). Composer Ernest Boulanger (1815–1900), father of Nadia and Lili, recipient of the Prix de Rome in 1835 and author of a dozen *opéras-comiques*, taught voice at the Conservatoire de Paris (see Spycket, *À la recherche de Lili Boulanger*, chap. 1, "De Marie-Julie à Raïssa," 17–89). The oil on canvas of Nadia's paternal grandmother is by Georges Rouget (1784–1869), c. 1825 (MM E.981.3.8.5). Marie-Julie Halligner (1786–1850) was a student of Pierre-Jean Garat at the Conservatoire. Her glory days at the Opéra-Comique were in the years 1810–20 (see Spycket, ibid.). The photographs of Lili are MM E.981.3.8.50 and MM E.981.3.8.148.

13. Lithograph by Pierre Audouin, n.d. (MM E.981.3.8.299). In the nineteenth century this honor was generally accorded to Vigée-Lebrun (1755–1852) when in fact it belonged to Anne Vallayer-Coster (1744–1818). See Eik Kahng and Marianne Roland Michel, eds., *Anne Vallayer Coster: Peintre à la cour de Marie–Antoinette* (Paris: Somogy, 2003).

14. Photograph of Dubois by Eugène Pirou, n.d. (E.981.3.8.224); of d'Indy by Henri Manuel, c. 1912 (E.981.3.8.225); of Vidal by Pierre Petit, 3 April 1906 (E.981.3.8.228); of Saint-Saëns (photographer unknown), 1917 (E.981.3.8.223); of Caussade by Nadar, c. 1910 (E.981.3.8.230); and the bust of Fauré by Emmanuel Fauré-Frémiet (c.1900), which is not currently at the Musée de la Musique.

15. The role of Nadia Boulanger's "Frenchness" in the development of her international career has often been pointed out, as was her preference for the methods and teaching traditions of the Conservatoire de Paris. For more on this topic, see in this volume my introduction to "The Beethoven Analyses" as well as Jeanice Brooks's essay, "Modern French Music: Translating Fauré in America 1942–45."

16. The director of the Conservatoire Femina-Musica was Xavier Leroux; three-quarters of its faculty were professors from the Conservatoire de Paris. On the Boulangers' attachment to the Conservatoire and the connections between it and the other institutions in which she taught, see in this volume Marie Duchêne-Thégarid's essay, "From Technique to *Musique*: The Institutional Pedagogy of Nadia Boulanger." See also Kendra Preston Leonard, *The Conservatoire Américain: A History* (Lanham, Toronto, Plymouth: Scarecrow Press, 2007), ix–xxix.

17. Beethoven was represented by a medallion on a silver plaque by Abel La Fleur, n.d. (MM E.981.3.8.153); Chopin by a portrait painted after the daguerreotype at the Warsaw museum, n.d. (MM E.981.3.8.278); Debussy by an engraving by Pierre Dujardin, after a photograph by Otto Wegener, 1917 (MM E.981.3.8.220); Bartók by a photograph, n.d. (MM E.981.3.8.140); and Stravinsky was represented several times, including two color photographs from 1960–65 (MM E.981.3.8.274): a photograph by Challs from summer 1936 (MM E.981.3.8.66) and a photograph dedicated to Nadia Boulanger, October 1944 (MM E.981.3.8.67).

18. Archives of the Conservatoire national supérieur de musique et de danse (CNSMDP), Paris, no shelfmark.

19. Olivier Messiaen thus taught under the watchful eye of Frédéric Chopin (see the photograph by Robert Doisneau, 1961, reproduced on the cover of Jean Boivin's *La Classe de Messiaen* [Paris: Christian Bourgois, 1995]). The busts from the Conservatoire were transferred to the Musée de la Musique in 1997 (E.995.6).

20. The portraits of Lili are so densely displayed (see the upper left corner of the drawing room in Figure 3) that it hardly seems possible it was unintentional.

21. Though the charcoal portrait of Lili (Figure 5, top image) hung in the dining room during Nadia Boulanger's lifetime, it was probably moved to the drawing room between 1979 and 1981. It is now kept in the photo archive at Centre international Nadia et Lili Boulanger (CNLB).

22. The crystal chandelier is item MM E.981.3.8.255. The descriptions of salons by Adolphe Bitard in *Le Livre de la maîtresse de maison et de la mère de famille* (Paris: Maurice Dreyfous, 1880); and by Alphonse Depras immediately after the war in *Le Français de tous les jours* (Paris: La Renaissance Universelle, 1920) could be those of rue Ballu down to the smallest detail, including the color of the draperies and the color of the wood furniture.

23. See M. D. Sheriff, *The Exceptional Woman: Elisabeth Vigée-Lebrun and the Cultural Politics of Art* (Chicago: University of Chicago Press, 1996).

24. Jeanice Brooks, "Nadia Boulanger and the Salon of the Princesse de Polignac," *Journal of the American Musicological Society* 46 (1993): 415–68.

25. *Vue de la terrasse de Jouy-en-Josas*, 1934 (MM E.981.3.8.7) and *Marine sur la lagune de Venise*, n.d. (MM E.981.3.8.8). On Princesse de Polignac, see esp. Sylvia Kahan, *Winnaretta Singer-Polignac: Princesse, mécène et musicienne*, trans. Charles Mouton, rev. ed. (Dijon: Les Presses du réel, 2018); English edition *Music's Modern Muse: A Life of Winnaretta Singer, Princesse de Polignac* (Rochester: University of Rochester Press, 2003).

26. When Rainier III came to power (1949–50), Nadia Boulanger was named *maître de chapelle* in Monaco, a post she occupied until her death (1979). Regarding the romantic feelings between Nadia Boulanger and Prince Pierre de Monaco (nephew of the Princesse de Polignac), see Alexandra Laederich and Rémy Stricker, "Les trois vies de Nadia Boulanger: Extraits inédits de la valise protégée," *Revue de la BNF* 46 (2014): 77–83. The portrait of Maria-José is a photograph from 1962 (MM E.981.3.8.142). On the genealogy of the Boulanger family and Raïssa's supposed aristocratic origins, see Spycket, *À la recherche de Lili Boulanger*, 17–89. Nadia's mother was the "Russian princess" Raïssa Mychetski, student and later wife of Ernest Boulanger.

27. Anne Martin-Fugier, *Les Salons de la IIIe République: Art, littérature, politique* (Paris: Perrin, 2003), 8–9.

28. Bruno Monsaingeon, *Mademoiselle: Entretiens avec Nadia Boulanger* (Paris: Van de Velde, 1981), 22.

29. A leaflet listing the times and fees for lessons in 1905 is reproduced in Spycket, *Nadia Boulanger*, 26.

30. "Le Code de l'élégance et du bon ton," in *La Grande Dame*, May 1894, cited in Martin-Fugier, *Les Salons de la IIIe République*, 101.

31. See Myriam Chimènes, *Mécènes et musiciens: Du salon au concert à Paris sous la III*ᵉ *République* (Paris: Fayard, 2004), 76.

32. In the first of these photographs, Mme Boulanger senior is seated to the right of the Cavaillé-Coll-Mutin organ. On the second, Loulou Gonet (a close friend of Lili and the Boulanger family) poses sitting in front of the chimney. The large Majorelle table (MM E.981.3.8.334), purchased around 1910, was later moved to the sitting room.

33. The open involvement of the Princesse in the career of Nadia Boulanger did not begin until the early 1930s.

34. Although filled with exotic objects (mostly from Eastern Europe) and copies of antiques (from China and Ancient Greece), there was no truly precious work of art in the drawing and sitting rooms of Nadia Boulanger except for the painting by Berthe Morisot, *Les sœurs Rouart dans un parc* (gift of Princesse de Polignac, and currently at the Musée d'Art Moderne de la Ville de Paris) and the undated painting by Georges Rouault, *Sacré Cœur: Esquisse pour le tabernacle de la chapelle de Voiron* (MM E 981.3.8.24).

35. The undated bust is MM E.981.3.8.268. CNLB photographic archives show that the bust of Isabelle d'Este was initially in the drawing room, but was moved to the sitting room and replaced by the bust of Lili.

36. Martin-Fugier, *Les Salons de la IIIᵉ République*, 9–10.

37. On the private house museum in France, see Anne Higonnet, *A Museum of One's Own: Private Collecting, Public Gift* (Pittsburgh: Persicope, 2009).

38. See especially Spycket, *À la recherche de Lili Boulanger*, 359–69; and Cédric Segond-Genovesi, "Lili Boulanger par Nadia Boulanger, 1918–1993: Disques, partitions et normes interprétatives," in *Les musiciens et le disque* (Lyon: AFAS-AIBM and Atelier Blaise Adilon, 2009), 25–38.

39. See Jeanice Brooks, "'*Noble et grande servante de la musique*': Telling the Story of Nadia Boulanger's Conducting Career," *Journal of Musicology* 14 (1996): 92–116. Brooks showed that for Nadia Boulanger to achieve the status of first woman to conduct all-male orchestras she had to erase all sexual identity and any demonstrated ambition, in aid of a figure who accepted her destiny as a simple "intermediary" at the *service* of a superior power: music. See also Jean Boivin, "Convictions religieuses et modernité musicale au Québec avant la Révolution tranquille: L'exemple de Nadia Boulanger et d'Olivier Messiaen, pédagogues et transmetteurs du renouveau musical," in *Musique, art et religion dans l'entre-deux-guerres,* Sylvain Caron and Michel Duchesneau, eds., (Lyon: Symétrie, 2009), 443–69.

40. The image of Lili as "sent from heaven," often implicit in Nadia Boulanger's remarks, seems completely believable, even more so because the musician thought of art as an expression of the divine. See esp. Monsaingeon, *Mademoiselle: Entretiens avec Nadia Boulanger*, 30.

41. Every year, around 15 March, the musician held a mass in Lili's memory in the Chapel of the Virgin. The photograph from 2005 in Figure 7a is evidently an incomplete rendering of the chapel as it must have appeared to Nadia Boulanger. Before the Second Vatican Council (1962–1965), the chapel was probably more richly furnished.

42. In the same perspective, one can compare the drawing room at rue Ballu and the main altar at Eglise de la Madeleine—another place familiar to Nadia Boulanger. She was the assistant of Henri Dallier at the organ beginning in 1906 and she gave a eulogy for Gabriel Fauré there on 4 November 1924.

43. The two arabesque sconces (not accounted for at Musée de la Musique) were installed around 1910. The wood trellis that covers the back (not accounted for at the Musée de la Musique) was installed in 1952. Before that, the alcove was covered by an embroidered silk shade (now lost) that was identical to the one that covered the other side, in the sitting room (MM E.981.3.8.370). It gave a stained-glass window effect that was even more striking behind the bust of Lili. CNLB photographic archive.

44. MM E.981.3.8.261 (undated).

45. Russian triptych in bronze and enamel; gift of Zygmunt Mycielski ca. 1952–53 (MM E.981.3.8.75).

46. The photograph of Stravinsky is by Challs, summer 1936 (MM E.981.3.8.66), and the photograph of Boulanger is ca. 1961–62 (MM E.981.3.8.44). On the friendship and professional relationship between Stravinsky and Boulanger, and Boulanger's role in the distribution and interpretation of Stravinsky's music, see Kimberly A. Francis, *Teaching Stravinsky: Nadia Boulanger and the Consecration of a Modernist Icon* (Oxford: Oxford University Press, 2015); and Kimberly A. Francis, ed., *Nadia Boulanger and the Stravinskys: A Selected Correspondence* (Rochester, NY: University of Rochester Press; and Woodbridge, UK: Boydell & Brewer, 2018). On the importance of Stravinsky's music in the cantata classes after 1945, see Cédric Segond-Genovesi, "Fin de règne?"

47. The undated crucifix is MM E.981.3.8.212.

48. The definition in the French dictionary *Littré* helps to make that analogy clear: "In the early Christian Church, the narthex held the catechumen [the people preparing to be baptised] . . . and the people who were allowed to be present during the divine service *outside the temple*" (my emphasis).

49. Miki Piré often watched over Lili's health, until the end. A photograph on page 55 in Spycket, *Nadia Boulanger*, shows her dressed as a nurse, with Nadia, at Lili's bedside. In the photograph taken just after the composer's death which was displayed in the drawing room (MME.981.3.8.149), she again appears as a nurse. The lamp is MM E.981.3.8.240 (undated).

50. See, for example, Franz Liszt, *Frédéric Chopin* (Paris: Buchet/Chastel, 1977), 157–67.

51. 36 rue Ballu remained above all a music school that charged fees; this led Nadia Boulanger to adopt the codes of the "five to seven" (or "five o'clock"—see Martin-Fugier, *Les Salons de la IIIᵉ République*, 102), which was more practical, modern, and intended for a wider audience than the aristocratic.

52. Anne Martin-Fugier stressed that during the Third Republic the people found at an aristocratic salon were also those found at church. Ibid., 102–3.

53. André Chastel and Jean-Pierre Babelon, *La Notion de patrimoine* (Paris: Liana Levi, 1994), 13–25.

54. The close private and professional relationship between Nadia Boulanger and Raoul Pugno is discussed by Alexandra Laederich (this volume) and Jeanice Brooks and Kimberly Francis (also this volume). See also Laederich and Stricker,"Les trois vies de Nadia Boulanger." The two musicians performed together regularly, and they collaboratively wrote the song cycle *Les heures claires* and the opera *La ville morte*. Pugno died in Moscow in 1914, while on tour with Nadia Boulanger.

55. The first photograph, by Roger-Viollet, can be found in Kendall, *Tender Tyrant*, whereas the other photographs are by Charles Leirens (from around 1960). CNLB photographic archives.

56. According to Boulanger's student Narcis Bonet (unpublished interview, 2 November, 2005), the move to Fontainebleau required no fewer than fourteen suitcases. CNLB archives.

# "What an Arrival!"
# Nadia Boulanger's New World (1925)

NADIA BOULANGER
TRANSLATED AND ANNOTATED BY JEANICE BROOKS
AFTERWORD BY GAYLE MURCHISON

Nadia Boulanger's diary describing her first tour of the United States provides a window onto a defining moment in her life. Produced as a set of letter-journals addressed to her mother, Raïssa Boulanger, Nadia's detailed account of her trip shows how her ideas about the United States were confirmed or overturned by the experience of traveling and working in the country. And the reception of her own performances as recitalist, organ soloist, and especially as public speaker and advocate for new music had a decisive impact on her personal life and professional career.[1]

Boulanger's visit lasted for two months, beginning when she embarked upon the *Aquitania* at Le Havre on 24 December 1924. After an unusually stormy passage, she arrived in New York on 31 December to start the new year in a new country. The schedule for her tour was packed (Figure 1). Beginning her visit in New York with short excursions to Philadelphia, she then traveled to Cleveland and Urbana before heading south to Houston. During the course of her return to the Northeast, she made appearances in Saint Louis, Minneapolis, Chicago, Indianapolis, and Cincinnati before finishing her visit with a series of concerts and lectures in Boston. During her trip, she would be the featured soloist with major American orchestras; play organ recitals at Harvard University and the New England Conservatory, and on the grand Wanamaker's organs in Philadelphia and New York; and give lectures and lecture-recitals at a wide range of venues including universities and colleges, schools, art museums, and hotel ballrooms. But despite this punishing schedule, Boulanger found time to write to her mother almost every day (and sometimes more than once) with a detailed journal of her activities, adding pages at regular intervals before sending the entire installment to Raïssa in France every two to three days. The result is a vivid day-by-day account of her tour as it unfolded, expressed in the familiar tone she employed with her family and intimate friends.

• 145 •

Mlle Nadia Boulanger

1 9 2 5.

- - - - - - - - - - -

Friday evening Jan 9th at 8.15 p.m.  Organ Recital
    at Wanamakers , Philadelphia, Pa.     *10J. 45 p.m. réception*
Sunday afternoon Jan 11th at 3 p.m.  Soloist With New York Symphony
    at Aeolian Hall, New York City.
Wednesday evening Jan 14th at    ,Lecture    *Diner Mannes*
    at David Mannes School, 157 East 74th St, N. Y. City
Thursday Afternoon, Jan. 15th at    , Organ Recital    *8.30 réception guild*
    at Wanamakers, Broadway & 10th Street, N. Y. C.
Saturday Evening at 7:30 p. m., Lecture Recital  *diner —*  *18 p.m. 3J. Sam*
    at Assembly Hall, Vassar College, Poughkeepsie, N. Y.  *18 — 3J. 5h Reynolds*
Monday evening Jan 19th at 8:15 p.m.  Lecture Recital  *5h Reynolds*
    at Town Hall, New York City  *diner Flagler*
Wednesday Evening, Jan 21st at 8:15 p.m. Lecture Organ Recital  *19 thé à 5h*
    at Museum of Art, Cleveland, Ohio
Thursday afternoon, Jan 22nd at    Private Lecture Recital
    at Laurel School, Cleveland, Ohio.
Friday evening Jan 23rd, at    Lecture Recital  *Préludes Debussy*
    at University of Illinois, Urbana, Ill  *French music modern*
Tuesday    Jan 27th at 8.15  Lecture Recital  *ultra-music*
    at The Rice Institute, Houston, Texas  *Stravinsky*
Wednesday    Jan 28th at 8.15  Lecture Recital  *meeting with teachers*
    at The Rice Institute, Houston, Texas  *faulK*
Thursday    Jan 29th at 8.15  Lecture Recital
    at the Rice Institute, Houston Texas
Monday    Feb 2nd at
    St. Louis, Mo  *3 Chicago ?*
Thursday    Feb 5th at
    Minneapolis, Minn  *organ and piano*
Saturday afternoon, Feb 7th at 3 p.m.  Lecture with Piano & Organ
  Travertine Room,Lincoln Hotel,Indianapolis, Ind
Monday morning, Feb 9th at 11 a.m.  Lecture with Piano  *8 for dinner Cincinnati*
    at Hotel Sinton,  Cincinnati, Ohio  *11th*  *10J. lunch*
Friday evening, Feb 13th at 8:15 p.m.  Recital
    at Assembly Hall of Cleveland Institute of Music, Cleveland, Ohio  *14 févr. Bryn Mawr*
Monday evening Feb 16th at 8 p.m.    Recital
    at Collection Hall, Swarthmore College, Swarthmore, Pa.
Wednesday afternoon Feb 18th at 12:50 noon  Lecture Recital
    at The May School, 339 Marlborough St, Boston, Mass  *— thé Caroline —*
Thursday morning, Feb 19th at    Rehearsal with Boston Symphony  *for concert Thomson*
    at Symphony Hall, Boston, Mass
Friday afternoon Feb 20th at 2:30 p.m.  Soloist with Boston Symphony
    at Symphony Hall, Boston, Mass
Saturday evening, Feb 21st at 8:15 p.m.  Soloist with Boston Symphony
    at Symphony Hall, Boston, Mass
Sunday afternoon Feb 22nd at    Lecture Recital  *Thé Caroline*
    at Womens City Club, Boston, Mass  *Swritti diner*
Monday Evening Feb 23rd at    Lecture Recital
    at Dartmouth College, Hanover, N. H.
Tuesday evening, Feb 24th at    Recital  *a.g. Blurr*
    at Harvard University, Cambridge, Mass  *Soirée Hill*
Wednesday afternoon Feb 25th at    Organ Recital
    at New England Conservatory of Music, Boston, Mass

*10    réception Dam*
*15 J.  réception Sealy*            *Goodrich 20 or 25 dinner —*
*16 ?        D'Carl*
*17  Vassar diner*

Figure 1. Draft schedule for Nadia Boulanger's 1925 U.S. tour,
with her annotations, undated (c. December 1924).

The tour was partly sponsored by the French Ministry of Foreign Affairs, and Boulanger's status as a cultural ambassador is apparent in much of her activity. Before leaving France she circulated a questionnaire about current trends to leading musical figures, and her lectures and concerts were largely devoted to informing American audiences about contemporary music and musical culture in France. At each stop on her journey she met local dignitaries, attended receptions and dinners, and explored the musical infrastructure of the city. At the same time, she pursued a personal mission of promoting her sister Lili's works to American audiences, including Lili's music in virtually all of her appearances; the performances of *Pour les funérailles d'un soldat* by the New York Symphony Society and the Boston Symphony were particular high points. Nadia's letters also reveal that she was then seriously considering a permanent move to the United States, and her trip was a precious opportunity to evaluate the professional and personal consequences of accepting a post at an American institution. A principal issue was her mother's well-being: Nadia was the only wage earner and sole surviving family member for the aging Raïssa, and her letters imply that there was no question of leaving her mother alone in France if Nadia did accept a job offer in the United States. Raïssa's own letters to her daughter are full of concerns about Nadia's health and the risks of traveling such a long distance. Nadia's constant repetition in her journal about how kind everyone is to her, her frequent mentions of their mutual acquaintances, and her reassurances that she would never accept any of the positions she was offered before consulting Raïssa all seem designed to reassure her mother, and provide revealing insights into how caring responsibilities affected Nadia's professional life. Nadia's gradual realization of her own powers as a speaker, revealed over the course of several installments and summarized near the end of her tour, is another thread running through her reflections on her professional future.

Boulanger's tour built upon a large network of personal relationships, many established during her wartime charity activity as a founder-director of the Comité franco-américain du Conservatoire de Paris or through her postwar teaching at the Conservatoire américain de Fontainebleau. Her most powerful supporter was Walter Damrosch, the conductor of the New York Symphony Society, whose work with American and French military musicians during the First World War was instrumental to the foundation of the Conservatoire américain. Harry Harkness Flagler, the principal financial backer of the New York Symphony, was instrumental in raising funds for her trip. Boulanger stayed in the Damrosches' New York apartment for most of the time she was on the East Coast, and her major concerts included an appearance as organ soloist with the New York Symphony for Handel's Organ Concerto in D Minor and the premiere of Aaron Copland's Symphony for Organ and Orchestra. Serge Koussevitzky, whose Paris concerts Boulanger had championed in her concert criticism of the early 1920s, returned the favor by welcoming her to Boston, where he had arrived only a few months before to become the conductor of the Boston Symphony Orchestra. Among the final engagements of Boulanger's tour were repeat performances of Copland's Organ Symphony and other works with the BSO.

But while her influential colleagues were crucial in securing the major engagements that punctuated her tour, her students were equally essential in assuring its success. The Philadelphia music teacher Katharine Wolff began studying with Boulanger at Fontainebleau in 1923 and rapidly became a member of her teacher's inner circle. Wolff accompanied Boulanger from France on the *Aquitania* and was indispensible in making travel arrangements within the United States and organizing Boulanger's schedule in Philadelphia. Former students—including Melville Smith, Aaron Copland, Virgil Thomson, and many others—assiduously attended her concerts and lectures and escorted her to musical and social events. Others, such as Walter Piston and Caroline McFadden, helped to organize her appearances at clubs, schools, and universities. The warmth of her students' welcome and Boulanger's immense gratitude form a frequent theme of her journal.

Although Boulanger had previously traveled widely within Europe and had made two trips to Russia, this tour represented her first sustained exposure to non-European cities and landscapes. In her attempts to understand and describe what she encountered, she filled her letters with comparisons, discussing not only architecture and landscape but the organization of musical and educational life, race and gender relations, and the meaning of "culture," among many other topics. Her comments often reflect common period assumptions about "Old World" versus "New World" achievements and values, especially in her attitudes toward narratives of technological progress, industry, and innovation. Her travels allowed her to hear American musical idioms in situ, including both jazz—at a concert by Paul Whiteman's band in Houston—and African American song forms. And her tour furnished her first personal exposure to American race relations and to segregation in practice. Her reflections on this experience particularly mark her letters from Houston, where she delivered three lectures on modern music.[2] Boulanger was the second speaker to participate in the newly created Rice Institute Lectures on Music, which were conceived as a contribution to the cultural aspirations of a rapidly growing provincial city. The first speaker had been John Powell (1882–1963), whose talks delivered in 1923 were explicitly dedicated to his racist vision of American music and the "problems" of immigration and of African-American influence. While Boulanger's lectures were devoted to modern French music rather than to American musical or political issues, her visit to Houston brought her into personal contact with black Americans affected by segregation, which encouraged her to reflect on American racial politics.

Boulanger's understanding of American racial oppression involved expectations and assumptions shaped through exoticized representations of the United States in early twentieth-century France. Her experience of American culture included not only the views of the country communicated by her students, but also built upon the experience of hearing traveling American musicians in France—including jazz bands and minstrel shows—as well as French musical and stage entertainments that portrayed stereotypes of black Americans. Her assumptions about race were shaped by discourses of French colonialism in the late nineteenth and early twentieth centuries, but also by the principles of French republicanism, the ideals of *liberté-égalité-fraternité*, and the belief that France was the international home of human rights through the French revolutionary and republican project. Boulanger's letters are particularly revealing on how these different strands could figure in an early twentieth-century Frenchwoman's experience of the United States. For example, her accounts of an earnest conversation about segregation with a Pullman porter on her train and her encounter with singing restaurant workers in Houston show her to have been concerned with human connections with black Americans and disturbed by segregation. Yet her descriptions of these experiences also reveal the beliefs and prejudices that conditioned her interpretation of structural racism, visible in her frequently patronizing stance. In musical situations, contemporary and sometimes contradictory assumptions about music and musical genres characteristic of her background, education, and aesthetic position further shaped her accounts of American culture. The belief in music as a universal language underpins her description of her encounter with black restaurant workers in Houston—an experience she clearly found deeply moving—but her report on a concert by the Whiteman band rests on the assumption that, unlike jazz, European art music is a superior and unmarked category of musical achievement.

Boulanger's journal of her tour reveals overlapping patterns of marginalization and privilege. Her letters show that she was often the only woman professional in her environment. For instance, her account of a lunch in her honor at the Damrosches' for nearly a hundred male guests, while all the other women present served the tables, provides a telling image of her exceptional situation. Her fees, though higher than those she was able to ask in France, were nevertheless far lower than those paid to male speakers and performers.[3] At the same time, she was celebrated as a representative of European culture by audiences eager to assimilate European models into American musical life, and she saw herself as occupying a superior cultural position to her American audiences. Her position as a white upper-class woman provided a privileged standpoint from which to interpret American culture and the oppressive power structures she observed. Her reflections, including those about her own performances as well as those of others, are a gold mine of information about contemporary musical life. Her letters provide a fascinating perspective on early twentieth-century American culture as well as insights into how the experience of American life helped to shape her subsequent career.

## Letters from Nadia Boulanger to Raïssa Boulanger, December–February 1925

*Boulanger's letters to her mother are held at the Bibliothèque nationale de France (F-Pn), NLa 282. Items 1–115 make up the journal of her American tour. The selections included here, organized by city, represent some of her more striking impressions. In some cases I have included extracts from a longer installment; cuts are indicated by ellipses in brackets [. . .]. Three dots appearing without brackets indicate suspension points or interruptions in thought—employed by Boulanger in the original French text. Underlined text in the manuscript letters has been rendered in italics.*

### EN ROUTE
**24 December 1924**. *Complete text.*

My dear Maman,
A little note before arriving at Cherbourg—to tell you everything I couldn't say to you when leaving. Katharine [Wolff] and Delaney[4] have been touching— Everyone was at the station—but . . . I am happier to have said goodbye to you at home. Now the page has turned—I have to try to make the best of things—thinking of you will help, it seems to me.

How strange things are, at once both simple and profound. One comes down the stairs just like every day, and it's the time for just us. You must take care of yourself, take advantage of me not being there to finally think of yourself a little. What to say to you—so much—but it is necessary to remain silent if one wants to stay brave—

My head is empty—and I don't really comprehend I have left—it is at times like these that one understands how little everything is worth, after a certain time in life—you'd laugh at yourself, if you didn't want so much to cry.

Figure 2. Nadia Boulanger in New York, in a photograph taken the day after her arrival by a professional who "thought himself a great artist."

But be calm—everyone is doing the impossible for me, and everyone is preparing to make everything easy for me—if I work a little at helping myself, things can go well. In any case, you have the certainty of knowing that I am surrounded by friends, which is a reassurance for you and a real relief for me. As soon as I set foot on land, [I will send] a telegram—it seems to me as if the trip will be good—perhaps some melancholy to start with, but one must get used to it. I gauge the idiocy of my letter—but forcing oneself not to say any of the words one feels would make even an intelligent person become a little stupid. But you understand—

My little Maman, I kiss you with all my heart, and dispense with saying anything else to you. How far away you are already!

Your little
Nadia

### NEW YORK

**1 January 1925**. *Complete text. This letter is written on stationery embossed "Walter Damrosch, No. 146 East 61st Street, New York City."*

What an arrival! In marvelous weather, an unforgettable, indescribable show—a city made of precious stones, rising little by little in the night, raising up towers, hills, sketching innumerable little streets, the whole illuminated in green, blue, red, gold—on the dark, silent water, the ferryboats passing like enormous glow-worms. To the left, the right, as far as one can see, the city; behind us, on a sea full of reflections, the boats with their lights forming such beautiful, varied lines—

Before disembarking, photographers, journalists, telegrams, agitation! Copland, Clurman, Thomson, Reynolds, Elliott, Mel, the Holdens, the president of the Guild of Organists, the representative from the New York Symphony, Engles's associate—everyone confused—they were not supposed to let me disembark until the following day![5] Thanks to my diplomatic visa, I was the only foreigner who did not have to spend the night on board!

You can't imagine my reception—arrival at the Damrosches', getting dressed in a hurry, supper with the Rogerses, supper again with just the four of us—the Damrosches, Fairchild, and me—exquisite.[6] I am at home—everything has been prepared, I can't tell you how well, a magnificent bedroom, bathroom, every little thing in order. Everyone sorry [to be unprepared] for my early arrival, which they no longer thought possible.[7]

Telegrams from Woodfin, Elliott, Moore, *Mrs. Cobleigh*, Annette, Thérèse, Irma, Surette, W. Carl, Mrs. Hilton, Reynolds. This morning, impressive flowers from Lucien Wulsin, the Flaglers—[8]

At noon, guest of honor for the Guild of Organists—a speech from the president, Mr. Seely, to welcome me, an admirable talk by the minister, who had said a prayer for the new year before we sat down—then, Hanson got up, and he explained what my influence is, what I have done, how much confidence so many young people have in me, what the new America owes me—and, even though I was a little embarrassed, I must say how much courage I drew from it.[9] Then, I improvised a response, not too badly, actually, and in all sincerity. They were all touched. The minister was delightful, telling me not to be afraid of my English, that words that come from the heart go to the heart—and all around me, an atmosphere like I have never had in my life. And that gives you strength, courage, the desire to feel really yourself. I am, as I have been since leaving the boat, still wobbly—but well. I am only worried about holding up—such a pedestal lifts you up or crushes you.

I am going to rest for an hour, before going to dine at Damrosch's daughter's house. Tomorrow lunch with Flagler, day after tomorrow a lunch here for 91 people!!

Monday is the first rehearsal with orchestra—a reception for several organizations—overall, a really special life.

A piano in my bedroom, which had to be moved in through the window—that seemed completely natural—how friendly these people are, and how vibrant.

Everyone sends you thousands and thousands of wishes—for myself, need I say how much I think of you, and remain your little

Nadia

General impression—an enlarged Holland—the houses very much in the same style—dining room in the basement.

Everything would please you. And really, now that I hear everyone saying that this crossing was unusually bad, I would not hesitate to see you undertake it, if ever I return.

## NEW YORK AND PHILADELPHIA

**5 January 1925**. *Complete text. Boulanger began this letter on Monday 5 January and continued to add installments covering the period up to 12 January. It is written on Damrosch's New York stationery, though part of the text was added in Philadelphia.*

Finally some letters—what a joy—I wasn't worried, but was finding it a long wait. And to recognize the writing, to know what you are doing, to find out how you are, was so sweet.

Wednesday, I haven't had a minute since yesterday—I am writing to you on the way to Philadelphia—so I don't forget anything, I will recommence the diary—

Friday on waking up, the city covered with snow, *marvelous*—lunch at Flagler's—in the morning, a walk with [Melville] Smith, a magnificent impression of this immense and colorful city, the snowflakes falling fast—a delightful lunch—a wonderful welcome, a sumptuous home.[10] At 3:00 went to the photographer's, for Murray (Baldwin—Wulsin)—a guy straight out of a comedy—steeped in his own importance—thinking himself a great artist. At 5:00 tea at Fairchild's with Madame Chanler, no need to tell you about the atmosphere—at 6:00 meeting with Silvia Saunders, faithful, devoted and touching—in the evening, Damrosch's concert, supper at his oldest daughter's, delightful.[11]

Saturday, went to see the organ at Aeolian Hall—difficult, interesting to work on—at 12:30, lunch at the Damrosches' for *91 people* with tables set up everywhere, his daughters serving alongside one or two friends and the servants, myself the only woman guest. What liveliness, what freedom—and how you would like the atmosphere in this house— After lunch (tables for 8 or 10 people set up everywhere) they took everything away in the blink of an eye, then they started to make music. Barrère singing Carmen, Kochanski dressed as an acrobat, playing the craziest things—everyone dancing, even me with Saminsky, a little Russian Jew, and Finletter—Smith sick over it (for Smith was invited)—he must have sent some cards to Paris.[12]

I fell asleep and just woke up while approaching Philadelphia—snow everywhere—but it is so mild that I had to give up the idea of wearing my fur-lined overcoat and it's a coat of Mrs. Damrosch's that has saved my life, at least until I take desperate measures.

Saturday night, I dined with Damrosch, Mrs. Damrosch was in bed, Polly was out—he went out to the concert—I went to bed.

Sunday, departure for Philadelphia at 10:00—I met Katharine [Wolff] at the buffet—lunch, invited by Smith—then Wanamaker's—an organ, a world—nothing can give you an idea—a little delay, because of the immense distance and the size—but an indescribable splendor. A little too beautiful for me—practiced, badly, because of the need to become familiar with it—but I will do anything for this to work. Dinner at 6pm, at K. Wolff's parents', a touching welcome—in general, incredible kindness—I have too many balls in the air not to be a little afraid—everyone is so touching—it's as if an exchange is established right away—but . . . it's a question of living up to their expectations.

Saw Silvia Saunders, who did not want to leave without assuring me once more of her affection.

Monday, first rehearsal with the orchestra—Damrosch wonderful in his goodness and care—the players extremely well disposed—we worked a lot—Copland's piece, difficult, but truly astonishing—[Lili's] *Funérailles* always sounds so good, and its emotion remains so great—everyone will have put their hearts into ensuring it goes well—Copland so grateful, so devoted—Engles talking of nothing but my tour next year—but it needs to be understood that everything here changes from one day to the next, and even very great artists have had a lot of difficulty in making a place for themselves—it is necessary to take a philosophical approach and admit that where everything is so easy there are bound to be hiccups—is this a question of pessimism? No, just of recognizing that everything is difficult.

But how much kindness—you can't even imagine—it's impossible to describe—it is unbelievable—the very abundance of confidence placed in me is frightening, I think, but how much comfort I find in it!

They are making the arrival announcement—is there any need to tell you what relief I feel at the thought that you have finally been to see Kouindjy[13]—but will you do what he tells you—think about what you mean in my life—I measure this more each day—and you will look after yourself. It's when one is far away, that one understands! And essentially, how I love our life—it's better I am sure—even if it is good to change from time to time, one learns so much.

With all my heart I kiss you tenderly, Maman, and remain your little

Nadia

**12 January 1925**. *Extracts. Dated 12 January and also written on Damrosch stationery, this installment may have been sent to Raïssa along with the preceding letter. Boulanger returned to New York for a lecture at Town Hall and rehearsals with Damrosch and the New York Symphony, then went back to Philadelphia for her organ recital at Wanamaker's.*

I take up my journal again—

Tuesday 6 [January]—orchestral rehearsal—everything comes into shape—I am getting used to the organ—I think this is going to work—delightful atmosphere—lunch with Engles and Murray, charming, full of confidence and kindness, astonished to see how well things are going. Went to Town Hall, tried out my voice. I don't think it will be difficult to be heard—it is not very big, and is very nice—afterward I went to see the Wanamaker's organ—less difficult than the one in Philadelphia. In the evening dined at the Damrosches' with Fairchild, went to the cinema—a good evening—[14]

Wednesday, rested in the morning—rehearsal at 1pm—at 3pm train for Philadelphia. Arriving to practice, found Bossi, who was ill and had not yet been able to give a concert, Dupré, Courboin—photos were taken, we talked and ... I gave up on practicing.[15] Hosted by Katharine's parents, adorable and attentive—such a cozy house!—her brother very intelligent and likeable—

Thursday 8—rested until 10:00. Very tired, Went to the organ, played a few minutes (every day between 11:00 and 11:30 the organ is played to give the sales employees some rest in this *enormous* store)—excellent lunch with the brother—saw Marguerite Bulle, engaged to an architect who we would politely call "café au lait."[16] Saw the [French] consul, affable and stupid, detesting America and saying so in front of Americans—what useful publicity! Afterward, a little walk—then the organ from 5:30 until 3am, so that I could arrange all the registrations, get used to it—all the security guards were so kind—

Friday 9 got up late—lunch with a friend of Katharine's and Reynolds's, very rich, very influential, very charming—and a friend of Saunders's —invitation for Bryn Mawr, conviviality, exchange—

Went afterward to the Philharmonic, *magnificent orchestra*—Stokowski very charming.[17] Discipline, order, a result *unheard of* in France—tea at the house of a cousin of the Marquisets, an exquisite woman, with around twenty people, each one kinder than the next—a reception that confirmed Armand and Madame de Laumont's affection once again.[18] At 5:00 Wanamaker's—at 7:00 Katharine brought me my dress, at 8:00 I dressed—at 8:30, hands on the keyboard, a nasty moment—a fairly weak start but no mistakes—all the registrations in order, *everything* prepared for the whole concert, it's really extraordinary—but there is delay, and

# Nadia Boulanger—*Organist—Composer*

*Mlle. Boulanger at her own organ in her
home in Paris*

THOUGH still in the years of her youth, Nadia Boulanger is by virtue of her genius the ranking woman organist of Europe. Her visit this winter to America is her first, and the first organ keys which her gifted fingers will touch in a public performance in this country will be those of the Wanamaker Grand Organ, the largest in the world, on January 9th.

Walter Damrosch says of Mlle. Boulanger: "Among women, I have never met her equal in musicianship and indeed there are very few men who can compare with her. She is one of the finest organists of France."

Mlle. Boulanger was born in Paris, of musical parentage. Her father was a professor in the Conservatory, a position which his father had held before him; while her mother was a daughter of Mychetzky. At an early age she entered the Conservatory, where she attained the highest honors, graduating at the age of 16. Soon afterward she became assistant to Dallier, professor of harmony at the Conservatory, and also as his assistant at the great organ of the church of La Madeleine. From the Conservatory she received, in 1898, first medal in solfeggio; in 1903, first prize in harmony; in 1904, first prize in piano accompaniment, organ, counterpoint and fugue, and in 1908, second Grand Prix de Rome.

She is professor of harmony at the American Conservatory, Fontainebleau; professor of organ, harmony, counterpoint and fugue at the Normal Music School of Paris; critic of the "Monde Musical," and is the author of a number of striking musical compositions. Of these one of the most notable is "La Villa Morte," produced by her in collaboration with the late Raoul Pugno. It is a four-act tragedy by d'Annunzio, who wrote for them a special version of his celebrated drama.

A course of lectures in modern music, to be delivered in the English language by Mlle. Boulanger, in various American cities, is being arranged by the Symphony Society of New York.

Figure 3. Program, Grand Court of Wanamaker's Department Store,
Philadelphia, 9 January 1925.

# Program

*"And the night shall be filled with music"*
*—Longfellow*

1. FINALE FROM THE FIRST SONATA . . . *A. Guilmant*

2 a PIECE IN D MINOR . . . . . . . . . . . . . . . . . . . . *D. Scarlatti*

b SISTER MONICA . . . . . . . . . . . . . . . . . . . . *Franc. Couperin*
Transcribed by A. Guilmant

c TOMB OF COUPERIN . . . . . . . . . . . . . . . . . . *Maurice Ravel*
Forlane
Rigaudon
Toccata

3 a PRELUDE AND FUGUE IN E MINOR . . . . *J. S. Bach*

b PRELUDE AND FUGUE ON BACH . . . . . . . *Franz Liszt*

4 a PIECE FOUNDED ON POPULAR FLEMISH AIRS
*Nadia Boulanger*

b CRADLE SONG AND FINALE FROM
"THE FIRE-BIRD" . . . . . . . . . . . . . . . . . . . . *Strawinsky*
Transcribed by Maurice Begby

c PIECE IN B MINOR . . . . . . . . . . . . . . . . . . . . . . *M. de Falla*

d CORTEGE . . . . . . . . . . . . . . . . . . . . . . . . . . . . . *Lili Boulanger*

5 FINALE, FIRST SYMPHONY . . . . . . . . . . . . . . . . . *L. Vierne*

*PROGRAM NOTE—Among the numbers on this program are several which have been transcribed for organ from piano and orchestral scores by Mlle. Nadia Boulanger, including works by Ravel, de Falla, and Lili Boulanger, the talented sister of Mlle. Boulanger, who in her brief life revealed the fire of real genius—a flame which was unhappily quenched at the early age of twenty-four.*

Figure 3. continued

physically I am awkward—I played the Liszt well—from that moment on it was better—*Cortège*, which I had to encore, made a huge impression and sounds so good on the organ—it is so sweet for me to feel our little Lili associated with it all—she would be so happy to help me.[19] General appreciation, good overall impression, continuous control.

A big crowd afterward, signed masses of programs, saw a heap of touching people, Al Holden, the Forests, Smith, who came from New York (which cost him, because he had to stay over) so nervous and so happy afterward—the Wanamaker's people *truly kind*—the organ maker *touching*—the Wolffs—*what can I say*! Elizabeth Moore, Alwyne—supper with Katharine, her brother, Smith and Bulle.[20]

Saturday 9am train for New York—Madame de Forest taking the train so she could travel with me—*so kind*—so confident in me.[21] 11:00: children's concert, Carnegie Hall filled with little faces, most of them lively and interested.[22] Lunch at the Damrosches'—rehearsal with the baritone and Sam [Dushkin] who will play the works of the poor little one [Lili Boulanger] at the reception.[23] 4pm, Beethoven Association, reception for me organized by Damrosch—warm, lively—a heap of people each more charming than the next—Gange sings the *Psaume*, Sam plays *Nocturne et Cortège*—emotion, empathy.[24]

Sunday 9am organ at Aeolian Hall until 12:45, still with Smith, Katharine and Copland—Smith succeeds in arranging the combinations—I am less nervous—lunch. At 3:00, concert—my heart in my throat a little—Damrosch prepares my entry [and] I feel the atmosphere is warm, generous—Handel goes well, good combinations—*Funérailles* made a very great impression—reception of Copland clearly warm, a success—I feel better. An obvious empathy everywhere—lots of people, many friendly faces—Whitney Warren *touching*—tea with Mr. Surette, then at the Flaglers'[25]—everything is going well, you feel the confidence, the esteem— You take heart, want to do better, and feel more self-confident, among all these people who support you and appreciate you, more than you would like perhaps, but it does you good every now and then. I saw Coates, prepared by Roger [Sessions], more than kind and who would like me to come to Rochester as a professor[26]—Damrosch at his brother's here— Overall, an atmosphere of admiration that I have never encountered anywhere before—Smith's and Katharine's joy is touching. The orchestra and the staff, *touching*.

This morning, washed my hair—[then went to] Wanamaker's—lunched in Lower Manhattan, invited by Smith and Katharine—a really strong impression—the port—and everywhere these immense skyscrapers—excellent elevators—truly easy subway. What a singular portrait people paint of America for us!

**16 January 1925**. *Extract*.

Wednesday will remain one of the great days of my life—this first lecture was an inconceivable thing—I was sick over it.[27] Once on stage, I felt completely different, lighter, more polished, and the words came so simply, so well, almost in good English—the audience visibly in sympathy, interested—and I hadn't prepared a single word, not a program. How strange one can be!

Yesterday, recital at Wanamaker's—not bad, not too good, but a *big* audience—and yet the atmosphere was so touching. Big success for *Cortège* here as well!

I received some proposals from the Mannes School, though unacceptable—but it's a start. I really think there will be others—we will see. I saw a ton of people, former students—the Damrosches are very amused by what they call my shadows! It must be said that Smith, Katharine, Gerry, and Copland and Clurman are touching. Each has their own ideas and works silently and usefully—how much they have done for me!

**17 January 1925**. *Extract*.

We leave New York at 10am in radiant weather, Katharine and I—how I wish that you could see us—you would realize that between the fears you have for me, and reality, there is an unbridgeable gap—

We follow the banks of the Hudson, the sky and the water are marvelously blue, the cliffs abruptly dominate the opposite bank—and the ice brings white amid these warm colors—it's an admirable spectacle. We are comfortably installed in large swiveling seats, which allow us to look at everything—the wide windows and very long car allow us to see very far— Here, the river is almost entirely frozen—on the right, there are series of pine trees, in the middle of which are scattered *tiny* little houses—it seems almost strange on leaving New York to find, almost all of a sudden, this uninhabited, wild nature, for we go for "miles" without seeing a sign of habitation.

I want so much to give you an idea of life as it is—you would feel so much more calm and would see everything more clearly. Truly, you measure what a difference there always is between reality and the imagination, which interjects images that absence renders more vivid than facts. I am, I have been above all, very tired, because I have been tormenting myself—but now I understand better what remains for me to do, and my cursed bad habits can't prevent me from seeing that everything is better than I [had expected].

## CLEVELAND AND CHAMPAIGN (URBANA)
**24 January 1925**. *Extracts.*

### On the way to Houston

Exactly a month since I left the house—it seems like a year—I have to look far into the past, to see myself in my usual life—I've done so many things that the days seem to me to have multiplied. The two days spent in Cleveland were exquisite and I think among the best I will have.[28] The recital was hard, because I felt nervous the whole time, but I played better than in my other concerts. Afterward a reception at the director's house, Mr. Whitney more than happy—saw Ernest Bloch there, unchanged—his wife, a big woman of German extraction I think, dull at first, but then so intelligent and sensitive—his eldest daughter with beautiful eyes, a very ardent, spontaneous manner— Some charming women, bourgeois, enthusiastic; some men of the flabby type, not very expansive or eloquent, others lean and intense.[29] Always, everywhere, the same thing—more attraction, more individual than artistic action—once together, a gift of persuasion that creates immediate, one could say irrational, empathy.

Thursday, lecture at Mary Sanders's school—as a director in front of the children, an impenetrable, impassable stone wall—once relieved of the mask she wears in front of her mannequins, an old she-wolf with soft eyes.[30] Saw Bloch and his daughter again, the Quimbys, Mrs. Pray, Weyman very excited, a crowd all enthusiastic, Mary really happy.[31] Spent an hour at the Blochs', dined with them, an abundant hospitality, not knowing what to do. They gave me a piece of Indian jewelry, a little basket—the children, who are remarkable, wanted to give me everything—saw Sessions again—after dinner, the Moores were invited, we heard the quintet and the two sonatas, then the train at 11:15 accompanied by the Moores.[32] I had forgotten how beautiful his wife is—she is adorable—and two lovely little girls. Poor Bloch has a strange tic—he sticks his tongue halfway out, then folds it—it gives him a senile look—there is also something in the way his thoughts do not follow—has he been using drugs? But like everyone else they have been touching.

[ , .. ]

Arrived yesterday noon at Champaign (Urbana), found the Director, a former pupil of [André] Guilmant, with his old car—very likeable—loosening up little by little, happy to laugh and to chat—lunch with his charming wife. Visited the university, a wonder, you can't even imagine this world—everything so well organized for work, for comfort—everything new and clean—studios for the professors, the students, practice organs, a concert hall with a four-keyboard organ, which was muffled by the way—the lecture room where I spoke, with 1,800 seats, and the stadium that can fit *60,000(!)* spectators. Everywhere there are fantastic ideas, everywhere suddenly a desperate lack of taste—new things mingled with naïve reconstructions—what a shame, one could create so much beauty with such extraordinary resources.

A peaceful city, *with no walls*, little houses, most of them charming—trees, gardens, snow, sunshine—but not a single time except yesterday in Chicago, any real sensation of cold.

Dinner at the hotel—lecture fairly good I think—reception at the Director's house with the notables of the area, at first stiff as poles, all chanting "a true joy, *yes* indeed, a true joy" in a rhythm like machines, then everything loosened up—projects, exchange—and finally, something to drink.

[ , . . ]

The more I think about it what is lacking here, where so many things are found, is a little beauty and sophistication—everything is good, but so functional—and at the root of all this cleanliness such negligence—as if, disciplined, yes, but well-groomed, no! You are already so far from the cosmopolitan atmosphere of New York—and there, I am in no position to judge—if you know what the Damrosches have been to me, and *Katharine*, and Reynolds, and Smith, and everyone—

I will not talk in detail about the proposals made by Frank Damrosch—if, as our D[amrosch] thinks, Mannes is added to that, one could think about it entirely freely but . . . I don't feel myself sure enough even to talk to you seriously about it yet. Here comes my train for Saint Louis—I will continue later—can you imagine how my thoughts are with you every minute of the day, Maman?

I kiss you with all my heart. Your Nadia

## HOUSTON

**25 January 1925**. *Extracts. This and subsequent letters are written on stationery from the Rice Hotel of Houston, Texas.*

My good Maman,

Here I am at the end of my long voyage, without news from France, alas, but very well settled. Arrival in the cities here is definitely the most monotonous thing in the world: everything is made according to a single model without any imagination—and after a few days, one yearns to see something *beautiful*, just as in their devilish trains, one yearns after cold.[33] The lack of beauty is so great that it almost ends up causing physical pain—at Vassar, in Urbana, there is a certain atmosphere of intimacy that the large cities do not have— Industry, coal, practical activity—one has everywhere the impression that people are part of a mechanism—they, I mean as a group, never seem cheerful, never spontaneous—suffocated as they are by a uniformly dispensed and accepted discipline—taken individually, they are so kind, so generous. En masse, the perhaps sly but always lively aspect of the Negro seems to me, up to now, to have infinitely more character. All day long, crossing this poor, primitive countryside, where here and there little temporary, truly ugly shacks of wood are placed as if by chance—It looks as if people have become tired, just stopped, and constructed a shelter, without thinking of anything except protecting themselves—no fence, no garden—land that appears to be uncultivated, a house, several kilometers, two or three houses, a hangar that one guesses is the church, more kilometers, and thus, everywhere, life in isolation. Thinking, loving, creating—no. Eating, sleeping, producing, and that's it. God knows that I am warmly welcomed and one can strive usefully here, but outside of New York (a furnace) or a college (seclusion), I ask myself how one can live here for a long time—it's true that to see everything growing from day to day must be a joy—but not to know how to stop, not to know the joy of doing nothing, what intellectual poverty!

One has something of the impression that it is necessary to know everything, learn everything, see everything in a given time, and with the right system, nothing is impossible. Giving, dreams, poetry: one has the feeling that these things that men have lived for, no longer have a place.

It's true that these words are dictated by my disappointment. Houston, two hours from the Gulf of Mexico: I saw myself in an exotic city, with palm trees, almost with the scent of the sea! The traffic lights, the noise, the shops, the elevators, the anonymity: it's a suburb of New York. Discouraging for someone counting on a picturesque trip! Where then in this country are the regions that are still wild? In a few years they will have yielded their place to factories, to coal, to this miserable struggle for money. Gargenville, our little house, how I love them at this moment— how necessary their charm appears to me—and how much I love France, with its flaws, its old customs, and its backwardness—yet it is France that is in advance, by so much. The life of the mind is not widespread [here], it is not a need—and there is all the difference. One shouldn't be surprised— but . . . in spite of oneself, one awaits, as if one was made to wait forever at Bois Colombes![34] But without ever reaching Paris—there is no Paris—

I feel I am being mean—and probably unfair—surely unfair, like someone going from the Gare de l'Est to the rue de Steinkerque and not admiring Paris[35]—but . . . I needed palm trees, colorful Negroes, beautiful landscapes and I am Rice Hotel no. 1019!

After all, my room is excellent and the people are delightful—come on, I feel it's I who am wrong—I am demanding what I had no reason to expect—and so . . .

Following your advice, I wrote to Mrs. Wulfsin that I couldn't think of bothering her, since her husband is still ill, and I think everything is in order—Engles has prepared everything, tickets are bought, rooms reserved, people alerted—I only have to follow my way, and thank them all. In one month, my final concert, three days later the boat—how my heart will beat![36] And yet, I have been offered a magnificent opportunity—and such a useful experience. I will have learned a lot and will have extracted a lot from myself.

[ . . . ]

Here, everyone speaks of the poor Little One [Lili Boulanger] with so much emotion—Bloch found her *Psalm* so beautiful, so moving—she is intermingled with my life, always—and not a day of my life goes by without saying her name, while she is in my heart so much that even if I laugh, I can't forget it.

And you, Maman, you to whom I owe so much, and who have given me so much, why can I not resemble you more? I understand better and better the richness of your sincerity and the gift of your heart, that heart that has lived only for your loved ones and has forgotten only itself—

Letters [from France] are so rare—you are so far away—and I miss you so much—how to tell you—you wouldn't believe me! Give my love to everyone and believe me, feel me always your little

Nadia

**[30 January 1925**.] *Extract. This undated letter is written on Rice Hotel statio-nery. Between the previous letter of 25 January and this installment, Boulanger sent her mother several postcards, without any extensive text but with greetings such as "Thinking of you." Three cards picture Hopi children in Arizona and New Mexico, and one depicts a group of ten black Americans, adults and children, posed in a field, with the legend "Down Where the Cotton Blossoms Grow." These images represent the materialization and commodification of the exoticized expecta-tions Boulanger had of the American South and Southwest.*

Here I am, on my way—and this trip to Houston, which I was going to consider as an isolation treatment, is over.

Oh well, as for the accuracy of that prediction—

I arrived on Sunday afternoon—18-story hotel, crowd—cigars, shopkeepers—room on the tenth floor—no staff members visible, but everything at your disposal—telephone—bathroom—four dollars a day—

Found a charming letter from Mrs. Morgan, whom I met at Fontainebleau!

Went to have ice cream, tea—saw a church lit up, went in—the minister, friends—tried out the organ—immediately friendly atmosphere.

Monday, got up very late, and, in what still seems to me to be a miracle: springtime, not our springtime, but one of calm, a little heavy, full of sap, and almost tiring— Put on my walking legs, went out, found two organists in their churches—their ugly new churches, where without any sense of proportion, everything is imitated, copied and deformed.

Nice organs—musical level, very simple—walked some more, among the palms and camphor trees, between the little houses, some of them really ravishing, so comfortable and welcoming—

Visited that marvel that is the Rice Institute—saw everything, Chemistry, Physics—realized, and deplored, my ignorance—

In the event went to a concert with Mrs. Lovett, the wife of the president, who is rich, cultivated, kind, but so "done": mind, heart, everything controlled.[37] She also lives at the Rice Institute, very kindly invited me to supper with her little 13-year-old boy. She has classified everything here—people and things—and is precious—precious a little in both senses of the word, despite her physique, which is a bit too rounded and substantial to fit with so much puritanism.

Tuesday—snow, cold—worked from 11:00 to 1:00, returned to work— an excellent hall, built by the Masons, but used for concerts.

I crossed through the room for secret meetings, with all the [Masonic] symbols—how ridiculous, and how impoverished seems the man who, having renounced a religious faith, sacrifices to stupid conventions, to which all the most primitive superstitions are attached besides.

All this under the guidance of Mrs. Lovett [who is] very touching.

Introduction made this evening by the Dean, a man of about *forty years old* perhaps (how that represents this young country)—using the words Damrosch wrote about me in his book—words that I should pay for in diamonds![38]

Nothing very precise [technical] to say—people wouldn't have understood—but . . . I immediately won over the audience. No enthusiasm [but] visible respect, an extraordinary silence and an increasing warmth—I feel that everything goes well—a little supper with the Lovetts.

Wednesday, got up late, escaped this city, without a name, without a personality, all the cities are the same, but once away from the center, my good Negroes, the trees, the sky— Ah yes, the terrace of the hotel, on the 18th floor—the whole city lost below and an immensely extended view—

At 11:00 Miss Parks came to get me to see their organ—

Lunch at the Country Club—an absolutely lovely spot—with beautiful pine trees, magnificent rolling hills—women-only lunch—but very nice—several of them really charming and clever—the place was ideal—to be able to stay there for a week, how peaceful and charming—spring has returned, the heat is back, and only flowers are lacking.

[ . . . ]

Second lecture—more people, even more attention—a particular impression made by Fauré, Roussel, and the poor Little One [Lili Boulanger]—this, everywhere—

Introduction by Watkins the architect, clever, artistic—a very good evening afterward, impression of being truly with friends

A little supper at Miss Morgan's, who was so happy, having done everything to welcome me well—modest, a teacher, a little house where she lives all alone—but such an atmosphere—

Thursday morning got up late, talk for the teachers, worked—lunch at Mrs. Baker's with Mrs. Lovett, two other ladies, and the professor of French literature, Mr. Oberlé—charming lunch in a pretty little house—how much you would like it! And what a dessert—with whipped cream, to die for!

At 2:30, the concert of the famous Whiteman jazz orchestra—as a music hall attraction, amazing; as a concert, adulterated—25 musicians, 25 virtuosos and among the 25, at least 10 marvelous clowns. One in particular who played eleven or twelve instruments almost at the same time, he changed between them so fast—priceless—and admirable. All of it *vulgar*.

At 5:00 we went to the YCG, and there the Negroes who serve in the restaurant sang for me—behind the counter in a row, short, tall, thin, fat, ugly—ten women and two men—and suddenly, they and I forgot both the restaurant and the time, and everything—they started to rock from side to side, letting out from their sleepy, yet so melancholy hearts, the slow, obstinate, fervent, and monotonous song—what an hour I owe them![39] And how happy they were when I thanked them and said to them that our feelings were one and that we could understand each other so well—

I gave them a tip, but it wasn't that that gave them most pleasure—"Come soon again, come soon again" they repeated with their eyes suddenly happy—and once we were in the kitchen you would have said they were a band of clowns suddenly delivered from fear. From that kind of fear that makes them sometimes sly—always sad, and as if they are solitary—

Lecture in the evening, on Stravinsky

Supper at Mrs. Spach's house, flowers from Miss Hogg—[40]

What useful work accomplished here—I am really pleased—it's not through talent that I won them over, but through the heart—and they all thanked me so much, and music won overall—

I came back at 1am, quickly did up my suitcase, went to bed—and at 6:30 Mr. Oberlé was there with his car to take me to Galveston. So I have seen the Gulf of Mexico, and that furnished me with some special hours . . . some hours of home, of our culture. Oh, I forgot to say that it was the philosophy professor, Mr. Tsanoff, a Bulgarian, who introduced me on the third evening, very kindly, and he was so happy with the lecture—that gave me so much pleasure.[41] Where was I?–Oberlé is a little Alsatian man, modest, doubtless a superior man, certainly very good, who adores his students, and speaks slowly with a true Strasbourg accent—so delighted to have European contact, and to drop the hypocritical veil of virtue that covers everything here—what a clean sweep would be needed to rediscover spontaneity, and from there, imagination. We came back at noon as he was so afraid I would miss my train, but we had 45 minutes. Mrs. Lovett had taken care of my ticket, brought my luggage, so all I had to do was chat with her at the station and get on the train. I found the same Negroes as on the outward trip, my strawberries and cream—I think a diet is going to be necessary—slept like a log—arrived here [Saint Louis] at 11:30 and—here I am after a sumptuous lunch, installed at Mrs. Kroeger's—[42]

How truly kind all these people are—a beautiful house, lovely room and so much simplicity—They are awaiting me for a walk, so I will continue my journal tomorrow—but Saturday the *4th* [March] departure—And I will miss this life to a certain extent—but . . . what happiness!

There is much more to say about Houston—they have the sun—and it's a hope of life—

Oh! I *had* to buy a coat there—after looking all over, wound up in a men's tailor's and found one for 25 dollars—otherwise it would have been at least 50 dollars.

I have to run—Maman, Maman, how I miss you, and how much more I admire you, compared to all this conventionality—

You'll come [to meet me] at Le Havre, won't you? But patiently, because there are often delays.

I kiss you with all my heart, your little Nadia

## SAINT LOUIS

**[30 January 1925]** *Complete text. This letter is written on three postcards from the Cleveland Museum of Art. Boulanger had purchased them there on her way through Cleveland before going to Houston. The first is a postcard of the exterior of the museum, and is marked "De Houston à St Louis," indicating these were written on the train and sent once she arrived. The other two cards show two views of the interior courtyard of the museum.*

### From Houston to Saint Louis

Here is where I played last Wednesday—a nice venue even though it is too new.

I've received the cards and will send them back to you right away.[43] The day finished this evening in such a moving manner, in a way that makes one feel infused with the spirit of God. I found again, in car R, my fine Negro porter who recognized me—we had a big conversation—how nice [*sympathique*] they are, those that are nice, for I don't know where they come from, and they are all very different from each other—one thing is the same, though, and that is the way they are treated. But it's a dangerous game, and I think the day that a movement begins it will be a lot worse than the Russian Revolution—one understands the problems that exist—but after all, these waiting rooms—"for whites" "for colored"—it's dreadful—and so painful—and besides, with all the white they make them wear, all starched and shiny—they have such an ugly, clumsy, and disguised air about them—

Tomorrow is Saturday—on the 4th [March] France—what a joy—though I am treated better here than I have ever been in France—the need, of you Maman above all, but also of our old streets, our old churches, the Past—how it is lacking here—it is beautiful to see life *growing* here—I understand, I feel it—but I need home.

Maybe tomorrow some letters from Saint Louis—not much to say now, this news is already so old—give everyone my best wishes, and to you, Maman, all my heart, Nadia

**2 February 1925**. *Extract. This letter is written on stationery from 5284 Westminster Place, Saint Louis, the home of the Kroeger family.*

My good Maman,

Just a note, before leaving Saint Louis—it has been a real success here—they would like me to come next year for at least three lectures—really made a great impression—many professionals [in the audience], serious—I had an excellent hour. The atmosphere was so friendly, I found myself in good form—and from my first words, felt that I could let myself be carried along by the emotion and interest that the subject inspired in me. For I improvise like nobody's business—I do a class, as if for friends, on a large scale—and with heart, with sincerity, one definitely forges immediate bonds.

You can't imagine what the Kroegers have been for me—everything was done to make my stay charming—and I am really touched. Saturday, 14 guests for lunch—the same thing yesterday—today, after the lecture, which was at 11:00, we went to lunch in a restaurant with Mrs. Kroeger, her daughter and a charming friend. Don't let anyone tell you the food is bad here: it's my downfall, I am reveling in it.

And then, I should say that this morning I had real joy in feeling that I could create emotion as I pleased—I never would have thought I could do that—and, to tell the truth, without nerves—beforehand, yes—but once on stage, I simply feel like myself. Today, though a different type [of talk], it went as well as it did at the Mannes School.

I received a pile of interesting letters—I think that Hanson is going to propose Rochester for me, Miss Ely is working on Curtis, the Damrosch family, both the brother and the sister, are wrestling over me— Maybe we will not accept anything, but how much I owe already to Fairchild, Damrosch and Flagler—oh yes, and Fairchild is working on Juilliard! Whatever the future brings, I will have gained great professional reputation—and friendships—and I should thank God. Marcelle [de Manziarly] counted so much on this trip! I am a little tired, but very well, in very good form—My voice makes its impression—and you can be proud of having worked so hard—I laugh—but sincerely, everything is going so much better than I expected.[44]

[. . .]

## BOSTON

**19 February 1925**. *Extracts.*

My dear Maman,
What a week—charming—successful—but what a whirlwind—I am dazed—I fall into bed at night like an animal without even thinking of reading, or of doing anything at all.

Much to tell you, but before tomorrow, very little time—for as soon as I'm alone, the spring releases, and I feel my need of sleep and am overwhelmed by an *inexpressible* lethargy. But I feel very well, happy and in absolutely excellent health. Only surprised to forget even that life is too fevered at the moment, as soon as I have something to do—

At Bryn Mawr, two truly unforgettable days—at Swarthmore, an exquisite reception—here . . . almost too many friends. Monday the talk for children was a veritable enchantment—as for the rehearsals with Koussevitsky, it's a joy—all is going well and I think that it will be a great success—yesterday evening Caroline, such a warm atmosphere—it's really touching.

I am completely in agreement about the projects and *have not made up my mind to come at all,* I am only happy to have so many offers—but how I will reflect on it before saying yes—and in any case, there was no question I would decide anything without having spoken to you about it. Could you really think that would have occurred to me? Besides, I think it would only be worth thinking about seriously starting at $15,000—otherwise there would be no point—and even in that case, I am not certain it would be the right step—we will see.

[ . . . ]

I received just now your letter with the news from Brussels—how sad I am not to have been there—I feel that truly, there was some of that emotion that escapes all analysis and that everyone gave the best of themselves to bring to life the works of our Little One. I will write to Madame DuBois and Mr. Systermans.[45] It is so sweet to think that little by little, the works are taking their rightful place, prolonging her memory, creating such tenderness, such emotion around such a poor, short little life. The other day, at Bryn Mawr, when I finished the *Psaume*, there was such a long moment of silence, that you would have thought hearts had stopped—then, such applause—and so many people coming up to me, having understood. The whole hall, all at once, united in such respect—I couldn't say anything further to those who rushed toward me, in order to go to Her. It is Fauré and [Lili] who will have dominated this trip—because in order to speak, between my admiration and my grief, the words came up from my heart to go toward others' hearts—and then, people understand.

The final days have come, and on the point of leaving, of finishing, it is toward our Little One that all my thoughts are turning—she put so much into my life that her memory has changed me—and it seems as if she guides and inspires me.

I think of you, Maman—and kiss you with all my heart, Nadia

**22 February 1925**. *Extracts*.

My dear Maman,
Now the two concerts are done—and I am so happy that everything went so well. I played fairly well—the Handel—and even if I definitely do not feel myself to be a virtuoso, the effect was really good. Friday, the audience was divided during Copland's Symphony—without *protesting* (that isn't done here) but you could feel how painful the breathing was—how much those dissonances shocked well-bred ears. Still, the really extraordinary ending forced people to emerge from their attitude and many of them sincerely showed an interest. The *Funérailles* was very well played, and listened to with an extraordinary and moving attention—the impression it produced was truly profound.

Yesterday, the whole program received a warmer welcome—and I played better.

At the end of the second movement of the Copland, a cipher forced us to stop—but everyone understood (it has happened frequently) and one felt a real sympathy from the audience besides—great success for Copland's work.[46] As for *Funérailles*, a welcome even more moving than the previous night—the orchestra, Koussevitsky, the audience—one felt that everyone was moved to the bottom of their hearts. As for the welcome received here—it's incredible—everyone so kind—I never knew I had so many friends here.

Tuesday dinner at the Greenes', Wednesday, after the rehearsal, children's talk, completely successful—all around me little attentive, laughing faces. Lunch at Miss Nourse's, practiced the organ, evening at Caroline's, very successful as I already told you—Thursday, rehearsal, lunch at the Koussevitskys'—very interesting—there is such a mix of sincerity, of emotion and of savvy in them—she is so intelligent, he, such a force, such intuition, without depths—but what a leader. Lunched in the Russian style, in a house all white and bright, at the edge of a little lake—

Rehearsal with the Glee Club, admirably directed by Davison and Thomson—what a lovely effect from those 250 young voices.[47]

[ . . . ]

This will no doubt be the last letter that you will receive before you see me—I haven't fixed any appointments—I think I will need a few days on coming home—for, besides the exhaustion, I need to see a few people at the Ministry, it's very important—and also to breathe a little—I've drawn from the well so much that I need to relax. But how happy I am to have made this trip, how much I have gained in authority, and how many friends I have made. This will mean more students in the future, unless something unexpected happens.

[ . . . ]

Is there any need to tell you how impatient I am—it seems to me as if Saturday will never come! With all my heart I kiss you my little Maman,

Your Nadia

# AFTERWORD:
## THOUGHTS FROM OUR CONVERSATION
### GAYLE MURCHISON

Jeanice Brooks ran into me in November 2019 at the Boston meeting of the American Musicological Society. She excitedly told me about the 2020 Bard Music Festival on "Nadia Boulanger and Her World" and her work in editing the festival companion volume. Among her own contributions was the translation of Boulanger's letters to her mother sent during a tour of the United States in early 1925. I, too, was excited about the Bard project, as I had written a book on Aaron Copland, and included chapters about Copland's study with Boulanger.[48] In conducting research in the Aaron Copland Collection at the Library of Congress in Washington, D.C., I had read courteous, respectful, and affectionate letters Copland wrote his teacher and mentor. Our conversation continued over dinner in early January in London.

In providing me with an overview of the letters project, Brooks's narrative centered around two events that occurred during Boulanger's trip. The first was a spontaneous performance by African American workers at a Houston restaurant where Boulanger was dining. The second involved Boulanger's conversation with an African American Pullman porter during two train trips coming and going from Houston. Having spent her youth in the United States, Brooks was aware of the importance of these two incidents, and thus, the need for addressing the issue of race in discussing Nadia Boulanger's 1925 tour of the United States. The topic of race—and racism—had to be addressed, but how?

Without a doubt, race is part of any discussion of American music, music in the United States, or the circulation of American music and musicians outside the country, as well as within it. And, as historical musicology slowly recognizes these facts and more musicologists adopt critical race studies as part of their methodology more broadly, race is being addressed in studies of the canon and Western classical music in general, alongside gender and, increasingly, class. All three of these issues come to bear, we both understood, on what Brooks was describing. Brooks sought my insight and advice on how to write about a subject so many in the Global North find to be a delicate and too often controversial topic even simply to talk about, and one that has been long in coming to the field of American modernist music. Over the course of our London conversation, Brooks sought something more formalized, and this essay began to take shape. As we talked, I took out my sketchbook, as sketching what interests me is one of my activities. Having come late to art, I seek less to capture my subject as though I were taking a photograph. Rather, I focus on what I see as the essence and try to present that as best I can.

And so it is with this essay. Rather than definitively trying to argue one thing or another about what is in the letters Brooks chose, my approach is rather to ask questions about the sources and what they *do not tell* or what they *do not do*. For what is absent in Boulanger's account reveals far more about her trip, and what she might have seen or learned or experienced, than what she actually describes in her postcards and letters home to her mother. In the course of reading the letters and Brooks's commentary, I came to realize that this is one of those situations in research where, given the source materials at hand and the scope of what one is asked to consider, one cannot possibly *answer* a lot of questions. Rather, one can only open avenues for future research by formulating a set of questions to ask, and offering suggestions about approaches to answering them. Thus, that is the primary focus of my essay.

Boulanger's missives are at once tender letters home and a travelogue. With respect to the latter, they are both in the spirit of Charles Burney's musical account of his 1770 voyage through Europe (albeit with descriptions of the music scene in the United States), and they are a diary of a visit to what for Boulanger (and other Europeans of the time) was an exotic place. Indeed, the United States was an ocean away, and a country known to her primarily through contact with her American students. Musically, the United States was unfamiliar terrain as well. It was a nation that was still developing with respect to the cultivated Western European classical tradition that Boulanger herself was helping to shape. The opening of the Conservatoire américain in 1921 positioned Boulanger to become, by 1925, one of the most influential figures then shaping American music, as her students such as Aaron Copland, Roger Sessions, Virgil Thomson, and others returned home and their works came to represent American musical modernism. For her American hosts, Boulanger represented the best of what French musical institutions and musical culture had to offer. They aimed to show her what they understood to be the best of American institutions. Narrowly, they were blinded by race.

**Institutions and Venues, and the Traces of Segregation**
I will examine the two incidents around which our conversation centered below. Now, I want to begin by examining the question not of what venues Boulanger was programmed into, but which venues were excluded. Or, if approached another way: which institutions—and thus, audiences—were excluded from Boulanger's itinerary? This forces the issue of segregation

directly to the forefront. We confront the question: what could Boulanger have known about segregation, both *de facto* and *de jure*?

No matter where she was in the United States in 1925, Boulanger moved in segregated spaces, and as a white European woman, moved with an ease and privilege of which she would have been largely unaware. As Boulanger traveled in the North and parts of the Midwest, she found herself in public spaces that were not legally segregated, but to which African Americans had limited access. Schools, universities, and conservatories largely denied admission to African American students and barred employment of African American faculty and instructors. When black students were admitted to conservatories such as Oberlin and New England Conservatory, they were forced to live apart from other students. While concert halls and other public venues in New York or Philadelphia did not deny entry to African Americans, the spaces were segregated through practices such as seating them in the balcony. In Southern states, African Americans were barred entry altogether. Thus, the venues where Boulanger spoke and performed were not spaces that permitted integrated audiences; these were not spaces where blacks were welcomed. One wonders if and how much Boulanger noticed the absence of African American or other students of color in the places where she was invited to speak and perform in the Northeast and Midwest, or whether she was aware that they were segregated in this fashion.

Boulanger's letters do not record encounters with any black musicians, instructors, faculty, teachers, or other black classical musicians. Yet there were prominent, well-known African American classical composers, singers, and instrumentalists in the places she visited, such as Roland Hayes, Nathaniel Dett, and William Grant Still, for example. The latter was a student of Edgar Varèse, and, here at the beginning of his career, his works appeared on the same programs as those of her own former student, Aaron Copland. By 1925, the Harlem Renaissance was well underway, and concert singers such as Roland Hayes, Jules Bledsoe, and Florence Cole Talbert had established themselves as major interpreters of the classical repertoire. As these musicians performed in venues such as Aeolian Hall and with major orchestras, one wonders why Boulanger's hosts such as Walter Damrosch did not introduce her to black classical singers or composers.

Another question comes to mind: Boulanger does not mention encountering the students and faculty from, or traveling to, historically black colleges and universities (HBCUs) where a vast number of black musicians, including classical and some jazz and church musicians, were trained. She certainly would have had opportunity to do so, for there are HBCUs in the places she visited. Philadelphia, for example, has both Cheney and Lincoln Universities; both schools were well-established and had been in existence long before her arrival—Lincoln since 1854 and Cheney since 1837. Cleveland offered two major ways for Boulanger to encounter black musicians. First, nearby Oberlin had long enrolled African American students in general, and admitted black musicians and artists as students. Second, two major HBCUs—Wilberforce and Central State Universities—are located within half a day's drive. Though they were further away than Oberlin, it would not have presented an onerous obstacle for organizers to connect Boulanger with blacks at these institutions. While in Houston, Boulanger could have visited Prairie View A&M in Prairie View and Huston-Tillotson in Austin, both of which were only two to three hours away by car. Boulanger's hosts could easily have reached out to area HBCUs; they could have invited music faculty, students, and ensembles from these schools to attend her lecture—or even perform for her—or arranged visits for her to these campuses. But in reality, such gestures would not have entered the minds of Boulanger's hosts, and she would not have known to ask. In short, there were numerous opportunities for Boulanger to have encountered both African American student musicians and faculty who were her peers. But, clearly, no one conceived of things this way.

There would have been an audience for Boulanger among African Americans. Both students and faculty—including French-language faculty— would have welcomed a chance to at the very least greet such an esteemed international figure. Having Boulanger meet African American classical musicians and HBCU students and faculty, as well as African Americans studying at predominantly white institutions, would have enriched Boulanger. She had encountered black Americans in France on a very limited basis, and had heard African American jazz while in France. Now, she was *in situ,* as Brooks writes. Here, I introduce the following question: had Boulanger seen, heard, and interacted with blacks in Europe—Francophone Africans and Caribbeans, for example? As students, for example, or in capacities in which she encountered them as workers? Where and how can we know more about such encounters and interactions? Is this to be found in diaries, letters, or other documents? And how would her earlier interactions with black people in general have informed her voyage to the United States? Would she have harbored prejudices against Africans who were French colonial subjects that she would not have harbored against African Americans? Would she have been more receptive to black Americans and their music, whether jazz or spirituals, than to the music of sub-Saharan or Caribbean people? Did she differentiate among these various groups? Or more bluntly: did she exoticize African Americans in a way that she did not black French colonial subjects?

### Gender: The Club Woman and Patron

A further question involves the intersection of race and gender in Boulanger's experience. In our conversation, Brooks underscored the importance of elite patronage as she discussed what brought Boulanger to Rice. Central to not just Rice, but Boulanger's visit more generally, was the patronage and private philanthropy of wealthy white American women. Whether from "Old Money" families or those with recently acquired industrial fortunes, these elite women were typically versed in music and art, with varying degrees of training, from dilettante to professional, included in their education or "finishing." One such woman, Ima Hogg, helped bring Boulanger to Houston, and throughout her tour she regularly spoke for, or was hosted by, cultural and community groups led by women.

There were parallels to these wealthy white philanthropists in African American communities. Among their leaders were many prominent middle-class, and sometimes affluent, college-educated women who were often referred to as "Club Women." These were members of Black Womens Clubs, which were also to be found in Texas; indeed, the state had a governing Texas Federation of Colored Women's Clubs. The Texas organization was part of a larger movement of black women's clubs, spearheaded by figures such as Mary Church Terrell, the founder of the National Association of Colored Women. Terrell and Josephine St. Pierre Ruffin brought together a range of black women's organizations when they founded the National Association of Colored Womens Clubs. The NACWC has as its motto (still today), "Lifting as we climb." It was more than a social organization, for it also provided a range of resources, educational and social services while working to improve the lives of women and children, including advocating women's suffrage. Also popular among middle-class and college-educated African Americans were literary and music clubs, as well as related community and professional musical ensembles that cultivated classical music. Had the organizers of Boulanger's tour reached out to members of various Black Women's Clubs, she could have lectured and performed for black classical music audiences and found patrons—and, potentially, students for her summer school, and private students among them. The experience would have further enriched Boulanger: she would have gained a gendered perspective on specific issues facing black American women, as well as learned much about African American women's social and cultural activism.

## Boulanger's Racialism

The excerpts Brooks provides do inform us of some of Boulanger's own attitudes toward race, albeit in a limited fashion. Her letter of 12 January 1925 is informative: here we see Boulanger making comparisons between light-complected African Americans in the United States and in France. In describing the architect Julian Abele, fiancé of her former student, the French pianist Marguerite Bulle, Boulanger writes that he is what "we would politely call *café au lait*." Here, Boulanger chooses to use a term that is less derogatory than others that referred to biracial or mixed-race persons of African and European ancestry. In other words, she clearly knew that a more racist term existed, but chose not to invoke it in this letter. Boulanger's politesse signals a genteel bourgeois sensibility that eschews vulgarism, yet is not uncomfortable with its own racialism.

In our conversation, Brooks particularly focused on Boulanger's letter of 30 January, written on three Cleveland Museum of Art postcards. After describing the venue to her mother, Boulanger recounts how she encountered the same Pullman porter on the outbound train who had attended her on the way to Houston from Cleveland and departing Houston for Saint Louis. Here, Brooks wisely chose this letter, for it offers Boulanger's frank assessment of racism and race relations. Boulanger clearly recognizes that segregation cannot be sustained. As she further exoticizes African Americans, she also is to a degree perceptive and recognizes their plight. Yet, both what she writes and the circumstances that gave rise to her writing are troubling. In referring to the "white they make them wear, all starched and shiny"—from the white uniforms of the restaurant staff she encounters in Houston to those of the Pullman porters—we learn that the African Americans Boulanger has interacted with have all been in service positions. The way she conjoins race and economics is clear. Boulanger learned from the porter about economic disparity at the very least, and she herself remarked upon what she saw of substandard housing. She was clearly aware that race aside, she held different social standing. Though living in somewhat genteel, financially straitened circumstances in France, she was both of high social status and education. Yet, she clearly was not tone-deaf, as it were, and she perceived nuances in the way the black restaurant staff behaved towards white patrons, sensing something perhaps her hosts did not. As a French woman with a Russian mother and knowledge of history, Boulanger understood not just the need for change in terms of the end of segregation, but also that a fundamental end to such inequities was needed.

Boulanger was largely left on her own when it came to encounters with black Americans. Had she been introduced to a wider range of African

Americans on her tour, her attitudes would have been more thoroughly challenged. The omission of formal introduction to the fullest possible range of members of the African American music community—from cabaret and nightclub entertainers such as Eubie Blake and others of *Shuffle Along*, to Louis Armstrong or Fletcher Henderson; to concert singers such as Roland Hayes and Paul Robeson, or composers such as William Grant Still or Will Marion Cook or countless others of whom Damrosch and Leopold Stokowski would have been aware; to the educators, students and patrons who cultivated music in every city she visited—shaped her tour in profound ways.

African American academics and scholars often speak of having conversations—of engaging in dialogue with canons, hegemonic discourses, or of (as Henry Louis Gates, Jr. would invoke) signifyin(g). And one core of African American intellectual history has always engaged with the question of what is missing from the record as the starting place for intellectual query and research. And so it is here. I have sketched what is missing from the present record in hopes that the essence of what could have been can now be envisioned. Moreover, what is presently documented can be seen in sharper relief as we understand that the essence of Boulanger's visit turned on segregation, which excluded her from a significant and rich part of American musical culture.

# NOTES

1. Further on Boulanger's tour, see Jeanice Brooks, *The Musical Work of Nadia Boulanger* (Cambridge: Cambridge University Press, 2013), 29–31; Léonie Rosenstiel, *Nadia Boulanger: A Life in Music* (New York: W. W. Norton, 1982), 174–89.

2. On the series and its goals, see Walter B. Bailey, "Ima Hogg and an Experiment in Audience Education: The Rice Lectureship in Music (1923–33)," *Journal of the Society for American Music* 5 (2011): 395–426; on Boulanger's Rice Lectures, see Kimberly Francis, "'Everything Had to Change': Nadia Boulanger's Translation of Modernism in the Rice Lecture Series, 1925," *Journal of the Society for American Music* 7/4 (2013): 363–81. And see Brooks, "Modern French Music," in this volume.

3. For example, Boulanger's fee in Houston was $500 less than that offered to other speakers; see Francis, "'Everything Had to Change,'" 364.

4. Robert Delaney (1903–1956), originally from Baltimore, studied at the Ecole Normale de Musique and privately with Boulanger between 1922 and 1927.

5. The list of people who met Boulanger at the dock included several former students—Aaron Copland, Virgil Thomson, Alonzo Elliott, Gerald Reynolds—and Copland's Paris roommate, the writer Harold Clurman, who had become an honorary member of the Boulangerie during Copland's studies. George Engles was the manager of the New York Symphony Society and the principal organizer of Boulanger's tour dates.

6. The American composer and diplomat Blair Fairchild (1877–1933) lived mainly in Paris but made frequent visits to New York. He collaborated closely with the Boulanger sisters on their wartime charity work and became an important mentor for Nadia.

7. The storms during the *Aquitania*'s crossing were so severe that the arrival was two days later than scheduled, and it was expected there would be even more substantial delays.

8. The telegrams were both from Americans welcoming Boulanger to the United States (Douglas Moore, Alberta Cobleigh) and her French friends and colleagues (Annette Dieudonné, Thérèse Hansen) sending good wishes for her trip. Harry Harkness Flagler, whose fortune came from the Standard Oil business cofounded by his father, was the president of the New York Symphony Society and a principal sponsor for Boulanger's tour. Lucien Wulsin II was the director of the Baldwin Piano Company, which he had inherited on his father's death in 1912. Baldwin was among the backers for Boulanger's tour, and advertisements asserting her endorsement of the company's instruments featured in many of her concert programs.

9. The composer and educator Howard Hanson (1896–1981) had been appointed director of the Eastman School of Music in 1924, the same year he made his conducting debut with the New York Symphony at Damrosch's invitation.

10. Melville Smith (1898–1962) began organ studies with Boulanger at the Ecole Normale de Musique in the autumn of 1920 after completing his degree at Harvard. He became the director of the Longy School of Music in Cambridge, helping to create a post for Boulanger there during World War II.

11. Margaret Chanler, née Terry (1862–1952) was a prominent New York socialite, author, and musician. Her son Theodore Chanler was Boulanger's student in Paris. Saunders is likely the noted American photographer Silvia Saunders (1901–1924).

12. Georges Barrère, who joined the New York Symphony in 1905, was a major exponent of the French style of flute playing in the United States. The internationally acclaimed Polish violinist Paweł (Paul) Kochanski had recently emigrated; he made his debut with the orchestra in 1921 and began teaching at Juilliard in 1924. The Ukrainian composer and conductor Lazare Saminsky had moved to New York in 1920; he was music director of Temple Emanu-El between 1924 and 1926 and founded the League of Composers in 1923. Lawyer Thomas Finletter was the husband of Damrosch's daughter

Gretchen. Melville Smith had an unrequited passion for Boulanger, who had rejected his advances in 1922.

13. Dr. Pierre Kouindjy (1862–1928) was a leading Parisian doctor, author of numerous works on physical therapy.

14. John Wanamaker's New York store already had an organ in the mid-19th century; a new instrument was installed in 1902, when a 1,300-seat auditorium was included in a new annex to the store. The Wanamaker Grand Court organ in Philadelphia is the largest functioning pipe organ in the world. Originally built for the 1904 Saint Louis World's Fair, it was substantially expanded between 1911 and 1917 after it was installed in John Wanamaker's department store in Philadelphia. On the importance of department-store concerts to American musical culture in this period, see Linda L. Tyler, "'Commerce and Poetry Hand in Hand': Music in American Department Stores, 1880–1930," *Journal of the American Musicological Society* 45/1 (1992): 75–120.

15. Boulanger's near-exact contemporary Marcel Dupré (1887–1971) was the most famous organist of their generation; his first, wildly successful, American tour had been in 1921, launching his career as a touring virtuoso. The Italian organist and organ composer Marco Bossi (1861–1925) had arrived in November for a recital tour of New York and Philadelphia; during his return he died at sea in February 1925. The Belgian organ virtuoso Charles Courboin (1884–1974) had overseen the expansion of the Wanamaker's organ in Philadelphia. Boulanger had arrived at the store intending to practice, but the presence of her famous colleagues and the press made it impossible.

16. The French pianist Marguerite Bulle studied with Boulanger in Paris before moving to New York. She married the leading architect Julian Abele in 1925. The first black person to graduate from the University of Pennsylvania in 1902, Abele was responsible for designs for Harvard's Widener Library, the Philadelphia Museum of Art, and the campus of Duke University.

17. Leopold Stokowski had become director of the Philadelphia Orchestra in 1912.

18. The Marquiset de Laumont family were part of Parisian high society; Armand Marquiset (1900–1981) studied with Boulanger and had some success as a composer in the 1920s before devoting his career to charity work.

19. Lili Boulanger's *Cortège* (1914) was originally written for solo piano, and the following year was premiered by Lili and the violinist Emile Mendels in a version for piano and violin. Her contract with Ricordi for the publication of both versions was signed in January 1918 a few months before her death, and Nadia supervised the publication herself in 1919. Nadia likely made the organ arrangement especially for her tour.

20. Horace Alwyne (1891–1974) had become the head of the music department at Bryn Mawr College in 1924. I have been unable to identify Elizabeth Moore.

21. Madame de Forest may be May de Forest Payne, who published a melodic index to the works of J. S. Bach in 1938.

22. Damrosch pursued a wide range of music appreciation activities with the New York Symphony and other organizations. Boulanger was particularly impressed with his children's concerts and had discussed them in an article on the orchestra's 1920 European tour. Nadia Boulanger, "Walter Damrosch et le New-York Symphony Orchestra à Paris," *Le Monde musical* 31/9–10 (May 1920): 156–57.

23. The violinist Samuel Dushkin (1891–1976) was a protégé of Blair Fairchild. After studies in Paris in New York he began an active touring career in 1918. He had made his first appearance with the New York Symphony in 1924, shortly before Boulanger's arrival.

24. Damrosch was an associate member of the Beethoven Association, a New York society founded by Harold Bauer in 1919. See Laura Tunbridge, *Singing in the Age of Anxiety: Lieder Performances in New York and London Between the World Wars* (Chicago:

University of Chicago Press, 2018), 101–3. Fraser Gange was a Scottish baritone who made his New York debut in 1924.

25. The American architect Whitney Warren had been the main sponsor of the Boulanger sisters' Comité franco-américain du Conservatoire during World War I. The composer Thomas Whitney Surette (1861–1941) was a crusader for music appreciation, which he promoted through his Concord Summer School of Music (founded in 1915) and at Bryn Mawr College. He was the first curator of the department of music at the Cleveland Museum of Art, where Boulanger gave an organ recital during her tour.

26. Albert Coates became the director of the Rochester Philharmonic Orchestra in 1923. Roger Sessions studied with Boulanger's friend Ernest Bloch at the Cleveland Institute. Sessions was close to Aaron Copland, and had met Boulanger in Paris the year before her tour. Bloch himself was teaching at the Eastman School of Music in Rochester in February 1925, and this passage suggests that Boulanger was being sounded out for similar work via this network.

27. Boulanger lectured at the David Mannes School, which had been founded in 1916 by David Mannes, former concertmaster of the New York Symphony (1903–12), and his wife, the pianist Clara Mannes, née Damrosch (Walter Damrosch's sister).

28. Boulanger played the new organ at the Cleveland Museum of Art, which had been dedicated in 1922. See William Osborne, *Music in Ohio* (Kent, OH: Kent State University Press, 2004), 201–2.

29. Boulanger had known the composer Ernest Bloch (1880–1959) since his studies in Paris in 1903–4 and admired his music. Bloch had come to the United States in 1916; he taught at the Mannes School from 1917 to 1920 and became founding director of the Cleveland Institute of Music, 1920–25. His oldest daughter, Suzanne, began studies with Boulanger in Paris later in 1925, and went on to become a noted lutenist and early music advocate.

30. I have been unable to identify Mary Sanders; Boulanger may have been referring to Martha Bell Sanders, a Cleveland musical activist and the first executive director of the Cleveland Institute of Music. Osborne, *Music in Ohio*, 195.

31. Boulanger's former pupil Arthur Quimby was teaching in the music department of Western Reserve University in Cleveland.

32. Douglas Moore studied in Paris in 1919–21 and attended Boulanger's group classes in rue Ballu. He moved to Cleveland in 1921 to take a post at the Cleveland Museum of Art under Thomas Whitney Surette. He gave Boulanger's *Airs populaires flamands* its American premiere there in 1922. Moore returned to Paris for a final year of study with Boulanger in 1925.

33. Boulanger admired the efficiency and layout of American trains—and included a drawing of her Pullman car in her previous letter—but found them overheated.

34. Bois-Colombes is a northwest suburb of Paris, about nine kilometers from the center, and was substantially built up in the late nineteenth century. Its development was relatively recent at the time Boulanger was writing, and from Paris it was necessary to go through or near it to get to the Boulangers' country house in Gargenville.

35. This route would take you from the Gare de l'Est, in front of the Gare du Nord and up through Barbès, seeing only the railway stations, a hospital, and the architecturally unremarkable poor and working-class areas around them.

36. Boulanger was originally meant to stay at the Wulfsins' on the way back from Houston.

37. Edgar Odell Lovett was president of the Rice Institute and the director of the lecture series.

38. Boulanger was introduced by William Ward Watkin, a professor of architecture. He quoted Damrosch's appreciation of Boulanger from *My Musical Life* (New York: Scribner, 1923), 265: "Among women, I have never met her equal in musicianship and

indeed there are very few men who can compare with her. She is one of the finest organ-ists of France, an excellent pianist and the best reader of orchestral scores that I have ever known."

39. There is no organization with the initials YCG in the 1925 Houston city directory; Boulanger may have been referring to the YMCA or the YWCA, which both had cafeteria restaurants. My thanks to Ginger Berni of the Houston Heritage Society for her help in tracking Boulanger's reference.

40. The Houston musical activist Ima Hogg was the principal financial backer and cofounder of the Rice Institute Lectures on Music. Mrs. Spach may have been a relative of Boulanger's pupil, the organist Barrett Spach, who studied with her in Paris in the mid-1920s.

41. Dr. Radoslav Tsanoff (1887–1976) was a professor of philosophy at the Rice Institute.

42. Boulanger stayed with the composer Ernst Kroeger (1862–1934) and his wife, Laura Kroeger, née Clark. Ernst Kroeger became director of the music department of Washington University in Saint Louis in 1925.

43. Likely a reference to samples for invitations to the memorial service for Lili Boulanger planned for March, discussed in several previous letters.

44. Earlier letters make it clear that before the tour Boulanger had taken lessons from her mother, who was a professionally trained singer, on vocal production and projection.

45. A concert featuring some of Lili Boulanger's works took place in Brussels while Nadia was away. Georges Systermans was a Belgian music critic.

46. A cipher is an unwanted noise on the organ caused when a pipe remains open. Some reviews of the concert noted that Copland's Symphony had to be stopped so that the tuner could fix the problem; see Rosenstiel, *Nadia Boulanger*, 189.

47. Archibald Thompson Davison (1883–1961) was appointed to the music depart-ment at Harvard University in 1904 and was the first faculty director of the Harvard Glee Club, which he directed from 1912. Boulanger's student Virgil Thomson had been assis-tant conductor of the group (including during its 1921 European tour) and continued to conduct occasional concerts.

48. Gayle Murchison, *The American Stravinsky: The Style and Aesthetics of Copland's New American Music, the Early Works, 1921–1938* (Ann Arbor: University of Michigan Press, 2012).

# Modern French Music:
# Translating Fauré in America, 1925–1945

JEANICE BROOKS

On 6 November 1940, after a fraught summer of indecision about whether to stay in France under German occupation, Nadia Boulanger arrived in New York. A week later, she made her first conducting appearance since her arrival in the United States, directing the Washington Choral Society at the National Cathedral in Washington, D.C. The concert featured J. S. Bach's Magnificat in D, BWV 243, and Gabriel Fauré's Requiem, Op. 48, and the program booklet included a short introduction linking the two composers:

> Mlle. Boulanger, herself, a pupil of Fauré gives us this bit of background and tribute: "One feels that he (Fauré) regarded death in much the same way that Bach regarded it, as a natural goal and not a danger, as a state to be desired rather than feared. Both were inspired by a similar, mystical view of religion and death, a view so high and serene that, in its presence, differences of creed and dogma fade into insignificance. If, as in the Requiem, he sings of the grief which death inspires, it is a grief so near to God as to be wholly free from vain revolt or lamentation. What dominates the quite impersonal tenderness of the music, is the sense of certain pardon, the serene expectation of eternal rest."[1]

The next day, the Washington musical activist Mildred Bliss wrote to Boulanger, "*Thank you*, Nadia. You enveloped my soul in serenity through the medium of Fauré. . . . All my tenderness and gratitude—I felt what it meant for you to exteriorize the Requiem at this moment."[2] This event in many ways encapsulates a significant development in the reception of Fauré's music in twentieth-century America. Heather de Savage has traced how appreciation of his songs, chamber music, and orchestral works was increasingly enhanced, and eventually surpassed, by reactions to the Requiem after its relatively late introduction to American audiences.[3] The Washington concert was also an important event in Boulanger's own work: it was part of a larger campaign of advocacy for Fauré's music stretching back for more than twenty years, and, as Bliss's message suggests, a moment in which Boulanger's personal understanding of the Requiem could be "exteriorized" in a meaningful collective context.

Boulanger was a key figure in Fauré's international reception, acting as what Marianne Wheeldon has recently described as a "reputational entrepreneur" on the composer's behalf.[4] In concert with French colleagues and American pupils, she aimed to represent Fauré as both indisputably modern and quintessentially French. In this vision, Fauré appeared as an exemplar of architectural principles and the perfection of form; an Olympian classicist above the tumult of the times; and a paragon of characteristically Gallic virtues such as clarity, reason, and order, elevated to universals within the context of a post–World War I turn to formalism. In her promotion of Fauré's music, Boulanger both adopted such common perspectives and took a more idiosyncratic view of the spiritual aspects of the composer's aesthetics. Drawing on her personal associations of Fauré's music with grief as well as broader concepts, she presented Fauré as a master of sacred music whose detachment from worldly concerns could provide consolation and inspire serenity in the face of loss.

Boulanger's advocacy for Fauré relied on a process of translation and retranslation that repeatedly crossed the Atlantic in both directions. Traces of the process appear in her articles, lecture texts, and concert program notes, and its effects can be seen in reviews and correspondence. In this essay, I review newly released documents that shed light on the development of Boulanger's relationship with Fauré and his music in the years before her first American tour in 1925. Taking a 1924 article by Aaron Copland as an example, I explore the portrait of Fauré communicated to Boulanger's American students in the early 1920s and how this could be reframed in American settings marked by Eurocentric cultural aspiration. I then explore how Boulanger herself conceived and presented Fauré as both "modern" and "French" for American audiences during her tour. My analysis of Boulanger's work in both oral and textual domains situates her advocacy for Fauré within a set of linguistic transactions that were marked by frequent shifts in authority and agency, as well as by the concepts of music, history, and nation to which Boulanger appealed. Finally, I show how Boulanger's sacralized vision of the composer was adapted to new contexts up to and including World War II.

## Boulanger and Fauré in France

Fauré's status as a modern was cause for debate in the early twentieth century.[5] Before 1900 he had patchy success with large-scale works. His songs, piano works, and chamber music were more consistently admired, but they were generally performed either by concert societies devoted specifically to the cultivation of new music, or in the context of progressive salons; his music was often considered too subtle for wider consumption. After his unanticipated appointment to head the Paris Conservatoire in 1905, he became significantly more famous and influential in France. He was still somewhat dogged by his reputation as a salon musician, however, and his early reputation as "too complicated" seems quickly to have turned to "outdated" in the teens, despite his creation of substantial new works throughout the period. Nevertheless, Fauré's final years were marked by national acclaim. He was awarded the Grand-Croix of the Légion d'honneur in 1920, the year of his retirement from the Conservatoire; in 1922 there was a national tribute at the Sorbonne, and a special number of *La Revue musicale* was published in his honor. On his death in 1924, an elaborate state funeral confirmed his status as a national figure. However, we might read this as a version of the monumentalizing phenomenon described by Matthew Head in his study of Haydn's final years: in the formal celebration of Fauré's achievement there is often a sense of placing the composer historically into the prewar past as a late-Romantic or transitional figure, rather than considering him a "modern," as this was understood after 1918.[6]

Boulanger was in regular contact with Fauré from early childhood and matured as a musician surrounded by his work.[7] She was born in 1887, in the same year Fauré began composition of the Requiem, a coincidence of which she was well aware.[8] Fauré was a colleague of her father, the composer Ernest Boulanger, and visited frequently when Nadia was a child; in 1901, the year after Ernest's death, she joined Fauré's composition class at the Conservatoire as an auditor. Fauré seems to have followed her progress attentively, and she was rapidly adopted by her older classmates. She would become particularly close to Jean Roger-Ducasse, Fauré's principal musical assistant.[9] Boulanger may have experienced the Requiem in one or more of the smaller-scale (without full orchestra) performances it probably received at the institution for which it was written, the Church of Sainte-Marie-Madeleine in Paris; she was Fauré's regular substitute at the organ at the Madeleine from 1903 until he stepped down to lead the Conservatoire in 1905.[10] She noted his nomination in her diary and was pleased to be photographed with him a month later, after the post was confirmed.[11]

That summer also marked the beginning of her personal and musical partnership with the pianist and composer Raoul Pugno (1852–1914). Boulanger's daybooks from the period, recently released from under seal, reveal much about the development of their emotional and professional lives. The consequences for Boulanger's compositional career are explored elsewhere in this volume; here I focus on the way in which Fauré and his music figured in their partnership.[12] Pugno, a close colleague of Fauré, frequently programmed his chamber and piano music. After Boulanger began piano studies with Pugno in 1905, she regularly worked on Fauré's piano music with him.[13] And the composer himself continued to participate in Boulanger's musical and social life, which was now thoroughly attached to Pugno's. The Glaswegian pianist and organist A. M. Henderson (1879–1957), who studied with Pugno in 1908, remembered hearing Fauré improvise twice on the Cavaillé-Coll organ in the Boulanger home at 36 rue Ballu. He also provides a vivid description of a Sunday afternoon gathering at "La Maison Blanche," Pugno's country home in Gargenville, where Henderson was living for the summer:

> On this particular afternoon Saint-Saëns and Fauré came to Gargenville together. After a careful rehearsal of Saint-Saëns's "Africa" (the purpose of the visit), it was suggested that they might now regale themselves with an arrangement for eight hands (two players at each piano) of the "Danse macabre" of Saint-Saëns. Pugno and Nadia Boulanger settled at one piano, while Saint-Saëns and Fauré took the other. Saint-Saëns acted as generalissimo, saying he would count aloud at the "difficult bits" which he did! The piece was received with acclamation.[14]

Although Boulanger could not wield the same clout as Pugno, she too vigorously promoted the music of her former teacher as her career developed. She worked on Fauré's music with her own students; for example, her daybook notes a sightreading session through the *Dolly Suite* and the incidental music to *Shylock* and *Pelléas* with her first American pupil, Marion Bauer, in 1906.[15] She was an enthusiastic advocate for Fauré's opera *Pénélope*, whose premiere at the Opéra de Monte-Carlo on 4 March 1913 she attended with Lili and Pugno, and which gave rise to her first piece of published musical criticism.[16] This early effort to join the ranks of Fauré's "reputational entrepreneurs" is notable both for the difficulties she had in placing the review in a leading journal, and for her adherence to several of the main tenets of Fauré's reputation among his French admirers.

Tropes picked up in her lengthy review include notions of restraint, simplicity, and clarity. She claims that Fauré disdains overt effects: he shuns outbursts and noise, as well as those complicated effects so many musicians spend time over. She underlines the innovation of his work, by using words such as "discovery," "ingeniousness," "unexpected," and "new," but at this stage makes few references to concepts of form or architecture. Nor is the national element of Fauré's achievement explicit, although in closing, she claimed Fauré for the nation by praising the Opéra de Monte-Carlo for promoting the "work of the great French musician."

In later daybooks, Boulanger looked back on this period as among the happiest in her life, but it would soon come to an abrupt and traumatic end. In December 1914, she and Pugno embarked upon a concert tour to Germany and Russia. Pugno had been unwell and his health rapidly worsened on arrival in Moscow; he died on the morning of 3 January. Boulanger's note in her daybook conveys the depth of her distress: "Mon petit, mon cher amour s'éteint à 11h15. Ma jeunesse s'achève aujourd'hui. Mon bonheur est fini" (My sweet one, my dear love passed away at 11:15. My youth is over today. My happiness is finished).[17] Stranded alone in Moscow, Boulanger raised funds to repatriate his remains and returned home to endure the funeral ceremony and burial. The ceremony took place at the Boulanger family church of La Trinité on 13 January, with the interment at Gargenville later in the afternoon. The orchestra of the Société des Concerts du Conservatoire, directed by André Messager, performed at the ceremony; one of the funeral orations was pronounced by Fauré.[18] Exactly a year later, Boulanger inscribed the repertoire and her feelings in her diary in an act of mourning and remembrance, "One year ago: Trinity – Gargenville. Afterward . . . to enter the library [of Pugno's house, where they frequently spent long days together] – how did I remain standing – " Underneath the comment she notated two musical citations—the main themes from the funeral march of Beethoven's Symphony No. 7 and the slow movement of Symphony No. 3 (Eroica)— and between them inscribed the words "Requiem de Fauré" (Figure 1).[19] On the same date in 1916 she noted only,"Trinité – Requiem Fauré," demonstrating both the association of the work with Pugno's funeral and her continued use of the Requiem to record and reflect upon her loss.[20]

Only a few years later, Fauré's music played a significant role in establishing Boulanger's postwar teaching career at the Ecole Normale de Musique (from 1919) and the Conservatoire américain at Fontainebleau (from 1921). In the final years of World War I she had seen the slow and agonizing death of her sister Lili, and Nadia again sought consolation in music for feelings of loneliness and grief. Her letters and diaries

Figure 1. Nadia Boulanger's daybook, entry for 14 January 1915.

record an intense period of study in which Fauré's music loomed large. In April 1919, she noted in her daybook, "Fauré—there is doubtless no other modern oeuvre that is more exclusively musical than this one, and it is thought, emotion, transcribed by the sounds without any association of color."[21] It is not clear which work(s) by Fauré inspired her remark, but these are the first allusions I have found to three ideas that come back repeatedly in her writing and speaking on the composer: he writes "pure music"; in doing so, he reifies ("transcribes") thought and emotion in musical form; and he is a musician of line, not color. All three of these notions were central to the developing rhetoric of international modernism during the postwar formalist turn, and they became hallmarks of modernity in Boulanger's pedagogy of the early 1920s. Aaron Copland, who studied with Boulanger from 1921 to 1924, remembered that Fauré was the composer Boulanger used to illustrate her concept of the *grande ligne*—the self-unfolding line at the heart of the masterwork, to which aspects of form and harmony are subordinate.[22] His memory is confirmed by extant course materials and correspondence; for example, a 1925 letter in which she described the first movement of Fauré's Second Piano Quintet as a masterpiece in which form and line are perfectly integrated.[23] And while studying Fauré's music and teaching it to her students, Boulanger also performed his work: she was the organist for concerts of the Requiem by the Société des Concerts du Conservatoire in January and February 1920, the year of Fauré's retirement, on a prestigious program featuring well-known soloists.[24]

Despite abundant evidence of Boulanger's deep engagement with his music, the composer himself seems not to have always been sure of her regard. In September 1920, in response to a letter that may have been sent on his retirement, and in which she apparently tried to convey what his music meant to her, he wrote:

> You are wrong, dear Nadia, things of the heart need to be said, and your excessive circumspection, over the last fifteen years, has made me believe in your indifference to me, and perhaps also, in a change of direction in your work. You should fix this: your charming letter is already a sign that has given me enormous pleasure.[25]

Fauré's words seem somewhat unfair; though he may have been unaware of her comments in diaries and personal letters, he certainly knew of her role in planning celebrations around *Pénélope*'s Paris performance and was aware of her praise for the work in *Le Ménestrel*. Her diaries show that she helped with the proofs of Fauré's *Le jardin clos* in 1915, and the number of his scores in her library, many with affectionate dedications from her teacher, suggests that he knew she regularly acquired his new work. Jean-Michel Nectoux posits that Boulanger's deep respect for Fauré made it difficult to establish a truly personal relationship of the kind he enjoyed with Roger-Ducasse and Ravel.[26] However, this letter may also reflect Fauré's own sensitivity to being thought a has-been at this moment during his late career—there is evidence he was profoundly hurt about being forced to retire from the Conservatoire—and could also serve as an index of the degree of overt deference he may have expected from a female student. He may also have been reacting to Pugno's assumption of the role of Boulanger's principal mentor between 1905 and 1914. Whether or not this is the case, Boulanger seems to have taken his reproach to heart, for she redoubled her efforts in the following years. Her daybooks show that she visited Fauré regularly, and she participated in major celebrations of his work, including the national homage at the Sorbonne in June 1922, which she attended with Roger-Ducasse.[27] She also contributed an article to the special number of *Revue musicale* in Fauré's honor that appeared in October the same year.[28]

The issue assembled a prominent group of Fauré's colleagues and former students, summarizing the views of his ardent defenders in France. His most vocal champion, Émile Vuillermoz, wrote the general introduction, and other contributors included René Chalupt on Fauré and poetry, Charles Koechlin on the stage works, Florent Schmitt on the orchestral music, Roger-Ducasse on the chamber music, and Alfred Cortot on the piano music. The issue also included an interview between Roland-Manuel and Ravel on the songs, an opening memoir by Fauré himself, and a musical supplement titled "Hommage à Gabriel Fauré" by seven former students—Ravel, George Enesco, Louis Aubert, Schmitt, Koechlin, Paul L'Admirault, and Roger-Ducasse—each of whom completed a short work using a theme based on the letters of Fauré's name. The articles convey a portrait of Fauré that emphasized originality, innovation, and independence in consistently anti-Romantic terms.[29] Praising Fauré's personal modesty and disdain for effect or fashion, the authors celebrated his originality while underlining his distaste for self-aggrandizement, claiming that his work was modern by inner necessity rather than from a desire for notoriety. They described Fauré's capacity for continuous self-renewal and his ability to break new musical ground without rejection of the past. This brand of quiet revolution is one reason Fauré is a "musicians' musician" whose subtlety is appreciated only by sophisticated and knowledgeable ears. There is relatively little overtly nationalistic rhetoric in the issue aside from a bombastic passage by Roger-Ducasse, but most authors worked to make Fauré a founding figure in a specifically French strand of modern music.[30] By presenting concepts such as clarity and simplicity as characteristically French and at the same time elevating these principles to the status of universals, the *Revue musicale* authors were able to nationalize Fauré yet remove him from the aggressive sphere of national politics. This position both echoed Fauré's own stance during World War I and chimed with Boulanger's views on music as existing on a plane outside the recent conflict.[31]

Boulanger, the only female contributor to the enterprise, accepted the task of covering Fauré's sacred music.[32] This was a complex assignment, for although Fauré was raised a Catholic and spent much of his life as a church organist, by mid-career his spiritual leanings were pantheistic or agnostic, and by the time of the *Revue musicale* celebration he was approaching atheism.[33] His distance from the Catholic establishment was well known in Parisian musical circles, and stood in direct contrast to the Church-sanctioned activities of contemporaries such as Vincent d'Indy and colleagues at the Schola Cantorum. Throughout the article, however, Boulanger brushed Fauré's religious unorthodoxy under the carpet, implicitly presenting him as a devout servant of the established Church. In her opening, she identified Christian thought as an enduring inspiration for great artists, providing a necessary overall direction that both constrains and liberates through its basis in collective feeling. And in her focus on the Requiem, she linked many of the by now common claims about Fauré's musical style to the signal attributes of musical modernity and to concepts of religious faith.

Her first move was to situate Fauré outside his own time, stating that "an artist as noble as Gabriel Fauré would not know how to consent to see in an epoch its tastes with no future, its unreasonable fervors, its little uglinesses and its fleeting trends" (105). She then touches on the familiar concepts of restraint, simplicity, and clarity, traits she associates with both timelessness and innovation:

> Everything in this work has been tempered by the well-judged and incomparable sense of order that constitutes its greatness and ensures its longevity. Without affectation and never with brutality, his strength charms, dominates, imposes itself—without systems, without overturning, without noise, his originality innovates, renews, builds. (106)

Throughout the article, she applies words such as *sweet, sober, grave, calm, confident, tender*, and *tranquil* to her analysis of Fauré's motets and other sacred works, but as in this passage, frequently juxtaposes them with words such as *new* and *inimitable* to highlight Fauré's originality. Her statement that Fauré becomes younger as he ages echoes Vuillermoz's remark that despite his age, Fauré was "young, younger than his students, younger than the most systematically young of our most recent youngsters" and underlines his continuing relevance to the most up-to-date musical developments.[34]

Turning to Fauré's religion, Boulanger obliquely refers to others' doubts about the composer's orthodoxy and counters them by placing his style within a legitimate strand of Catholic thought:

> Just as it can absolve and sustain us, the Church can judge, condemn. This, the Maître has never expressed, any more than he has cared to follow the dogmatic spirit of the text. One could say that he understands religion rather in the manner of the sweetest episodes in the Gospel according to Saint John—rather according to Saint Francis of Assisi than according to Saint Bernard, or according to Bossuet. He sees in it, finds in it a source of love and not of fear. This must be accepted if one wants to understand him. No severity in the Little Flowers, no sternness in the Golden Legend, and I am not aware that anyone has reproached either Saint Francis, or Jacobus de Voragine (107).[35]

Boulanger presents all of Fauré's sacred music, including his motets and the *Messe basse*, as springing from this element of Christian faith, but sees the Requiem as its most perfect expression: "The Requiem is not only one of Gabriel Fauré's greatest works, but is also among those that most honor Music and Thought. There is none greater, none purer, none that is more definitive." Using the language of postwar formalism to describe its musical content, she emphasizes that the "essential causes" of the piece's greatness are "its musical fabric, its architecture, its reason and its order." But she also attributes its effects to the serenity of Fauré's musical style: "Not a single exterior effect alters its sober and somewhat severe expression of pain, neither anxiety nor agitation trouble its profound meditation, not one doubt tarnishes its unshakeable faith, its sweet confidence, its tender and tranquil expectation" (110). Here she links her comments on formal architecture to an existing strand of criticism around the Requiem, and to Fauré's own comments about the piece and his perception of death as happy release.[36] This sentiment pervades her statements about Fauré's music as consolation, before she closes by reiterating the idea of service to the Church:

> In the Requiem, it is the pain that is left behind by those departures without return that the music sings; a pain so close to God

that it is without rebellion, without noise, without gestures. And, if the grave warnings arise, if the weighty, sad songs unfold, what dominates is the certainty of forgiveness and the serene promise of eternal rest. To have given this to our unhappy hearts, to have mingled Charity with Beauty, Hope with Love, is not this the most beautiful way to participate in the work of the Church (111).

This passage, which, in English translation, was the central element of Boulanger's program note for her Washington concert in 1940, would become an indispensable part of her future presentation of the Requiem.

Just over two years later, Fauré would make his own "departure without return." In her daybook for 4 November 1924, Boulanger noted "Fauré died last night—how many memories, and what a light extinguished."[37] In his account of the funeral, *Le Monde musical*'s editor Marc Pincherle noted that the most moving part of the service was Fauré's own Requiem, given by many of the same musicians with whom Boulanger had performed the piece in 1920.[38] Roger-Ducasse was asked to speak on behalf of Fauré's students, but fearing he would break down in an unmasculine way, he requested Boulanger to act on his behalf.[39] In addition to her speech, she wrote a tribute to her former teacher that was published in *Comoedia* on the day of the funeral, and reprinted later in the month in *Le Monde musical* alongside the text of her funeral oration (Figure 2).[40] In her tribute, she applied words she had used in *La Revue musicale* to describe his music to talk about Fauré himself: "His presence spread such clarity over all things"; as he aged, he renewed himself, and "an ineffable serenity developed within him, stripping his thought of any ornament that would have distorted the purity of the forms"; he is now "sheltered from futile distress" but even in his absence, his presence can be felt by contemplating "the admirable order, the radiant certainty, the total lack of self-interest, [and] the incredible simplicity" of his life. In her analysis of Fauré's funeral, Jillian Rogers remarks on the impersonality characteristic of the post–World War I obituary, characterized by a strong tendency to frame loss in national or collective terms and distaste for overt displays of personal grief.[41] Boulanger's speech, pronounced on the steps of the Madeleine directly after the ceremony, supports this reading: she addressed Fauré directly, "at the moment when you go to rejoin those whom all of us mourn," associating the loss of her teacher with that of her lover and her sister but sublimating her own loss into collective expression.

Boulanger's positions as expressed in her writing and teaching of the early 1920s were typical of other Fauré reputational entrepreneurs who

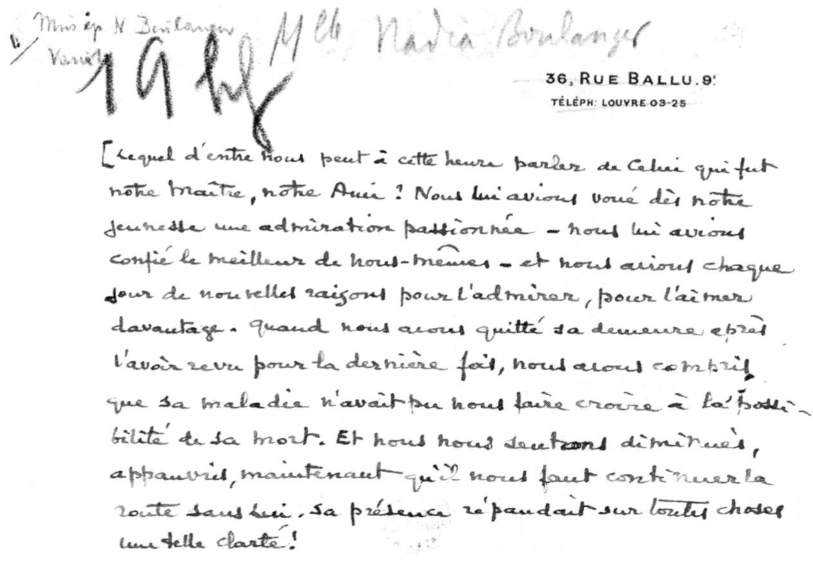
Mlle Nadia Boulanger
36, Rue Ballu. 9e
Téléph: Louvre 03-25

[Lequel d'entre nous peut à cette heure parler de Celui qui fut notre maître, notre Ami ? Nous lui avions voué dès notre jeunesse une admiration passionnée – nous lui avions confié le meilleur de nous-mêmes – et nous avions chaque jour de nouvelles raisons pour l'admirer, pour l'aimer davantage. Quand nous avons quitté sa demeure après l'avoir revu pour la dernière fois, nous avons compris que sa maladie n'avait pu nous faire croire à la possibilité de sa mort. Et nous nous sentons diminués, appauvris, maintenant qu'il nous faut continuer la route sans lui. Sa présence répandait sur toutes choses une telle clarté !

Figure 2. Manuscript of Boulanger's tribute to Gabriel Fauré.

adapted their praise of the composer to neoclassical and formalist strands within the emerging vocabulary of international modernism. Though other critics had often commented on the quiet and tenderness of the Requiem, Boulanger placed unusual emphasis on religious thought and the notion of consolation in loss. There is a notable lack of explicit national rhetoric in her writing and teaching, especially in comparison to some colleagues such as Roger-Ducasse, but she continually cited attributes that were used in contemporary French aesthetic discourse: grace, order, clarity, disdain for effect, internalized or abstracted rather than overt emotion. These would be more explicitly nationalized in her advocacy for Fauré abroad, as she repurposed her claims of Fauré's modernity within the context of transnational exchange.

**Fauré, Copland, and Boulanger's First American Tour (1925)**

When Fauré died in November 1924, Boulanger was deeply involved in preparations for her first American tour, and almost exactly a month later she embarked on the *Aquitania* for New York. A visit to the United States had been in the cards for some time, urged both by American colleagues with whom she had worked on wartime relief and cultural efforts, such as Blair Fairchild and Walter Damrosch, and by her increasing numbers of American students. Like other French composers and performers who toured America in the interwar period, Boulanger profited from the American turn away from its former heavy reliance on German musical traditions, already evident by 1910 and given further political impetus by reactions to the war.[42] She was also able to secure French state support for her trip, building on her wartime charity work and postwar international links.[43] She circulated a questionnaire to her French colleagues before departing and was engaged to speak to cultural organizations about French musical life and to gather impressions of the American musical world that she could report on her return. Boulanger's tour was thus not only an opportunity to build personal prestige, but also to further her reputation as an internationalist and ambassador for French culture. The tour began in New York in January 1925 and involved extensive travel up and down the Eastern seaboard, through the Midwest, and as far southwest as Houston. She did not include works by Fauré in the organ recital she played in several major cities, but the composer figured prominently in her lectures, which were her first large-scale presentations in English.

Her way had been partly prepared by Aaron Copland, who had returned in early summer 1924 from three years of study with Boulanger in Paris and Fontainebleau, and distilled the understanding of Fauré's music that he had gained there in an article for the October issue of *The Musical Quarterly*, titled "Gabriel Fauré, a Neglected Master."[44] In their influential work on transnational cultural transfer, Michel Espagne and Michael Werner have described how access to foreign cultural elements can be a source of power within the receiving culture.[45] This power may be exercised in a variety of contexts, including in the symbolic realm represented by Pierre Bourdieu's concept of cultural capital, the social assets that affirm the status of individuals in relation to high culture.[46] In translating Fauré for American audiences, both Copland and Boulanger instrumentalized their linguistic fluency in French as well as in the "language" represented by Fauré's music. This established their musical authority and accrued cultural capital by appealing to American understandings of the French language as a marker of distinction. Analysis of their strategies sheds light on common frameworks as well as the differing situations and expectations that affected each musician's advocacy for Fauré in the United States.

Annegret Fauser has persuasively discussed how Copland's developing identity as an "American composer" was shaped not only by his own self-image but by the pressures of the views and stereotypes of America he experienced during his years in France.[47] His *Musical Quarterly* article shows a similar process, demonstrating how he could draw upon both his French experiences and American understandings of France upon his return. Copland began by claiming that Fauré's music was known and appreciated only in France: "Perhaps no other composer has ever been so generally ignored outside his own country, while at the same time enjoying an unquestionably eminent reputation at home . . . in America, and one might add, in all other countries except France, his work is practically unknown" (573). As Heather de Savage has shown, Fauré was not as neglected in the United States as Copland claimed.[48] However, in characterizing Fauré as unknown among his compatriots, Copland positioned himself as a cultural insider, with the ability to translate French music and culture for American readers.

Copland's summary of Fauré's career touches on several existing biographical tropes, including modesty and the idea of renewal in old age. He claims that Fauré's critics misunderstand him by focusing on his early works and considering him "a composer of a sort of super-salon music." But Fauré's most important music dates from his late career, when his works have become "ever more spiritually youthful and serene as he becomes physically older and weaker" (573–74). Copland's account of Fauré's musical style emphasizes the neoclassical vocabulary of postwar modernism: his music displays "absolute clarity in formal texture," but this apparent simplicity masks great complexity, as difficult as "Schoenberg's later manner" (576). In his comments about Fauré's late works, Copland invokes Boulanger's favorite concept of the *grande ligne*, observing that "continuity of the architectural line is very characteristic of Fauré's last style" (581). Fauré's music displays a classical beauty "if we define classicism as 'intensity on a background of calm' and his late music in particular is "limpid, clear . . . seemingly effortless" (583). The Second Piano Quintet, the work that Boulanger characterized as a masterwork in its integration of form and content, is a "pure well of spirituality, a humanizing force such as is found in only the greatest masters. For those who love Fauré's music, it is the 'holy of holies.' . . . The entire composition is extremely classic, that is to say, it is as far removed as possible from the romantic temperament" (584). *Pénélope*, "one of the best operas since Wagner," partakes of the same "classical emotion" as the chamber music, overflowing "with a deep feeling that shuns all exterior display" (585).

Copland projects expertise according to the traditional (and normatively masculine) conventions of specialist publications such as *The Musical Quarterly*, including the citation of authorities to support his points. Almost all of his cited sources are French, and he relied heavily on the 1922 *Revue musicale* special issue. We might read his essay as a verbal parallel to his 1923 composition for string quartet, originally titled *Hommage à Gabriel Fauré*, in which the second movement spells out the letters of

Fauré's name in imitation of the procedure used in *La Revue musicale*'s musical supplement.[49] Copland cites Cortot and Roger-Ducasse by name in borrowing material from their *Revue musicale* articles for his discussion of Fauré's piano works and chamber music. And his brief comment on the Requiem quotes directly from Boulanger's essay on the religious music, although without explicit attribution: "Fauré has been called the St. Francis d'Assisi of music, and nothing could better exemplify his humble, modest attitude towards life than this 'Requiem' where 'no inquietude or agitation disturbs the profound meditation'" (579). In discussing Fauré's "Frenchness," however, Copland imagined a new role for himself and other advocates in America. He pointed out: "It has been many times written and said that Fauré's art is so extremely Gallic in its very essence that it is hardly possible for anyone without the French temperament and mind to understand it and appreciate it. One cannot export him, they tell us, just as one cannot export Racine" (573). But, Copland remarks, until the composer's work is better known outside France it is impossible to evaluate such claims. Citing Willem Mengelberg's efforts in promoting Mahler (and foreshadowing Boulanger's own on behalf of Fauré), he outlines the need for "Fauré-propaganda" as the first step toward "a just appreciation of this Frenchman's work." Until then, Fauré will remain a connoisseur's musician. Copland imagines that his style "must be disconcerting to the uninitiated" (576), and quotes Vuillermoz's introduction to the *Revue musicale* special number to praise those—like himself—who have moved beyond such initial incomprehension: "To love and understand Fauré constitutes a privilege from which it is difficult not to derive a sort of innocent pride. It is the mark of a subtle ear, the flattering indication of a refined sensibility" (585).

This passage from Vuillermoz accumulated new meanings in the transnational context of Copland's text. Like Vuillermoz, Copland positioned himself in an inner circle of connoisseurs with whom readers are implicitly encouraged to align to achieve the same levels of sophistication. In Copland's case, however, the status of French culture and language in the United States adds further complexity to his rhetorical move. French fashion, food, and wine represented international chic in America; French was the language of diplomacy, and the principal foreign tongue cultivated by American elites, particularly in the northeastern cities where European high culture was most conspicuously present. Fluency in French remained the mark of an expensive education and experience of travel. Concert programs featured publicity for imported French fashion and cosmetics, and newspapers in Boston and New York were full of advertisements for lessons from native speakers.[50] Copland's own French was reasonably

fluent and like many other members of the "Boulangerie," in some contexts he presented himself as an honorary Frenchman. In a 1923 letter to
Boulanger reporting on a concert in Vienna, he commented, "The Ravel
and Stravinsky that you and me—that is to say we (all of us French people!)—have known for a long time, were acclaimed by the whole hall."[51]
Copland's transition from "vous et moi" (you and me) to "nous autres
français" (all of us French people) is revealing. In his presentation of Fauré
for *The Musical Quarterly* he similarly draws upon and overdetermines his
insider knowledge as a recent resident of Paris, presenting his understanding of Fauré not only in terms of access to musical knowledge and beauty
but also to French culture. The role of the language in conveying this status is underlined by using a quote in the original French from Charles
Baudelaire's "Invitation au voyage" from *Les fleurs du mal* to sum up Fauré's
achievement and to close the article. Copland does not identify or translate
the poetic citation, projecting his own cultural knowledge and assuming
it in his readers. In a final sentence that seems almost prescient in light of
Fauré's later American reception, he remarked: "The world at large has
particular need of Gabriel Fauré to-day; need of his calm, his naturalness,
his restraint, his optimism; need, above all, of the musician and his great
art: "Là, où tout n'est qu'ordre et beauté / Luxe, calme, et volupté" (There,
where all is order and beauty / Luxury, peace, and pleasure) (586).

Copland's article can thus be read as an effort by an ambitious, but
not college-educated, young musician to capitalize upon his French
apprenticeship when launching himself as a critical voice within specialist
musical circles, and as an attempt by a New Yorker of recent immigrant
family origins to deploy the French language in line with established concepts of sophistication among the wealthy elite of early twentieth-century
America. When Boulanger arrived in the United States some weeks later,
her concerts, lectures, and social appearances took place within a similar
environment of Eurocentric cultural aspiration. Unsurprisingly, in her
talks on Fauré she deployed many of the same concepts as Copland did in
his article; but her strategies and reception were inflected by her status as
a pupil of Fauré, a French national, and a woman. And unlike Copland,
she was a native French speaker communicating largely in imperfect
English to non-specialist audiences.

Fauré was the starting point for her presentations on modern music,
and comments in her daybooks and letters suggest that she was particularly successful at conveying his importance to American audiences. After
a lecture at the Mannes School in New York, she noted "lecture – probably
my best evening – Fauré" and in a letter to her mother after speaking
in Houston, she wrote that she had made "a particular impression with

Fauré, Roussel, and the poor Little One [Lili Boulanger] – this, every-where."[52] In another letter near the end of her tour, she attributed this success in part to her emotional experience of recent loss:

> It will have been Fauré and [Lili] who dominated this trip –
> because in order to speak, between my admiration and my
> grief, the words came up from my heart to go toward [others']
> hearts – and then, people understand.[53]

Boulanger saw this "speaking from the heart" as a way to compensate for her inability to convey her thoughts in a second language. Although she had begun learning English in 1905 and had been teaching in the language for several years by the time of her tour, her concerns about the difficulty of making herself understood permeate letters to her mother. She recounted with relief that at a lunch given in her honor by the American Guild of Organists in New York, her impromptu speech in response to a flattering introduction had gone over well; she added that the minister responsible for the blessing was reassuring:

> The Pastor was exquisite, telling me not to be afraid of my
> English, that words that come from the heart go to the heart
> – and all around me, [there was] an atmosphere like I've
> never had in my life – and that gives you strength, courage,
> the desire to feel you are really yourself.[54]

Although texts for most of Boulanger's 1925 talks do not survive, a valuable glimpse of what they were like is provided by the stenographer's transcripts of her lectures in Houston.[55] Boulanger was invited to speak in a series founded in 1922 by the Rice Institute's director, Edgar Odell Lovett, and the wealthy Houston musical activist Ima Hogg in an effort to enhance the intellectual and cultural life of the rapidly expanding provincial city. Boulanger was the second speaker in the series, which would welcome Ravel in 1928 and Arthur Honegger in 1929. Houston in the 1920s hosted many foreign musicians as the city's musical clubs and patrons attempted to match the offerings available in older East Coast centers and build a high-culture environment very different from the vernacular traditions, including black and rural musical idioms, that existed in the region.[56] The cultural ambitions of the Rice Lectureship are clear in the documents surrounding Boulanger's visit. As one of her hosts claimed on presenting her to the Houston audience: "It is essential in education that a general study of the Fine Arts be made a part of that education; that the inspiring qualities of painting and sculpture, architecture and music have a part in the making of a man."

The topics for Boulanger's three lectures were "The Twenty-Four Preludes of Claude Debussy," "French Music, Modern and Ultra-Modern," and "Igor Stravinsky." All three of the talks were to be about recent or new music, underlining Boulanger's role as spokesperson for modern French music, which had gained her official support for the tour. At the same time, as Kimberly Francis has shown, she had to adapt her presentations to the limits of her amateur audience's technical knowledge and the challenges of expressing herself in English. As Francis remarks, "Her discussion of music *outside* of France was inherently bound to the act of translation through her adoption of the English language."[57] After the Rice Lectures, Boulanger wrote to her mother: "No very precise things to say – people wouldn't have understood – but [I] was able immediately to win over the audience."[58] To do so she invoked concepts of both personal and cultural authenticity.

For her lecture on "French Music, Modern and Ultra-Modern" on 28 January, Boulanger plunged immediately into a long discussion of Fauré, implicitly casting Debussy (whom she had covered the previous evening) as a precursor to the "modern" despite the nearly twenty years that separated Fauré's birth in 1845 from Debussy's in 1867. Her opening emphasized Fauré's greatness while establishing her personal connection with the composer and her emotional reaction to his recent death:

> The first man of whom I will speak is a man whom I believe to be one of the greatest artists of all time. I cannot speak of him without the deepest emotion. He died only a few weeks ago, and he was my old master – I mean Gabriel Fauré.[59]

From the outset, Boulanger's text shows her effort to transcend her difficulties with the English language and the inability of her audience to follow a more technical talk by "speaking from the heart" about her emotional life. Her subsequent summary of Fauré's importance to his students roughly summarizes several sentences from her funeral tribute, claiming, "When Gabriel Fauré was with us, we knew we owed him much . . . but today, when we know we will see him no more, we understand that what he brought to our youth was an extraordinary gift." The usual claim of Fauré's youthfulness in old age is rendered personal as Boulanger describes how his renewal was communicated to students like herself: "Even as a very old man, and very ill, his spirit was so young that when we needed to go forward, when we needed to find our way, we had only to enter in the room where he was, and we understood where was the truth" (3).

Having established her credentials as an intimate of the composer, Boulanger remarked upon his unjust neglect. In contrast to Copland, she claimed that his music was not yet fully appreciated in France, while agreeing with Copland that Fauré was virtually unknown in America. This difference reflects Copland's desire to present Fauré as an established French "product," and Boulanger's wish not to offend her audience by appearing to doubt their cultural knowledge. Her subsequent comment, "I don't mean to come here and say you don't know Fauré" (although this is exactly what she just said) seems to confirm this reading. Boulanger went on to describe Fauré as a classic artist and thus "perhaps the most modern of the modern," characterizing his work in terms such as modesty, serenity, and purity. She made a glancing reference to his reputation as a salon composer by describing him as "in society a most charming man," but encouraged her audience to look beyond the charming surface to the "perfection of form, the perfection of expression, and the perfection of feeling." As in Copland's article, this appeal invokes the chic of Parisian social life while using the claim of underlying substance to fend off potential associations with frivolity. Boulanger then moved on to discuss the Requiem, the first specific piece to be mentioned in her talk. Her initial summary duplicates the content of her description of the work in *La Revue musicale*, while showing the challenges she faced in conveying these ideas in a foreign language:

> When quite young, Fauré wrote a requiem. This requiem is perhaps one which is based on the idea of death, which we can suppose. He is before his God with the feeling of his responsibility, and with the feeling that the hour is grave, but he has also such a belief that death is a way where one has to go, is an aim, and is not a danger. Generally, the requiems we have to hear are imbued by a terrible feeling of fright. In his requiem his principal idea is that death is rest, and I know too well his idea of death to not thank him for giving us such a consolation when sorrow comes.[60]

Boulanger's subsequent presentation of the Requiem's music, however, allowed her to deploy two languages in which her fluency was indisputable: music and French. Moving to the piano, she played three extracts from the work—the opening "Requiem eternam," the "Pie Jesu," and the closing "In paradisum," interspersing her performance with comments on the music's classic perfection and purity. After allowing her audience to hear the sounds of this unfamiliar music, Boulanger again emphasized the personal connection: "I recently had occasion to hear the [Requiem] under very sad circumstances, and so I can say what is sung in the right place, in the right moment, this work brings to us." She may have been thinking of Fauré's funeral, but her failure to say exactly which sad circumstances she had in mind suggests she may have been reliving the experience of mourning Pugno. Boulanger concluded her presentation of the Requiem by citing poetry, a move she employed frequently in her lectures and concert reviews, and one which, as we have seen, Copland also employed in closing his Fauré article with Baudelaire. Her Houston lecture is the first documented appearance of her application of a quote from Paul Valéry's recently published *Eupalinos* to Fauré:

> It is two years now since a wonderful book was published, which is not yet translated, which is called [*Eupalinos*] and it is written by Paul [Valéry] and in this book he says—excuse me if I try to translate; I shall do the best I can—have you not remarked when going through the city that certain edifices which are built, are silent, and certain of them are speaking, while others are singing. That is the idea here, which is so beautiful, and in French it comes: [Reciting] "N'as-tu pas observé, en te promenant dans cette ville, que d'entre les édifices dont elle est peuplée, les uns sont muets; les autres parlent; et d'autres enfin, qui sont les plus rares, chantent." The words come in such a beautiful manner, and when I think of this, I always have those words in my memory.[61]

Her move from indifferent English into poetic French, marked by her own fluency and by the musicality and rhythmic control of Valéry's text, must have been as striking as her musical examples. Boulanger's framing of the quote both indicates a desire to translate and the ultimate impossibility of doing so; the beauty of the French language, like the beauty of Fauré's music, partakes of a form of desirable mystery.

Boulanger's work in Houston was marked by complex intersections of marginality and authority. Francis provides a compelling interpretation of Boulanger's efforts to establish herself as a master teacher despite her outsider status as a foreigner and as a woman within the masculine scholarly environment of the Rice Institute. Drawing on Gilles Deleuze and Félix Guattari's concept of a "minor literature," the use of a dominant language by a minority presence, Francis shows how Boulanger turned speaking from the margins to her advantage.[62] By frequently excusing herself for

Figure 3. Nadia Boulanger, ca. 1925. Photographer Edmond Joaillier.
This widely distributed publicity portrait posed Boulanger in the rococo interior
of the Hôtel Allard du Cholet (built 1881), home of the Ecole Normale de Musique.
The historical setting underlined her role as ambassador of French culture.

her poor English and by using inclusive pronouns to introduce unfamiliar music, she cultivated a self-deprecating stance in order to charm and
persuade. The status of French as the *lingua franca* of cultural sophistication and the efforts of Houston's institutions and elite individuals to shape
the city's culture on European and American northeastern urban models

added a further layer to Boulanger's performance. Boulanger's presentation of Fauré drew on elements of authentic Frenchness to counterbalance her marginality, and her performative fluency in languages—both French and the "language" of modern music—that her audiences wished to know, but had to struggle to understand, provided access to other forms of authority within the environment of American cultural aspiration (Figure 3). Her heavily accented and idiosyncratic English lent authenticity to her claims about Fauré's music, while a further layer of authenticity sprang from Boulanger's evocations of personal connections to the music and its composers, and through her "speaking from the heart" about her experience of grief and consolation.

The Rice Institute lectures were published upon Boulanger's return to France, appearing in 1926 as a record of her successful tour and extending the influence of her work in America beyond her visit. The *Rice Institute Pamphlet* in which the talks were published included a note that implicitly presented them as faithful renditions of the stenographer's transcriptions.[63] But comparing the texts reveals a thorough revision of both content and language. Boulanger prepared the significantly expanded published versions with the help of her former student Howard Hinners, who reworked Boulanger's words into idiomatic English for the *Rice Institute Pamphlet* to create the image of an accomplished linguistic performance very different from what her audiences heard in Houston.[64] She added a large amount of new technical material (including abundant notated musical examples that went well beyond the number of excerpts she had performed in Houston) and radically reduced the personal evocations, endowing her text with the assured and scholarly tone of specialist musical writing. And just as Copland had done, she deployed extracts from the 1922 special issue of *La Revue musicale* in translation, resulting in a portrait of Fauré that resonated strongly with the work of the composer's reputational entrepreneurs in France but which also effaced the personal and emotional connections to Fauré and his music that she had introduced into her Houston talk.

Boulanger's new text, now titled simply "Modern French Music" and appearing first rather than second in the series of three lectures, begins with nine completely new pages exploring the scales and chords of modern music before moving on to discuss composers and works. Fauré remains the first composer to be covered, but is introduced by a bolder statement about his importance and her readers' ignorance of his work than she had made in her talk:

> Fauré, Debussy and Stravinsky are, of course, the chief figures
> in the musical history of the last thirty-five years. The work of

> Debussy and Stravinsky is known, if it is not always understood,
> the world over; but Fauré, who is perhaps the greatest of the
> three, is still practically unknown outside of France (122).

Before moving on to discuss the music, she inserted several pages of material on Fauré's biography and personality, though with little mention of her personal connection and without reference to her own experience of emotion or grief. In her discussion of the music, she changed the order of the pieces, beginning with the song "Le soir" and the Second Piano Quintet before moving on to the Requiem. She cites many more of Fauré's works than she had covered in her talk, so that the coverage more closely approaches the overview of the composer's oeuvre that Copland's article had attempted. She also placed much greater emphasis on neoclassical notions of line and architecture: for example, she claimed that in the Allegro of the Second Piano Quintet, "the entire movement represents a single, long line," and she characterized Debussy's use of harmony as an element of color in contrast to Fauré's as a feature of design (126).

These points are fleshed out with newly added quotes and summaries of previously published material, mainly from *La Revue musicale*. Her account of Fauré's training at the Ecole Niedermeyer quotes the composer's own memoir in the special issue, and in her treatment of the Requiem, she used a long passage from her own essay on the religious music.[65] Her text on Fauré's spirituality is not only translated but expanded by a comparison of Bach, the "great Protestant cantor," with "Fauré, the Catholic." This juxtaposition invokes Bach's indisputable musical authority while appealing to the largely Protestant confessional allegiances of the American audience; the assertion of the similarity of the two composers' spiritual sensibilities is the first appearance of the English words she would use in concert programs, such as her Washington appearance in 1940:

> One feels that [Fauré] regarded death in much the same
> way as Bach regarded it, as a natural goal and not a danger, as a state to be desired rather than feared. . . . Works,
> for instance, like Bach's Choral Prelude for Organ, "O Man,
> Bewail Thy Grievous Sin," and Fauré's "Requiem," are both
> inspired by a similar, mystical view of religion and death, a
> view so high and serene that, in its presence, differences of
> creed and dogma fade into insignificance. The Church can
> absolve and sustain, but also judge and condemn us. Unlike
> Bach, Fauré has never given expression to this latter and
> menacing aspect of his faith. Religion, he understands more

in the manner of the Gospel according to St. John, in the manner of Saint Francis and Fra Angelico, than of Bossuet or Saint Bernard. He finds in it a source of love, not of fear. If, as in the "Requiem," he sings of the grief which death inspires, it is a grief so near to God as to be wholly free from vain revolt or lamentation. What dominates the quite impersonal tenderness of the music, is the sense of certain pardon, the serene expectation of eternal rest (128–29).

In comparison to its presentation in the Houston talk, however, the sacred aspect of Fauré's work is a less prominent strand in the published version. Boulanger added literary citations to her lecture text, including a quotation from André Gide (124) as well as two new passages from Valéry to replace the one she had used in the Houston talk (129–30).[66] The Valéry citations conclude her discussion of the Requiem directly after her litany of religious authorities from St. John to Bossuet; here she supports her assertion of Fauré's classicism through the authority of classical antiquity rather than Catholic thought. She describes Fauré's delight in beauty as "Greek rather than Christian" and claims, "Like Plato, he feels a sort of ecstasy before the austere though sensuous beauty of form or line" (129), then cites Valéry's description of the formal genius of the classical architect Eupalinos (139).

The published record of Boulanger's lecture is thus a more strongly worded, technically grounded, and textually authoritative case for Fauré's status than her speech had been. "Modern French Music" is like Copland's article in that Boulanger asserts Fauré's modernity through formal concepts and technical language that connects to broad cultural knowledge rather than to emotional or personal ties. Boulanger's individual Frenchness is also given a more impersonal turn in the representation of her lecture in print: in smoothing out Boulanger's English, Hinners helped remove idiosyncratic French constructions and "false friends" from the representation of reported speech. The idea of France remains strong in Boulanger's revised text, however, and she makes bolder statements on the national character of Fauré's music than in earlier writing or in her Houston talk. And she goes well beyond Copland in elevating Fauré's "French" characteristics to the status of universals, and in tying appreciation of these characteristics to musical expertise and to a specific form of cultural distinction linked to class identity. Observing that Fauré is principally "a 'musician's composer,'" Boulanger continued:

The unique concentration of his style, his refinement and his grace are of the sort that sum up centuries of previous culture and development, which can be loved by any sensitive spirit, but which only the trained musician can perhaps fully appreciate. For a foreigner the problem is perhaps even more difficult, for Fauré's music, like the dramas of Racine, is essentially French. Before its deceptive elegance, an Anglo-Saxon or a German sometimes feels those movements of impatience and irritation which the music of Brahms or Mahler tends to provoke in a Frenchman. But in all such cases of national differences, longer acquaintance is an easy and a certain remedy, and in the end one finds oneself loving the very qualities which at first seemed so repellen (124).

Boulanger continues by explicitly linking Fauré's simplicity and classicism to notions of class and sophistication, perhaps in an appeal to the sensibilities of the American audiences she encountered on her tour. She characterizes Fauré as a patrician, his music possessing "the charm of an aristocrat; it is the cloak of discretion and restraint that go with gentle manners and high breeding" (125), adding a sophisticated veneer to her scholarly contribution to the Rice Institute's project of intellectual uplift through association with European high culture.

### (Re)translating Fauré in Europe and America
Following her 1925 trip, Boulanger would not visit the United States again until 1937. Fauré continued to figure prominently in her pedagogy, however, and she reused her American work in the public lectures that increasingly supplemented her classroom and private teaching in France. In the 1925–26 academic year, she reworked some of her tour material for six public lectures on "La Musique moderne" at the Ecole Normale de Musique. As in Houston, a stenographer was employed to record the lectures, and an edited account was published over three issues of *Le Monde musical* in spring 1926.[67] Although most of the published text represents summaries of Boulanger's sessions by the journal's editor Marc Pincherle there are also extensive quotes from the stenographer's transcripts. These show considerable overlap with the published versions of Boulanger's Houston lectures; for example, her exposé of the scales and chords of modern music closely matches the material added to "Modern French Music," and the account of her discussion of rhythm matches additions to her published Rice lecture on Stravinsky. These correspondences suggest that she was working on a French revision of her Rice lectures with the intention of reusing the material for the public lectures at the Ecole Normale, and provide a further context for the technical turn her

Houston material took in publication. At the same time, the public lecture series at the Ecole Normale represented a new pedagogical initiative that owed much to the success of her American tour the year before.

The reports in *Le Monde musical* are partial, but they confirm that Boulanger did not restrict herself to discussing French (or French-based) composers in her account of modern music as she had done in the United States: Prokofiev, Szymanowski, Bartók, Hindemith, Casella, and Malipiero joined composers such as Stravinsky, Debussy, and the younger French generation of Les Six in her sessions. While her sponsors and audiences in the United States expected her to speak for France, in Paris she could project a more international modernism. Although the stenographers' transcripts for her comments on Fauré do not figure in the publication, Pincherle's summaries confirm that the composer appeared in her survey of the modern, and that, as in the Houston lectures, she used quotations from Valéry to support her claims.[68] Fauré took an even greater place in her next series of public lectures at the Ecole Normale in the 1926–27 academic year, which were devoted to analysis of modern dramatic works and included a session on *Pénélope*.[69] Reworking this material into English for American publication appears to have been a project that arose at about the same time. Correspondence with Minna Lederman, the managing editor of the New York–based League of Composers' journal *Modern Music*, reveals that Boulanger was commissioned to write an essay on *Pénélope* specifically to convince American readers that Fauré was indeed a composer of "modern music." Lederman wrote:

> I should like to add that we feel, if possible, that we would like you to point out to us in what respect you, or any other admirers in France, consider Fauré a modern. In America, where only his earlier works, his songs principally, are known, he is not ranked in this category. We have felt that this would be a good opportunity, as you so thoroughly know his work, to get the other point of view about him. If you could, in your discussion of "Pénélope," give us some larger estimate of the man so that we can understand what his true significance is for France and perhaps even for us, we would get a discussion most interesting from the point of view of our magazine.[70]

Boulanger never completed the commissioned article; if she had, it would be fascinating to see how the incipient neoclassical vocabulary she had employed in reviewing *Pénélope*'s premiere in 1913 had developed in the aesthetic climate of the 1920s. But she continued to analyze and discuss

Fauré, sometimes using the same materials, in her teaching in French at the Ecole Normale and in English for the American pupils who came to study with her at Fontainebleau through the later 1920s and into the 1930s.

In the interim Boulanger's work took a distinctive new turn that would profoundly affect her activities in America in the late 1930s and during World War II. Performance became an important mode of advocating for Fauré as her career as a conductor developed, while her own and others' earlier writing on the composer served to frame and comment upon this new work. From 1933, when her career as a conductor began to develop, Boulanger's teaching was reinforced by demonstration in public performances. Fauré became one of the "moderns" she juxtaposed with early music in an argument about the timeless nature of the masterpiece, a strategy that involved, for example, juxtaposing Stravinsky with Bach, and Lili Boulanger with fourteenth-century motets. When exported, this transnational and transhistorical programming practice aimed at illustrating her understanding of the modern often clashed with concert organizers' desire for her to represent something characteristically French.

In this regard, Boulanger's performance projects in the United States in the late 1930s became closely tied to her work for Britain and the BBC. Her first concert visit to London in 1936 included an engagement to produce five programs in the BBC music-historical series *Foundations of Music* with her Parisian vocal ensemble; the broadcasts would each cover a range of early music and contemporary works, including pieces by Boulanger's students Jean Françaix, Léo Preger, and Marcelle de Manziarly as well as the premiere performance of Francis Poulenc's *Litanies à la Vierge noire*.[71] Fauré was represented in the fourth broadcast by his Madrigal, which figured alongside secular chansons by Josquin and Lassus. This short work was dwarfed, however, when the decision was made to include the Requiem on a concert at Queen's Hall during the week of Boulanger's trip. The concert was intended to showcase Heinrich Schütz's *Historia der Auferstehung* (Story of the Resurrection) which had been a major success when Boulanger conducted it at the Salle Gaveau in Paris the previous spring.[72] French cultural organizations, including the Ministry of Beaux Arts in Paris and the French Embassy in London, were more interested in using Boulanger as a national ambassador, however, and pressured her to include a major French work on her program. This would be the first performance of the piece in Britain by any conductor; but it is worth noting that although she had performed the Requiem as an organist, Boulanger had at this point never conducted the work in France.

When asked for material to aid Edwin Evans write program notes for the Fauré, Boulanger instructed her assistant Annette Dieudonné to send him the 1922 *Revue musicale* special issue.[73] Evans borrowed directly from Boulanger's article for his analytical notes, prefacing them with a new translation of the same paragraph on the Requiem that Boulanger herself had frequently deployed:

> According to Mlle. Boulanger, "No external effect detracts from its sober and somewhat severe expression of grief: no disquiet or agitation disturbs its profound meditation, no doubt tarnishes its unassailable faith, its quiet confidence, its tender and peaceful expectation. . . . The music tells of the sorrow that is left behind by those who depart without return, a sorrow so near to God that it is without revolt, cry, or gesture, And if grave utterances are made, if grief-laden song unfolds itself, they are dominated by the assurance of forgiveness and the serene promise of eternal peace."[74]

The concert was an outstanding critical success, and Boulanger's achievement was mingled with Fauré's in many of the press reactions. For example, Francis Toye remarked, "It would be unfair not to ascribe much of the success [of the Fauré] to the exquisite performance achieved by Mademoiselle Boulanger. . . . Indeed, as an essay in restraint, in delicate tones, this performance was perhaps the best I have ever heard anywhere, proclaiming Mademoiselle Boulanger as a great interpreter of music."[75] Boulanger was immediately engaged for a return visit during the following year to repeat the Fauré performance, although this time she would become the first woman to conduct the orchestra of the Royal Philharmonic Society. International media coverage of this significant milestone helped to establish Boulanger's association with the Requiem. Her status as a pupil of Fauré was almost invariably invoked in the press to underscore the legitimacy of her interpretation, and as in Toye's review the year before, many accounts conflated the clarity and serenity of the piece with the character of Boulanger's performance. For the concert program, Edwin Evans's notes from 1936, including the quoted passage from Boulanger's *Revue musicale* article, were reused. And though public accounts of the concert tended not to stress the consoling concepts of peaceful death evoked at the end of Boulanger's quote, some reactions from her inner circle did connect her work to these ideas. In a letter to Boulanger on the 1937 performance, her assistant Cécile Armagnac wrote:

> I ask myself sometimes if the souls of those in heaven see from above what is happening on earth—and in any case for

myself, I think I believe this absolutely—and I thought how much your own [souls in heaven] must delight and rejoice in your glory—you were so beautiful, Mademoiselle, and the Requiem so peaceful and great, the atmosphere itself so full of meaning and yet so calm and confident.[76]

Enthusiastic reactions to Boulanger's London performances paved the way for the successful export of the Requiem to America during concert tours in 1938 and 1939. In the spring of 1938, she became the first woman to lead the Boston Symphony Orchestra, conducting the Requiem before taking the organ part for Saint-Saëns's Symphony No. 3. The concert program included not just a paragraph from Boulanger's 1922 essay in *La Revue musicale*; instead, almost the entire article was used in an anonymous translation, including all of the passages about Fauré's service to the Church.[77] Boulanger's authorship and the source of the text is noted at the top. The program continued with a long unsigned article drawing liberally from other essays in the 1922 issue (including Fauré's own memoir), and also mentioning Copland's 1924 article and subsequent books by Koechlin and Paul Landormy. Boulanger's words on the spiritual meaning of Fauré's music are relocated here amid the voices of the large crowd of "reputational entrepreneurs" who had worked to promote Fauré's music in France, similar to how they had appeared on first publication in *La Revue musicale*. Here, however, they were used to authorize the performance of a work Boulanger had still never conducted in her own country. In January 1939, she conducted the Requiem in Columbus, Ohio, and again at Oberlin Conservatory in a performance that was broadcast nationwide on the NBC radio network.[78] Thus although both tours included frequent performances of Fauré—including extracts from *Shylock* and *Pelléas*, the Violin Sonata, and many songs—the Requiem reached more listeners, and generated more publicity for Boulanger's status as conductor and Fauré expert than any other single piece. Within the space of a few years, the Requiem had become a signature work over which she had particular authority not only as critic but as performer, setting the stage for the vision of Fauré that would come to dominate her reception in America during World War II.

When Boulanger arrived in New York in 1940, she was not a musical diplomat from the capital of European fashion as she had been in 1925, or a visiting virtuoso as she had been in the late 1930s, but an exile from a suffering country. Letters from American friends and admirers regularly mention their sympathy for Boulanger and hopes for France's salvation in terms reminiscent of condolence letters. Unlike many refugees, she was already well established in American musical circles, and in addition to the job at the Longy School in Cambridge that provided her living expenses, she was able to continue taking the same kinds of concert and lecture engagements as on her prewar American tours. However, the narratives surrounding her work reflected new concerns. Building on by now well-established tropes of restraint and serenity, the "quiet" of Fauré's music was explicitly juxtaposed with the noise of war, and the French origins of both the music and Boulanger herself were welcome to wartime audiences as an alternative to German works. Performances of the Requiem in particular aimed at an atmosphere of transcendence, aided by Boulanger's practice of insisting that the work figure last on her concert programs and that it should not be followed by applause.[79]

Her most high-profile performance after arriving in the United States was aimed at European war relief, a context in which Fauré's music could figure as spiritual consolation and a contribution toward material aid. At Carnegie Hall on 4 April 1941, Boulanger directed the New York Philharmonic and the Potsdam State Crane choir for a concert in honor of the pianist and cultural diplomat Ignacy Paderewski. The concert was given to benefit the Paderewski Fund for Polish Relief; as the flyers note, the event was a "Concert of Religious Music to honor Mr. Paderewski on the Golden Anniversary of his American debut (1891–1941) and to help him relieve the suffering of his exiled countrymen in Great Britain and Switzerland."[80] The program was a near-repeat of Boulanger's London concert of 1936, featuring Schütz's *Historia der Auferstehung*, the Fauré Requiem, a fragment of Karol Szymanowski's *Stabat Mater*, and a fourteenth-century Polish hymn in an arrangement by Boulanger. The concert program reused the notes on the Requiem and the Schütz that Edwin Evans had written in 1936, including Boulanger's *Revue musicale* quote on Fauré's attitude toward death. Although this rendition of the Requiem was the most prominent of her efforts, Fauré also figured in more intimate concerts and in lectures as Boulanger adapted her musical advocacy to the wartime environment. In May 1941, she included Fauré on a Washington recital of small-scale vocal music in aid of the Coordinating Council of French Relief Societies. A special conference in June during the Indiana University summer session included two talks on "The Role of the Arts in Time of Crisis," though it is unclear whether Fauré's music figured in these lectures, the title gives some indication of how Boulanger saw the new context for her work.[81]

In other respects, Boulanger continued to promote Fauré's music in lectures, recitals, and publications that not only echoed her earlier efforts, but often used the same materials and texts she had created for previous engagements. Much of this work took place in educational settings; for example, 1942 performances of the incidental music from *Shylock*, chamber music, and songs at the Longy School were similar to those she had produced at the Ecole Normale de Musique and at Fontainebleau. The same month, a talk at the Phillips Gallery in Washington was billed as a "discussion, with musical illustrations, of the music of Gabriel Fauré" in an echo of her work for "Modern French Music" at Rice nearly twenty years before.[82] In 1943, she produced an article for the Francophone cultural journal *Amérique française* that demonstrates how the texts prepared for earlier publications continued to be circulated and adapted.[83] Her article used several paragraphs verbatim from her *Revue musicale* article from 1922, but interestingly does not discuss the Requiem or Fauré's religious affiliations. Instead, the choice of material strongly promotes the image of Fauré as the founding father of modern French music. Beginning with an account of his modesty, charm, and serenity, the article continues with a direct quote from Boulanger's *Revue musicale* article to describe Fauré's sensibility in neoclassical terms:

> Everything in this work has been tempered by the well-judged and incomparable sense of order that constitutes its greatness and ensures its longevity. Without affectation and never with brutality, his strength charms, dominates, imposes itself—without systems, without overturning, without noise, his originality innovates, renews, builds—without posing, without useless exclamations, without shouts, this music of such profound emotional character thinks, loves, and suffers. (10)

After a further paragraph taken from *La Revue musicale*, on Fauré's youthfulness in old age, Boulanger added new remarks that even more forcefully stated the case for the composer's originality, emphasizing the anti-Romantic aspects of his work and describing how, "in complete tranquillity, with the most ingenuous grace, the musician had, without shattering anything, changed something in the musical language and begun to trace . . . the uninterrupted arc that would, continuously renewed, be crowned with the String Quartet in 1924" (10).

But there is considerable evidence that such efforts to promote Fauré's modernity to North American audiences were eclipsed by Boulanger's fame as a conductor of the Requiem and by the desire for musical responses to wartime concerns. At the end of the war in 1945 Boulanger was eager to return to France, but her final months in the United States were marked by different events of commemoration. The first was a week-long festival of

Figure 4. Aaron Copland, Nadia Boulanger, and Walter Piston at the appropriately named Old France Restaurant, during the Harvard University Fauré Festival, 1945.

Fauré's music mounted at Harvard University in 1945 to celebrate the centenary of the composer's birth. Boulanger was deeply involved in the effort, conducting the first and last of the five concerts and accompanying Fauré's songs on the fourth. The festival concluded with her direction of a concert performance of *Pénélope*, the first performance of the work in the United States. The textual framing of Fauré's music in the program booklet moved firmly into the realm of the scholarly: an unsigned note, possibly written by Boulanger and her former pupil Tillman Merritt, opens with an overview of Fauré's career and music, and closes with a catalogue of the composer's works listed by opus number.[84] As in 1924, Aaron Copland joined his efforts to hers, writing an article in the *New York Times* to promote the festival.[85] By now an established composer and critic, Copland had become a significant authority in his own right as the voice of American musical modernism. Nevertheless, there is an echo of the young man recently returned from Paris in his reassertion of the sophisticated nature of Fauré's quintessentially French music and the people who appreciate it. Copland again claims, "It has never been easy to convince the musical public outside France of the special charm that attaches itself to Fauré's art. . . . Outside France the public has been slow to appreciate his delicacy, his reserve, his imperturbable calm—qualities that are not easily exportable." Fauré remains a connois-seur's musician, however, "those aware of musical refinements cannot help but admire the transparent texture, the clarity of thought, the well-shaped proportions" and "the true believer in the genius of Fauré is convinced that to hear him is to love him."

Within the panorama represented by the festival, and despite the draw of *Pénélope*'s premiere, Boulanger's rendition of the Requiem seems to have overshadowed the rest. All of the concerts were well attended, but a letter from the poet May Sarton—who was turned away at the door despite arriving well in advance—suggests that the crowds came out especially for this first concert, and also expresses something of what the audience expected from the piece and the performance:

> What desolation to arrive 40 minutes in advance and not to be able to enter for the Requiem! In the dark, in the hell of outside I watched the chapel illuminated by the presence of Fauré, and a star near the spire—o despair! I was one among at least eight hundred others—could the Requiem not be redone for this multitude? . . . I'm told that you are returning to France. What happiness for France! May all that means civilization, soul, unite now for the never-ending struggle towards the Light![86]

Boulanger's student Ruth Culbertson was among those who managed to get a seat, and her own letter suggested that the performance succeeded in bringing some listeners to the light-filled realm that Sarton's letter con-trasted with the hell of external darkness:

> The concert was so noble—profound—so truly a memorial—a dedication of love. To these ears—this heart—it was the case of listening to that inner hearing, that inner pulse—no confusion —no noise.[87]

While Culbertson may have been thinking of the performance as a loving memorial to Fauré himself within the context of the festival, two perfor-mances of the Requiem within the month were explicitly dedicated to commemoration of those lost in the war. At the Toledo Museum of Art in Ohio on 9 December 1945, Boulanger conducted a memorial concert of Bach chorales and Fauré's Requiem in honor of the Toledo war dead. There was no program note, but Boulanger gave a public talk on Fauré's music and its meaning the evening before, allowing her to communicate her understanding of the timeless and consoling aspects of the work. She followed the same procedure later that month for a concert of the Requiem for the Crane Department of Music at Potsdam State Teachers College in New York State's "North Country," giving a lecture on Fauré the day before the performance.[88] This performance was presented as a celebration of the centennial of Fauré's birth, but the program dedicated the Requiem to the memory of eleven students from the college who had died in Europe. When framed as a wartime memorial and contextualized by Boulanger's words, these performances of the Requiem read as a musical manifestation of "speaking from the heart," which had garnered so much success on her first visit to America, and which became more meaningful to many in her audiences in the wake of wartime loss.

After her return to France in 1946, Boulanger continued to champion Fauré for the rest of her teaching and performing career. Her association with the Requiem continued to grow, with postwar performances in Europe (Paris, London, Warsaw, Monaco, Winterthur) and return engagements in America, from landmark performances such as those with the New York Philharmonic in 1962 to appearances at educational institutions, including a return visit to the Crane Department of Music in Potsdam. Her performances were widely broadcast and twice recorded, and her interpretation of the Requiem continues to be a principal aspect of her legacy as a conductor. As Heather de Savage's account of the Requiem in postwar American culture makes clear, Boulanger's wartime performances of the work were a step toward the role it holds in American culture today, in which it is frequently used in memorial contexts and to benefit humanitarian causes by communities facing loss, up to and including 9/11.[89] In the popular imagination, Fauré's status as a "modern French composer" has faded from view, while the image of consolation that marked Boulanger's relationship with his work has persisted.

Boulanger's speech at Fauré's state funeral concluded: "Of our admiration for you, Maître, it is not appropriate for me to speak here—we must prove it."[90] Her own efforts to do so rendered her a forceful advocate for Fauré's status as a modern composer. Within the transnational context, whether teaching American students in France or lecturing to United States audiences, Boulanger's ability to represent French culture and music through language and performance lent authority and distinction to her interpretation. Her work drew on thorough familiarity with the claims of Fauré's reputational entrepreneurs in France, many of whom were close friends, but was also inflected by her personal religious beliefs and experience of mourning. Her early work in France as the spokesperson for Fauré's religious music allowed her to consolidate a strand of Fauré interpretation that framed the composer's formal clarity and restraint in terms of spirituality. The transnational reception of her work increasingly centered around this aspect of her understanding of Fauré's music, particularly in reaction to the development of Boulanger's conducting career and the need for musical responses to collective trauma during World War II. Paradoxically, Boulanger's success in promoting the spiritual framework for Fauré's work undercut her own efforts to present him as a composer of wider significance. When Boulanger first came to the United States in 1925, her presentation of Fauré produced a deep personal impression; and despite her consistent efforts to "formalize" his music and represent the composer as the standard bearer for "modern French music," it is the use of his work for personal and emotional needs of commemoration and memorialization that produced the most enduring effect on her American audiences.

# NOTES

1. Program, Washington Cathedral, 14 November 1940; copies in the Bibliothèque nationale de France (F-Pn), Rés. Vm. dos. 195, and the Centre international Nadia et Lili Boulanger, Paris (CNLB). Boulanger conducted only the Fauré, and the Society's usual leader, Louis A. Potter, directed the Bach.

2. Mildred Bliss to Nadia Boulanger, 15 November 1940, F-Pn, N.L.a. 56 (249), in French. This and all subsequent translations are my own. On Boulanger and Bliss, see Jeanice Brooks, "Collecting Past and Present: Music History and Musical Performance at Dumbarton Oaks," in *A Home of the Humanities: The Collecting and Patronage of Mildred and Robert Woods Bliss*, ed. James N. Carder and Robert S. Nelson (Washington, DC: Dumbarton Oaks, 2010), 74–91.

3. Heather de Savage, "The American Reception of Gabriel Fauré: From Francophile Boston, 1892–1945, to the Broader Postwar Mainstream" (PhD diss., University of Connecticut, Storrs, 2015), 266–304.

4. Marianne Wheeldon, *Debussy's Legacy and the Construction of Reputation* (New York: Oxford University Press, 2017), 29–64.

5. On the problem of Fauré's historical position, see Carlo Caballero, *Fauré and French Musical Aesthetics* (Cambridge: Cambridge University Press, 2001), 8–9: and Tom Gordon, "Introduction: Rearguard or Avant-Garde?," in *Regarding Fauré*, ed. Tom Gordon (Amsterdam: Gordon and Breach, 1999; repr., London: Taylor and Francis, 2013), xiii–xxiii. On Fauré's fluctuating status as old guard or modern during his late career, see Jean-Michel Nectoux, *Gabriel Fauré: A Musical Life*, trans. Roger Nichols (Cambridge: Cambridge University Press, 1991), 424–37.

6. Matthew Head, "Music with 'No Past'?: Archaeologies of Joseph Haydn and the *Creation*," *19th-Century Music* 23 (2000): 191–217. Head describes how late eighteenth-century efforts to honor Haydn entombed the composer in history years before his physical death by consigning him to the pre-Romantic past. On the state celebration of Fauré, see Nectoux, *Gabriel Fauré*, 424–28 and 467–68.

7. Jean-Michel Nectoux, "Nadia Boulanger: La rencontre avec Gabriel Fauré," in *Nadia Boulanger et Lili Boulanger, témoignages et études*, ed. Alexandra Laederich (Lyon: Symétrie, 2007), 33–47.

8. Boulanger's heavily annotated copy of the full orchestral version of the Requiem (1901) can be found at F-Pn, Vma. 1938a. The date the composition was begun is printed at the top of the first page.

9. The friendship is traced in their abundant correspondence; see Jean Roger-Ducasse, *Lettres à Nadia Boulanger*, ed. Jacques Depaulis (Sprimont: Mardaga, 1999).

10. Byron Adams, "*Lux aeterna*: Fauré's Requiem, Op. 48," in *Fauré Studies*, ed. Carlo Caballero and Stephen Rumph (Cambridge: Cambridge University Press, forthcoming), considers how Fauré's piece was used in different versions in the Church. See also Vincent Rollin, "Chants et musiques des cérémonies de funérailles à Paris sous le régime concordataire (1802–1905)," *Revue de musicologie* 99/2 (2013): 235–70; and Nectoux, *Gabriel Fauré*, 117–24.

11. Daybook entries for 13 June and 11 July 1905, F-Pn, Rés. Vmf. ms. 145.

12. On Boulanger's relationship with Pugno and the opera *La ville morte*, see Alexandra Laederich, "The Strange Fate of *La ville morte* by Nadia Boulanger and Raoul Pugno," this volume, and Jeanice Brooks and Kimberly Francis, "Serious Ambitions: Nadia Boulanger and the Composition of *La ville morte*," also this volume.

13. One daybook notes a session on Fauré's *Ballade*, describing the "velvet sonority" that Pugno was able to achieve and his encouragement for Nadia's own piano technique. See entry for 22 September 1905, F-Pn, Rés. Vmf. ms. 145.

14. A[rchibald] M[artin] Henderson, "Memories of Some Distinguished French Organists—Fauré," *The Musical Times* 78/1135 (1937): 818. My thanks to Byron Adams for alerting me to this source.

15. Boulanger daybook entry for 12 July 1906, F-Pn, Rés. Vmf. ms. 146.

16. Nadia Boulanger, "Semaine Théâtrale," *Le Ménestrel* 79/11 (15 March 1913): 82–83. Boulanger first offered the review to *Le Figaro* but was brusquely dismissed by the editor, Gaston Calmette; see *Nadia Boulanger: Thoughts on Music,* ed. Jeanice Brooks and Kimberly Francis (Rochester, NY: University of Rochester Press, in press). Later that year, Boulanger joined Ravel and Roger-Ducasse as the principal organizers of the banquet in Fauré's honor after *Pénélope*'s Paris premiere on 10 May. Roger-Ducasse, *Lettres à Nadia Boulanger,* 37.

17. Boulanger daybook entry for 2 *(sic)* January 1914, F-Pn, Rés. Vmf. ms. 152.

18. Edward R. Phillips, *Gabriel Fauré: A Guide to Research* (New York: Garland, 2000), 21.

19. Boulanger daybook entry for 14 January 1915, F-Pn, Rés. Vmf. ms. 153. The Beethoven examples had long been associated in France with mourning. In a later review, Boulanger commented extensively on death as the "principal idea" of the slow movement of the "Eroica." See Nadia Boulanger, "Walter Damrosch et le New York Symphony Orchestra à Paris," *Le Monde musical* 31/9–10 (May 1920): 156–57.

20. Boulanger daybook entry for 14 January 1916, F-Pn, Rés. Vmf. ms. 154.

21. Boulanger daybook entry for 3 April 1919, F-Pn, Rés. Vmf. ms. 157.

22. See Aaron Copland, *A Reader: Selected Writings, 1923–72,* ed. Richard Kostelanetz (New York: Routledge, 2004), 349; Aaron Copland and Vivian Perlis, *Copland: 1900 through 1942* (New York: St. Martin's Press, 1984), 67. Further on the development of Boulanger's ideas on form, see Jeanice Brooks, *The Musical Work of Nadia Boulanger: Performing Past and Future Between the Wars* (Cambridge: Cambridge University Press, 2013), 42–76.

23. Nadia Boulanger to Marcelle de Manziarly, 5 October 1925, F-Pn, N.L.a. 289 (127–31).

24. Two performances on 25 January and 1 February 1920 were conducted by Philippe Gaubert, with soloists Jeanne Campredon from the Opéra and Charles Panzéra from the Opéra-Comique.

25. Gabriel Fauré to Nadia Boulanger, 15 September 1920, F-Pn, N.L.a. 69 (265).

26. Nectoux, "Nadia Boulanger: La rencontre avec Gabriel Fauré," 38.

27. Boulanger daybook entry for 20 June 1922, F-Pn, Rés. Vmf. ms. 90.

28. Special issue on Gabriel Fauré, *La Revue musicale* 4/11 (October 1922).

29. Caballero, *Fauré and French Musical Aesthetics,* 125–27.

30. In his conclusion "La musique de chambre," Roger-Ducasse claimed that "French music today reigns sovereign over the world" before listing the flaws in the musical cultures of other European nations, starting with Germany (60–70).

31. Carlo Caballero, "Patriotism or Nationalism? Fauré and the Great War," *Journal of the American Musicological Society* 52/3 (1999) 593–625.

32. Nadia Boulanger, "La musique religieuse," *La Revue musicale* 4/21 (1922): 104–11. (Page numbers in parentheses that follow refer to this article.) For a complete English translation, see Brooks and Francis, eds., *Nadia Boulanger: Thoughts on Music.*

33. Nectoux, *Gabriel Fauré,* 109–12. For a detailed examination of Fauré's religious beliefs in relation to his musical aesthetics, see Caballero, *Fauré and French Musical Aesthetics,* 170–218.

34. Émile Vuillermoz, "Gabriel Fauré," *La Revue musicale* 4/21 (1922): 11.

35. The *Golden Legend,* compiled by Jacobus de Voragine, is a collection of saints' legends, which has been in continuous circulation since the thirteenth century. The *Fioretti* or *Little Flowers* is a collection of legends about Saint Francis of Assisi. Both texts are associated with a popularizing approach to devotion. Fauré himself pointed to the broad range of possible approaches to faith in an early interview published in 1903, in which he remarked that Saint Teresa of Avila was still a saint although her mode of expressing

her faith was ardent to the point of seeming licentious to some. See Caballero, *Fauré and French Musical Aesthetics*, 182–83.

36. Ibid., 187–90.

37. Boulanger daybook entry for 4 November 1924, F-Pn, Rés. Vmf. ms. 92.

38. Marc Pincherle, in *Le Monde musical* 35/21–22 (November 1924): 364.

39. Jillian Rogers, "Grieving Through Music in Interwar France: Maurice Ravel and His Circle, 1914–1934" (PhD diss., University of California, Los Angeles, 2014), 68.

40. *Comoedia* 18/4339 (Saturday, 8 November 1924): 2 (tribute only); *Le Monde musical* 35/21–22 (November 1924): 362–63 (tribute) and 365 (funeral speech). Boulanger's autograph manuscript for the tribute is held in the Staatsbibliothek zu Berlin—Preussischer Kulturbesitz, Mus. ep. Boulanger, N. Varia 1. See Edward R. Phillips, "Two Fauré Sources in the Deutsche Staatsbibliothek, East Berlin," *Canadian University Music Review* 11 (1991): 99–100.

41. Rogers, "Grieving Through Music," 41–44.

42. James R. Briscoe, "Debussy in Daleville: Toward Early Modernist Hearing in the United States," in *Rethinking Debussy*, ed. Elliot Antokoletz and Marianne Wheeldon (Oxford: Oxford University Press, 2011), 225–28; Nicholas Gebhardt, "The Historical Context for Ravel's North American Tour," in *Ravel Studies*, ed. Deborah Mawer (Cambridge: Cambridge University Press, 2010), 92–113.

43. Contracts and other documents relating the tour are held in F-Pn, Rés. Vm. dos. 137.

44. Aaron Copland, "Gabriel Fauré, a Neglected Master," *The Musical Quarterly* 10/4 (October 1924): 573–86. Page numbers in parentheses that follow refer to this article. Copland would be a main beneficiary of Boulanger's tour; among her most notable appearances were as organ soloist for the premiere performances of his Symphony, whose commission she had brokered, in Boston and New York.

45. Michel Espagne and Michael Werner, "La construction d'une référence allemande en France: Genèse et histoire (1750–1914)," *Annales. Économies, Sociétés, Cultures* 4 (1987): 969–92.

46. Pierre Bourdieu, *Distinction: A Social Critique of the Judgement of Taste*, trans. Richard Nice (London: Routledge, 1984).

47. Annegret Fauser, "Aaron Copland, Nadia Boulanger and the Making of an 'American' Composer," *The Musical Quarterly* 89 (2006): 524–54.

48. De Savage, "The American Reception," 124–211.

49. On Copland's Two Pieces for String Quartet, in which the second movement "Rondino" spells Fauré's name, see Gayle Murchison, *The American Stravinsky: The Style and Aesthetics of Copland's New American Music, the Early Works, 1921–1938* (Ann Arbor: University of Michigan Press, 2012), 40–47; Edward R. Phillips, "Fauré, through Boulanger, to Copland: The Nature of Influence," *Gamut* 4 (2011): 299–309; and De Savage, "The American Reception," 225–26.

50. See De Savage, "The American Reception," 56–58, for examples of the marketing of French language, food, and culture as symbols of sophistication in late nineteenth-century Boston.

51. Aaron Copland to Nadia Boulanger, 12 August 1923, Library of Congress, Aaron Copland Collection; available in digital facsimile at https://www.loc.gov/resource/copland.corr0059.0?st=gallery.

52. Boulanger daybook entry for 14 January 1925, F-Pn, Rés. vmf. ms. 93; Nadia Boulanger to Raissa Boulanger, n.d. [February 1925], F-Pn, N.L.a. 282 (51-56). Extant programs for lectures in New York (Town Hall, 19 January) and Indianapolis (Lincoln Hotel, 7 February) give her title as "Modern Music and Its Evolution." See CNLB and F-Pn, Rés. Vm. dos. 195.

53. Nadia Boulanger to Raissa Boulanger, 19 February 1925, F-Pn, N.L.a. 282 (105–10).

54. Nadia Boulanger to Raissa Boulanger, 1 January 1925, F-Pn, N.L.a. 282 (15–17).

55. Kimberly Francis, "'Everything Had to Change': Nadia Boulanger's Translation of Modernism in the Rice Lecture Series, 1925," *Journal of the Society for American Music* 7/4 (2013): 363–81.The transcripts, held by the CNLB, were discovered in preparing Brooks and Francis, *Nadia Boulanger: Thoughts on Music* (in press), and are edited there in entirety.

56. Walter B. Bailey, "Ima Hogg and an Experiment in Audience Education: The Rice Lectureship in Music (1923–33)," *Journal of the Society for American Music* 5/3 (2011): 395–426.

57. Francis, "'Everything Had to Change,'" 379.

58. Nadia Boulanger to Raissa Boulanger, n.d. [1 February 1925], F-Pn, N.L.a. 282 (51–56).

59. Stenographer's notes for Nadia Boulanger, "French Music, Modern and Ultra Modern," 28 January 1925. Typescript, CNLB, 1–2.

60. Stenographer's notes, 3.

61. Stenographer's notes, 4–5. The stenographer left blanks for the title and the poet's name, suggesting she did not catch the words; but she transcribed the entire French citation, which Boulanger may have supplied in advance (and which translates as, "Have you not remarked, in strolling through this city, that among the edifices with which it is filled, some are mute, others speak; and others still, which are the rarest, sing."). *Eupalinos* was first published in 1920; for the cited passage, see Paul Valéry, *Oeuvres*, ed. Jean Hytier, 2nd ed., 2 vols., Bibliothèque de la Pléiade (Paris: Gallimard, 1992–93), 1:93.

62. Francis, "'Everything Had to Change,'" 366–68.

63. Nadia Boulanger, "Lectures on Modern Music delivered under the Auspices of the Rice Institute Lectureship in Music, 27, 28, and 29 January 1925," *The Rice Institute Pamphlet* 13/2 (April 1926). The "Modern French Music" lecture appears on pages 113–52 and is available online at http://dspace.rice.edu/handle/1911/8733.

64. Hinners's correspondence with Boulanger can be found in F-Pn, N.L.a. 75 (354–71).

65. Boulanger, "La musique religieuse," p. 122; Fauré, "Souvenirs," 6.

66. Boulanger quotes from Valéry's *L'âme et la danse* (1921) and from *Eupalinos*; for a discussion of these two citations, see Brooks, *The Musical Work*, 62–65.

67. "La Musique moderne: D'après la sténographie des cours à l'Ecole Normale de Musique," *Le Monde musical* 37/2 (February 1926): 59–61; "Les Cours de Mlle Nadia Boulanger, à l'Ecole Normale de Musique," *Le Monde musical* 37/5 (May 1926): 201; and "Les Cours de musique moderne de Nadia Boulanger," *Le Monde musical* 37/6 (June 1926): 242–44. Translations appear in Brooks and Francis, *Nadia Boulanger: Thoughts on Music*.

68. Pincherle wrote: "I do not know of a more deeply penetrating analysis of Fauré's genius than that which she extracts, by analogy, from Paul Valéry's marvellous *Eupalinos*," in "Les Cours de Mlle Nadia Boulanger," 201.

69. An announcement for the series and flyers for some individual sessions, which were illustrated with performances by singers from the Opéra, can be found in F-Pn, Rés. Vm. dos. 195. Boulanger reused the material in later years; documents in F-Pn, Rés. 127 indicate that she analyzed *Pénélope* in her Ecole Normale composition courses in the 1935–36 academic year.

70. Minna Lederman to Nadia Boulanger, 19 March 1927, F-Pn, Rés. Vm. dos. 139.

71. See Alexandra Laederich, "La première audition à Londres des *Litanies à la Vierge Noire* par Nadia Boulanger (novembre 1936)," in *Francis Poulenc et la voix: Texte et contexte*, ed. Alban Ramaut (Lyon: Symétrie, 2002), 153–67.

72. For details on the Paris performance and London trip, see Jeanice Brooks, "Nadia Boulanger and the Salon of the Princesse de Polignac," *Journal of the American Musicological Society* 46 (1993): 437–44.

73. The note to Dieudonné appears in a letter from the concert organizer Robert Mayer to Boulanger, 1 October 1936, in which he wrote that Evans would be asked to write the program notes and requested material from Boulanger to help him. CNLB, folder "Londres 1936."

74. Concert program, Queen's Hall, 24 November 1936; copies are held in F-Pn, Rés. Vm. dos. 195 and CNLB.

75. Francis Toye, *Morning Post*, 26 November 1936.

76. Cécile Armagnac to Nadia Boulanger, F-Pn, N.L.a 51 (62–63). Boulanger's mother had died in 1935, and Nadia was now the sole surviving member of her immediate family.

77. The program was performed twice. A copy of the concert program for Symphony Hall, 17–18 February 1938, is held at CNLB.

78. Brooks, *The Musical Work*, 102.

79. The order of some high-profile concerts—including for example the Paderewsky testimonial discussed below—was switched after programs went to press, to allow Boulanger to achieve her desired order. See Brooks, *The Musical Work*, 207–9.

80. Flyer and concert program are both held at CNLB.

81. Flyer, Indiana University summer session, 1941, CNLB.

82. Ticket, 25 April 1942, preserved among the concert programs at CNLB.

83. Nadia Boulanger, "Gabriel Fauré," *Amérique française* 2/4 (January 1943): 9–12. *Amérique française* was published in Montreal between 1941 and 1955; it is unclear how the article was commissioned. Large sections of the article are identical to an undated lecture text preserved at CNLB, though it has not been possible to determine which text came first.

84. Correspondence between Merritt and Boulanger is preserved in Harvard University Archive, Records of the Music Department: Correspondence, 1936–1959, UAV 587.17, Box 4. It shows that Merritt and Boulanger rejected a short text by Edward Burlingame Hill that had been written for the program, but does not indicate who wrote the replacement.

85. Aaron Copland, "Fauré Festival at Harvard," *New York Times*, 25 November 1945.

86. May Sarton to Nadia Boulanger, 30 November 1945, F-Pn, N.L.a 103 (299); original in French. Irving Fine's review of the festival cast the Requiem and *Pénélope* as the highlights, and identified Boulanger's "proselytizing fervor" as a component of their success. Fine, "Symphonic Words and Fauré Anniversary," *Modern Music* 23 (1946): 55–57.

87. Ruth Culberton to Nadia Boulanger, 27 November 1945, F-Pn, N.L.a 64 (272).

88. Program for 15 and 16 December 1945, F-Pn, Rés. Vm. dos. 195. The Crane chorus had been her singers for the 1941 Paderewski concert at Carnegie Hall; the work played such a large part in the mind of Boulanger's former pupil Helen Hosmer, the department's director, that on her own death in 1989 she had a passage from the Requiem engraved upon her tombstone.

89. De Savage, "The American Reception," 266–304, esp. 283–91.

90. Boulanger, funeral speech for Fauré, *Le Monde musical* 35/21–22 (November 1924): 365.

# For Nadia Boulanger:
# Five Poems by May Sarton

## INTRODUCED BY JEANICE BROOKS

It is unclear when the American poet and novelist May Sarton (1912–1995) first met Nadia Boulanger, though it is likely they encountered each other in Cambridge, Massachusetts, through musical and academic networks. Sarton's Belgian father, a historian of science, was employed by Harvard University, where Boulanger pupils such as Tillman Merritt and Walter Piston held posts in the music department. On her American tours in 1938 and 1939 Boulanger stayed in Cambridge with the family of Edward Forbes, director of Harvard's Fogg Art Museum, and during her wartime exile in the United States between 1940 and 1946, she taught at the Longy School and made Cambridge her principal base.

The earliest extant correspondence between the two women dates from 1939. Over the following years, Sarton sent Boulanger several poems, some of which were subsequently included in her books and others that were apparently never published. The most personal are two poems Sarton wrote after attending a concert at Boston's Symphony Hall, conducted by Boulanger and largely devoted to works by Nadia's sister, Lili. The concert was given to benefit the newly established Lili Boulanger Memorial Fund and featured the combined Harvard Glee Club and Radcliffe Choral Society, accompanied by members of the Boston Symphony Orchestra and E. Power Biggs at the organ. Soloists included Hugues Cuénod, Noémie Pérugia, and Natalie Kédroff, singers Boulanger had brought with her from Paris for parts of her 1939 American tour. After a first half devoted to Bach, Beethoven, and the American premiere of extracts from Gian Francesco Malipiero's *San Francesco d'Assisi*, the second half featured large-scale sacred works by Lili Boulanger, including her *Pour les funerailles d'un soldat*, Psalm 130 (*De profundis*), and Psalm 24. Sarton apparently wrote her "Elegy at a Concert in Memory of Lili Boulanger" directly after the event, and sent it from her family home in Cambridge the next day with a note:

Mademoiselle—

I am humbly a poet in addressing you—for I would need
to be a musician to thank you *correctly* for the power, the joy,
the tenderness of yesterday evening's concert.

It is one thing to celebrate poetry with a musical setting
that transforms and magnifies it—it is another thing to celebrate music with a poem, alas!

But I was furious about the lack of *silence*—and perhaps a
poem carries the emotion and the gratitude that this multitude of applauding hands served only to obliterate.[1]

A week later, Sarton sent or gave Boulanger another poem, "Memory,"
reflecting further on the connection between music, death, and mourning. Sarton was clearly struck by Boulanger's role in bringing her sister's
music to life in performance and interpreted it through a mystical lens
that resonated with Nadia's own conception of her responsibility toward
Lili and her work.[2]

Three further typescript poems in Boulanger's archive were signed and
dedicated in 1945. No framing correspondence survives, so Sarton may
have given these to Boulanger personally in Cambridge during the war.
These include "The Tortured," one of Sarton's best-known poems today,
which was published in her collection *Cloud, Stone, Sun, Vine* (1961) and
in several subsequent editions of collected poems, and which Sarton analyzes in *Writing on Writing* (1980). "Night Storm" was included in Sarton's
*The Lion and the Rose* (1948). "Where Thought Leaps On" appears never
to have been published; it returns to some of the same themes of death
and memory that imbue Sarton's powerful elegy with the music of Lili
Boulanger and her sister's acts of faith in resurrecting it in the world.

## NOTES

1. May Sarton to Nadia Boulanger, 7 March 1939, Bibliothèque nationale de France
(F-Pn), N.L.a 103 (297). The letter is in French, translation by Jeanice Brooks.
2. "Memory" is preserved in the archives of the Centre international Nadia et Lili
Boulanger, without accompanying correspondence. The other four poems here are held
in F-Pn, N.L.a 103 (298 and 301–3).

## Elegy
### at a Concert in Memory
### of Lili Boulanger

Silence, silence be hers
Wherever she is
About whom this music stirs:
Not this applause.

There in the ravaged bone,
The soundless case of skull
Under the heavy stone
Lies music's living will.

Match death if you dare.
You who have not stood,
But seated sit and hear
(That music in your blood.)

Go, go, since you are filled
As fountains are with sound,
Before you too are stilled
And music underground.

Spend all this given grace,
Live back her darling breath,
Her heart, her unknown face—
You must transform her death.

Remember where she lies
Lies music's living will
That looks out from your eyes:
Go forth and live. Be still.

May Sarton
For Nadia Boulanger
March 7 [1939]

**Memory**
**For Nadia Boulanger**

Ah, what is memory but a holy gift:
To keep the whole heart open, where
Split, and to hold death in the rift:
Within all living still to die with her.

Within all dying still with her to live.
Wherever the pure Absolute of Pain
Leaps unarmed from the heart, you give
Her back to earth, merciful as the rain.

Wherever Joy, that holier than Grief,
Pours pure as music from the anguished mind,
There you are living back her heart's belief:
Your joy is brought back to her on the wind.

Between this ardent life and cruel death
Take up your station, heart, and there stand blazing
That for her sake while you draw living breath
Remembrance may become the gift of praising.

That she, the living dead, the pure translator
Of Glory visible into triumphant sound
May now translate invisible and greater
Glory through you: Heart, praise the wound!

March 16, 1939
May Sarton

# The Tortured

Cried Innocence, "Mother, my thumbs, my thumbs!
The pain will make me wild."
And Wisdom answered, "Your brother-man
Is suffering, my child."

Screamed Innocence, "Mother, my eyes, my eyes!
Someone is blinding me."
And Wisdom answered, "Those are your brother's eyes.
The blinded one is he."

Cried Innocence, " Mother, my heart, my heart!
It bursts with agony."
And Wisdom answered, "That is your brother's heart
Breaking upon a tree."

Screamed Innocence, "Mother I want to die.
I cannot bear the pain."
And Wisdom answered, "They will not let him die.
They bring him back again."

Cried Innocence, "Mother, I cannot bear
It now. My flesh is wild."
And Wisdom answered, "His agony is endless,
For your sake, my child."

Then whispered Innocence, "Mother, forgive,
Forgive my sin, forgive—"
And Wisdom wept, "Now do you understand, Love,
How you must live?"

For Nadia Boulanger
May Sarton
1945

# Night Storm

We watched the sky torn by the terrible light,
Bright presences whose jagged swords lash out
While their feet thunder on the stairs of cloud,
The flash of wings where light and darkness crowd.
We watched it all and, trembling, thought of Blake
For whom these powers were angels and did speak:
The wings rushed past. The clouds were overthrown.
We lay there where the naked light leapt down,
Exposed to God's impersonal and distant eyes
That gazed on us and on the Pleiades.
And then against your heart I leaned my fear
And heard it beat and knew that God was near:
The Love that binds the stars' sweet influence,
Heart-beat and thunder in a single Presence:
The angels did not speak a single word
And yet we were transfixed by what we heard.

May Sarton, 1945

## Where Thought Leaps On

### 1

I saw a man bend to a flowing stream
To drink where light and shadow made a fish,
A leaping liveness: this was not a dream.
I saw the man bend down as if to wish
And all around him the green leaves were still,
Leaf folded upon leaf, by the sun drenched.
I saw the man drink deep of miracle.
He made his wish. His dusty thirst was quenched.
And then I knew what I had only guessed:
How past flows into future every hour
And we are by the dead continually blest.
Their lives are a bright stream of power
And we can drink there deeply if we will,
Where thought leaps on although the mind is still.

### 2

The dead are with us when we know it least,
When given up to grief, when most alone,
When the dear angel has become a beast
And there is only crying in the bone,
When death is with us, then the dead can give
What life obscures with its multiple shadow—
They rise, implacable, demanding that we live.
Their saving thoughts go with us where we go
And we are loved best when we know it not;
When out of darkness shines the core of faith
And the angelic presence in the night
Seizes the heart and almost stops the breath,
The dead are with us and their live belief
Makes a great flaming tower out of grief.

For Nadia Boulanger
May Sarton
1945

# Friend and Force: Nadia Boulanger's Presence in Polish Musical Culture

ANDREA F. BOHLMAN AND J. MACKENZIE PIERCE

On 11 October 1956, Nadia Boulanger commanded the room at the Polish Composers' Union, or Związek Kompozytorów Polskich (ZKP), the main professional association of Poland's composers. She had been accompanied by her dear friend and former student, Zygmunt Mycielski, on the walk from her apartment at the luxurious Hotel Bristol—accommodations only accessible to visitors from abroad at the time—to a gathering of her former students on the upper floor of a building facing Market Square in Warsaw's newly rebuilt Old Town. Boulanger was one of the most fêted guests at the first Warsaw Autumn Festival for Contemporary Music, and this stop was one of many during an extended visit to the Polish capital (see Figure 1). The trip was the first of several she would make to Poland over the following two decades. The bustling activity of the festival kept her busy, as her luminescence bequeathed importance on what would become one of the "most significant zones of cross-border cultural contact during the Cold War."[1] Boulanger reportedly attended all the festival concerts, made time for individual meetings, participated in musicological discussions, was welcomed by visiting delegations from nations East and West, and even observed and gave feedback in some of the rehearsals. She contributed to the festival's ceremony, but also to the informal encounters that would become the festival's trademarks.

On October 11, all eyes were directed at Boulanger. "My Polish students are like a large family among whom I now arrive with joy. I feel at home among them. Over the course of these meetings, the years fall away and the old Parisian memories return," the Union's newsletter reported her saying when pressed about her sense of occasion. The gathering was musically intense as she pored over and critiqued newly composed scores, gifts from the union's members.[2] Her remarks underscore her familial ties to Poland and Polish music, capture the intimate sociability and sense

Figure 1. Former students Grażyna Bacewicz, Kazimierz Serocki, and Zygmunt Mycielski, (left to right), welcome Nadia Boulanger, center, at Warsaw's train station in 1956.

of care—even responsibility—she felt toward the dozens of students from Poland she interacted with throughout her lifetime.

Of the twenty-four people gathered at the Union, she had taught nineteen. By the end of her life, more than fifty Polish pedagogues and composers would have studied with her. In her last letter to the Union, composed 9 January 1979, her opening salutations expressed how touched she was by the organization's "loyalty and affection."[3] Boulanger's Polish students extend across generations; some lived and worked abroad (Michał Spisak, Stanisław Skrowaczewski, Marta Ptaszyńska, Zygmunt Krauze, and Elżbieta Sikora), but most returned to Poland after studying with Boulanger in Paris. In the twenty-first century these former students still occupy leadership positions at the nation's top conservatories and musical organizations: the French composer's "Polish family" continues to grow.

In this essay, we consider Nadia Boulanger as a vital force for Polish musicians and musical institutions across the twentieth century and show how her intellect, energy, and eminence interacted in personal, musical, and institutional encounters. In the interwar period, Paris attracted not only composers but instrumentalists from across independent Poland. Boulanger student Grażyna Bacewicz, for example, also studied violin with André Touret during her sojourns there (1933–34, 1935). The

Association of Young Musician-Poles in Paris (Stowarzyszenie Młodych Muzyków Polaków w Paryżu) facilitated their community and nurtured their professional network. Here, Boulanger played a key pedagogical role: young composers from Poland were expected to join in her composition classes even if their stay in Paris was brief—a practice that would continue until her death. Those who studied longer and more intensely with her, such as Witold Rudziński, Bolesław Woytowicz, and perhaps most notably Zygmunt Mycielski, maintained epistolary relationships with their French mentor upon returning to Poland, where they took up leadership positions at Polish music institutions before and after the Second World War.

Her personal and professional relationships with Poles evolved as a result of the devastation of the war, which affected every aspect of everyday life as well as musical life in both Paris and Warsaw. The People's Republic of Poland shaped classical music as a triumphant marker of its modernization, and Boulanger came there to bestow international status on it, for example, as a juror for the International Chopin Competition in 1957. She welcomed students to Paris year after year, and both the Polish and French states funded these students' rigorous instruction in counterpoint and orchestration.[4] The new music scene in Poland thrived in contradistinction to other countries in the Eastern Bloc because of its international connections and exchange, as Lisa Jakelski has shown in her study of the Warsaw Autumn Festival.[5] Nurturing a connection to Boulanger was a crucial component of its vitality. This work was not only symbolic cultural diplomacy: her friendship with Mycielski, a prominent public intellectual, persisted through emotionally laden correspondence that reveals a compassionate mutual respect and affection. Boulanger cherished the reception and valued the community she had in her Polish family. Her relation with Poland and Polish musicians raises larger questions concerning the role of pedagogy as a source of prestige and even power during the Cold War, and of the role that the politics of friendship play for the realization of internationalist exchange. This essay follows the contours of her relationships to Poland, Polish music, and Polish musicians to historically—and musically—ground the affective warmth in her statements at the Composers' Union that October afternoon in 1956.

**From Warsaw to Paris**
The hundreds of Polish musicians who headed to Paris in the 1920s and 1930s chose to live and study there not only because of the city's unquestioned status as a center of modernist culture, but also because of the significance that France had acquired in the Polish cultural imagination

after the First World War. In 1918, Poland had regained statehood after having spent over a hundred years under partition. For independent Poland, France stood a safe distance from the onetime partition-era capitals of Berlin, Vienna, and Moscow, making it especially appealing to the state-backed funding organizations that supported studies abroad.[6] Many Polish Boulanger students traveled under the auspices of these official scholarships, while others were funded by the wealthy pianist (and former statesman) Ignacy Jan Paderewski, who was aware of Boulanger's support of Polish music and appreciated her efforts.

Those whose musical lives flourished in Paris noted specific affinities between Poland and France that had resonance in debates about the stakes and sounds of modernism. The ideological justification for the musical turn to Paris was provided by Karol Szymanowski (1882–1937). As a rare defender of new music in a highly conservative cultural environment, the composer of *King Roger* (1924) was respected and listened to by the younger generation of composers headed to Paris. In a series of widely read polemics from the 1920s, he argued that after Chopin's death Poland had become cut off from the culture of the West, engaging instead in a "hopeless plumbing of the depths of a once splendid past."[7] Rejecting the marriage of a tired academic style with folk-inspired tropes in the music of composers such as Władysław Żeleński (1837–1921) and Zygmunt Noskowski (1846–1909), Szymanowski claimed that Chopin's exile in France (and subsequent international fame) was proof that Polish music could be both nationally distinct while partaking in the mainstream of Western music history.[8] Though he did not endorse a return to Chopin's harmonic idiom or formal language per se, he insisted that France—standing in for civilization and modernity at large—was the arena in which Poland's musical ambitions ought to be realized. Szymanowski put his agenda into action, personally advising Mycielski, among others, to make the trip to Paris.[9] In return, Boulanger promoted Szymanowski's music in her public lectures on modern music in the mid-1920s and brought his compositions to her students.[10]

Poland's composers framed their studies abroad as serving a domestic agenda of musical nationalism that was underwritten by the purported closeness of French and Polish culture. The Association of Young Musician-Poles in Paris (1926–1950) justified their choice of city on ideological terms: "One must take into consideration the contemporary movement within Polish intellectual life (and especially within music) that aspires to establish close contact with Latin culture, in opposition to the prewar generation of musicians, who were educated chiefly in Germany."[11] The phrase "Latin culture" had ties to a discourse of racial purity in interwar

France. As used by right-wing French writers such as Charles Maurras and Maurice Barrès, it denoted an unbroken continuity with Mediterranean civilization that they believed was guaranteed through the French race.[12] It is unclear to what degree the Association's members were familiar with the anti-immigrant connotations of this discourse, especially since working-class Poles were part of the "problem" that these writers described. It is clear, however, that the Association used this rhetoric to paint Poland as part of a Western cultural orbit, linkages underlaid by their shared Roman Catholicism and the Latin script of the Polish language.

Not all Polish musicians who traveled to Paris were composers and not all the composers studied with Boulanger. Yet it was often her students—including Bolesław Woytowicz, Zygmunt Mycielski, Feliks Łabuński, Witold Rudziński, Michał Spisak, Tadeusz Szeligowski, Michał Kondracki, and Antoni Szałowski—who occupied leadership positions among the community abroad.[13] One reason for this was that Boulanger quickly brought her students into contact with the latest musical trends of Paris. Mycielski's notebooks contain a hurriedly sketched copy of Stravinsky's *Symphony of Psalms* that he made from Boulanger's copy of the score when she lent it to him for a night before its premiere on 13 December 1930.[14] In such cases, connections to Boulanger promised access to the latest unpublished and even unpremiered compositions and offered insider insight into new musical thought. Unsurprisingly, many of her students adopted elements of the neoclassical aesthetics with which she was associated. Bacewicz's 1935 Trio for Oboe, Violin and Piano, for example, calls to mind the textural clarity, propulsive accompaniment figures, and prominent use of wind instruments that Stravinsky had pioneered over a decade earlier in his Octet.[15] Working with Boulanger enabled Poles to shape transnational social networks that long outlasted their Parisian sojourns.[16] Back in Poland, the musical press tracked Boulanger's public advocacy for her former students, reporting on, for example, the 1938 radio broadcast of her performance of Antoni Szałowski's jocular perpetuum mobile Overture (1936) at the helm of the BBC orchestra.[17]

Another likely reason for Boulanger's popularity among Poles was a compatibility between her pedagogy and Polish cultural politics, both of which were engaged in balancing the (national) individual with the wider universal of a cultural heritage. As Annegret Fauser has documented, Boulanger aimed to bring out the distinctive voices of her students from around the world while still analyzing works from across music history in terms of universal principles like *la grande ligne*.[18] Some students also recalled a deeper set of cultural similarities between France and Poland. Looking back in 1958 on her studies with Boulanger, Maria Modrakowska recalled that Boulanger "often said that Polish culture (which she knows superbly) is so related to French culture that nothing divides them except language."[19] Indeed, Boulanger displayed a growing interest in Poland itself during the interwar period, expressing a wish to visit the country as early as 1934.[20]

Members of the Association of Young Musician-Poles recognized the cultural visibility that Boulanger could lend to their projects. In 1930, she became an honorary member and gave the Association financial support over the following years.[21] In return, its members nominated her in 1932 for the Order of Polonia Restituta, an award given by the Polish state for exceptional contributions to Polish culture. In justifying the successful nomination, the Association highlighted her role in frequently discussing Polish music in her lectures at the Ecole Normale de Musique, for helping to arrange performances of Polish works at the Société Musicale Indépendante, and in general her role in "informing French and international musical opinion about the direction of Polish music and the role that it plays in the general progress of musical culture."[22] By virtue of her eminence, she lent significance to this repertoire by programming Polish new music alongside that of France—"providing a sort of consecration to the concert of the young composers," as one review described.[23]

Zygmunt Mycielski (1907–1987) was among the Polish students who studied with Boulanger for the longest time. In the official biography for his application to the Polish Composers' Union, he reported that his studies lasted the decade between 1926 and 1936.[24] In addition to private composition lessons, he also took her courses in music history at the Ecole Normale, with notes from the 1934–35 school year showing Mycielski analyzing examples from Delphic hymns to Monteverdi madrigals.[25] The early 1930s were also the start of a long-lasting friendship. "[Mycielski] is— as you know—profound, understanding, and loyal," Boulanger described him at this time.[26] He was a conscientious student and composed consistently throughout his life, but Mycielski's larger impact on Polish musical culture—somewhat to his own regret—was as a critic, taste-maker, editor, and, in the decade after the Second World War, cultural official, when he served as vice president, then president, of the Composers' Union.

Mycielski owed his success as a writer to an ear for concise prose and a sensitivity for articulating the more complex issues of Poland's cultural politics. His essays were peppered with acerbic wit and playful irony, interlinking music with the arts and broad societal concerns. He shared Boulanger's desire to stay open-minded when hearing new works that eschewed his compositional principles. Upon hearing Krzysztof Penderecki's *Threnody for the Victims of Hiroshima* (1961) at the Warsaw Autumn Festival in 1964, he wrote that the work, which he critiqued for its static formal blocks, its orchestration defying common sense, and a near absence of pulse "should be bad, but it is good. It is music like oysters, snails, and vodka."[27] After Mycielski took a public stand against the Soviet invasion of Czechoslovakia in 1968 in the most influential émigré publication in Paris, *Kultura*, his published editorials addressed not just cultural politics, but the political questions at the heart of the opposition to state socialism (especially in the Catholic *Tygodnik Powszechny*). After the military crackdown on the Solidarity movement in December 1981, the pages of his journal were occupied equally with drafts of letters to the imprisoned opposition leader, historian Adam Michnik, as they were with sketches of his *Liturgia Sacra* (1983–84), which would receive a commendation from one Warsaw-based arts council associated with the opposition to state socialism in 1986.

Among his peers, Mycielski also amassed clout because his brand of criticism activated long-standing beliefs that the intelligentsia had inherited the aristocracy's role as the spiritual leaders of the nation.[28] Echoing the rhetoric of earlier generations, he often emphasized the obligations of the artist to society and reflected on Poland's accomplishments or shortcomings from a bird's-eye perspective. Although not all members of the intelligentsia in Poland were descendants of the nobility, Mycielski was; this aristocratic background he shared with Boulanger. Although he often downplayed his class origins, all were aware of them—he was even occasionally referred to as "the Count." This position, of both acknowledging and denying his class, allowed him to slip with some ease into his chosen role as a member of the intelligentsia, and to be taken seriously when he attempted to speak on behalf of Polish culture.

Though he remained closeted during his lifetime, Mycielski's homosexuality was an open secret among the social circles of the intelligentsia of Communist Poland. Beginning in the 1950s he lived with a partner, Stanisław Kołodziejczyk, and socialized extensively with other gay male writers and artists, as he details in his posthumously published diaries.[29] Kołodzieczyk and Mycielski visited Boulanger together; in Paris, at least, she referred to the composer's sexuality openly.[30] In Poland, the social stigma against public discussion of male homosexuality allowed someone of his class and educational background to acquire power—or at least leave behind a historical record in which any homophobic retaliation he experienced must be read between the lines.[31]

Mycielski is certainly not among Boulanger's most famous students. Among those from Poland, Wojciech Kilar, who composed the score to Francis Ford Coppola's *Bram Stoker's Dracula* (1993), would probably earn that label on an international scale. But he played an outsized role in mediating her relations with Poland and is the key figure for the story that unfolds in this essay. In the years prior to Boulanger's first visit (1956), he translated for her what was happening in Poland with more detail, passion, and cogency than any of her other Polish students. Across dozens of letters, he explained what the traumas of war and efforts at rebuilding meant to Poland. During her subsequent visits to Warsaw, he accompanied and guided her, hosting her at social gatherings in his home. After her visits, he was the most insistent of her former students promoting her cultural significance and defending her relevance, as when he published her impressions of Warsaw and the Warsaw Autumn Festival in *Przegląd Kulturalny* (see "A Letter from Professor Nadia Boulanger" in this volume). He explained that other countries would follow Poland's musical example because of the blessing implied by her presence. "By attending our festival," wrote Mycielski, "Professor Boulanger made a gesture that has great significance, one that will doubtlessly echo in the musical life of many countries."[32] Boulanger's relations to Poland are also a reminder of how friendships animate the histories of cultural exchange: her visits brought officials from the French Embassy to dinner tables with Poland's ministers of arts and culture and were essential to cultural diplomacy, even if Boulanger refrained from discussing politics on the record.

### Wartime Intimacies

As the Second World War threw Poland under German and Soviet occupation, many of Boulanger's Polish students, including Mycielski, corresponded with her. For some, connections to Boulanger became a source of hope for escape. For Tadeusz Szeligowski, then in Lithuanian-ruled Vilnius, Boulanger's letter of support for his efforts to secure a French visa was like "a message from heaven."[33] Friends and family of Bolesław Woytowicz and Roman Palester likewise believed that letters from her could somehow extract these composers from occupied Warsaw.[34] Former Polish students who had remained in France also appealed for help, with Antoni Szałowski seeking written endorsement as he worked to obtain visas for himself and Michał Spisak to go to the United States.[35] In none of these cases was Boulanger able to secure exit visas for her students.

Students had begun to see her as a life-line to the musical and diplomatic world at large. Those who were already in the United States also asked for assistance with employment.[36] The wartime aid with the broadest impact was probably the April 1941 concert that Boulanger conducted that benefited Ignacy Jan Paderewski's Polish Relief Fund in New York City.[37] The program, built entirely of religious music, brought together selections from her trademark repertory (including Fauré's Requiem) and a landmark of early twentieth-century Polish music, a movement of Szymanowski's *Stabat Mater*, with what Gary A. Galo has suggested was her own arrangement of the first piece of chant notated in the Polish language, the "Bogurodzica" ("Mother of God").[38]

Mycielski did not so much ask Boulanger for aid as he made her into an audience and witness to his trauma. His letters to her, preserved today in the Bibliotèque Nationale de France, read like a journal of his wartime experiences. After the campaign against the German and Soviet invasions of Poland failed, Mycielski fled across the Hungarian border. "All that I can tell you is that I am still alive," he wrote on 22 September 1939, a few days after the Red Army's attack. "But I don't know anything about the fate of my family and friends—of my brothers, mother, family, not to speak of everyone, of the entire country."[39] That he wrote to Boulanger at such a critical moment is telling of the importance he gave to this friendship. But it also presaged his course of escape, as he would eventually join the Polish Army in France.[40] "I didn't know anything of our army here [in France], but I decided to serve in any army that was fighting with Germany or Russia. . . . We are defending mankind. All that is not mankind—all that is beyond humanity—must be destroyed."[41]

Mycielski rarely tallies the everyday events of war for Boulanger, but instead shares his military mindset as they approach battle. In February 1940, while preparing in France, he described to her how

> we are learning to organize this terrible thing, war . . . it's a very different thing than "the civilian" believes to see, believes to know. War has its aspect of craft, of well-done work. Its classic aspect. . . . It's not that I equate war with art, but that art, like every human creation, is an act composed of an end and a means.[42]

After Mycielski saw action and was captured during the Battle of France, his attitude changed. Boulanger became a source of escape and ethical support while he performed forced labor in Germany. "All the days, during the long hours of work, during the nighttime hours, I talk with you. Your conscience is a guide, your heart a force."[43] We do not know how Boulanger responded to these letters and we cannot be certain of how she felt being Mycielski's absent dialogue partner.[44] Yet in many ways, the intensity of their intimacy at a distance, established first during Mycielski's captivity, would continue to her death in 1979.

A focus on the quotidian mindsets of those struck by trauma is equally present in Mycielski's correspondence to Boulanger after the war. Indeed, on the very day he was liberated, he wrote to Boulanger and two of her close associates describing, in a long and extraordinary letter, his angst and conflicting desires to return to Poland and see them in France. (See English and French versions of the letter, titled "What Awaits Them Now," in this volume.) After returning to Poland in late 1945, he continued to relay to Boulanger the sensibility of Poles living amid widespread loss. "For us, it is necessary to be content, yes, content, with all the beauty, sun, and rays that one day brings—this is already enormous."[45] He writes of musical events that signal renewal—the conductor Grzegorz Fitelberg's return, the premieres of pieces by Andrzej Panufnik—yet the emphasis is upon the rupture of the war and the all-consuming need of reconstruction. His desire to partake in a national, collective effort led to his decision to remain in Poland, when he could have easily sought exile in France.[46] His attitude and conviction extended beyond the early postwar moment. In 1950, he explained to her how, in Poland, "each person, according to his strength and means, should fight until the end. Each year—really, each month, each week, even each day—is a year, month, or day that we have won. We have won this time so that we may live, so that we may build again. All that matters is life. No one can grasp this who has not seen war from close up."[47]

## Postwar Aesthetics and Cultural Diplomacy

In the decade following the Second World War, the significance of France within the Polish cultural imagination changed in ways that were both minor and significant. Musicians still sought to study in France and with Boulanger, but fewer managed to do so.[48] Critics and composers did not immediately reject the compositional techniques that they had learned from her in the 1930s, yet even Francophiles expressed skepticism about the formerly unquestioned status of Paris as the center of the musically modern.[49] In 1945, Mycielski described that in Paris "the rhythm of musical life flows along the old paths, depleted, rather than enriched, by the experiences that shocked that country."[50] But he also wrote to Boulanger that "it is useless to explain to you how much I wish to renew the bonds, already old, that connect almost all of us to French musical life."[51]

During the advent and debate over socialist realist aesthetics in Poland during the late 1940s and early 1950s, ambivalence toward neoclassicism and the lessons learned from Boulanger peaked. For Marxist commentators, French aesthetics cued up decadent Western excess.[52] But state doctrines that advocated for aesthetics founded in socialist ideology were largely abandoned by policy makers and composers when the cultural thaw of the mid-1950s reoriented classical music's institutions to the international avant-garde. By the time of Boulanger's first visit in 1956,

France had lost some of its prewar status in the Polish cultural imagination, even as the explicitly political discourse critical of her school of composition had dwindled. Instead, France was one player within the broader category of Western countries whose works and artists were aggressively sought out for programming at the Warsaw Autumn.[53]

Responding in part to these changing aesthetic and political circumstances, Boulanger's prewar students often reframed her ideas in order to maintain their relevance to new music in Poland. Early accounts, such as Mycielski's extended exegesis on her pedagogy from 1947, highlight the content (and ideology) of her teaching.[54] In the 1950s students lauded her tireless labor orchestrating, conducting, and teaching. Mycielski pointed to her moral authority, claiming, "She was concerned with the entirety of her students' artistic, psychological, intellectual, and even moral development."[55] Maria Modrakowska likewise focused on the dedication and commitment that Boulanger required of her students, recalling how in preparation for the performance or study of unpublished works her apartment "turned during the nighttime into a medieval monastery, where instead of monks, students copied out scores."[56]

However much the aesthetic debates of early 1950s Poland had disengaged Boulanger, by the time she visited in 1956, she was unquestionably a star and would remain so through her returns. "Among the many musical celebrities from all of Europe [at the Warsaw Autumn] Nadia Boulanger reigned supreme," wrote Jerzy Waldorff, comparing her with the Queen of Belgium.[57] The Composers' Union designated her the "most influential guest."[58] When she entered the National Philharmonic for the festival's first concert (mere moments before the lights dimmed), she received her own round of applause.[59] Her presence was amplified through newspaper reviews—at least twenty-three papers mentioned her attendance. The press coverage is littered with photos of her—arriving at the train station, in conversation with former students and cultural dignitaries at concert receptions, and in the Union offices, articulating her ubiquity and magnanimity.[60] One critic indicated how familial her relationship to former students was by describing her as the fount of Polish new music, a "friend of all young Polish composers over the last 35 years."[61] Another noticed that works by Boulanger's former students had a prominent place on the festival's program.[62]

Above all else, she was a selfless devotee of music. Commentators noted her seemingly ceaseless ability to attend every concert in the jam-packed week. Writing a color piece for the newspaper for younger readers, a journalist asked Boulanger as she passed through the lobby of the Hotel Bristol if she was going to take a rest. She replied, "A break? Never!"— and then lauded the sound of a Polish choir.[63] Such portrayals recycled well-established tropes that had surrounded her in the 1920s, when critics reconciled her gender with the traditionally masculine work of conducting by painting her as a "servant" of music.[64] If her public image was somewhere between that of a celebrity and musical votary, Boulanger engaged specialist audiences of students and composers with what she considered the pressing issues of the music of the day. In a talk she gave to one such group at the Chopin Institute in 1956, she argued that the exhaustion of tonality had brought contemporary music to a decisive and dangerous crossroads. Boulanger claimed that "patience" was needed, that composers and listeners would need to go through several aesthetic systems—including dodecaphony—before finding a system that would be capable of equaling the accomplishments of tonality.[65] Opinions would necessarily be "extremely divergent and fragmented," a claim her former student Witold Rudziński heard as support for the festival as a platform for debate.[66] While positioning herself as a forward-looking advocate for new aesthetics, however, she remained skeptical of dodecaphony itself. Romuald Twardowski, writing after her death in 1979, would credit her postwar pedagogy with helping him "listen internally" and avoid pressure to follow trends and pressures from sounds beyond his "own musical creation."[67]

If Boulanger weighed in on particular works, she did so privately. Even as the Polish premiere of Stravinsky's jazz-inflected *Ebony Concerto* generated some of the most enthusiastic reviews from the festival, the connection between Boulanger and the Russian émigré, whom one organ of the Communist Party praised as the "father of modernism," went unmentioned.[68] But after the festival Boulanger would pay particular attention to Polish music, pointing to "those works that contain imagination, sonic sensitivity, vitality and rhythmic energy, and, ultimately, an originality of the melodic line and harmonic inventiveness"—all values that, albeit somewhat vague, reveal how she discerned a fundamental concern for melody and harmony in the new Polish music.[69] (See the translation "A Letter from Professor Nadia Boulanger" following this essay.) Thus Boulanger's written responses to the Festival, while seeking support for her own positions within music from Poland, also weighed into ongoing Polish debates about the direction of the avant-garde.[70]

## A Public Friendship

Boulanger and Mycielski had likely seen each other in 1939 and again in 1949, when he visited France as part of a delegation sent to coordinate celebrations for the Chopin centenary.[71] Her 1956 visit to the first Warsaw Autumn was thus not their first reunion. But it was Boulanger's first visit to Poland, an occasion she did not take lightly. "If my arrival is important for you," she wrote to Mycielski, "think of what it represents for me—I don't know how to tell you."[72] Several commentators noted that Mycielski and Boulanger were to be found side-by-side throughout the festival, and what had been an intimate epistolary friendship took on an element of public performance and allegiance.[73]

It was at this time that Mycielski presented Boulanger with an inscribed manuscript copy of two songs from his cycle *Ocalenie* (*Rescue*).[74] Composed in spring 1946, these songs were no longer congruent with his compositional outlook. But the gift was a powerful, even therapeutic, echo of the exchanges about war, suffering, and destruction that he had had with his French teacher, mentor, and friend over the preceding fifteen years. (The musical offering was reciprocated. In the 1950s, when imports were hard to come by in Poland, Boulanger helped rebuild Mycielski's long-playing record collection, gifting him new music from the West, such as Stockhausen, Boulez, and Nono, as well as pressings of her own recordings, notably a much-cherished recording of Rameau.)[75] The cycle sets a selection of poems from Czesław Miłosz's 1945 collection with the same title. *Rescue* is a literal description of the volume's contents—the publication contains poems his wife, Janina, was able to take with her when she fled Warsaw during the uprising at the end of the Second World War.[76] But it also summons a haunting specter: the failure of Catholic Poles to prevent the liquidation of the Warsaw Ghetto. The canonic poems from *Rescue*, such as "Campo di fiori" and "A Poor Christian looks at the Ghetto," are about witnessing the Holocaust and the textual trace (or effort) of Miłosz's own experience as witness of the Ghetto's annihilation. Mycielski certainly would have been familiar with these texts laden with efforts, however impossible it seemed, to represent the barbaric murder of the Holocaust. His choice to set the concluding poem, "Dedication" ("Przedmowa"), of the second cycle in the collection ("The World: Native Poems"), maintains genocide's reality as a haunting presence—in the specific, dark and silent prelude that unfolds before his melody.

In his *Rescue*, Mycielski treated each of that poem's five stanzas as the text for a short song. He pared down the musical composition for Boulanger, choosing the first and third verses as his gift, thereby creating a thematically coherent selection that moves from the evocation of a lost acquaintance in the first stanza to the grave of the lost one in the third:

> You whom I could not save
> Listen to me.
> Try to understand this simple speech as I would be
>     ashamed of another.

I swear, there is in me no wizardry of words.
I speak to you with silence like a cloud or a tree.

. . . . . . . . . .

Here is a valley of shallow Polish rivers. And an immense
    bridge
Going into white fog. Here is a broken city;
And the wind throws the screams of gulls on your grave
When I am talking with you.[77]

By choosing these two songs, Mycielski omitted the more didactic—and historically specific—songs of this cycle. In the second the speaker suggests their mourned acquaintance was unable to resist encroaching ideologies of hate. Mycielski supplies the fourth with a recitative-like setting that asserts "Poetry which does not save / Nations or people" is a "connivance with official lies." The pairing for Boulanger avoids the verses that grapple with complex responses to death (relief, retaliation), focusing instead on a more universal portrait of loss that dwells upon the closeness between the narrator and the dead as well as mourning's expressive difficulty.

Mycielski's settings strip musical language down to a core of counterpoint that, unmoored from a harmonic context, produces unforgiving and even grating harmony. Perhaps Mycielski anticipated that these techniques would resonate with Boulanger's own pedagogical emphasis on line and counterpoint. Still, one wonders what Boulanger had to say about this raw rendering, this caustic musical language, since she and Mycielski spoke often of Polish-language poetry and its musical settings.[78] In the opening of the third song, for example, the moment in which the speaker points to the landscape in which the grave is situated is set by using two staccato clusters a whole step away from each other (see Example 1). Mycielski distributes the pitches across octaves, reducing somewhat their dissonance. Yet they are still a harsh accompaniment for a melody that is disarming in its simplicity and limited ambitus. All told, there is only one moment of consonance in the entire song: the bare, open-octave A♭s in the fourth-to-last measure. These are wiped out in the following measure by another cluster (distributed across four octaves), which "resolves" via stepwise motion to a four-octave C and C♯ chord to conclude the song. This final chord thereby recalls the first song, which begins and ends with motion between C and D♭ (see Example 2). Perhaps because of this harsh musical language, Mycielski's settings remained private utterances, and the songs were never published during his lifetime. For the Polish

Example 1. Zygmunt Mycielski, *Ocalenie*, 3.
"Here Is a Valley of Shallow Polish Rivers," mm. 1–8.

composer they were intimately linked with Boulanger: he revisited them after her death as part of the mourning process, as he listened to choral music by Gesualdo and recalled her lectures on the madrigals.[79] In fact, the songs' existence was only brought to attention when the manuscript he had dedicated to Boulanger was found in her papers after she died.[80]

Mycielski's view of Poland's recent wartime past—and the obligations it spelled for the future—were echoed in Boulanger's reactions to the Warsaw Autumn Festival. She emphasized the collective effort needed to carry out the event and linked this energy to the war and Poles' recovery from it:

> And, finally: Warsaw. I finally saw—next to her terrific destruc-
> tion and ruins, which shake with their ghastliness—the reborn
> and rebuilt New and Old Towns. They are happy and colorful;
> they speak to your past and of a present being built through
> great effort, so that you may have a beautiful future.

Example 2. Zygmunt Mycielski, *Ocalenie*, 3.
"Here Is a Valley of Shallow Polish Rivers," mm. 27–31.

. . .

> Thanks to my friends, I could also perceive that which has
> vanished from Poland as well as that which was systematically
> annihilated through the terrible historical events that struck
> your land. But I observe that your nation is full of life, that it
> finds inspiration in its past, that your grace depends on your
> values. Here, heroism has become an everyday matter.

To be sure, Boulanger's rhetoric played into the founding ideologies of
the Warsaw Autumn. The leaders of the postwar music scene, gathered
at the Polish Composers' Union, saw the new music festival as a crucial
means to combat cultural isolation and compensate for lost time. Lisa
Jakelski has shown that it was none other than Mycielski who took the
lead on this matter behind the closed doors of the Union: he worried that
Poland would become a "backwater."[81] In Boulanger's comments, however, she exudes empathy toward her Polish family and their experiences
rather than focusing on the vitality of their institutions. She understands
survivors as the resilient bearers of cultural heritage, that past and present are visible through human effort. Indeed, she had considerable
interest in seeking out the present remains of the past while attending
the festival, visiting key monuments of Polish early modern history in
Cracow.[82] Throughout Boulanger's published letter of gratitude, she
holds herself to her students through pledges to act as well as displays of
intimacy. She presents herself as a leader for and cultural force within the
postwar Polish milieu. Her private thanks to Mycielski ran even deeper,

describing how he "left me with something so profound that I do not know how to describe it—we so often forget what matters."[83]

Boulanger's presence at the first Warsaw Autumn Festival adorned the new institution with prestige; her feedback and enthusiasm underscored that the visit was no mere performance. The Polish Composers' Union symbolically marked this special relationship by distinguishing her with an honorary membership in 1957, to be celebrated during her next visit to Warsaw as a juror for the International Chopin Competition that September. In the decades that followed, Boulanger's visits to Poland deepened not just her friendships—her sense of Polish family—but her official institutional relationships and responsibilities. At the helm of the Union, Boulanger's former students did the administrative work for the Polish Artists' Agency (PAGART), seeking out choirs Boulanger might conduct, conservatories she might visit, and reminding bureaucrats that the guest of honor would only travel by train.

Composers communicated with Boulanger in ways both official and unofficial after the 1956 festival, often using her connections with the Union as a means for strengthening their contacts. The organization sent messengers to Paris and received materials in return. A Mrs. Zacharzewska brought an official letter wishing Boulanger a happy seventieth birthday in 1957, an occasion upon which she received the Commander's Cross with a Star from the Ministry for Foreign Affairs in recognition of her "outstanding pedagogical achievements in the education of Polish musicologists and contribution to the deepening of Polish-French friendship."[84] Włodzimierz Kotoński was charged with picking up tapes and vinyl from Boulanger on his trip to Paris in 1959, though his luggage (and thus recording bounty) was breached upon his journey into Poland.[85] That encounter no doubt generated an interesting, if now lost, meeting between Polish music past and present. Kotoński surely learned some of Boulanger's pedagogy through his teacher Tadeusz Szeligowski in Warsaw, but as a student at the Darmstadt Summer Courses in 1957 he had been electrified by serial techniques and was in Paris to study not with Boulanger but with Pierre Schaeffer. His *Study on One Cymbal Stroke* (1959), a pioneering work of *musique concrète* and an attempt at total serialism, is one of the first pieces realized at the Experimental Studio of Polish Radio. As Boulanger sent scores and recordings from Paris, the composer's lifelong commitment to promoting her sister Lili's music also shaped her gifts to and activities with the Union. After a 1960 visit she sent via Mycielski's hands an LP of Lili's music for the Union's library, where it is still accessible. In 1964, Nadia conducted Lili's psalm settings in Cracow.

As Boulanger and Mycielski continued their correspondence over the years, he racked up some regrets—for example, that he could not manage

Figure 2. Nadia Boulanger delivering a lecture to students at
Warsaw's music academy, with Zygmunt Mycielski observing (1967).

to write something for her seventieth birthday when commissioned by Michał Spisak and that it was Lutosławski, not himself, who traveled to celebrate that milestone in Villars sur Ollon.[86] But he did travel to visit her in the 1960s and 1970s and welcomed her to Warsaw every time she traveled to Poland. Mycielski modeled his own discerning attention to new compositions on her powerful and engaged presence when she was teaching, as we observe in a photograph of her lecturing at Warsaw's music academy in 1967, with Mycielski perched beside the piano, peering at and over her (see Figure 2).

Mycielski remained devoted to Boulanger during her final months. After eating dinner with her in February 1979, he noted that her "mind and memory functioned with complete clarity."[87] She reflected upon that visit in what would be her last letter to him: "You are with me as in 1935, as always."[88] He visited her again in August as she convalesced, cared for by a Polish nurse, Anna. In this last conversation—held at a whisper, according to the composer's diary account—Boulanger tried to speak about Mycielski's ongoing compositional projects.[89] Till the end, their relationship was personal and intimate, threaded by a responsibility to music.

Mycielski's connections to Boulanger gave him networks in the West that put him on the radar of the Security Service (Służba Bezpieczeństwa). In the late 1960s, the government watchdog opened an investigation into him in response to private anti-regime statements as well as his criticism of the 1966 celebrations of the Polish millennium of Christianity.[90] An informant reported:

> On the topic of Mycielski, one must note first and foremost that he is one of those people who had the exceptional ability to study at the famous school of composition led by NADIA BOULANGER in Paris. The very fact of completing studies in this school places the student more or less on a pedestal, as far as all musical values are concerned—and besides, Mycielski is talented as both a composer and a writer. Going further, studies at that school gave him the support of friends among many of the famous figures of the musical world. Because of this Mycielski has no problems—and I mean none—if he finds himself in France, England, Germany, or the United States. [The studies with Boulanger] were the first and perhaps most important moment of his career. A second area of concern is his international connections with many pederasts [*z wieloma pederastami*], whose only guiding principle is to aid one other. The third is that his title is that of Count.[91]

In this discriminatory profile, Mycielski's education under Boulanger trumps what were, in the contemporary political climate, understood as international (and internationalist) conspiracies against the People's Republic of Poland: homosexuality and aristocracy.[92] The informant was providing a depiction preordained by the Security Service. At the same time, the report mirrors Mycielski's own self-portrait of his relationship with Boulanger as wrapped up in his connections with her. When he spent time with Aaron Copland during the American composer's stay in Warsaw in 1965, their conversations lingered on cherished recollections of Boulanger and a shared distance from the avant-garde. Copland's note to Boulanger upon returning home signals her importance for Mycielski: "When I was in Warsaw last week (conducting) we spoke of you constantly, especially with Mycielski. What a charming fellow he is!"[93]

## Boulanger's Polish Echoes

For Boulanger's eightieth birthday, the Union of Polish Composers rolled out the red carpet during a thirteen-day visit in December 1967.[94] Though her death twelve years later would spur another wave of reflection on her importance for musicians from Poland at concerts, across personal reflections, and through published obituaries, the 1967 visit consecrated Boulanger in the eyes of Poland's composers, performers, and politicians as the most important international figure in music of the twentieth century. In the words of the funding requests the Union sent to governmental agencies and the invitation she received, she was "inextricable" from Polish music.

Although Boulanger's visits were by then nothing exceptional, this trip involved a volume of commitments and service that spoke to the immense weight Poles attached to her presence. They hoped that the birthday celebration would rival, in both lavish ceremony and musical substance, recent celebrations for her in Monaco and Madrid. Boulanger's demanding schedule allotted one and a half days to listen to tape recordings of new compositions and radio performances at Polish Radio. For meetings, the demand was so great that Union members were convened in groups: her former students (forty-nine of them), young composers, and others with an interest in speaking with her. There was a press conference and a cocktail hour at the French Embassy. She was received at the Ministry of Arts and Culture twice. She attended Mussorgsky's *Khovanshchina* at the National Opera and many rehearsals of local ensembles. She delivered two lectures and conducted a concert at Warsaw's music academy (now the Fryderyk Chopin University of Music). A ceremonial banquet that took up a third of her entire visit (and cost nearly 19,000 złoty) was held at Jabłonna Palace; at the table with her former students she was seated next to Mycielski and

Bacewicz, while cultural ministers and diplomats shared a second.[95] She was presented with the scores of works dedicated to her—many published by the Polish Music Publishers (PWM), and was honored as a teacher with a concert by the National Philharmonic of her students' compositions, including Tadeusz Szeligowski's *Epitafium on the Death of Szymanowski* (1937), Michał Spisak's *Concerto Giocoso* (1948), and Wojciech Kilar's *Riff 62* (1962).[96]

Boulanger's unprecedented agency within the Polish musical milieu drew in equal parts on her musical, diplomatic, and interpersonal acumen. Likewise, her focus on musical aesthetics—commentary to young pianists, hours spent listening, and vibrant public addresses—kept her disengaged from any critique of the political realities of everyday life under state socialism, from which the Union also worked to distance itself. What had begun decades earlier as a modest promise of entrée into the Paris musical scene for young students had grown in scope and ambition. By the height of the Cold War, not only had her "Polish family" grown by dozens, but this matriarch had become a metonym for a broader set of values, standing in for composers' desire for international prestige, their search for foreign cultural capital, and their hope that avant-garde music could be both cutting-edge and relevant. Her public persona, bolstered by a dense network of private friendships, became a symbol for selfless dedication and the aesthetic evenhandedness that the Polish musical milieu had come to see as its calling card within Europe and the world at large.

Yet, at the conclusion of her final visit in 1967, it was not her countless roles behind the scenes and inside the classroom that mattered most, but rather that she embodied the power of the sounds she helped to create. This visit highlighted her role as a conductor, and she concluded her trip by leading a work that had long been dear to her: Fauré's Requiem. The applause that followed the concert was without a doubt even more thunderous than that which greeted her in the same hall eleven years earlier at the Warsaw Autumn Festival. Certainly, it was an accumulated expression of gratitude for fifty years of generous inspiration, demanding musical scrutiny, and compassion for an unfolding traumatic history. But it was also an immediate response to Boulanger's effort to revitalize Fauré on the Polish stage. It is poignant that, though her importance to musicians from Poland resonates profoundly across her many contributions to music in the twentieth century, her final appearance in Warsaw was on the stage, guiding an orchestra to rest after a magnificent performance. She was seen, heard, and applauded making music.

# NOTES

1. Lisa Jakelski, *Making New Music in Cold War Poland: The Warsaw Autumn Festival, 1956–1968* (Oakland: University of California Press, 2017), 1.

2. *Biuletyn Informacyjny Związku Kompozytorów Polskich* 3 (1956): 6.

3. Nadia Boulanger, personal file (86A), Polish Composers' Union (ZKP), Polish Music Information Center, Warsaw.

4. Romuald Twardowski, who studied with Boulanger in 1963 on a stipend from the French government, waxed poetic about the school's beauty and the paradox of NATO's nearby presence, a clear sign of the Cold War circumstances that brought about his sojourn. Romuald Twardowski, "Nadia Boulanger," *Kultura*, 25 November 1979, 14.

5. Jakelski, *Making New Music in Cold War Poland*.

6. Jan Piskurewicz, *W służbie nauki i oświaty: Stanisław Michalski, 1865–1949* (Warsaw: PAN, Instytut Historii, Nauki, Oświaty i Techniki, 1993), 137.

7. Karol Szymanowski, "On Contemporary Musical Opinion in Poland," *Szymanowski on Music: Selected Writings of Karol Szymanowski*, ed. and trans. Alistair Wightman (London: Toccata, 1999), 73–94.

8. Barbara Milewski, "The Mazurka and National Imaginings" (PhD diss., Princeton University, 2002), 111–65.

9. Teresa Chylińska, ed., *Karol Szymanowski: Korespondencja*, vol. 3 (Cracow: Musica Iagellonica, 1997), 318.

10. "Les Cours de musique moderne de Nadia Boulanger," *Le Monde musical* 37/6 (June 1926): 242–44.

11. *Stowarzyszenie Młodych Muzyków Polaków z Paryżu: Dotychczasowa działalność, cele i dążenia* (Warsaw, 1930), 4. By 1935, the Association had 111 members; its main objectives were providing information, financial support, and performances for Polish musicians arriving in Paris. See "Członkowie Stowarzyszenia Młodych Muzyków Polaków w Paryżu," Collection of the Association of Young Musician-Poles in Paris (SMMP), Archive of Polish Composers (AKP), University of Warsaw.

12. Ihor Junyk, *Foreign Modernism: Cosmopolitanism, Identity, and Style in Paris* (Toronto: University of Toronto Press, 2013), 16.

13. "Zarządy Stowarzyszenia Młodych Muzyków Polaków w Paryżu," SMMP, AKP.

14. "Notatki: 1930–31," Zygmunt Mycielski Collection, National Library of Poland (Biblioteka Narodowa) (henceforth PL-Wn), Warsaw, II14345.

15. A full evaluation of Bacewicz's life, including her relationship with Boulanger, will need to wait until her heirs allow unrestricted access to her papers at the National Library of Poland. Our understanding of Polish neoclassicism builds on Zofia Helman, "Neoclassicism in Polish Music of the Twentieth Century," in *The History of Music in Poland*, vol. 7, trans. John Comber (Warsaw: Sutkowski Edition, 2015), 487–683. This chapter is a complete translation of Helman's earlier *Neoklasycyzm w muzyce polskiej XX wieku* (Cracow: PWM, 1985).

16. For example, Mycielski communicated with Henry Leland Clarke at the University of California, Los Angeles, into the 1950s. Zygmunt Mycielski, *Dziennik 1950–59* (Warsaw: Iskry, 1999), 187.

17. "Co słychać w świecie muzycznym?," *Rampka: Tygodnik teatralny, filmowy i muzyczny* 3 (1938): n.p.

18. Annegret Fauser, "Aaron Copland, Nadia Boulanger, and the Making of an 'American' Composer," *The Musical Quarterly* 89/4 (2006): 534–37.

19. Maria Modrakowska, "Wspominając studia u Nadii Boulanger," *Ruch Muzyczny* 11 (1958): 11.

20. Łabuński to Boulanger, 19 May 1934, Bibliotèque nationale de France (henceforth F-Pn), N.L.a. 78(336).

21. AKP, K-LXIV/109; AKP, K-LXV/56.

22. AKP, K-LXIV/195. She received the award in 1934.

23. A.M., "Association de Jeunes Musiciens Polonais," *Le Monde musical*, March 1935.

24. Zygmunt Mycielski, personal file (239A), ZKP.

25. PL-Wn, IV 1407.

26. Boulanger to Maria Modrakowska, n.d., PL-Wn, Rps 12373. The letter was likely written in 1935 or 1936, since Boulanger alludes to Mycielski composing a ballet at the time (likely *Narcyz*, 1936) and to a presumed male lover whom Mycielski had while living in Paris.

27. Zygmunt Mycielski, "Przeżyłem VII Warszawską Jesień," *Ruch Muzyczny* (1–15 November 1964): 5.

28. Aleksander Gella, "The Life and Death of the Old Polish Intelligentsia," *Slavic Review* 30/1 (1971): 1–27.

29. In the 1980s, Mycielski writes aware that his diaries' posthumous circulation—first to Barbara Stęszewska, to whom he left his papers—would make his private life, including his homosexuality, public. In Zygmunt Mycielski, *Niby dziennik ostatni, 1981–1987* (Warsaw: Iskry, 2012), 240.

30. Ibid., 299.

31. Krzysztof Tomasik, *Homobiografie: Pisarki i pisarze polscy XIX i XX wieku* (Warsaw: Krytyka Polityczna, 2008). For example, Kołodziejczyk was fired from a bureaucratic position at the Composers' Union in 1951, a decision immediately clouded by political rumor, as discussed in David G. Tompkins, *Composing the Party Line: Music and Politics in Early Cold War Poland and East Germany* (West Lafayette, IN: Purdue University Press, 2013 ), 82n97.

32. Zygmunt Mycielski, "Przyjazd prof. Nadii Boulanger na Festiwal Muzyki Współczesnej," *Przegląd Kulturalny* 38 (1956): 6.

33. Szeligowski to Boulanger, 18 January 1940, F-Pn, N.L.a. 109.

34. Wanda Woytowicz to Nadia Boulanger, 23 January [1940], F-Pn, N.L.a. 118; Antoni Szałowski, Michał Kondracki, and Michał Spisak to Boulanger, 31 January 1940, F-Pn, N.L.a. 294.

35. Szałowski to Boulanger, 14 August 1940, F-Pn, N.L.a. 109, 301.

36. Łabuński to Boulanger, 12 March 1942, F-Pn, N.L.a. 78.

37. Gary A. Galo, "Nadia Boulanger: The Polish Relief Benefit Concert—4 April 1941," *ARSC Journal* 38/2 (Fall 2007): 183–93. Paderewski died two months later, so the concert was not, as some have suggested, a memorial.

38. Galo bases his hypothesis on a harmonic analysis of the choral arrangement and the fact that Boulanger asked the members of the chorus to return their parts. Galo, "Nadia Boulanger," 189–91. If this is in fact true, this concert would represent a unique moment in Boulanger's reciprocal relationship with Poles, in which she responded *through music* to Polish culture. The chant, a supplication to the Virgin Mary, had been a touchstone for cultural nationalism during the nineteenth-century partitions.

39. Mycielski to Boulanger, 22 September 1939, F-Pn, N.L.a. 89.

40. Mycielski to Boulanger, 2 December 1939, F-Pn, N.L.a. 89.

41. Mycielski to Boulanger, 18 February 1940, F-Pn, N.L.a. 89.

42. Mycielski to Boulanger, 8 February 1940, F-Pn, N.L.a. 89.

43. Mycielski to Boulanger, 9 June 1941, F-Pn, N.L.a. 89.

44. His papers, held at the National Library of Poland, include Boulanger's letters beginning only in 1952, catalogued as IV14368.

45. Mycielski to Boulanger, 21 May 1946, F-Pn, N.L.a. 89.

46. Mycielski to Szałowski, 2 August 1947, PL-Wn, Rps 10300 III, 41. After being freed from forced labor in 1945, Mycielski first went to Paris for several months before returning to Poland.

47. Mycielski to Boulanger, 1 November 1950, F-Pn, N.L.a. 89.

48. For one account see "Życie muzyczne Paryża (rozmowa ze St. Skrowaczewskim)," *Ruch Muzyczny* 4 (1949): 12.

49. Helman, *Neoklasycyzm*, 50 and 76.

50. Zygmunt Mycielski, "O naszej pracy uwag kilka," *Ruch Muzyczny* 5 (1945): 5. Graz'yna Bacewicz echoed Mycielski's sense of lost Parisian time. See "Rozmowa z Grażyną Bacewiczówną," *Ruch Muzyczny* 10 (1947): 12.

51. Mycielski to Boulanger, 9 April 1946, F-Pn, N.L.a. 89.

52. Zofia Lissa, "Aspekt socjologiczny w polskiej muzyce współczesnej," *Kwartalnik Muzyczny* 6/21–22 (1948): 104–43, at 135.

53. Jakelski, *Making New Music in Cold War Poland*, 38–39.

54. Zygmunt Mycielski, "Wspominaja c wykłady N. Boulanger," *Ruch Muzyczny* 17 (1947): 2.

55. Zygmunt Mycielski, "Przyjazd prof. Nadii Boulanger na Festiwal Muzyki Współczesnej," *Przegla d Kulturalny* 38 (1956): 6.

56. Maria Modrakowska, "Wspominając studia u Nadii Boulanger," *Ruch Muzyczny* 11 (1958): 11.

57. Jerzy Waldorff, "Festiwal Muzyki Współczesnej: Z dużej chmury...," *Stolica Warszawa*, 4 November 1956.

58. *Biuletyn Informacyjny Związku Kompozytorów Polskich* 3 (1956): 6.

59. Ludwik Ludorowski, "Pierwszy koncert 'Warszawskiej Jesieni,'" *Sztandar Ludu*, 17 October 1956. Lisa Jakelski analyzes the ritual pomp of the first concert, including Boulanger's portrait as figurehead, in *Making New Music in Cold War Poland*, 29.

60. These claims are based on the folder of press clippings assembled by ZKP (11/2) for its own internal reference.

61. Jerzy Młodziejowski, "Warszawska jesień," *Ekspres Poznański*, 15 October 1956.

62. M.B., "Uczniowie Nadii Boulanger," *Słowo Powszechne*, 17 October 1956. The critic, likely musicologist Michał Bristiger, mentions Antoni Szałowski's Overture (1936), Stanisław Skrowaczewski's *Night Music* (1952), and Bolesław Woytowicz's Second String Quartet (1947). He also notes that Tadeusz Szeligowski's tonally conservative and sumptuous string orchestra lament, *Epitaph on the Death of Szymanowski* (1937), was his favorite.

63. Stefan Wysocki, "O festiwalu z dygresjami," *Sztandar Młodych*, 20–21 October 1956.

64. Jeanice Brooks, "*Noble et grande servante de la musique*: Telling the Story of Nadia Boulanger's Conducting Career," *Journal of Musicology* 14/1 (1996): 92–116.

65. Summarized in Jerzy Waldorff, "Po 'Jesieni Warszawskiej': Zachwyty, zawody, niepokoje," *Świat*, 28 October 1956.

66. Witold Rudziński, "Jeszcze o 'Warszawskiej Jesieni'," *Życie Warszawy*, 2 November, 1956.

67. Twardowski, "Nadia Boulanger."

68. M. F., "I Międzynarodowy Festiwal Muzyki Współczesnej," *Żołnierz Wolności*, 19 October 1956. It is worth noting that the first jazz festival in Poland also occurred in 1956 with state support, in the vacation town of Sopot.

69. The Polish avant-garde's propensity for expression and reinvention of traditional sonic means has often been noted. For example, Lisa Jakelski, "Górecki's Scontri and Avant-Garde Music in Cold War Poland," *Journal of Musicology* 26/2 (2009): 205–39.

70. Lisa Cooper Vest, "The Discursive Foundations of the Polish Musical Avant-Garde" (PhD diss., Indiana University, 2014), 302–47.

71. "Sprawozdanie z pobytu delegatów Komitetu Roku Chopinowskiego w Paryżu od dnia 4–17-ego lutego 1949," Archive of Modern Records (AAN), Warsaw, 366/12 238.

72. Boulanger to Mycielski, 26 September 1956, PL-Wn, IV 14368, 21.

73. See, for example, articles by Jerzy Młodziejowski and Jerzy Waldorff in ZKP, 11/2.

74. PL-Wn, Rps 14173.

75. Zygmunt Mycielski, *Dziennik 1950–59*, 233 and 253. Mycielski's hearing of Darmstadt's darlings is also shrouded in wartime trauma as he journals, "This music—it sounds like the hydrogen bomb has already exploded." The Rameau recording was most likely Boulanger's 1953 release of opera excerpts on the Decca label.

76. Bożena Shallcross, *The Holocaust Object in Polish and Polish-Jewish Culture* (Bloomington: Indiana University Press, 2011), 72–73.

77. Czesław Miłosz, *The Collected Poems 1931–1987*, trans. Czesław Miłosz (New York: Ecco Press, 1988).

78. Zygmunt Mycielski, *Niby-dziennik* (Warsaw: Iskry, 1998), 67. Here Mycielski recalls a conversation about another internationally renowned poet from Poland, Zbigniew Herbert.

79. Mycielski, *Niby-dziennik ostatni, 1981–1987*, 231.

80. Zofia Helman, "'. . . Tylko to jest ocalenie': Zygmunt Mycielski—pie ͵c ́ pies ́ni do słów Czesława Miłosza," in *Melos, logos, etos: Materiały sympozjum pos ́wie ͵conego twórczos ́ci Floriana Da ͵browskiego, Stefana Kisielewskiego, Zygmunta Mycielskiego*, ed. Krystyna Tarnawska-Kaczorowska (Warsaw: ZKP, 1987), 141–58. Mycielski's *Ocalenie* was subsequently published by PWM in 1989.

81. Jakelski, *Making New Music in Cold War Poland*, 19–21, at 19.

82. Maria Modrakowska, "Prof. Nadia Boulanger zachwycona Krakowem," *Echo Krakowskie*, 16 October 1956.

83. Boulanger to Mycielski, 30 November 1956, PL-Wn, IV14368.

84. Nadia Boulanger, personal file (86/A), ZKP.

85. ZKP, 16/19.

86. Mycielski, *Dziennik 1950–59*, 283, 289.

87. Mycielski, *Niby-dziennik*, 123.

88. Boulanger to Mycielski, 16 March 1979, PL-Wn, IV14368.

89. Mycielski, *Niby-dziennik*, 157.

90. Danuta Gwizdalanka, "Głosy i dygresje do 'teczek' i *Dzienników* Zygmunta Mycielskiego (1)," *Ruch Muzyczny* 57/3 (2013): 13.

91. Institute of National Memory (IPN), Warsaw, BU 0246/998.

92. See the study of Michel Foucault's security service file by Anna Krakus and Jessie Labov (forthcoming) for a discussion of the organization's practices and discourse around homosexuality, class, and Western intellectuals.

93. Copland to Boulanger, 20 November 1965, Aaron Copland Collection, Library of Congress, https://www.loc.gov/item/copland.corr0474/.

94. The records of the visit were kept in Boulanger's personal file (86/A) at ZKP.

95. It is difficult to offer a useful historical conversion for the złoty because of the currency's periods of volatile inflation under state socialism, but as a point of reference her twelve-night stay in an apartment in Warsaw's most luxurious hotel cost approximately 3,000 złoty.

96. Originally she had proposed conducting Mycielski's Second Symphony, among other works, on a concert of Polish music, but this did not come to pass.

# "What Awaits Them Now?"
# A Letter to Paris

ZYGMUNT MYCIELSKI
TRANSLATED AND ANNOTATED BY J. MACKENZIE PIERCE

*This letter was written by Polish composer and Boulanger student Zygmunt Mycielski as he was freed from a German labor camp in May 1945. At the outset of the Second World War in 1939, Mycielski had joined the defense of Poland against German and Soviet invasion but fled to Hungary when Poland's defeat became inevitable. He then journeyed to France and joined the Polish Army there, but was captured on June 17, 1940, while defending the Maginot Line during the Battle of France. He spent the next five years performing forced labor as a prisoner of war. Throughout his captivity he wrote to Boulanger, upholding a correspondence that would continue until her death. He received in return several letters from Boulanger and her former pupil and close friend Marcelle de Manziarly (1899–1989), a pianist and composer with whom Mycielski had a lifelong correspondence (and who accompanied Boulanger to the Warsaw Autumn Festival in 1956). In addition to Boulanger and Manziarly, the letter below is addressed to Annette Dieudonné (1896–1991), another former pupil who worked closely with Boulanger on both pedagogical and performance projects. The letter is held in the Bibliothèque nationale de France, N.L.a. 89 (241–44).*

Sonderlager
Kr. Gef. Arb. Kdo. 98 [*Kriegsgefangenen-Arbeitskommandos*]
Quickborn-Himmelmoor II
The day of the cessation of hostilities —<u>4th of May 1945</u>

Dear friends—Yesterday the barbed wire was broken down; it's the end of bars, padlock, cells, doors, and keys. Yesterday, we left—I can write these words—finally, finally. Your three letters from America and three from Marcelle were the big events of this life here—nothing else arrived.

But you know that your presence, your memory, never left me; it was my strength, each day, every day, most of all here, in captivity—for nearly 2,000 days.

I write to you all, *together*. Time is pressing. Impossible otherwise—but you all know how I bring you together in my heart, as if I never left you. Annette who stayed there [in Paris], who suffered cruelly, remaining alone after the loss of her father.[1] I never knew how to express [this] well, out of fear of weakness, out of a lack of strength for all that is sensitive and to which we were no longer entitled, out of a lack of courage. There are no more tears or laughter, one must be a piece of wood; Annette, for-give me, but you know, don't you; friendship, all this, no, I close my eyes again; it is no longer possible, but is still the same thing, it's profound, much more profound, centered, buried, let us not touch it, there is no more *sentimentality*, it's too profound.—And I remember, from far away, your remark: "I don't like it when France is criticized"—it was then that I understood what you are, from the tone of this remark—and then I saw you, but I never said anything. Then, here, I measured all whom I had the opportunity to approach; according to their true worth, according to the worth of that which remains in us for all the long days; each of you left me such a plain, clear, strong, evident yardstick, that I could carry this friendship inside me without growing weak and, in the decisive moments, think about you and know how to act: Mademoiselle Boulanger was so much the benchmark for gesture, for action: saying (of whom???), "He would never let a child be beaten in front of him."—When I saw a (Polish) twelve-year-old beaten, kicked—(she was there)—I took this phrase to my mother—in action—and still today, when the tanks rolled out—when I could touch them, when it was over, you understand, over—and the old ladies sitting in the ditches, and the gray columns, wobbly, bags, cars full of children—after what I had seen, with us [in Poland], with you [in France] (you, us, them???)—this is why I talked with them, offering the little that I had—since it is their turn for the kicks of the cowardly, of the weak, of those without courage.[2] Nadia, why is man the way he is? To ask for nothing, but one cannot sleep. It is them, now. Justice, but why the cowardice? It is as difficult to be oppressed as it is to oppress (since it's always about oppression). That which is, is always the same thing. Should one keep quiet? Keeping quiet is also cowardice, the worst kind, perhaps? So, always dying, without bearing fruit?

In front of these broken barbed wires, this change in role from one hour to the next, where man the master became from one minute to the next the slave, and the slave has his toys again: revolvers, rifles, rancorous

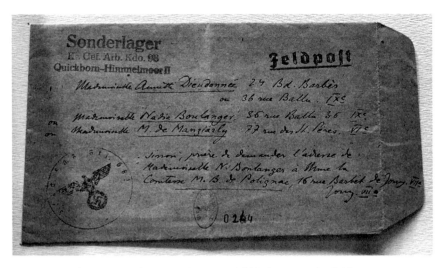

Figure 1. Envelope containing Mycielski's letter sent by field post
from Labor Subcamp Quickborn-Himmelmoor to three possible Paris addresses.

looks, the look of a whipped dog who can die without fear. Let's spit out
the word, kill without fear—even without danger! I think about you, about
Marcelle's laughter, about your world, about your lives, about all that you
give to others in terms of strength, courage, and true nobility. If humans
could only resemble you! But it is not so: they are cruel, stupid, cowardly,
mediocre, and yet, no, they are not evil. They are poor. We were not able
to keep them busy, to fill their hours of life with anything other than a war.
Because egoism is at the root of our projects, our "systems," of our organizations. Because we are cowards, who fear death, poverty, and suffering.
One must <u>always</u> search for sin in the "grand people," *always.*

I once heard Mme Rot[hs]child (I name her, yes) talk of poverty. I had
enough of that. Enough. It is worse, it was worse than truncheons, kicks,
bayonets, bullets in the neck. (But the system that our century invented of
mass deportations is the worst of all.) Take me at my word, it is what she said.[3]

If I write to you, it is because I must go over there [to Poland], to
my mother, my brothers, children, all my brothers. You know that I am
not a chauvinist. But it was evident that in [19]40 it was necessary to be
with you, and now—over there, after what they have gone through. What
awaits them now, what is happening in Central Europe?

But I would like to be able to visit you for several months. Yes. Imagine
that I would like to write several symphonic works, see Marcelle often during

this work, then hear my compositions quickly. Don't jump from indignation. This is what I want to do. But first it is necessary to be over there, in Poland.

If they deport me to Siberia or elsewhere as a "lustful viper of capitalism," know that nothing physical affects me. Besides, my heart is broken to the core and I would not hold up for even a few months of forced labor. My lovely health—it is done, and it's good like this. It facilitates a wisdom, belated, but a certain wisdom. (Without the smile of Anatole France.) One must love life, but not fear death—neither one's own nor that of others.[4]

To talk with you, to speak to you about what is going on in Poland is too grim to attempt. The last letters I received from my mother were too simple to try to explain to you: the facts, too poor, poverty? All of civilization is a function of wealth and poverty; but there is also something else. Marcelle knows this very well, you know it very well; all of you; the simplicity of all this. Like your mother. She was also like [my] Mother; because of what my mother had seen, she has become like the women of the people, very varied—in France, what one sees with the Breton women, who, as shown in *images d'Epinal*, are a symbol of virtues in face of the Ocean where the husband, man, son expose themselves and perish, but the women remain "themselves."[5] The concentration camps of Oświęcim [Auschwitz], Dachau, Warsaw and all our territory took away one by one, and martyred in a manner that is too cruel to express in words, our dear ones, our dearest ones; months and years passed without any news. And my mother put all this in a card, without being able to name it, to say it—but one understands all: "He was able to take a little linen away with him"—and *voilà*—that is all my mother was able to write to me, but she said it, and she is there and I will take a bicycle and go over there, trying not to die, in order to be once more, a little bit, near to her, who has none of us four close to her.

Let us never again ask why such a world surrounds us, never again ask for the reasons, for the cruelties, all that, so that they may forget it, that they may stop, no longer accumulate, no longer do these shameful things.

Nadia, Marcelle, Annette, I can write to you because I remained honest. Often a real idiot, but I never asked for anything, I never signed anything, never calculated anything for the cowardly "pros." It's negative, but there is always that, otherwise I would not have the courage to write this first letter after what is called liberty. Only my failed escapes complicated my captivity.—It was too long. If for the few millions on only one side of the globe for whom all this has happened, and this debris, this burning sky, this Ocean of misery, if our poor Europe can no longer live otherwise than on the towline of a bloody injustice, well, always remember that, over there, somewhere, there will be strength until the end. Mother knows it—she wrote me, often speaking of you.

Otherwise, perhaps we will see each other again. And then I know what I will find in you, with you, my dears, my very dear friends whom my heart unites—and you know, understand, how and why.

Z. Mycielski
From the location where disciplinary Kommando of Himmelmoor (Holstein) was.

[Addressed to:]

Mademoiselle Annette Dieudonné 24 Bd. Barbès or 36 rue Ballu IXe
Or Mademoiselle Nadia Boulanger 36 rue Ballu IXe
Or Mademoiselle M. de Manziarly 77 rue des St Pères VIe

If not, please ask for the address of Mademoiselle N. Boulanger from Mme la Comtesse M.B. de Polignac, 16 rue Barbet de Jouy VIIe

## NOTES

1. Dieudonné remained in Paris during the war and moved into Boulanger's flat during the Occupation to prevent it from being requisitioned.

2. It is unclear what, if any, specific scene of early postwar hardship and displacement Mycielski is describing. In any case, his generosity and sympathy toward the German civilians, whom he believes will now suffer from the Allies, is striking.

3. Although Mycielski is criticizing Rothschild, it is unclear if he thinks it is her hypocrisy or the experience of poverty that is worse than war.

4. Mycielski alludes to Anatole France's statement, one often quoted by Boulanger: "The artist should love life and show us that it is beautiful. Without him, we would have doubts" ("L'artiste doit aimer la vie et nous montrer qu'elle est belle. Sans lui, nous en douterions"). *Le Jardin d'Epicure* (Paris: Calmann Lévy, 1895), 33. Thanks to Jeanice Brooks for this source.

5 . *Images d'Epinal* are brightly colored, inexpensive prints, especially popular in rural France, that tend to project a traditional, simplistic view of the world in depictions of rural life, fables, and famous battles, among other topics.

# A Letter from Professor Nadia Boulanger

*Przegląd Kulturalny* vol. 10 (1956), issue no. 46

## TRANSLATED BY J. MACKENZIE PIERCE

*Written following Boulanger's visit to the first Warsaw Autumn Festival of Contemporary Music in 1956, this letter was likely intended for publication. The French-language manuscript is held in Mycielski's papers (National Library of Poland, IV14368). The Polish translation that appeared in* Przegląd Kulturalny (The Cultural Review) *is presumably by Mycielski, though he is uncredited. The paragraph on audiences was excerpted, in the original French, for a pamphlet advertising the second Warsaw Autumn, held in 1958.*

*A letter from Prof. Nadia Boulanger, written while she was returning to France, has arrived in Mycielski's hands, along with authorization to publish it in our periodical.*

As I leave Poland, I wish to send my regards, my thanks, and my admiration to all of you. Your undertaking was tremendous, and it would have been impossible had you not all taken part in it and used all the means available in service of this enormous result.

You offered all of your time, all of your energy, you completely forgot about yourselves in order to bring this idea to realization. And you were rewarded with complete success.

Petty minds will debate about the selection of this or that work, about this or that artistic orientation, and also about the program's omissions and inclusions. From the 10th to the 21st of October, we could hear 78 works from 53 composers hailing from twelve countries—works performed by nine symphonic orchestras from six European countries. There were works performed by two Polish choirs and two quartets—one Hungarian, one French. Fifteen soloists and sixteen conductors performed. Among these performers, some are already well known across Europe, but the true revelation was the younger cadre of conductors. They are already outstanding, and we were filled with admiration for the seriousness and musical authority with which they worked with ensembles.

I was completely impressed by your audiences. The impartiality with which they applauded works and performers. They seem to measure a performance's success only through the emotions it conveys or the lack thereof. The audiences amazed me thoroughly, always showing concentration and attention without regard for the accompanying social environs. In my view, the audience was as impressive as the festival itself: an amazingly attentive, enthusiastic, and impartial public filled the halls throughout the festival, a public that could not be distracted on those evenings. They demonstrate that your efforts are not just for show, nor are they cordoned off from the vital artistic needs running deep in your society.

Over eleven days we listened to works from abroad that represented the most disparate, even opposite tendencies. Next to works of Khachaturian, Berger, or Dutilleux, who belong to the generation of 1903, 1905, and 1916, we heard works by Alban Berg, Myaskovsky, Bela Bartók, and Stravinsky, all of whom were born between 1881 and 1885. Hearing Polish works alongside these allowed us to better evaluate the great fecundity, vitality, and artistic weight of the Polish School. Previously, such an evaluation had only been possible through score reading. In the course of those eleven days, we were able to evaluate the excellent discipline and exceptional quality of orchestral sound of several unfamiliar ensembles, including both the Moscow and Bucharest orchestras, as well as—from Poland—the Warsaw orchestra and the two orchestras of the Polish Radio, from Katowice and Cracow. And finally, your marvelous choirs, so well rehearsed, with such a subtle and balanced sound. The quality and value of soloists, the diligence of their work, their talent and technical level—all of it was, in most cases, a great revelation for us, since these ensembles are not well known throughout the world.

As guests we received ceaseless care from the festival's organizers. They attended to the smallest details of our stay and itinerary. Thanks to this, our stay was not only a pleasure but will remain in our memory as an unforgettable experience.

And, finally, Warsaw. I finally saw—next to her horrific destruction and ruins, which shake with their ghastliness—the reborn and rebuilt New and Old Towns. They are happy and colorful; they speak to your past and of a present being built through great effort, so that you may have a beautiful future. I saw people deep in prayer and beautiful children who were happily playing, like birds on the street. I saw your excellent concert hall, marvelous, and—moreover—not overdone. By removing some of its old decorations, you created a new image for the hall that loyally draws on the Warsaw Philharmonic's famous old hall.

I admired your artistic taste while visiting the Chopin Society in the old Ostrogski Palace on Tamka Street. It shows the best, simply refined taste, in which nothing has been overlooked: the walls, the floor, the furniture, the upholstery—everything there emanates effort and love. This palace has been turned into a true temple of art.

I visited the music schools and conservatory where you prepare children and youth in a serious manner for serious work, which should then become a source of joy. I could see that you remember that both training and artistic work must be connected to joy.

Thanks to my friends, I could also perceive that which has vanished from Poland as well as that which was systematically annihilated through the terrible historical events that struck your land. But I observe that your nation is full of life, that it finds inspiration in its past, that your grace depends on your values. Here, heroism has become an everyday matter.

All of these impressions are thanks to your festival, which I consider an amazing undertaking. It also proved that your energy, if shaped by the intrinsic conviction of your cause's righteousness, can surmount all difficulties.

Thanks to this meeting, I conversed again with my friends. Neither time, nor distance, nor historical events—which separated us for so long—were able to break those bonds that only death can sever. In my friends' music I heard expression that was deep, serious, fundamental, original, and unique.

I would like to be able to articulate my admiration, respect, and attachment to my friends' work through action. I wish to work so that these compositions that show their art's specificity are better known. I am thinking specifically of those works that contain imagination, sonic sensitivity, vitality and rhythmic energy, and, ultimately, an originality of melodic line and harmonic inventiveness. This inventiveness is sometimes hidden by an overly rich sonic apparatus, and a saturation of orchestral techniques. But it is also possible that such a sonic sumptuousness is the price that must be paid in exchange for the inexhaustible store of creative energy that infused the Polish works performed at the festival.

As I leave you, my mind returns to all of you. My ears and my heart ring with something more than the sounds of individual, dazzling compositions. My mind returns to those works full of the specificity of your poetry. It returns to those works that were especially moving, in which the full phenomenal vision of the soul of your greatest artists pulses—artists who have achieved universal significance while remaining distinctly Polish. I still have much to say about this. But today I wish only to make note of these impressions. They are for me full of deep significance. I feel a great responsibility as I become aware of what I experienced with you. I wish that my friends will learn of my feelings and accept my most heartfelt thanks for this stay.

# THE LONGY SCHOOL OF MUSIC

PRESENTS

THE NOTED LECTURER, TEACHER, CONDUCTOR, ORGANIST

# NADIA BOULANGER

NADIA BOULANGER, long recognized throughout the world for her unusual qualities of musicianship, her unquestioned contribution as a teacher with whom such composers as Igor Markevitch, Aaron Copland, Walter Piston, Roy Harris, Jean Françaix and Marcelle de Manziarly have studied, has given similar lectures in Paris.

To hear Mlle. Boulanger lecture is a privilege that both the trained musician and the layman appreciate. With those in all walks of life she shares, in her informal talks, an intelligence so keen, a love for music so strong, such rare scholarship and understanding that the genius of the composer is revealed.

## *in* TWO LECTURE SERIES

I:  Beethoven—The String Quartets and the Missa Solemnis

PERFORMANCES BY THE STRADIVARIUS QUARTET

II:  Bach—The Cantatas

PERFORMANCES BY THE BACH CANTATA CLUB

Figure 1. Poster for the lecture series given at the
Longy School of Music in Cambridge, Massachusetts, 1941.

# The Beethoven Lectures for the Longy School

INTRODUCED BY CÉDRIC SEGOND-GENOVESI
TRANSLATED BY MIRANDA STEWART

Alongside Bach's cantatas and the works of Stravinsky, Beethoven's quartets counted among the fixtures of Nadia Boulanger's classes and lectures on musical analysis. As early as 1928, she produced a series of public lectures on these compositions for the Ecole Normale de Musique, accompanied by the Quatuor Calvet's live performance of the works.[1] This is probably the period when Boulanger added numerous annotations to the scores she had purchased in 1919, now held at the Conservatoire national supérieur de musique et de danse in Lyon.[2] In 1940–41, she revisited this material in preparation for a series of lectures at the Longy School of Music, in Cambridge, Massachusetts, where Boulanger taught during the Second World War. By way of illustration, she provided a single-page analytical "summary" of each movement of the quartet, representing aspects of form, thematic material, harmony, and voice leading.[3] These documents offer valuable and comprehensive evidence of Nadia Boulanger's analytical tools at the end of 1930s. In particular, they allow us to assess the wide range of models she employed.

First, let us take the area of harmonic analysis. Many of Boulanger's students have mentioned and, on occasion, regretted, the rigorous and slavish application of Théodore Dubois's *Treatise* (1921) to her teaching, in the purest tradition of the Paris Conservatoire.[4] Yet Boulanger's analysis of the Rondo, Op. 18, No. 4 shows the extent to which she departed from this work. She did so directly and overtly; for example, using Roman numerals for chords both as an analytical tool and in teaching harmony, whereas Dubois, embedded in the French teaching tradition, concentrated primarily on intervals and the rules governing their production (voice leading).[5] Boulanger broadly adopted the tools and conventions of the German-speaking and, incidentally, English-speaking countries: systematic numbering of chords, keys noted below the staff (if space permitted), use of uppercase/lowercase to distinguish between major and minor chords and keys, crossed-out scale degrees for diminished chords, etc. We can speculate that she adopted these technical tools because of the regular, virtually daily, contact with her English-speaking colleagues and students, beginning in 1906 and particularly after 1919, once the Ecole Normale de Musique opened, followed by the Conservatoire américain of Fontainebleau. Boulanger quickly added to her personal library several works by American composition teacher Percy Goetschius in which the learning of harmonic analysis is based on scale degrees, progressions, and harmonic functions.[6]

Between 1890 and 1900, Boulanger became aware of similar approaches in Emile Durand's 1893 *Abrégé du cours d'harmonie théorique et pratique,* the *Cours de composition* (first volume in 1899) by Vincent d'Indy, who widely disseminated Germanic *Musiktheorie* in the French-speaking countries; and Ernst Friedrich Richter's *Lehrbuch der Harmonie,* translated into French by Gustave Sandré (fourth edition in 1894) and recommended by Fauré, Boulanger's teacher from 1901 to around 1904. These works could all be found in her personal library.

Her library also embraced, at a deeper level, a more Germanic, and incidentally Anglo-American idea of harmonic tonality than that favored by the French. At the beginning of his treatise Théodore Dubois, with scant originality, based his theory of tonality on the "Rameau school" premise of harmonic resonance. However, he immediately set himself apart from his predecessor Henri Reber's 1862 *Traité d'harmonie* when he noted that the "chord given by the resonance of the sonority (*do-sol-mi-sib-ré,* etc.) is placed on the *dominant*: the resolution of this chord alone gives rise to a tonic chord." He thus concluded: "1. That the most important chord in the scale from the tonal point of view is the *dominant,* and not the tonic, despite the fact that the latter lends its name to the key due to its conclusive nature; 2. That the dominant-tonic order is the *enchaînement-type* (primary sequence) given by nature."[7] In other words, it is the V–I resolution and not the tonic alone that is the basis of tonal harmony. This premise has the practical effect of assuming a new tonality for every V–I sequence (and consequently, modulating), which is effectively what Dubois suggests in his *Traité* (Figure 2).

Boulanger adopted a different approach. In addition to the principle of pivot chords (which create a logical and fluid connection between the original and the destination keys), she favored the use of secondary dominants—V of IV, for example, in her analysis of the Rondo, Op. 18, No. 4—which allowed her to assume large, stable, non-modulating tonal areas, an approach clearly more akin to Schoenberg than to Dubois.[8] The concept of secondary dominants was refined and disseminated by Walter Piston, a student of Boulanger, in *Principles of Harmonic Analysis* (1933), a

Cédric Segond-Genovesi

Figure 2. Théodore Dubois, "Bass lines to figure and realize,"
*Traité d'harmonie théorique et pratique* (1921).

signed copy of which she owned. It bears the inscription "In memory of the years 1924, 1925, 1926 / Walter Piston / June 21, 1933."[9]

As can be seen in her analysis of the Rondo, Boulanger's analytical tools were borrowed less from Théodore Dubois (and the tradition of the Conservatoire) than, via various go-betweens, from the German- and English-speaking worlds. This enabled her to grasp Beethoven's harmony (and architecture) by prioritizing large, stable tonal areas, rather than chopping up and excessively segmenting the musical discourse.

This relates to another essential feature of Boulanger's approach to analysis: the consideration given to horizontal (melodic and contrapuntal) phenomena and the voice leading at different levels revealed by melodic reduction. When Nadia Boulanger was asked by Bruno Monsaingeon in 1978, "What is the precise purpose of your analysis classes?" she replied: "The ability to hear!! Hearing music not as a vertical phenomenon but as a *horizontal* one."[10] This principle, which Boulanger also successfully applied to Stravinsky's works, proved to be particularly comprehensible and effective in her analyses of Beethoven's quartets.[11] Her melodic reductionof the first theme of the Allegro con brio, Op. 18, No. 1—on the first staff, principal notes without rhythms, presented in reduction on the 2nd, 3rd, and 4th staves—reveals a generative melodic segment F–G–A–B♭ (marked by a horizontal line), which is fairly inexplicit in the first part of the phrase due to the descending G–B sixth that interrupts the ascending movement, then developed, and finally spread throughout the polyphony with a fairly unexpected voice leading (Figure 3). On other occasions, Boulanger offers more complex linear reductions, as in

• 265 •

Figure 3. Beethoven's String Quartet, Op. 18, No. 1, Allegro con brio, mm. 21–29, voice leading suggested by Boulanger's reductional analysis.

the case of the third movement (Allegro) of Op. 18, No. 3 on three staves: "melodic outline," "melody," and "harmonic outline" (Figure 4) and the initial Allegro of Op. 18, No. 2, the development of which is reduced to its "harmonic outline" on two staves (Figure 5).

It is tempting to compare this "outline" or *grande ligne*, as Boulanger referred to the concept of unfolding form in her teaching, to the Schenkerian *Urlinie*. Both reduction methods are similar in many ways: suppression of rhythmic patterns, octave displacement of certain lines, smaller script for structurally secondary notes, slurs indicating relationships over distance, etc. Among Boulanger's students and close friends were several

Figure 4. Detail of analysis of Beethoven's String Quartet, Op. 18, No. 3, Allegro.

Figure 5. Detail of analysis of Beethoven's String Quartet, Op. 18, No. 2, Allegro.

Figure 6. Analysis of Beethoven's Violin Sonata Op. 24, in Maurice Emmanuel,
*L'histoire de la langue musicale*, vol. 1, 1911.

Americans well acquainted with Schenker's writings, particularly Israel Citkowitz, "the guru of an important, though largely forgotten, New York Schenker-circle," and Citkowitz's teacher and former Boulanger pupil, Roger Sessions, whose copiously annotated personal copy of Schenker's *Harmonielehre* (1906) featured in Boulanger's personal library.[12]

However, it can safely be said that Boulanger's reduction, which was considerably less systematic and developed than Schenker's, probably derived from older models. Nadia Boulanger's library (partly inherited from her father, the composer Ernest Boulanger),[13] contained, in addition to Vincent d'Indy's *Cours de composition*, Reicha's 1818 *Cours de composition musicale* which includes a section on "fugue analyzed in relation to harmony," superimposing different reductions of the same fugue "reduced to its simplest expression and free of any incidental notes," and another on "principal notes and chords in fundamental basses" or harmonic realization of a fundamental bass. Her library also contained Maurice Emmanuel's 1911 *L'histoire de la langue musicale* (Figure 6), which was one of the main sources for Boulanger's music history class, and which she recommended highly. Even more clearly, the lessons in counterpoint taught by André Gédalge at the Paris Conservatoire appear to have enduringly influenced Boulanger's teaching and analytic tools. Although Gédalge's treatises were unfortunately only partially published, evidence of the influence of his teaching methods can still be gleaned from a variety of sources.[14] As Barbara Kelly notes, "Milhaud's increasing preoccupation with linear textures and melodic writing in the late 1910s was inspired by the guiding influence of his counterpoint teacher at the Conservatoire, André Gédalge."[15] Another student of Gédalge, Maurice Ravel, also used successive linear reductions to explain harmonic dissonances in his *Valses nobles et sentimentales*.[16]

In her analysis of Beethoven's quartets, Boulanger's formal diagrams (see pages following this introduction), which emphasize symmetrical relationships, hierarchical levels, and proportions, also reveal, more loosely, a different influence—that of Russian musical theory and, in particular, the metrotechtonic analysis developed between 1900 and 1920 by the Franco-Russian theorist Georgy Eduardovich Conus. Boulanger boasted Russian ancestry from her mother, Raïssa Mychetski, and taught numerous Russian-speaking students.[17] Her working library, which included a handwritten translation of Taneyev's treatise on counterpoint (*Podvizhnoi kontrapunkt strogogo pis'ma*, 1909),[18] also showed a clear interest in Russian musical theory. Boulanger was featured alongside Michel Delines (pseudonym of Mikhail Osipovitch Achkinazi) among the "contributors" responsible for the section on Russian music in the *Encyclopédie de la musique et dictionnaire du Conservatoire* by Albert Lavignac and Lionel de La Laurencie.[19] Everything suggests that she intended to take advantage of her tour through Russia with Raoul Pugno in the winter of 1913–14 to compile the information she needed—a project that was unfortunately aborted due to the sudden death of Pugno in Moscow, in January 1914.[20]

As Manfred Kelkel observes, metrotechtonic analysis

> allows us to express the form of a work in figures through a type of *spatial projection of durations*, revealing its architecture measured strictly. You start by outlining the results of a formal analysis, and replace the staff by a horizontal line, the bar lines by vertical lines and the boundaries of musical phrases by different types of brackets to indicate the quantitative value of phrases, which corresponds to the number of measures in the phrase. This offers an overview of a piece of music and reveals the numerical relationships between the different parts of the musical architecture, placing a complex whole into a limited area. The duration of the phrases is expressed by a series of numbers, which represent its beats (eighth note, quarter note, half note or measure, according to the unit chosen) and this produces a spatial projection of durations.[21]

According to Conus, the symmetry of a piece of music, considered and analyzed as architecture over time, ensures its perfection. This is precisely what formal diagrams seek to demonstrate (Figure 7).

No copy of Conus's *Metro-tektonicheskoe issledovanie muzykal'noi formy* (French-Russian bilingual edition, 1933) is currently in Boulanger's library, but she may have met Conus in 1913–14, and it is even more likely that she attended his lectures in France between 1923 and 1928. And her annotations to her copy of Chopin's *Etudes* (edited by Raoul Pugno, c. 1915) show that she was clearly aware of Conus's theories: the "quantitative values" of

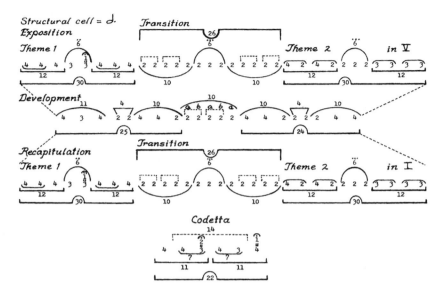

Figure 7. Georgy Eduardovich Conus, metrotechtonic plan of the syntactical motion in Beethoven's Piano Sonata, Op. 90, No. 1.

phrases, expressed in numbers of measures, are arranged around vertical and horizontal axes, or interlinked to show structural symmetries.[22] In her analysis of Beethoven's quartets, she appears to have abandoned any systematic search for formal symmetries, but continued to use the tools and certain graphic conventions of metrotechtonic analysis.

This list of models and influences could be further supplemented by Hugo Riemann's 1890 *Katechismus der Harmonielehre,* for which Boulanger possessed a handwritten French translation; Paul Hindemith's 1937 *Unterweisung im Tonsatz*, which Boulanger at one point considered translating;[23] and thousands of other diagrams and references, both from France and abroad, not to mention the early treatises that featured prominently in the library at 36 rue Ballu (Fux, Mattheson, etc.). Consequently, to assess Nadia Boulanger's *musical world*, we must go beyond countries, institutions, and activities and explore her mental and technical tools. A brilliant synthesis of French heritage and foreign influence, poised between modern theory and ancient tradition, emerges clearly in the analyses contained in the Beethoven Lecture Series—Longy School, reproduced below.

Boulanger's analysis of the opening Allegro con Brio of Beethoven's Opus 18, No. 1.

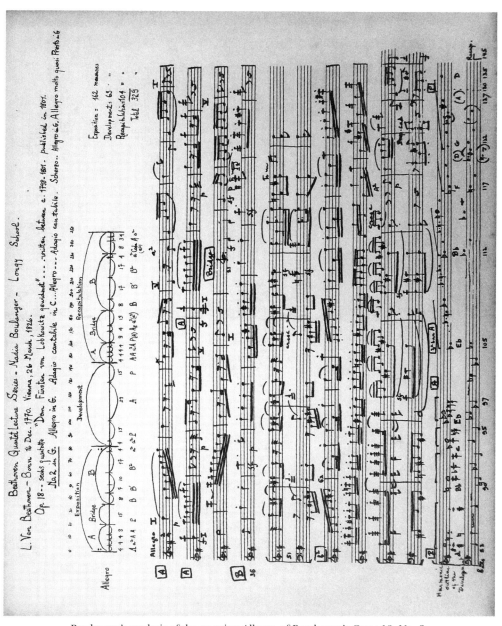

Boulanger's analysis of the opening Allegro of Beethoven's Opus 18, No. 2.

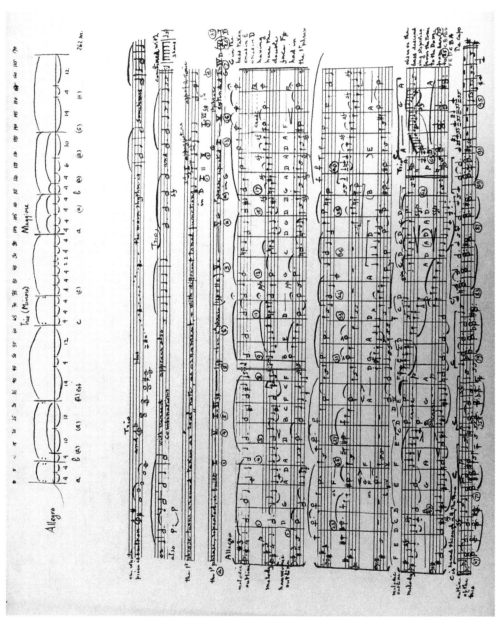

Boulanger's analysis of the third movement (Allegro) of Beethoven's Opus 18, No. 3.

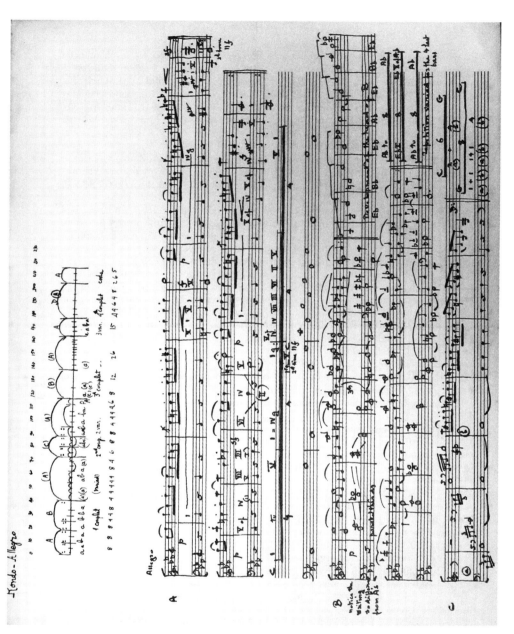

Boulanger's analysis of the Rondo Allegro of Beethoven's Opus 18, No. 4.

# NOTES

1. Correspondence with the Quatuor Calvet's agent, 5 and 18 October 1927, Bibliothèque nationale de France (F-Pn), Rés. Vm. dos. 127 (1–2). The nine sessions, held on Saturdays at 2 p.m., were advertised in *Le Monde musical*: 24 March (Op. 18, Nos. 1 and 2); 31 March (Op. 18, Nos. 3 and 4); 21 April (Op. 18, Nos. 5 and 6); 28 April (Op. 59, Nos. 1 and 2); 5 May (Op. 59, No. 3 and Op. 74); 12 May (Op. 95 and Op. 127); 19 May (Op. 130 and Op. 135); 26 May (Op. 131); and 2 June (Op. 132 and Op. 133). The audience "was invited to bring along scores." See "France: Composers: Boulanger," a page from *Le Monde musical*, n.d., F-Pn, Fonds Montpensier, Bob. 28255.

2. Ludwig van Beethoven, *Quartette . . . Partitur*, 4 vols., ed. F. A. Roitzsch (Leipzig: Peters, c. 1900). Boulanger noted the date of purchase on the cover of each volume. Conservatoire national supérieur de musique et de danse de Lyon (F-LYc), UFNB ME BEE 246.

3. Boulanger left France for the United States in November 1940, and returned to Paris in January 1946. She was responsible for these classes at the Longy School of Music: "Madrigal group," "Advanced counterpoint and fugue," "Seminar in composition" and "Reading class." Sets of Boulanger's analyses including varying numbers of the single-page summaries are preserved at F-LYc, the Eda Kuhn Loeb Music Library at Harvard University, and the Centre international Nadia et Lili Boulanger (CNLB).

4. According to Robert Levin, for example, "She had a sense of instrumentation, of texture, of rhetoric, the importance of rests as much as the importance of sounds. And beyond that she displayed a contradiction, which to me this very day, remains completely inexplicable. Which is that she relied, for the most part, on teaching materials that in some respects are thoroughly unremarkable and, indeed, mediocre. Nadia Boulanger sang the praises of [the theory texts of] Theodore Dubois and she celebrated his musicianship. She lived with that contradiction because that was the way it was taught to her. She did not challenge it." Robert Levin, "Boulanger's Pedagogy," unpublished paper delivered at "Nadia Boulanger and American Music: A Memorial Symposium," University of Colorado, Boulder, 7 October 2004, cited in Barrett Ashley Johnson, "A Comparative Study Between the Pedagogical Methodologies of Arnold Schoenberg and Nadia Boulanger Regarding Training the Composer" (PhD diss., Louisiana State University, Baton Rouge, 2007), 217–18.

5. See also "Cours d'harmonie de Nadia Boulanger" (Nadia Boulanger's Harmony Lessons), mimeographed copies of which are held in various Boulanger collections: F-LYc, CNLB, Conservatoire américain de Fontainebleau archives. Chapter 3 of Dubois's *Traité*, "Harmonization of cantus firmus: Influence of the different chords," suggests a hierarchy of scale degrees: I–IV–V, then II–VI, then III–VII. This is the only time in Dubois's entire work when Roman numerals appear and, incidentally, are solely used to refer to scale degrees in the text and sequences by movements (intervals) of the fundamental bass (broadly in the tradition of the Rameau school). Théodore Dubois, *Traité d'harmonie théorique et pratique* (Paris: Heugel, [1921]), 35–39.

6. Percy Goetschius (1853–1953) studied and taught in Stuttgart before returning to the United States to teach at Syracuse University and the New England Conservatory, among other institutions. Boulanger owned several of Goetschius's treatises; her copies are today held at F-LYc. See especially part II ("The Succession or Connection of Chords") in Goetschius's *The Material Used in Musical Composition: A System of Harmony* (22nd ed., based on the revised [14th] ed.) (New York: Schirmer, 1889); Boulanger's copy is F-LYc UFNBL 68 GOE M. See also David M. Thompson, *A History of Harmonic Theory in the United States* (Kent, OH: Kent State University Press, 1980), chap. 2, 37–73; and Arthur Shepherd, "'Papa' Goetschius in Retrospect," *The Musical Quarterly* 30/3 (July 1944): 307–18.

7. Dubois, *Traité d'harmonie*, 1.

8. For example, the first bass line proposed by Dubois (mm. 1–8) would be considered entirely in C major (with V of vi, V of IV, and V of V), rather than containing successive modulations toward A minor, F major, and G major. See esp. Arnold Schoenberg, *Structural Functions of Harmony* [1933–1951] (London: Williams and Norgate, 1954).

9. Musée de la Musique, Paris, item E 981.3.8. See Thompson, *A History of Harmonic Theory in the United States*, 127–28.

10. Bruno Monsaingeon, *Mademoiselle: Entretiens avec Nadia Boulanger* (Paris: Van de Velde, 1981), 62.

11. See for example Boulanger's comments about the primacy of line in Stravinsky's music, in the published account of her 1925 lectures at the Rice Institute in Houston, Texas: "Stravinsky's dissonance is far more contrapuntal than it is harmonic, that is, it results from the clash of melodic lines rather than the structure of chords. . . . To appreciate such music, it is obvious that we must establish new habits of hearing, reacquire a new sense of the old linear values which were the pride of the Renaissance and the glory of Bach." Nadia Boulanger, "Lectures on Modern Music," *The Rice Institute Pamphlet* 13/2 (1926), 178–95.

12. Robert W. Wason, "From *Harmonielehre* to *Harmony*: Schenker's Theory of Harmony and Its Americanization," in *Schenker-Traditionen: Eine Wiener Schule der Musiktheorie und ihre internationale Verbreitung*, ed. Martin Eybl and Evelyn Fink-Mennel (Vienna, Cologne, and Weimar: Buchet-Chastel, 2006), 188. Citkowitz was one of the first to translate and disseminate Schenker in the United States. For Roger Sessions's thoughts on Schenker, see "Heinrich Schenker's Contribution," *Modern Music* 12/4 (1935): 170–78; "Escape by Theory," *Modern Music* 15/3 (1938): 192–97; and "The Function of Theory," *Modern Music* 15/7 (1938): 257–62. See also Milton Babbitt, "I Remember Roger," *Perspectives of New Music* 23/2 (Spring–Summer 1985): 112–16. Boulanger's copy of Schenker's *Harmonielehre* is F-Lyc, UFNBL 63 SCH N.

13. Some works that had belonged to Ernest Boulanger, such as Choron's 1808 *Principes de composition des écoles d'Italie*, were subsequently annotated by Nadia Boulanger.

14. Some of Gédalge's unpublished work is preserved in his manuscript *Traité de contrepoint et de fugue* (F-Pn Musique MS 14960); this was partially published in *Traité de la fugue* (Paris: Enoch, 1901). See also the manuscript F-Pn Vmb. ms. 122, "Le Contrepoint, copie de Edmond Maurat, du manuscrit inachevé d'André Gédalge," of which only one part, the introduction, was published: André Gédalge, "Les rapports de l'harmonie et du contrepoint: Définitions et considérations générales," *La Revue musicale* 4/13 (1904): 326–29.

15. Barbara L. Kelly, *Tradition and Style in the Works of Darius Milhaud 1912–1939* (Aldershot: Ashgate, 2003), 154. See also Gédalge, "Les rapports de l'harmonie," 326: "The art of counterpoint essentially consists of producing, in terms of musical effect, two or more melodies independent in rhythm and nature, *without, however, attenuating the relief of the lead melody*" (emphasis added).

16. In René Lenormand's *Etude sur l'harmonie moderne* (1913), 64–65.

17. See, in particular, Jérôme Spycket, *A la recherche de Lili Boulanger* (Paris: Fayard, 2004), 60–69.

18. Boulanger archives, F-LYc, file 4.2.3.

19. Albert Lavignac and Lionel de La Laurence, eds., *Encyclopédie de la musique et dictionnaire du Conservatoire*, 1/1 (Paris: Delagrave, 1921, copyright 1913), viii.

20. On 5 July 1913, Delines wrote to Nadia Boulanger: "You have undoubtedly seen that Mr. Lavignac's *Dictionnaire Encyclopédique* is now in print and that we appear as contributors for the history of Russian music. . . . Have you finished your work? If you could tell me a bit more about it, I would be delighted." F-Pn. N.L.a. 66 (192–93).

21. Manfred Kelkel, *Alexandre Scriabine* (Paris: Fayard, 1999), 243–45.

22. Boulanger's copy of Pugno's Chopin edition is preserved in F-LYc, UFNB M 111 CHO.

23. Boulanger's copy of Hugo Riemann's *Katechismus* can be found in Paris at the Musée de la Musique, item E 981.3.8. Regarding the possible translation into French of Paul Hindemith's *Unterweisung*, see Gertrude Hindemith's letter to Nadia Boulanger of 9 January 1937: "My husband is extremely grateful for your very kind letter and is delighted at the prospect of working together with you. . . . If you want to translate his book, you will need a great deal of peace and quiet." F-Pn, N.L.a. 75 (350–51). A letter from Louis Saguer to Paul Hindemith of 27 June 1945 inquiring whether Schott was considering publishing a French version of his book and whether he had chosen a French translator, and reminding Hindemith of Nadia Boulanger's interest, is quoted in Bruno Schweyer and Laurent Feneyrou, eds., *Louis Saguer: Œuvres et jours* (Paris: Basalte, 2010), 243. The American translation of *Unterweisung im Tonsatz* (*The Craft of Musical Composition*, 1942) was ultimately provided by Arthur Mendel, one of Nadia Boulanger's students in the 1920s.

# Boulanger and Atonality: A Reconsideration

## KIMBERLY FRANCIS

In an excerpt from his *Paris Diaries* written in the early 1950s, Ned Rorem describes in detail a visit to one of Nadia Boulanger's Wednesday group classes. His words are not kind:

> Boulanger's shimmer [of influence] exploded into flame just before the war, in Boston, where she was the chief guide for any composer anywhere. . . . The flame's extinction . . . came in the late forties, when the new young Americans emigrated to Paris like good shepherds bearing dubious gifts. But they found (with the change of air) they didn't now need her. . . . Now, at her "Wednesdays," she moves like an automaton.[1]

Rorem's criticism derides Boulanger for her choice to cleave to an antiquated affection for the neoclassical aesthetic after 1946. Accounts of her pedagogical focus on tonality and counterpoint grew in the postwar climate like a malignant brand. American music critic Harold Schonberg echoed Rorem's sentiments in 1950, writing that Boulanger's influence was "not as strong today as it was."[2] Similarly, Pierre Boulez claimed that after the war "no one had any use for Boulanger."[3] The important voices of the time were Olivier Messiaen—whom Boulanger detested—and René Leibowitz. Even her own biographer, Léonie Rosenstiel, depicts Boulanger as "impervious to the changes sweeping the musical world. She continued to pass on what she had learned from her own teachers. . . . It was her manner, rather than her materials, that was unique" after the war.[4] Cast as an almost tragic figure, Boulanger stands in the historical record as stubbornly ignorant of atonal and serialist musics, even to the detriment of her career following her return to Paris after the Second World War.

Turning instead to annotated scores found in Boulanger's teaching library in Lyon, France, and building on her published and unpublished writings—lecture notes, published criticism, and correspondence—I explore Boulanger's manipulation of post-tonal analytical techniques as well as her long-standing familiarity with the works of atonal and extended-chromatic composers. To show the breadth of Boulanger's knowledge of the wide variety of musical techniques employed by composers during her lifetime, I begin with her annotations to Igor Stravinsky's *L'oiseau de feu* (*The Firebird*), annotations that likely date from the 1920s or '30s when Boulanger provided editorial oversight to his *Symphonie de psaumes*. Her annotations to Stravinsky's *Firebird* score reveal an interest in the intervallic collection that would later—in 1963—be termed "octatonicism" by Boulanger pupil Arthur Berger.[5] I then turn to Boulanger's lectures on Béla Bartók, which show her to be a champion of Bartók's music. His was an oeuvre she knew well, taught widely, and discussed in terms of its "irresistible logic" and deceptively beautiful dissonances. I discuss her annotations to Bartók's second violin concerto, where Boulanger analyzes various compositional elements, including the piece's dodecaphonic second theme. Thirdly, I turn to the serialist compositions in her collection and the annotations she added to her score of Anton Webern's String Quartet, Op. 28, and her thorough analysis of Pierre Boulez's first entirely serial work, the Piano Sonata No. 1. Both of these scores reveal the fluidity of Boulanger's analytical knowledge as well as her interest in works that employed serialist techniques, particularly their contrapuntal and motivic potential. Overall, my assessment of Boulanger's work pushes back against those who claim for her a myopic interest in post-tonal musics, broadening our understanding of the musical literacy of one of the twentieth century's great musicians.

### The Firebird

Boulanger's love of *The Firebird* began the night of its premiere on 25 June 1910. Boulanger attended the performance and was enraptured by the work's unique counterpoint and intriguing timbres. This impression evolved into a lifelong adoration of the piece. Even as late as 1970, Bruno Monsaingeon's interviews capture on video Boulanger's arthritic, trembling hands on the piano as they delicately play through *The Firebird*'s "Berceuse" movement, entirely from memory.[6]

Boulanger's first engagement with the score to *The Firebird* likely dates from 1923, when Stravinsky sent her a copy of the newly reorchestrated version of the piece. A year later, in September 1924, he sent her a copy of his "Berceuse-Finale" and "Ronde des princesses" arrangements.[7] Boulanger inserted registration indications in her copy of the "Berceuse" score, likely in preparation for performances executed while on tour of the United States the following year. She lectured on the work as part of her earliest recorded public speaking engagements at the Rice Lecture Series in Houston, Texas.[8] These scores were later designated by her estate as not belonging to her teaching library, and so were gifted to the Bibliothèque nationale, where they remain in general circulation. Three other versions of *The Firebird* score appeared regularly within Boulanger's teaching practices, and those scores were sent by her estate to what would become the Médiathèque Nadia Boulanger in Lyon, France. The Lyon collection holds two copies of the full orchestral score, one purchased by Boulanger in Chicago in 1941 for a cost of two dollars and the other bearing no annotations whatsoever.[9] The third score is a well-worn copy of the original 1912 solo piano reduction.[10] This document contains clues that reveal the depth of Boulanger's knowledge of the musical content of this piece (see Figure 1).

Boulanger's tight, ornate handwriting indicates the aspects of the piece she found most interesting, including intervallic oscillations, combinations of major and minor thirds, and Stravinsky's idiosyncratic rhythmic properties. Boulanger's interest in the major and minor thirds and, presumably, the major and minor seconds found in the opening motive, also suggest she was drawn to the building blocks of Stravinsky's octatonic materials. Not all of the content highlighted by Boulanger is octatonic, though some octatonic cells can be picked out, including the trichord A♭–C♭ and B♭–D♮ dyads in the right hand highlighted by Boulanger in the second system. But I doubt the octatonic collection was Boulanger's primary concern. Instead, Boulanger seems more interested in the oscillation of intervals in their immediate musical context than the result of artificially chaining these oscillating intervals together.

Unfortunately, Boulanger never dated her analytical work, and the date of the piano reduction analysis is a bit of a mystery. That said, Boulanger's script changed in the mid-1930s as her eyesight became progressively weaker and she gradually lost the ability to read her minuscule handwriting. The annotations found in the piano reduction score predate this shift. For this reason, Jeanice Brooks and I place the handwriting found on her copy of the 1919 *Firebird* score as roughly contemporaneous to its publication. I would further hypothesize these analytic notes coincide with Stravinsky's *Firebird* gift copies from the early 1920s.

Curiously, despite this engagement with the score, there is no additional evidence that Boulanger taught *The Firebird* in a lecture setting beyond her 1925 Rice Lectures. The piece appears nowhere on the syllabi related to her weekly Wednesday afternoon classes, and Louise Talma's meticulous notes of Boulanger's lectures at Fontainebleau during the

Figure 1. Boulanger's annotations to Stravinsky's *L'oiseau de feu*,
major and minor thirds.

1930s contain no mention of the work.[11] Instead, Boulanger's annotations
appear driven by curiosity or perhaps for discussion during specific one-
on-one lessons. Other analyses produced by Boulanger appear equally
as private, including her serial analysis of Stravinsky's *Elegy for J.F.K.*[12]
Given the sheer volume of Boulanger's teaching activities, it is impossible
to say whether the piece came up in conversation, but unlike other pillars
of her pedagogical work, such as the Monteverdi madrigals, the chorales of

Figure 2. Boulanger pores over a score with Stravinsky, 1945.

Johann Sebastian Bach, or Gabriel Fauré's Requiem, *The Firebird* remains oddly absent, despite Boulanger's engagement with the piece as audience member, performer, and analyst.

The aspect of Boulanger's analytical work that resonates the most with her pedagogical efforts involves voice leading. Boulanger embedded her interest in voice-leading possibilities in the chord progression exercises she required her students to practice. These repetitive exercises, well known among her alumni, required students both to hear and feel in the piano's keys the options offered by the twelve notes of the scale. She designed these chord progressions so her students could understand how one could arrive at a sonority and then depart from it, regardless of tonality. Students would memorize the patterns in all keys and learn to transpose at will. Ideally, in mastering these relationships, successful students could work fluently with the language of music, beyond the bounds of tonality and rigid, inorganic voice-leading principles.

Thus, the extended tonal practice highlighted by Boulanger within her annotated copy of *The Firebird* score connects with the stream of her musical thought that valued the linear, the melodic, and the spontaneous. Her conception of music appreciated the vitality of the contrapuntal over the stagnation of the horizontal, and thus, for her, music needed to be driven by the movement of sound through time in unique, expressive ways. I read this tenet of Boulanger's not as an opposition of tonality vs. atonality, but rather a celebration of the organic elements of sound over

more artificially controlled ones. Boulanger read these elements in myr-
iad composer's works, including the music of Béla Bartók.

## Béla Bartók

From February to June 1926, *Le Monde musical* published transcriptions of
Boulanger's analysis classes at the Ecole Normale de Musique.[13] They published these three installments under the title of "La Musique moderne,"
producing a series of texts that serve as an invaluable resource for understanding Boulanger's teachings in the late 1920s. A substantial portion
of her lectures at that time were dedicated to the forty-five-year-old Béla
Bartók. It was an odd time to be championing Bartók. It had been three
years since Bartók had composed anything. His most recent work dated
from August 1923.[14] Yet Boulanger discussed the composer at length in
her classes. Her glowing account of Bartók's biography celebrated his "brilliant studies at the Budapest Academy of Music" and praised his efforts
to explore "the folksongs transmitted by the preceding ages. In reuniting
them, he offered to his country an inestimable treasure, and at the same
time animated his own melodic inspiration." Boulanger celebrated these
Hungarian songs, equating them to the music of the "extreme-Orient" that
inspired Saint-Saëns and to the Russian songs that inspired Debussy.

Boulanger's analytical discussion echoes the annotations found in the
*Firebird* score, with her focus on the linear qualities of Bartók's folksongs.
Here, Boulanger lauded how, "instead of typical old formulas, [chromaticism]
gave the example of new, fresher, more vigorous contours, of rhythms that
were freer, [and] more expressive." Innovative linearity lent an inventiveness
to Bartók's music, whereas his harmonies did not require experimental elements. Indeed, Boulanger taught that "Bartók, who had lived through the
development of modern harmony since *Tristan*, held to Bach as his harmonic
basis." Boulanger allowed that Bartók's melodic language eventually generated new harmonies, creating certain "affinities of sound" that appeared as
"cloudy and incomprehensible without resolution." But she warned those
who would reject Bartók because of these qualities that "the majority of these
hated dissonances are melodic in origin. The conflicts, the sournesses, are
caused by combinations of two or more melodies." For Boulanger, Bartók's
music was not so distant from that of Bach. Her analytical point of view
emphasized that the overriding importance of the melody permitted the
generation of these sorts of sounds. In understanding the importance of
melody, one uncovered the "secret to Bartók's dissonances." Boulanger's
lecture contains a lengthy argument in support of tolerating the "noisy
racket" required by the passing of melodies that "hasten vigorously to their
goal." Two conflicting melodies did nothing more than heighten the melodic

imperative—or "melodic accent"—increasing a sense of tension that resulted in only more beautiful moments of release. Boulanger argued that this "was what gave Bartók's style its tight character, this irresistible logic, this expression of absolute necessity."

Louise Talma's lecture notes of 24 August 1931 reveal that Boulanger taught her students about Bartók's formations of new chords and his superimposition of different intervals, which subsequently created unique dissonances.[15] Nine years later, on 31 December 1940, alumna Katharine Wolff wrote to Boulanger to say that she was traveling to Washington for the Coolidge Festival, sponsored by the American patroness Elizabeth Sprague Coolidge.[16] The guest of honor that year was Bartók. "Wish you could be there!" Wolff kindly lamented. A year later, on 23 July 1941, Boulanger herself was in the United States, where she bought Bartók's *The Hungarian Folk Song* in Santa Clara, California, a purchase contemporaneous to that of buying the *Firebird* score in Chicago.[17] After returning to France in 1946, references to Bartók appear throughout Boulanger's archives. She programmed Bartók's music as part of the classes she gave at the Bryanston summer camps in 1948.[18] Her Wednesday afternoon classes discussed the Music for Strings, Percussion, Celesta (in 1959–60), the Suite 14 (in 1961–62, and 1971), the Second and Third Piano Concertos (in 1958–59 and again in 1972), and *Bluebeard's Castle* (in 1973–74).[19] In 1950, Boulanger wrote to Stravinsky that she was disappointed that people still disliked Bartók. In 1960, Boulanger created a master timeline of Stravinsky's works, comparing his compositions to those of his contemporaries to show affinities and ruptures. In this list of comparable masterworks, Boulanger noted three of Bartók's pieces: the Music for Strings, Percussion, and Celesta (1936), the 1944 Concerto for Orchestra, and the Second Violin Concerto (1937–38).[20] Turning to Boulanger's materials for the Bryanston summer camp reveals more technical and intriguing details about her treatment of Bartók's music, particularly the 1937–38 Violin Concerto.

### Bartók's Second Violin Concerto

Boulanger taught the Second Violin Concerto on several occasions, first as part of the Bryanston Summer Music classes she taught from 1948 to 1949 and later listing it as part of her 1958 Wednesday afternoon classes.[21] Her score for the work bears the annotation "Bryanston," likely because this was the first time she prepared a formal analysis for the work.

Bartók's concerto was dedicated to and written for Zoltan Székely, and premiered in 1939 with the Concertgebouw Orchestra of Amsterdam, under Willem Mengelberg's direction. Bartók intended the piece to have only one movement and be in theme and variations form, but Székely insisted on three movements.[22] The work is not serial, but it does contain dodecaphonic themes, including the arresting second violin melody first heard at rehearsal number 73. Bartók would later tell Yehudi Menuhin that he wished the piece to show Schoenberg that serial music could exist in a tonal setting.[23] Boulanger numbers this serial theme as a "prime row," labeling all twelve notes of the scale as they appear sequentially (see Table 1). She then labels subsequent variations of the melody by noting any reordering of the original pitches:

Table 1. Prime row and first two variations of
the main theme of Bartók's Second Violin Concerto

| Appearance of the theme | Pitch classes | Boulanger's labels: |
|---|---|---|
| P₀ | A B F B♭ F♯ C♯ G D♯ C E G♯ D | 1, 2, 3, 4, 5, 6, 7, 8, 9, 10, 11, 12 |
| First variation | A B F F♯ B♭ C♯ G D♯ C E G♯ D | 1, 2, 3, 4, 6, 5, 7, 8, 9, 10, 11, 12 |
| Second variation (P₅) | D E B♭ E♭ F♯ B C F G♯ A G C♯ | 1, 3, 4, 2, 6, 5, 8, 7, 9, 12, 10, 11 |

The first melodic variation, which begins at rehearsal number 76, switches pitches five and six and eight and nine. Boulanger caught this in her numbering system, which she placed above the staff. The second variation occurs at rehearsal number 79, beginning on P₅, or the row transposed up a perfect fourth, a transposition that no doubt delighted Boulanger for its connection to tonal principles. This variation contains even further manipulation of the order of pitch classes. Boulanger annotated this in her analytical system, again placing the reordered numbers above the staff. She made only one error here, confusing the order of the last two notes (see Figure 3).

Boulanger's annotations, therefore, reveal that she understood the fundamental principles of dodecaphonic theory such as it existed in 1948. Moreover, her analysis of this particular piece resonates with those found in the current secondary literature, analyses published decades after she prepared her lecture notes for Bryanston.[24] Also intriguing is that her engagement with dodecaphonic principles predates Stravinsky's exploration of serialism by at least four years. Therefore, Boulanger's knowledge of the principles of serial music existed before Stravinsky's switch to this process in 1952 and was not catalyzed by it. Boulanger's interest in serial methods continued well beyond her work at the Bryanston Summer Camp

Figure 3. Boulanger's annotations to Bartók's Second
Violin Concerto, twelve-tone analysis.

in 1948, seeming to gather steam in the 1950s with the music of Anton
Webern and Pierre Boulez.

## Anton Webern's String Quartet Op. 28

During the 1950s, Boulanger was open to learning and teaching more
about serialism and atonal musics. Though Boulanger's analysis of Bartók
was catalyzed in the 1920s through her interest in his contrapuntal and

melodic idiosyncrasies, her interest in the Second Viennese School blossomed after Boulanger's return to Paris in 1946. A program tucked into her copy of the score to *Wozzeck* reveals that Boulanger attended the French premiere of the work on 9 November 1950 at the Théâtre des Champs-Elysées under the direction of Jascha Horenstein.[25] Boulanger would later include *Wozzeck* on the same master timeline mentioned earlier on. Boulanger's library contains four books about Arnold Schoenberg.[26] The only one of these books that bears annotations was the French translation of H. H. Stuckenschmidt's *Domaine Musical: Schönberg*, an edition that appeared in 1956. Inside, Boulanger inserted a copy of a flyer advertising that same year's Domaine Musical concerts at the Petit Théâtre Marigny, which included works by Stravinsky, Messiaen, Webern, Luigi Nono, Karlheinz Stockhausen, Pierre Boulez, and others. These more tangential pieces of evidence paint a picture of Boulanger's engagement with the music of the Second Viennese School and the then-emerging second generation of serial composers. Documents relating to Webern, however, reveal an even richer connection to strictly serial compositions.

The first reference within Boulanger's archives to Webern is a rather vague one, found in the postscript to a letter from 10 June 1954, in which Boulanger asks Stravinsky "not to forget Webern."[27] Stravinsky's response five days later clarifies that Boulanger had asked him for a copy of Webern's Bach Ricercar, a work it would seem they had either discussed over the phone or in person. What Boulanger did with the score is a bit of a mystery. No further mention of it appears in the archives, and she did not own a copy of the score.

Two years after this exchange, Boulanger's Wednesday Afternoon syllabus listed that students would study the "works of Stockhausen, Webern, Nono, and Boulez."[28] For the fastidious Boulanger, whose Wednesday classes' syllabi typically listed the details for the works to be studied down to the opus number, this is a rather throwaway statement, which could be read as only the most superficial of carrots to entice students to Paris to study with her. The scores, however, suggest this may not have been a disingenuous advertisement. On 18 January 1957, Stravinsky wrote to Boulanger, asking if she had taken the time to photograph the Webern microfilms he had sent to her (with Robert Craft) in November.[29] Up to five months later, Stravinsky was still asking Boulanger to return the score to him, suggesting she had hung on to it, though for what purpose is unclear.[30] That same year, Boulanger drew up a detailed chart titled "Pieces of Interest," listing relevant publication information for specific contemporary works, in all likelihood a tool for students seeking supplementary study scores. Included on that list were Webern's Symphony, Op. 21; "Deux lieder Op. 8"; and

Four Songs, Op. 13.[31] Thus, Boulanger's engagement with Webern in the 1950s was multifaceted and extended beyond the superficial. Additional clues lie in her library.

Boulanger's collection of scores contains sixteen Webern compositions (Table 2). The only serial composer to exceed this number was Schoenberg, for whom Boulanger owned eighteen scores.[32]

Table 2. Scores by Webern in Boulanger's collection

| Title of Work | Date Published by Universal Edition | Type of Score |
|---|---|---|
| Fünf Lieder aus "Der siebente Ring," Op. 3 | No date | |
| *Entflieht auf leichten Kähnen*, Op. 2 | 1921 | Photocopies |
| Fünf Sätze für Streichquartett, Op. 5 | 1922 | Pocket Score |
| Fünf Stücke für Orchester, Op. 10 | 1923–1951 | Pocket Score |
| Fünf Lieder nach Gedichten von Stefan George, Op. 4 | 1923–1951 | |
| Sechs Bagatelles für Streichquartett, Op. 9 | 1924–1952 | Pocket Score |
| Drei Lieder für Gesang, Es-Klarinette und Gitarre, Op. 18 | 1927 | |
| Fünf Canons nach lateinischen Texten, Op. 16 | 1928–1956 | Pocket Score |
| Symphonie für Klarinette, Bass-klarinette, Op. 21 | 1929–1956 | Pocket Score |
| Drei Gesänge aus 'Viae inviae,' Op. 23 | 1936 | |
| Variationen für Klavier, Op. 27 | 1937 | |
| Streichquartett, Op. 28 | 1939–1955 | |
| Drei Lieder, Op. 25 | 1956 | Piano/vocal |
| Variation für Orchester, Op. 30 | 1956 | Pocket Score |
| *Das Augenlicht*, Op. 26 | 1956 | Pocket Score |
| Kantate für Sopran-Solo, Op. 29 | 1957 | Pocket Score |

Two of Webern's scores contain annotations: the Fünf Canons nach lateinischen Texten, Op. 16 (1923–24) and the String Quartet, Op. 28 (1936–38).[33] Boulanger's comments on the Canons are largely isolated to inserting translations of the Latin text into the score. Curiously, Boulanger translated Webern's sources into English instead of her usual practice of translating into French.[34] Beyond this aspect, the annotations lack significance. Her more interesting work rests in her copy of Webern's String Quartet, Op. 28.[35]

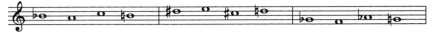

Example 1. Webern-derived row, Opus 28.

Webern's Opus 28 employs a derived row, forged from manipulations of the B–A–C–H motive (Example 1). Boulanger was deeply familiar with the B–A–C–H motive, and it is not difficult to imagine that she would have aurally picked up on this collection of intervals within Webern's piece, atonal treatment or not.[36] In another interesting point of overlap, preparations for the premiere of Webern's Opus 28 coincided with Boulanger's tour of the United States during which time she oversaw the premiere of Stravinsky's Concerto in E-flat *(Dumbarton Oaks)* in May 1938. Webern's piece was commissioned by Elizabeth Sprague Coolidge and the string quartet premiered five months after *Dumbarton Oaks*. Indeed, the performance of Webern's Opus 28 took place at the same Coolidge Festival that Katharine Wolff would write about to Boulanger two years later.[37] The 1938 festival was held in Pittsfield, Massachusetts, on 22 September, just a six-hour drive from where Boulanger premiered *Dumbarton Oaks* in May. Though she was not stateside in September, it is tempting to imagine the discussions among American patrons in the later months of 1938 concerning the Stravinsky and Webern premieres. It is also intriguing to consider the autobiographical connection Boulanger may have associated with the string quartet when she analyzed the piece decades later.

The handwriting on the score clearly betrays the analytical work as dating from a later era than the 1930s, though the lack of explicit information again makes the date of the work difficult to pinpoint. The shakiness of the handwriting, particularly the larger graphics, implies that the analysis took place post-1950. Boulanger's accentuation of the rests and her insertion of timings above the score also suggest that it was prepared for performance.

Boulanger's analysis has much in common with her work on Stravinsky's *Firebird*. She traced the dodecaphonic collection, but not as stringently as in the Bartók example. Instead, her interest lay in the intervallic relationships produced in this delicate texture, with the major thirds and the minor seconds that underlie the content of the B–A–C–H motive. Throughout, whenever possible, Boulanger marked areas of imitation. For example, at measure 10, Boulanger noted a point of imitation at the sixth (see Figures 4a–c).

Formally, Boulanger grouped the entire movement into smaller sets. She began by highlighting tetrachordal groupings. At measure 16, she switched to trichords, and at measure 22, Boulanger's annotations demarcate both dyads and tetrachordal pitch collections. Certainly, she focused

Figure 4a. Boulanger's annotations to Webern's String Quartet, Op. 28.

less on this piece's manipulation of the twelve-tone collection and more on its cellular content. In this way, she could view the piece as functioning in a manner similar to the Renaissance counterpoint with which both Webern

Figure 4b. Boulanger's annotations to Webern's String Quartet, Op. 28, continued.

and Boulanger were so familiar. In a manner similar to the Bartók analysis, the first page of Boulanger's work shows her highlighting points of harmonic interest, moments when the contrapuntal movement generated

Figure 4c. Boulanger's annotations to Webern's String Quartet, Op. 28, continued.

interesting sonorities. She abandoned these sorts of annotations, however, after the first page.[38]

These in-score examples drawn from the music of Stravinsky, Bartók, and Webern are all compelling if for no other reason than that they show a sincere engagement with principles of music (atonality, serialism, pitch-set theory) thought missing from Boulanger's analytical tool kit. Scores relating to Stravinsky's serial music reveal that this engagement was far from short-lived and continued well into Boulanger's later years—for example, the treatment of *Elégie pour J.F.K.*[39] But by far the lengthiest treatment of an atonal work, and arguably the most original, can be found tucked into the cover of Boulez's First Piano Sonata, revealing a detailed engagement with the work by Boulanger.

### Pierre Boulez and the First Piano Sonata

Perhaps the most oft-repeated comparison of Boulanger and Boulez involves their shared musicality. To quote David Wilde, in an interview for the British Broadcasting Corporation following Boulanger's death, "[She] had the best musical ear—comparable to Boulez, but Boulanger was more musical."[40] Boulanger must have known of Boulez from his time as a student at the Conservatoire under Olivier Messiaen, with whom she maintained an acrimonious relationship. Her dislike of Messiaen extended well beyond her irritation over his proclivities as organist at her local church, La Trinité. Boulanger characterized Messiaen's music as possessing empty, "mystico-chromatic chords," and she accused him of hollow religious expression in his compositions.[41] Perhaps because of Messiaen's prodding, and certainly with his foreknowledge, the young Boulez was involved in a minor scandal on 27 February 1945 when he joined a group of young students to protest the first postwar performance of Stravinsky's neoclassical music in Paris.[42] The students blew whistles and yelled to disrupt the performance, by the Orchestre national under the baton of Manuel Rosenthal, and critics subsequently took sides about Stravinsky's latest works, both those in favor and those opposed. Soulima Stravinsky was in Paris at the time and wrote to Boulanger immediately afterward to tell her about the incident.[43]

I find it somewhat surprising that Boulanger did not hold it against Boulez that he participated in such an activity. Perhaps she chalked it up to a release of postwar angst by this emerging generation of musicians, or perhaps she was later assuaged by his musical aptitude. Whatever the reason, the answers are not to be found in her correspondence with Boulez. Instead, her letters to Stravinsky from 16 April to 16 May 1957, clearly show that Boulez won Boulanger over, sometime after her return to Paris in 1946. Boulanger wrote to Stravinsky of her deep respect for Boulez, and that she was hopeful about his future within the classical music world.[44] It was Boulanger who, reflecting upon conversations she had with Boulez after he traveled to America and met with Stravinsky, characterized Boulez as a "*good* musician, [without] . . . tricks or bluffs."[45]

Boulanger's interest in Boulez transferred to his scores, and like the other extended-tonal and atonal composers mentioned in this essay, Boulez features prominently in Boulanger's teaching catalogue. She owned eight Boulez works, dating from 1950 to 1959 (Table 3).

Boulez's music appears three times in the Wednesday afternoon syllabi, including unspecified works in 1966 and 1969, and *Pli contre pli*, listed in 1975.[46] In the previously mentioned list of "Pieces of Interest" from 1957, she listed Boulez's Second Piano Sonata.

Table 3. Boulez scores in Boulanger's collection

| Title | Publisher Information | Date of publication |
|---|---|---|
| Deuxième Sonate pour piano | Paris, Heugel | 1950 |
| Première Sonate pour piano | Paris, Amphion | 1951 |
| Sonatine flute et piano | Paris, Amphion | 1954 |
| *Le marteau sans maître* (facsimile of the autograph manuscript) | Vienna, Universal Edition | 1954 |
| *Structures* | Vienna, Universal Edition | 1955 |
| *Improvisation sur Mallarmé* | London, Universal Edition | 1958 |
| *Le soleil des eaux* | Paris, Heugel | 1959 |
| *Le visage nuptial* | Paris, Heugel | 1959 |

Evidence of Boulanger's analytical attention appears in her copy of the score for the First Piano Sonata, Boulez's first entirely serial work. Composed in 1946, Boulez's First Sonata contains two movements: the first slow, the second fast. Boulanger's score is undated, and she did not annotate her copy, in contrast to the other pieces discussed here. Instead, Boulanger wrote out a detailed and careful analysis of the work on staff paper, which she then folded into the cover of the score. Such analytical care by Boulanger was extremely rare, reserved for works such as Stravinsky's *Symphonie de psaumes* and *Elégie pour J.F.K.*, Josquin's *Missa Pange Lingua*, and Gabriel Fauré's Requiem.[47] Boulanger's detailed engagement with Boulez's First Sonata, then, is remarkable.

Her analytical work condenses all intervals found in the composition, sometimes inverting the melodic contour and sometimes erasing octave displacement (see Figures 5a and 5b.)

Boulanger's analysis then groups the musical content into pentachords. She considered all material in both movements of the sonata as related to the sonata's initial five-note set (Example 2).

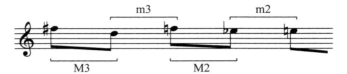

Example 2. Boulez, generative cell, first movement.

The generative pentachord isolated by Boulanger contains numerous sonic possibilities through its construction and ordering. In normal order, the set contains the same intervals as the B–A–C–H motive with the exception of an added fifth note that provides access to the interval of a major third (Example 3).

Interestingly, Boulez orders his pentachord so that the first interval presented in the sonata is that of the major third, albeit inverted as a minor sixth. Boulanger's marginal annotations for both the first and second movements of the sonata show that she viewed harmonic inversions as equal in quality to their smaller inverted counterparts—the minor sixth, therefore, was equal to that of a major third, and so on. In this way, Boulanger views Boulez's generative set as a series of intervals, each a semitone smaller than the last, containing a major third followed by a minor third, major second, and a minor second. There are additional ways in which Boulanger's analysis is uncharacteristically invasive. Not only did she eliminate the distance between notes—which she always honored and explored at length in Stravinsky's music—but she also controlled the reading of simultaneities, treating them strictly so that she could arrive at her pentachordal groupings.

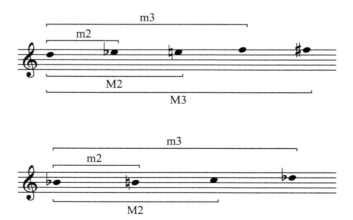

Example 3. Boulez, generative cell, first movement compared with the B-A-C-H motive.

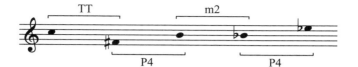

Example 4. Boulez, generative cell, second movement.

In both the first and second movements, Boulanger acknowledges the appearance of motivic content in inversion with "C" (*contraire*), as happens in mm. 5, 21, 17–19, 23, and 24 of the first movement and mm. 10 and 12 of the second movement. She also lists the cell's appearance in retrograde inversion—"RC" (*rétrograde contraire*)—as happens in mm. 12 and 15 of the first movement and in the final two measures of the second.

Boulanger's work with the second movement was arguably less successful than that of the first (see Figure 5b). Boulanger acknowledges the introduction of a new pentachordal collection in the second movement, a set that contains the intervals of the tritone, the ascending perfect fourth, the descending minor second, and the ascending perfect fourth again (see Example 4).

Boulanger's writing in the margins of this folio emphasizes the particular importance of these new intervals to the second movement. In an additional prose annotation at the bottom of the folio, Boulanger explains that she thought of this movement specifically in terms of dodecaphonic collections: the "12 notes [appear] in groups of three, based upon the final cell of the sonata's first movement."[48] Thus notes 3, 4, and 5 of the initial generative cell provide the seminal material for the second movement. That said, despite Boulanger's explanation of the connection between the first movement's trichord and the second movement's dodecaphonic contents, the analytical nomenclature contained in the folio never employs the numbers 11 and 12. Also, Boulanger's analysis of the second movement is somewhat complicated by the invariant relationship between pitches 4–5 of the original first movement pentachord and 8–9 of the new second movement pentachord. Therefore, when the minor second dyad appears in isolation in the second movement, Boulanger appears to have been uncertain how to label it, as one sees in measure 2 of her analytical notes. Indeed, Boulanger finished her comments on the second movement at measure 12, not even completing an analysis of the first page of the printed score. Although she does include a brief discussion of the final two measures of the sonata, her engagement with the second movement lacks the detail of her work on the first.

A discussion of the overall form of the piece is also curiously absent from this analysis. Boulanger's concerns about form, symmetries, and

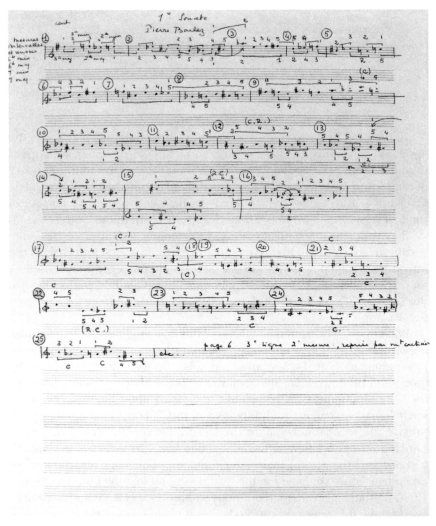

Figure 5a. Boulanger's analytical notes, Boulez's Piano Sonata No. 1, first movement.

structural balance are a hallmark of her analytical work.[49] Her analysis of the first movement of Boulez's piano sonata does contain an annotation explaining that the opening material is reprised in contrary motion at measure 69. But for the second movement, Boulanger provides no comments about form, though she traces every instance of Boulez using the harmonic interval of a perfect fifth.[50] Otherwise she does not address any sort of formal properties within the work in her analysis, treating

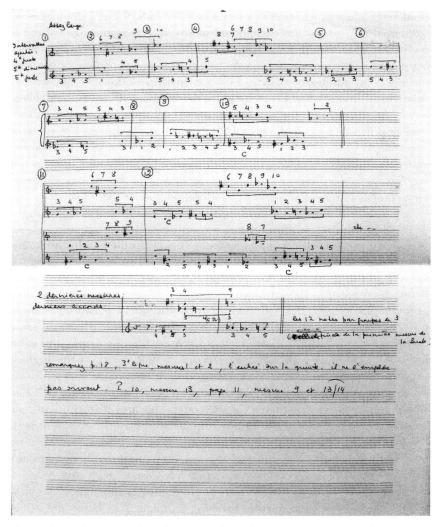

Figure 5b. Boulanger's analytical notes, Boulez's Piano Sonata No. 1, second movement.

the entirety of the sonata as more of a through-composed, contrapuntal exercise than an example of formal balance and proportion.

Boulanger's pentachordal approach does result in sections where the music breaks down, creating moments such as that found in the first movement, mm. 14–15, where she is left with nothing but a sequence of semitones. There is no formal reason for the set to dissolve at this point, such as a relaxation of tension or the introduction of new textures. Honoring her system,

Boulanger labels this section as a series of 4–5 dyads, though she makes no additional note about the exceptional nature of this section, and there is no further indication that she flagged this point for discussion in her teaching practices. Perhaps she sensed the lack of fit in her approach, or perhaps there was an additional layer to her nomenclature otherwise not written down, as is implied with her discussion of the complete dodecaphonic collection in the second movement despite a lack of twelve-tone labels. Regardless, analytical flexibility is a hallmark of Boulanger's work, as seen elsewhere in her analysis of Stravinsky's Symphony in C.[51] While Boulanger's analyses aimed to uncover underlying qualities in a given piece of music, she did not require absolute adherence to analytical cleanliness for a work to be valid nor for a composition to be worthy of consideration.

A hint as to further details within Boulanger's analytical thought might lie in Idil Biret's liner notes for her recording of Boulez's piano sonatas, produced in 1995.[52] Biret, a pianist from Turkey, studied with Boulanger as a young prodigy beginning in 1949, and it is possible that Boulanger's analysis of the Boulez sonatas may have coincided with Biret's studies.[53] Biret discusses the 1946 Boulez sonata as containing a series of five motives. She writes: "In the first four bars of the work the composer presents five characteristic and very different figures, easily distinguishable by the listener."[54] Biret elaborates that these involve "a simple and calm interval, a low note with an appoggiatura, a single note in the highest register, a rapid and impetuous figure leading to a deep stressed note, a broadly spreading polyphonic chord, low and high in register." The remainder of Biret's discussion of the sonata deviates from Boulanger's analytical work, and Biret does not connect the second movement with the first the way Boulanger clearly did. But Biret's emphasis on the first movement as a sort of theme and variations resonates with Boulanger's own treatment of the piece as based upon a five-note generative cell.

Boulanger's work in this instance is unique. Most other theorists view Boulez's sonata as a serial work, focusing on his manipulation of twelve-tone techniques.[55] Boulanger's idiosyncratic use of five-note segments clashes with the mathematics of serial composition, which so often hinge on segmentations of 3, 4, 6, or 12. I cannot help but wonder if there is a connection between Boulanger's examination of this work as based on groups of five and Stravinsky's *In Memoriam Dylan Thomas: Dirge Canons*, composed in 1954 and itself a serial work that manipulates groupings of five within an atonal framework.

## Conclusion

From the early 1920s until late into the 1970s, Boulanger's scores, lecture notes, correspondence, and syllabi show that she engaged with music outside of the tonal realm. From advanced post-tonal techniques to entirely serial musics, Boulanger studied scores across the spectrum of musical composition. For the most part, Boulanger's analyses reveal her focus to have been on smaller-scale relationships between pitches in music: intervals and recurring motives. Her lecture notes underscore her interest in the contrapuntal genesis of new dissonances and the linear motion that propelled music forward. Boulanger also understood serial music as containing contrapuntal techniques, such as inversion and retrograde inversion, though it is not clear if she felt these treatments particularly satisfying or effective. Though she sought to better understand the underlying principles behind a music's construction—be it a composer's chaining of major and minor thirds or the manipulation of a sequence of all twelve pitches—an underlying theoretical construct need not be fixed throughout an entire work. A piece's materials could bend and flex as the music required. Boulanger's analytical work then falls short of the stringent positivistic work that the generation of students trained by her would eventually produce.

What these scores do reveal is the complexity of Boulanger's musical knowledge. Though it may not always have transferred into her lessons, her musical vocabulary was vast and her acumen far more comprehensive than previously believed. It remains a curious question, then, why Boulanger limited her public lectures to certain concepts. Why paint herself as somewhat monochromatic? I suspect the compositional and analytical landscape shifted at such a tempo that Boulanger chose to avoid the possibility of speaking incorrectly. After all, Boulanger's analytical efforts read as organic and spontaneous, regardless of whether she chose to tackle a tonal piece or an atonal work. I suspect Boulanger conducted herself publicly in such a way so as to leave room for her own private discourse to evolve, even as she awaited the next musical experiment that would challenge her thinking.

# NOTES

1. Ned Rorem, *The Paris Diary of Ned Rorem* (New York: G. Braziller, 1966), 19.

2. Cited in Leonie Rosenstiel, *Nadia Boulanger: A Life in Music* (New York: W. W. Norton, 1982), 353. Rosenstiel cites this as part of an unnamed article in the April 1950 issue of *The Musical Courier*.

3. Ibid. Rosenstiel does not cite the source for this comment beyond stating that it took place during a conversation between Boulez and Carlos Moseley, manager of the New York Philharmonic.

4. Ibid., 354.

5. Arthur Berger, "Problems of Pitch Organization in Stravinsky," *Perspectives of New Music* 2/1 (1963): 11–42.

6. For further details concerning the premiere and development of *The Firebird* see Stephen Walsh, *Stravinsky: A Creative Spring, Russia and France, 1882–1934* (New York: Alfred A. Knopf, 1999), 138–43; and Richard Taruskin, *Stravinsky and the Russian Traditions: A Biography of the Works through Mavra* (Berkeley: University of California Press, 1996), 555–660.

7. Igor Stravinsky, *L'Oiseau de feu* (Paris: Editions Russe, 1923), Bibliothèque nationale de France (hereafter F-Pn), Vma. 4007; and Igor Stravinsky, "Ronde des princesses" and "Berceuse et Finale" (Paris: Edition Russe, 1924), F-Pn, Vmg. 22962.

8. The published version of the Rice Lectures differs drastically from what Boulanger actually said in her Houston lectures. It is important to keep this in mind when discussing what she taught to her audience in 1925. Kimberly Francis, "'Everything Had to Change': Nadia Boulanger's Translation of Modernism in the Rice Lecture Series, 1925." *Journal of the Society for American Music* 7/4 (2013): 363–81; and Jeanice Brooks and Kimberly Francis, eds., *Nadia Boulanger: Thoughts on Music* (Rochester, NY: University of Rochester Press, in press).

9. Igor Stravinsky, *Suite de L'Oiseau de feu* (London: Chester, 1920), Conservatoire national supérieur de musique et de danse de Lyon, Médiathèque Nadia Boulanger (hereafter F-LYc), UFNB MEp STR 400; Igor Stravinsky, *Firebird Suite (Suite de l'Oiseau de feu)* 1919 (New York : E. F. Kalmus, 1941), F-LYc, UFNB ME STR 400.

10. Igor Stravinsky, *L'Oiseau de feu: Conte dansé en 2 tableaux* (Leipzig and Moscow: P. Jurgenson, 1912), F-LYc, M. 111. 01 STR.

11. Louise Talma Papers, "1931, History of Music," Library of Congress, Box 21/1–13, 32/1–9.

12. For a discussion of Boulanger's analysis of the *Elegy for J.F.K.*, see Kimberly Francis, *Nadia Boulanger: Teaching Stravinsky* (New York: Oxford University Press, 2015), 212–213; companion website, "Into the Archives, Exploration 5, *Elegy for J.F.K.*" https://global.oup.com/us/companion.websites/fdscontent/uscompanion/us/static/companion.websites/9780199373697/pdf/exploration_5.pdf

13. "La Musique moderne: D'après la sténographie des cours à l'Ecole Normale de Musique." *Monde musical* 37/2 (February 1926): 59–61; "Les Cours de Mlle Nadia Boulanger, à l'Ecole Normale de Musique," *Monde musical* 37/5 (May 1926): 201; and "Les Cours de musique moderne de Nadia Boulanger." *Monde musical* 37/6 (June 1926): 242–44. All quoted material in this paragraph is from Boulanger's analysis.

14. David Cooper, *Béla Bartók* (New Haven: Yale University Press, 2015), 200–206.

15. Louise Talma Papers, "1931, History of Music."

16. Katharine Wolff to Boulanger, 21 December 1940, F-Pn, N.L.a. 117 (195–96). In this same paragraph, Wolff also wondered why Coolidge had not extended an invitation to Stravinsky to participate in the festival.

17. Nadia Boulanger "Biographie/List of Books Owned by Boulanger," F-Pn, n.d., Rés Vm. dos. 124.

18. The initial invitation to teach at the Bryanston Summer School of Music came from John Amis on 21 February 1948. Boulanger accepted on 4 March 1948. The invitation was repeated the following year. Boulanger was paid 120 pounds for her efforts. Boulanger's correspondence with Amis shows that she went to Bryanston primarily to speak about Stravinsky. This detailed discussion of Bartók's Violin Concerto, then, is a bit of a surprise. Nadia Boulanger, F-Pn, Rés. Vm. dos. 153 (48–54).

19. Nadia Boulanger, "Les Cours de mercredis," F-Pn, Rés. Vm. dos. 128.

20. Boulanger, "Timeline, 95 Q," Centre international Nadia et Lili Boulanger (hereafter CNLB).

21. Boulanger, "Bryanston Summer Music Class," F-Pn, Rés Vm. dos.153 (52–53).

22. Cooper, *Béla Bartók*, 201–5.

23. Yehudi Menuhin, *Unfinished Journey* (London: Macdonald and Jane's, 1976), 164. Menuhin and Boulanger worked together professionally on numerous occasions. Rosenstiel, *Nadia Boulanger*, 392–94. Though beyond the scope of this essay, the links between Menuhin, Boulanger, and Bartók and any possible transference of ideas along this continuum would be interesting to trace.

24. See, for example, Cooper, *Béla Bartók*, 201–5.

25. Alban Berg, *Wozzeck* (Vienna: Universal Edition, 1926), F-LYc, UFNB M 451 BER W.

26. Boulanger's holdings in Lyon reveal she owned the following books on Schoenberg: H. H. Stuckenschmidt, *Domaine Musical: Schönberg*, trans. Alexandra von Spitzmüller and Claude Rostand (Monaco: Éditions du Rocher, 1956); Benjamin Boretz and Edward T. Cone, *Perspectives on Schoenberg and Stravinsky* (Princeton: Princeton University Press, 1968); René Leibowitz, *Schoenberg et son école* (Paris: J. B. Janin, 1947); and René Leibowitz, *Schoenberg* (Paris: Editions du Seuil, 1969). The Boretz and Cone book was a Christmas gift from Claudio Spies in 1968.

27. Kimberly Francis, *Nadia Boulanger and the Stravinskys: A Selected Correspondence* (Rochester, NY: University of Rochester Press, 2018), 224–25.

28. Boulanger, "Les Cours de mercredis," F-Pn, Rés. Vm. dos. 128.

29. Francis, *Boulanger and the Stravinskys*, 252.

30. Ibid., 254–55.

31. Nadia Boulanger, "Les Cours de mercredis," 1957, F-Pn, Rés. Vm. dos. 128 (15).

32. Boulanger also owned scores to four of Alban Berg's works, including the Violin Concerto (Vienna: Universal Edition, 1936); String Quartet, Op. 3 (Berlin: Schlesinger, 1920); Lyric Suite (Vienna: Univerisal Edition, 1927); and *Wozzeck*. The Schoenberg works in Boulanger's collection included *Pierrot Lunaire* (Vienna: Universal Edition, 1914); Sechs Kleine Klavierstücke, Op. 19 (Vienna: Universal Edition, 1913) ; and *Pelleas und Melisande*, Op. 5 (Vienna: Universal Edition, 1911–1920). None of the Schoenberg scores are annotated. All these scores can be found in the Lyon collection (F-LYc).

33. Anton Webern, Fünf Canons nach lateinischen Texten (Vienna: Universal Edition, 1928), F-LYc, UFNB M. S11.2 WEB; and Webern, Streichquartett, Op. 28 (Vienna: Universal Edition, 1955), F-LYc, UFNB MEP WEB 246. According to the cover page of the Fünf Canons, Boulanger acquired her score in Copenhagen in 1963.

34. See, for example, Jeanice Brooks and Kimberly Francis, eds.,"Bach Concert, 1947," in *Nadia Boulanger: Thoughts on Music*.

35. It is also possible that Boulanger acquired the score after someone else had used it for a performance, though I am inclined to think that this was her score originally.

36. For one example of Boulanger's interest in the B–A–C–H motive in contemporary contexts see Kimberly Francis, "Mediating Modern Music: Nadia Boulanger Constructs Igor Stravinsky" (PhD diss., University of North Carolina at Chapel Hill, 2010), 336–39.

37. Ralph Locke and Cyrilla Barr, *Cultivating Music in America: Women Patrons and Activists since 1860* (Berkeley: University of California Press, 1997), 185–208 and 238–39. For more on Webern and Coolidge see Hans Moldenhauer and Rosaleen Moldenhauer,

*Anton von Webern: A Chronicle of His Life and Work* (New York: Alfred A. Knopf, 1979), 488–94.

38. For additional discussion of this score, see Cédri Segond-Genovesi, "Fin de Règne?: L'Enseignement de Nadia Boulanger après la seconde guerre mondiale," in *De la Libération au Domaine musical : Dix ans de musique en France (1944–1955)*, ed. Laurent Feneyrou and Alain Poirier (Paris: Vrin, 2018), 200 and 209–13.

39. For a discussion of this analysis as well as reproductions of Boulanger's work, see Francis, *Teaching Stravinsky* website, "Into the Archives, Exploration 5, *Elegy for J.F.K.*" https://global.oup.com/us/companion.websites/fdscontent/uscompanion/us/static/companion.websites/9780199373697/pdf/exploration_5.pdf

40. David Wilde, "Nadia Boulanger Is 90 Today," British Broadcasting Corporation, 28 April 1981.

41. Francis, *Boulanger and the Stravinskys*, 144; and Nigel Simeone, "Messiaen, Boulanger, and José Bruyr: Offandres Oubliées 2," *The Musical Times* 142/1874 (2001): 17–22.

42. Leslie A. Sprout, "The 1945 Stravinsky Debates: Nigg, Messiaen, and the Early Cold War in France," *Journal of Musicology* 26 (2009): 85–131; and Sprout, *The Musical Legacy of Wartime France* (Berkeley: University of California Press, 2013), 151–84.

43. Francis, *Boulanger and the Stravinskys*, 123–24.

44. Boulez did correspond with Boulanger, although the content of their correspondence is rather perfunctory. Pierre Boulez to Nadia Boulanger, 1950–1965, F-Pn, N.L. a. 57 (207–211).

45. Francis, *Boulanger and the Stravinskys*, 255.

46. Boulanger, "Les Cours de mercredis."

47. Boulanger's analyses of the *Symphony of Psalms* and the *Elegy for J.F.K.* can be found in Francis, *Teaching Stravinsky*, 37–53; and companion website, "Into the Archives 3 and 5." https://global.oup.com/us/companion.websites/9780199373697/resources/archives/pdf/. Boulanger's analysis of Josquin's *Missa Pange Lingua* is as of yet unpublished. Josquin, *Werken van Josquin des Prez: Uitgegeven door Prof. Dr. A. Smijers, Drie en Dertigste Aflevering, Missen, XVIII, Missa Pange Lingua* (Amsterdam: G. Alsbach & Co., 1952), F-LYc, U. Mon. Jos. W. 33. For more on Boulanger's take on Fauré's Requiem, see Jeanice Brooks, *The Musical Work of Nadia Boulanger: Performing Past and Future Between the Wars* (Cambridge: Cambridge University Press, 2013), esp. 102–9.

48. "Les 12 notes par groups de 3 (cellule finale de la première mesure de la Sonate)."

49. See, for example, her work on Stravinsky's *Symphonie de psaumes*, in Francis, *Teaching Stravinsky*, 37–53; and Francis, "A Dialogue Begins," 36–40. See also Brooks, *Musical Work*, 102–9.

50. Boulanger writes: "Consider p. 18, third line, measures 1 and 2, the entry on a fifth. He rarely employs this: p. 10, measure 13; page 11, measure 9 and 13–14."

51. For Boulanger's analysis of the Symphony in C, see Francis, *Teaching Stravinsky*, companion website, "Into the Archives: Exploration 2" https://global.oup.com/us/companion.websites/fdscontent/uscompanion/us/static/companion.websites/9780199373697/pdf/exploration2.pdf

52. Idil Biret, liner notes to Boulez, Piano Sonatas 1–3, Naxos NA 8.553353 (1995), CD.

53. For Biret's correspondence with Boulanger, see F-Pn, N.L.a. 56 (1–80); for Biret's reflections on studying with Boulanger, see "Souvenirs de disciples de Nadia Boulanger," in *Nadia Boulanger et Lili Boulanger: Témoignages et études*, ed. Alexandre Laederich (Lyon: Symétrie, 2007), 17–32.

54. Idil Biret, "Pierre Boulez 1," Major Projects, http://idilbiret.eu/pierre–boulez–1/.

55. Franck Jedrzejewski, "La mise en oeuvre du principe dodécaphonique dans la 1ère sonate de Pierre Boulez," *Analyse musicale* 7 (1987): 69–76; Barbara Dobretsberger, *Première und Deuxième Sonate von Pierre Boulez: Phänomene strukturalistischen Denkens* (Frankfurt: Peter Lang, 2005); and Jonathan Goldman, *The Musical Language of Pierre Boulez: Writings and Compositions* (Cambridge: Cambridge University Press, 2011).

# Why Music? Aesthetics, Religion, and the Ruptures of Modernity in the Life and Work of Nadia Boulanger

### LEON BOTSTEIN

Nadia Boulanger was one of the twentieth century's most revered and celebrated teachers of music. Her students include its leading performers and composers, including Aaron Copland, Elliott Carter, Walter Piston, Grażyna Bacewicz, Dinu Lipatti, Julia Perry, George Walker, Virgil Thomson, Igor Markevitch, Jean Françaix, Astor Piazzolla, and Philip Glass, to name just a few. The achievements, modest and great, of the incredible number, range, and diversity of her students help define her legacy. But Boulanger's place in music history is secured as well by some historic recordings; her tireless advocacy of the music of a neglected genius, her younger sister Lili Boulanger; her published criticism; and her close and influential association with Igor Stravinsky.

Boulanger abandoned composition early in her career. She concentrated on teaching and performing. As a performer, she gave concerts, organized concerts, made recordings, and was among the first women orchestral conductors to break major barriers in the twentieth century. Except for the war years of the 1940s, Boulanger lived and worked in France, based in her native Paris. She was an ardent French patriot with a keen sense of France's cultural superiority.[1]

Owing to the large number of Americans who studied with her and her wartime sojourn in America, a substantial body of admirable recent scholarship on Nadia Boulanger has emerged on both sides of the Atlantic. A historical assessment of her teaching of music and her deeply held convictions about music, religion, and the momentous events of her time is now possible.[2] This essay places Boulanger within a context of the history of ideas as a representative figure within French and European intellectual history. The essay seeks as well to understand Boulanger's approach to music in the light of how major twentieth-century theologians and social theorists, her contemporaries, construed the role of the arts, particularly music, within the terrifying realities of the twentieth century.

Paeans to the singularity, beauty, and power of music are constant and unexceptional. However, for the generation of Nadia Boulanger—Europeans who came of age at the turn of the century and reached adulthood before the outbreak of the Great War—defining and praising music as a form of life assumed uncommon urgency and significance. At the fin de siècle, more was at stake than the philosophic prominence music had gained as the quintessential expression of art of Romanticism. As the plethora of opera houses and concert halls constructed in Europe's major cities between 1850 and 1900 testify, by 1887, the year of Boulanger's birth, music had pressed beyond the boundaries of aristocratic privilege and exceptional wealth. Music had become pivotal to the public culture and domestic life of Europe's growing urban populations. It figured in debates over politics and society in nations facing the unprecedented existential challenges of modern industrial society. By the 1890s, the years of Boulanger's childhood, music was at the center of a broader search for meaning in the wake of radical discontinuities created by the momentous economic, political, and social changes Europe experienced in the century that followed the French Revolution.[3]

From the very beginning, more was at stake for Boulanger than music alone. Born into a culture in which music truly mattered in life, her generation grappled with its place in a future whose continuity with history was shattered by two ruptures in the fabric of culture and society. The first rupture was the violent transformation of Europe brought about by World War I. That rupture had its decisive prehistory in the realm of ideas: a late nineteenth-century challenge to the idea of progress in history, the logic of reason, the conduct of science, the nature of language, as well as the justification of imperialism and the preeminence of the West. This challenge was in full swing when Boulanger was in her teens and early twenties. The second rupture was the ethical, social, and political aftermath of the distinctively modern technological and bureaucratic barbarism of World War II that led to the atomic age and the Cold War. It defined the last period of Boulanger's career.

### Culture and History after the Great War

Boulanger was just a month shy of twenty-seven in August 1914. She was already an accomplished, versatile, and brilliant musician. The musical culture to which she had been exposed in Paris was dominated by intense disputes about music and modern life that dated back to Baudelaire, the 1860s, and the controversy over Wagner. In Boulanger's youth, epigones and innovators trapped in the framework of Wagnerian Romanticism and an eclectic, late nineteenth-century historicism (whose leading protagonists were Saint-Saëns and Brahms) dominated. They held sway over educational institutions and set the tone of public musical life, as Boulanger understood all too well from her ill-deserved, disappointing encounters with the Prix de Rome competition.

But between 1894, when Debussy's *Prélude à l'aprés-midi d'un faune* had its first performance, and 1913, the date of the notorious premiere in Paris of Stravinsky's *Le sacre du printemps*, Boulanger witnessed funda-mental departures from Wagnerian conceits and the aesthetics of late Romanticism. She welcomed these new developments with considerable enthusiasm.[4] But the outbreak and brutal—and unexpected—length of the Great War placed these disparate and novel prewar aesthetic challenges (represented by Debussy, Fauré, Roussel, Ravel, and Satie in particular) to the premises and practices of the nineteenth century in a new light. In the context of the war, the rejection of the past and the foregrounding of the self-consciously modern took on new meaning; it threatened to undermine the prominence and prestige in society and culture that music had achieved. Boulanger's determination to advocate for new music after 1918 was per-manently shadowed by a sense of foreboding.

Although the artistic and philosophic rebellion that surrounded the young Boulanger before the outbreak of the war targeted established practices in musical composition and public performance, the critique of dominant approaches to writing and performing music possessed unmis-takable overtones directed at politics and mores.[5] Boulanger understood, as her many references to the listening public in the music criticism she published after the Great War suggest, that the fin-de-siècle aesthetic rebellion entailed a repudiation of an established but tacit alliance between cultural taste and social and economic power. Expectations about what music was and how it ought to function and convey meaning—music's established rules, rhetoric, and perceived significance—were shared by a dominant segment of the French public, including patrons, listeners, composers, performers, and critics. Musical culture emerged from the war as a symbol of an inherited and discredited order.

Boulanger's musical training, however, as well as her emergence as a composer, performer, and teacher, unfolded in a context in which music was taken to be a unique and privileged art form, central to the social, political, and spiritual life of the human community and contemporary life. The pre-1914 aesthetic rebellion was, for the most part, contained within art and directed against the Wagnerian and late Romanticism that had captivated an astonishingly large public. After 1918, self-consciously anti-Romantic modern movements in music could no longer be separated from a critique of the culture that nurtured, affirmed, and sustained the war. Advocates of the new were accused of being subversive beyond the confines of aesthetics.

The challenges to continuity from before 1914 were pursued with renewed urgency after 1918. They were aimed at monumentality, best represented by the orchestral forces employed by Mahler and Strauss; an extravagant and exaggerated expressive rhetoric of emotion and narration achieved by extended chromaticism; surface sentimentality; an absence of formal restraint evident in the penchant for music of lengthy duration sustained by repetition; and a reliance on color and sonority—decorative sound effects. New music intentionally shattered these inherited expectations and placed music's comprehensibility and entertainment value in doubt. Some forms of radicalism in new music (for example, Antheil and Satie) heard in Paris after the war overtly threatened music's cultural complacency and public appeal. Others, like Stravinsky's Octet, which shocked the Parisian audience in 1923, pointed in Boulanger's view to a valid and necessary future for music in modernity.[6] The Octet displayed structural logic, formal integrity, transparency, and an evocation of tradition, even with irony, in a resolutely modern manner.

What became apparent to Boulanger was that a direction for new music was required in the postwar era that could preserve and even augment the prewar cultural significance of music as a form of life and communication, notably in France, and yet be modern. A prewar ambivalence among composers of new music toward the terms of popularity and success within the traditional audience had to be supplanted not by heightened confrontation, ridicule, and the exposure of the philistine and hypocritical, but by a constructive aesthetic. After the war, Stravinsky became the model of what new music might aspire to. To support a modernism Boulanger regarded as exemplary, the education and reeducation of musicians and listeners became imperative, not merely in the service of music but in the culture and soul of the French nation, whose most cherished cultural virtues were at risk in the social and political unrest that dominated the interwar era.

The challenge Boulanger took on was to help composers emancipate new music from its dependence on nineteenth-century Romanticism, thereby rendering music modern but without separating the modern from all of history. Her solution was to exploit music's independent character as a form of art and open up a novel foundation in history that extended back to the Middle Ages and the Renaissance. The uniqueness of music in Boulanger's view resided precisely in its stable non-linguistic character, its self-referential capacity to communicate apart from words and images, reconcile complexity and clarity, transform the subjective perception of time and duration, and at the same time convey contemporary sensibilities and meanings. Music's logic and formal attributes had been cultivated most persuasively before early Romanticism. Therefore, precedents from before the nineteenth century provided modern music a potent legitimacy rooted in history and tradition that could secure music's centrality in European culture and society for the present and future.

The task Boulanger undertook after 1918 as teacher, writer, and performer was to lead a cultural "renewal" for France and the postwar world. That renewal required new works of music that honored and drew inspiration from music that preceded the Second French Empire. Her appeal to a selective history and tradition was in turn based on the belief that all works of music, including new ones that possessed true beauty and greatness, demanded normative qualities, no matter how "persuasive their emotion may be, that carry within them the rule of intelligence, the desire for order, and the beauty of form."[7] By being rooted in the longer arc of past aesthetic practice that honored music's unique nature, modernism could go beyond rebellion and an undisciplined surface "novelty," both powerful temptations in the culture of the immediate postwar years.

Boulanger's invocation of normative standards of beauty and truth present in all great music required a recalibration of history that foregrounded a neglected past with exemplary precedents for contemporary composers and the audience. In this way, the early twentieth century's philosophical and aesthetic rupture with the nineteenth century on behalf of a uniquely modern age of music could be extended and legitimated. The integration of a pre-Romantic musical heritage distant from the modern world became an antidote to the shabby and tired rhetoric bequeathed by the nineteenth century and the threats to art, culture, and civility unleashed by the Great War. A modern music could emerge that would be acceptable to a conservative and skeptical public.

The past that Boulanger enlisted on behalf of the modern centered on, among others, Pérotin, Claudio Monteverdi, Heinrich Schütz, William Byrd, Jean Baptiste Lully, Jean-Philippe Rameau, and J. S. Bach, as well as Mozart and Haydn. Most of this music had a subordinate place during the second half of the nineteenth century in music making on the stage and in the home. Bach, in particular, came to occupy the center of Boulanger's efforts as teacher and performer to mobilize history on behalf of the modern. Boulanger used him as a moral exemplar. Bach demonstrated how new art might display clarity, complexity, and unity in aesthetic form, all in the service of faith and the spiritual.

Boulanger's turn to the music of the sixteenth and seventeenth centuries was not unique. One of Paris's key art patrons, with whom Boulanger became closely associated in the 1930s, Winnaretta Singer, the Princesse de Polignac, exhibited similar instincts in her musical salon soirees before 1914. Bach became a source of inspiration in modern painting, as evident in Georges Braque's cubist *Aria de Bach* from 1913 and his several *Still Life* versions. In the first decades of the new century, Bach emerged as an ideal for visual composition independent of both Impressionism and Expressionism.[8] The appropriation of Bach as master of counterpoint was not limited to France, as the prewar and wartime canvases of Marsden Hartley, August Macke, Vassily Kandinsky, Paul Klee, and Lyonel Feininger suggest.[9]

Boulanger's strategy debunked two uses of history dominant before 1900. One assumed progress as central to the logic of history. The second privileged history over philosophy. Nineteenth-century historicism suggested the fundamental contingency of cultural values and mores. Historicism contested the validity of absolutes in aesthetics and ethics. Differentiations among historical periods mean that each age revealed distinct and ultimately equivalent claims to truth. Boulanger's construct of history offered an alternative: the notion that music retained a special, consecrated, and constant criteria of merit throughout history, without variation. For the listener—the lay public—these invariant aesthetic norms linked present music to music from the past.

Historical progress was displaced in favor of a selective discontinuous history within which a consistency of qualities was audible beneath disparate styles. Evidence of the normative criteria of aesthetic judgment could therefore be located in Medieval, Renaissance, Baroque, Classical, even Romantic (Boulanger revered Chopin, for example), and contemporary music. A concert Boulanger gave at Harvard's Sanders Theater on 3 March 1938 with members of the Boston Symphony was typical of her approach. It included works by Stravinsky, Poulenc, Hindemith, and a Corsican-born composer, Léo Preger, who was thirty-one.[10] These were mixed in with music by Tallis, Palestrina, Purcell, and Bach, as well as an anonymous work from the thirteenth century. In this concert structure, new music could be judged as aspiring to traditional values. The modern became more palatable, despite discordant and discontinuous hallmarks of the contemporary.

Boulanger lent the history of music a universal metaphysical logic. This logic brought history and philosophy to bear in defense of the moderation of the instinct that the novelty of technology and industry and modern life alone would lead to great art. Boulanger promoted the idea that music's beauty and proper and central place in the conduct of life derived from absolute, not relative, criteria of excellence located in the objective essence of music and musical time, and therefore not from changes in history.[11]

Aesthetic value and musical beauty, as constants of truth, suggested parallel objective standards and values in ethics. If one could persuade the listening public, not only composers and performers, of a continuity in aesthetic truth and the presence of an underlying unity within history, one could sustain a culture of music that did not depend on easy recognition or familiarity with surface rhetoric and sonorities. This might open up, in modern times, a window on an underlying unity of truths shared by the making of art and the conduct of private and public life. France and Europe had to "come out of those terrible years with new glory," Boulanger declared in 1919, not only culturally but also socially and politically in a "useful" way, even though "life is resuming from a different angle." The stability of values within music's character could inspire contemporary life to "come up from the ruins," as Boulanger put it, "in spite of all the gazes bound to the past, in spite of all the mourning amassed during these years of holocaust, of all the sacrifices."[12]

The immortality of meaningful music that transcended history possessed, for Boulanger, a dual nature. It was material and logical as well as intuitive and spiritual, and therefore beyond rational comprehension. The fundamental law of music, for Boulanger, was that beauty comes forth, whether we realize it or not, from a mix of an "indefinable mystery" with its logic and rules: "its organization." "Truth" in music derived from the "abstractions that rule the world." Those abstractions defied "individualism" and the concrete, and therefore an "exaggerated weight placed on technique."[13]

Boulanger's "abstractions" behind criteria of beauty in music possessed a family resemblance to those of goodness and virtue. Ethical qualities required the formal consistency demanded by music. Not only individuality—originality and style—made music beautiful and profound, but universal standards of balance, structure, and moderation. Modern music, just as modern life, needed to resist the historically contingent and transitory—the immediate situation—that Boulanger characterized as inspiring a "fierce and narrow egoism."

If the new remained true to music's invariant logic it might retain its cultural power. An aesthetic renascence within the modern would parallel a moral and political one. Music's abstract and unreal nature—its synthesis of the opaque (the intuitively subjective) and the transparent (the intellectually objective), lent it an appeal that connected modern art to contemporary life. In May 1919, Boulanger concluded:

Nothing is better than music—when it transports us out of time, it does more for us than we have the right to expect; it expands the limits of our sorrowful lives, it forms a halo over the sweetness of our hours of happiness, by erasing the pettiness that diminishes us, by bringing us thus pure and new towards what was, towards what will be, towards what it creates for us. In music everything is extended, everything is constructed, and at the end of the enchantment, when we are still bathed in its clarity, our solitude is attended by new hope, between the self-compassion that makes us more gentle and more understanding, and the certainty of finding something that lives forever within it.[14]

The dualist vision Boulanger put forward in the years after 1918 concerning the immutable logic of beauty in music as the consequence of intellect and intuition was comparable to a tradition in the history of thought that sought to reconcile the truths derived from use of reason, primarily the findings of empirical science, with the truths of revealed religion. The reconciliation of rational logic and non-rational intuition—a necessary aspect of both Boulanger's and her friend Stravinsky's aesthetic—deepened the relevance of music to the prospect of restoring the human community in the wake of the Great War. Forming a harmonious community, particularly after the divisive Treaty of Versailles, depended, like a work of music, on a "concept of the whole," the presence of a comprehensible totality, a shared sensibility that the war had shattered. Possessed of "a general arc," Boulanger reasoned, new music could reveal a true synthesis for modernity of "mind and heart, thought and feeling, reasoning and intuition."[15] Music of beauty, like moral goodness, could affirm body and soul and the whole of the human character, a task desperately needed after the confrontation with the inhuman during the war. Aesthetics, grounded in reason and non-rational human intuition could lead politically, healing the nation and the world.

The "neoclassicism" of the interwar years derived its character, in Boulanger's view, from the idea that form and structure in music were subject to objective judgment and therefore justified the prestige of the term "classical." Boulanger, as her students repeatedly reported, stressed the necessity of an overarching linear shape in a work of music: *la grande ligne*. Coherence was attained by a structural logic that unified the use of the materials of music in contrast to the aesthetics of late Romanticism that privileged subjectivity, originality, narration, theatricality, and expansiveness.

Boulanger's invocation of anti-Romantic normative criteria worthy of the status "classical" had its origins in and outside of France before 1914. The 1890s saw a Mozart revival in France (led in part by Saint-Saëns) and Germany. In 1891, the young Hugo von Hofmannsthal anticipated Boulanger's postwar focus on the overriding principles of form. In music, Hofmannsthal declared, "Beethoven is the rhetoric of our soul, Wagner its feelings, and Schumann perhaps its thoughts: Mozart is more; he is form itself."[16]

Boulanger, like many of her contemporaries, read Nietzsche, her generation's most frequently cited inspiration for a transvaluation of meaning, the critique of conventional wisdom (including Wagnerian conceits), and inherited pieties. She made frequent references to his writings in her published criticism from the late teens and early 1920s. Nietzsche was also an influence in Hofmannsthal's lifelong allegiance to the unique power of music and his acute sense, prior to 1914, of the poetic bankruptcy of modern language use. These twin sensibilities cemented Hofmannsthal's collaboration with Richard Strauss after *Elektra*.

For all that separated Boulanger from Strauss and Hofmannsthal—politics, nationality, and personality—their postwar fears and prejudices, despite a wide divergence in tastes and beliefs, were similar. In both cases a nascent skepticism deepened toward late Romanticism and early Expressionism. This led them toward the idea of a revival of pre-Romantic aesthetic ideals contained in the eighteenth century as best represented by Watteau and Mozart. Boulanger's 1919 praise of music reads like an echo of the words and music Hofmannsthal and Strauss gave the composer in the prologue to the 1916 revision of *Ariadne auf Naxos*.

Music was the "holiest of all the arts," the composer sings, ending in a triumphant E-flat major, "for it gathers to itself all forms of courage, like cherubs around a shining throne."[17] In the midst of a brutal war, music of a certain classicist character was resilient in the face of the toll taken on any shared sense of beauty and virtue. Music's substance, form, and experience represented a field of pure aesthetic endeavor, unsullied and promising for the cultural and ethical task that lay ahead.

### Ancients versus Moderns: Pascal and Ernest Renan

Nadia Boulanger's understanding of music depended on the validity of metaphysics and the resultant truth value of universal notions of beauty and the good. This led Boulanger to the belief that the secularization characteristic of the second half of the nineteenth century required a modern defense of religion. Boulanger's postwar rhetoric about music assumed the tone of a call to religious renewal. Her premises were frankly theological and rooted in her ultramontane Roman Catholic faith. Biographers and contemporaries noted her religiosity; her strict routine; her regular ritual devotions in memory of the dead, especially her sister; her nun-like self-presentation; and her evident and obvious devotion to Catholicism.[18] She even sought to persuade Louise Talma, one of her American protégées, to convert to Catholicism, and her relationship with her British pupil Lennox Berkeley was predicated in part on their shared Catholicism.[19] The aesthetics of music and a religious sensibility were inextricably intertwined.

Two minor biographical anecdotes shed light on Boulanger's faith. Elliott Carter, who studied with her in the 1930s, recalled that the last time he saw Boulanger as a student was when he was preparing to return to America. Boulanger helped Carter pack and get gifts for his parents. But she also gave him a present: Pascal's *Pensées*, which Carter described as "very typical of her and a deeply touching reminder of her religious devotion."[20]

Some twenty years later, in the 1950s, Joyce Mekeel, an American student from Radcliffe College, came to Paris to study with Boulanger. On her first visit, Mekeel failed to notice the "do not touch" signs on many of Boulanger's bookshelves and pulled Ernest Renan's *Life of Jesus* from one. When Mekeel, "terrified," asked about the book, Boulanger was evasive and dismissive in tone, observing that "she hadn't read half the books in her library."[21] Of all of the books in Boulanger's library, Renan's skeptical and controversial 1863 bestseller was an unlikely candidate for membership in the unread portion of the book collection. If she had never read it, why was it shelved in the "do not touch" section?

For Boulanger's generation, Ernest Renan (1823–92) was emblematic of the essence and core commitments of the nineteenth century—the smug sense of superiority, the pride regarding progress, and a modern advance over all things ancient. *The Life of Jesus*, purported to be a scholarly and accurate biography of Jesus, not as the son of God but as a mere, albeit exceptional human being, was astonishingly popular and became, in its many translations, among the most widely read and debated books of the century. It was lauded as brilliant, a "work of art," as Sainte-Beuve put it. Renan stripped the figure of Jesus of all mystery and association with miracles and the supernatural. Jesus was, as one critic put it, "reclaimed to history and the normal life of man."[22] No wonder the book was controversial.

Mid-nineteenth-century scholars, notably Bruno Bauer and David Friedrich Strauss in Protestant Germany, had begun to subject the New and Old Testament to the rigors of scholarship, treating them as texts of history and not as divinely inspired and revealed. What made Renan different was that his literary secularization and humanization of Jesus emerged within the French Catholicism Renan and Boulanger both grew up in, and in which Renan received his initial academic training. Lutheranism was far more tolerant; rational critical scholarship of the Bible did not require a rejection of faith. Renan's book caused his removal from a professorship at the College de France.

Renan did more than craft a historical account of who Jesus might have been. He "brought him alive," as Albert Schweitzer observed, so much so that his readers "thought to see Jesus" and the landscape of the Holy Land.[23] Renan's lyricism and painterly prose depicted Jesus's transition from being a young Jew to becoming a follower of John the Baptist and then emerging as the thoroughly human proponent of "an unparalleled subversion in human affairs," a charismatic prophet who proclaimed "the principle upon which society has reposed for eighteen hundred years," a "gentle" social revolution based on spiritual virtues, not material things such as wealth and power, but on faith and love.[24]

Renan, who was a scholar of Semitic philology and became notorious for a dismissive but unstable obsession with Jews and Judaism, was attacked for turning the life and death of the son of God into a garish piece of sentimental theater, stripping Jesus of the authority of the supernatural, and contesting the mystery and the sacred that was out of reach of human reason. Renan was, as Schweitzer put it, a man of "indefinite" positions who was "at bottom a skeptic." What was most appalling about *The Life of Jesus,* Schweitzer concluded, was not its dismissal of mystery and miracles but "the lack of any definite ethical principles in the writer's outlook on life."

His critics in and out of France notwithstanding, Renan became as world-famous as any Frenchman of his generation. His eventual interment in the Panthéon during the aggressively secular Third Republic was a tribute to the success of his cause—historical scholarship based on evidence, the rigorous conduct of science, a conservative secular republicanism and ardent nationalism based on civic participation, and a belief in progress. Renan represented his century's triumph of reason, science, and the secularization of Christianity.[25]

Boulanger was five years old when Renan, a representative figure of her father's generation, died. Although many compatriots took aim at Renan's demystification of religion and conservative Catholics understood him as subversive and heretical, it was the aesthetic character and style of *The Life of Jesus* that evoked, for Boulanger's generation, the worst of the later nineteenth century—crass sentimentality, overwrought expressiveness, grandiose theatricality, and an absence of simplicity and clarity.

It represented the garishness of fashion, the destruction of a spiritual community of faith, and the privileging of materialism and empiricism over the spiritual, the mystical, and the magical. Boulanger and her generation believed they had been bequeathed a deficit of belief, clothed in a florid and mannered style, denying truths that transcended verifiable experience. Boulanger had placed *The Life of Jesus* in the "do not touch" category not arbitrarily and not merely on account of Renan's skepticism of the miraculous in the Gospels' account of the life of Jesus Christ. The aesthetics of Renan's prose mirrored the excesses of late Romanticism.

Boulanger's gift of Pascal's *Pensées* to Carter was equally carefully considered. The *Pensées* contained a philosophical framework diametrically opposed to Renan, one in which Boulanger found a basis for her concept of beauty and truth in art, and therefore the criteria by which to judge not only the music of the present but that of the past. Unlike Richard Strauss, who adhered to the end of his life to the anti-Christian atheism inspired by Nietzsche, and consistently rejected idealized justifications of the function and meaning of music by celebrating rather its link to the "all too human," Boulanger took refuge, after the war, in Pascal's premodern but existentialist dualist acceptance of the subordination and dependence of reason within ardent and unquestioning faith, without an epistemological resolution of the human with the divine, into a unity of being.

Pascal's austere depiction of the human predicament—one of wretchedness and suffering derived from original sin and the fall from grace—appealed to Boulanger. The paradox in the human condition was that the acceptance and pursuit of reason required faith, not the reconciliation of the two. One had to balance intellect—thought and reason—with faith—heart, feelings, and intuition. Boulanger stuck to Pascal's belief that only "those who serve God, having found him" can be deemed "intelligent and happy." Living with God enabled the artist to listen to the heart and pursue feelings and intuition and apply the distinct criteria of human logic and reason.[26]

Boulanger followed Pascal in embracing, axiomatically, an overarching allegiance to God, grounded in faith in the truth and authority of the Catholic Church. She shared Pascal's understanding that faith, and belief in God, did not require a defense by reason but actually defied it. Boulanger's beliefs about music owe a debt to Pascal's belief that there is more to learn than what can be gained from applying inductive and deductive reasoning to experience. A realm of mystery, miracles, metaphysics, and the supernatural surrounds human existence and bestows a unity over the contradictions we experience. Everything in the world of nature is "made and guided by the same master."[27]

Boulanger's suspicion of Romantic individualism detached from faith mirrored Pascal's notion: "Knowledge of God without knowledge of man's wretchedness leads to pride. Knowledge of man's wretchedness without knowledge of God leads to despair."[28] Faith in God permitted the reconciliation of the basic dualism of body and soul. Pascal's observation "Miracles and Truth are both necessary, because the whole man must be convinced, in body and soul,"[29] inspired Boulanger's belief that craftsmanship, technique, and a command of musical logic—human gifts grounded in reason, Pascal's "truth"—needed to be complemented by the intuitive spiritual "miracle" of distinct talent and genius. Music was at once a matter of rational truth in the mastery of its elements and the mysteriously inexplicable, those gifts of the soul beyond external and observable reality. Since music was free from a reliance on words and images and closely allied to heart, feelings, and intuition, music could communicate Pascal's root of faith, the spiritual recognition of man's wretchedness.

Although music demanded a clarity and form that mirrored thought, reason, and the mind, its true source rested on intuitions that bypassed reason. Pascal argued that scientific knowledge, based on reason, could never "console" an individual for "the ignorance of morality." Such knowledge rested on a faith in God not based on reason. Music, for Boulanger, was uniquely equipped to communicate faith, which could console the human being ignorant of all "external things."[30] But a musician without the miracle of intuition could not create the bridge between aesthetics and ethics and was, in the end, far worse off than the musician with just craft and technique.

Music's capacity to encompass the worlds of reason and faith without the need for reconciling them rested in the requirement of an overarching form in the work of art, an order and unity reflective of the omnipresence of God. God offered the potential gift of grace and salvation, and framed Christian love (something Boulanger never tired of invoking) amid incredible distress, weakness, and disparity in the world. In Pascal, Boulanger found a stable theological and philosophical justification for a plurality of historical and personal styles. Boulanger's commitment to a universal spiritual basis of human action in faith explains her legendary enthusiastic encouragement of every student to find a distinctive voice, a virtue to which practically all her students, notably her American protégés, including Aaron Copland, Virgil Thomson, Roy Harris, Carter, and even George Gershwin (who flirted with studying with her), testified. But she favored composers who, like Stravinsky, Fauré, Poulenc (in the 1930s) and Lili Boulanger, no matter the genre, system of pitch organization, or surface sonority, produced works that in their form and use of musical time revealed most clearly human reason and the presence of God in a non-mystical synthesis within a single work of art.

Boulanger's gift to Carter was indeed perfect, for it represented her underlying system of values for the conduct of life and the proper character of music. Human reason needed to reside alongside a religious acceptance of the unknowable, immune from validation by reason in a human condition of "inconstancy, weariness, and disquiet."[31] Music represented the human embrace of God's gift of freedom, the possibility of grace, the immortality of the soul, and the immutable and immanent presence of the divine. Her reach back to Pascal, France's leading writer, mathematician, scientist, and thinker of the seventeenth century, matched her rejection of all that Renan represented. It was also consistent with Boulanger's irrepressible French patriotism and cultural chauvinism. Music's vulnerability in a modern world dominated by reason and science led Boulanger to find ideas from the seventeenth century that could guide new music to resist the postwar threat of cultural decline and the trivialization of art.

### Bergson, Time, and the Aesthetic Discourse in France

The most influential figure in French thought in Boulanger's lifetime was Henri Bergson (1859–1941). Bergson, along with William James, Ernst Mach, Edmund Husserl, and Wilhelm Dilthey, was crucial in the transition away from the intellectual and cultural triumphalism of the generation of Renan and Wagner. References to Bergson appear directly and indirectly in Boulanger's own writing. But Boulanger was not a philosopher, so the importance of Bergson for her, as for most of her contemporaries, derived from the extensive popularization (not without distortion) of his thought. Bergson's reputation rested on pioneering the introduction of contingent human perception and experience in the construct of external reality, empirical observation, and the laws of nature, augmenting the use of categories supported by mathematics and mechanics. Bergson was credited for his theories of intuition and creative evolution. The most oft-quoted and misunderstood phrase associated with him is the vital "spirit" or "gesture," the *élan vital*. This lent him the reputation of an apostle of the distinction between intellect and intuition, a conception of the human mind that included mental operations well beyond cold calculation. Bergson loosened the spiritually bankrupt iron grip of secular instrumental reason, of reductive assumptions about sense-perception, positivism, and materialism.[32]

For musicians, and particularly Boulanger, Bergson's most influential ideas were those that dealt with the understanding of time. Bergson's first significant book, *Matter and Memory*, was published in 1896. In it, he put forward a conception of time as duration. In this reformulation of duration, "clock" time became more than a series of successive measurable units. In sleep and in our memory, "we no longer estimate past time mathematically"; even in the waking state, "daily experience ought to teach us to distinguish between duration as quality, that which consciousness reaches immediately . . . and time so to speak materialized, time that has become quantity." The formulation of duration allowed Bergson to foreground the qualitative impact of psychic perception.[33] A notion of "inner time" and the "continuity of our inner life" emerged as valid universals. Without taking "immediately perceived duration" into consideration, Bergson argued, "we would have no idea of time."[34]

Bergson's notion of duration suggested a nonlinear approach to time.[35] Duration integrated layers of consciousness and subjective impressions, blurring the boundary between past and present. It complicated the idea of the elapsed and the simultaneous. "The present contains nothing more than the past, and what was in the effect was already in the cause," Bergson argued.[36] "Basic time" required understanding "multiplicity without divisibility" and "succession without separation." Bergson used the example of a musical melody to buttress his concept of duration. Music, experienced both in clock time and in memory, erased the sharp distinction between starting points and endings. Listening to music provided empirical proof of "multiplicity without divisibility" and the fact of duration.[37]

For Boulanger and her contemporaries this supported a focus on coherence and unity within the elapsed time of a single work of music. The sources of unity in a composition stretched from the beginning to the last note, and erased the priority in the temporal sequence of earlier over later. Bergson's notion of music vindicated the idea of duration as transcending the mere passage of time. Boulanger's understanding of musical form and its experience was indebted to Bergson; duration legitimated the requirement of an overarching unifying dynamic form over the elapse of musical time, in which distinct events have their place not only along the lines of clock time succession but also retrospectively, through duration, the memory of the total experience. In Boulanger's vocabulary, that dynamic form would become the "*grande ligne*" that needed to be present in all great music.[38]

The introduction of the psychology of perception into the account of reality also led Bergson to defend differences in the human character. Although identifying individuality and achieving it are difficult, "life nevertheless manifests a search for individuality" in a context where "the whole of the universe is constructed or reconstructed by thought." Bergson's assertion of an objective role for subjective perception in understanding reality provided a scientific, reasoned basis for Boulanger's philosophical dualism. Using time and memory as evidence, Bergson reaffirmed "the reality of spirit and the reality of matter." His aim, he confessed, was "frankly dualistic."[39] Whereas Pascal saw two modes of human activity, reason and faith, in conflict, both resulting from the grace of God, Bergson reconciled mind and matter within human reason through an expanded definition of realism. Intuition was the spiritual part of reasoning and intellect. Intuition in life led the search for individuality and revealed the *élan vital*, the vital force and impulse that drove existence. Bergson's intuition was not logical or rational and not convertible into a measurable form, any more than duration could be broken down into a discrete sequence of events.

### Beyond Bergson: Apollinaire, Golberg, and Benda
Bergson was revered by artists, writers, and musicians. But his emphasis on individual perception and intuition gained detractors before 1914 among those in search of more substantive absolutes in art and ethics. By the 1920s, Bergson also came under attack from proponents of empirical science. Their target was the idea of duration. The most famous break took place in 1922 around a legendary confrontation between Einstein and Bergson. At issue was the relationship between time and space.[40] Bergson held that duration proved that they were distinct and not equivalent.[41] Einstein's theory of special relativity exploded the idea of "absolute" time and space, and made clear the equivalency (hence the origins of the term relativity) between the frames of reference that challenged the distinction between time and space. Einstein maintained a Spinoza-like pantheism and argued a fundamental unity within reality, including an equivalence between space and time.[42]

For Bergson, time was duration and an autonomous part of reality that shaped a dynamic and spiritual continuity in life. Reality was "becoming" with infinite possibilities that were out of the grasp of a relativistic equivalence of space and time. Bergson objected, philosophically, to relativity. Artists, particularly musicians, never wholly abandoned Bergson's idea of duration and his defense of time as an autonomous factor in reality.

By foregrounding intuition and creativity within cognition and logic, Bergson cast doubt on the priority of the material and mechanical in reality and suggested a distinct realm of the metaphysical—the spiritual—perceptible through the role of consciousness and memory in the construct of duration. However, despite his assertion of the aesthetic as proof of a metaphysical realm, in the postwar context this defense of the spiritual seemed halfhearted. Bergson was considered too tied to a tradition of philosophy indebted to Kant, and to the rational and the scientific. Intuition seemed little more than a form of deformed reasoning, not reflective of an autonomous spiritual experience of the sort suggested by theories of the soul and its immortality put forward by Pascal.

Furthermore, in the first two decades of the new century artists, despite sympathy for Bergson's defense of the dynamics of intuition and the creative impetus, found his plea for individuality perilously close to the cult of personality that flourished in Romanticism. An echo of this response found its way into Boulanger's thinking. By not going far enough to assert the autonomy of the spiritual, and thereby undermining the historicism and materialism of the age of Renan, Bergson's thought seemed not to offer an adequate defense of metaphysical normative values in art. Bergson failed to provide an adequate critique of monism, the view, held by Ernst Mach and others, that there is no true distinction between mind and matter, and that there is just one reality in which subjective psychological perception, and geometrical space, constructs of perception, physiology and material reality, can all be reconciled under a comprehensive dynamic theory comparable to evolution.

Guillaume Apollinaire took a step beyond Bergson's blurring of conventional wisdom about consciousness, memory, and reality. The French writer, of Polish origin, (famous in part because of his link to Cocteau and Satie in their collaboration on *Parade*), provided a philosophical theory for a new aesthetic distinct from Romanticism and Bergson in his 1913 *Les peintres cubistes: Méditations esthétiques*. Everyone in Boulanger's generation either read it or heard about it: it was the subject of lively debates in journals and the press. Apollinaire proposed a fourth dimension in consciousness to which painters had access: an immense, eternal space without any stable directional vector. That fourth dimension, accessed purely by intuition (unlike the other three dimensions described by Euclid), could be expressed through art. It revealed a metaphysical, stable presence of a pure, true, and universal spiritual realm. Art for Apollinaire therefore became the medium by which one might draw out of nature an inherent invariant metaphysical truth in reality. Geometry expressed universal truths about space, and the relationships within space. Therefore, the virtue of the Cubist movement was its dedication to the geometric and aesthetic absolutes in a spiritual reality rendered concrete by the intuitive imagination through art.[43]

This post-Bergson effort to locate absolute truths in art may have been most famously expressed by Apollinaire in 1913, but Apollinaire was indebted to a tract published in 1908 by a friend, one Mécislas Golberg

(1869–1907). Golberg's wide influence came from his theory of the transcendent truth value of art argued in a pamphlet, *La morale des lignes*. Golberg, Polish-Jewish in origin, was a legendary and shady Parisian gadfly who traveled widely among the city's leading painters and sculptors. He was equally notorious as an anarchist (whose son had the misfortune to be the last anarchist guillotined in France in 1922). Although Golberg died in 1907, his posthumous pamphlet earned him a potent notoriety in Parisian circles.

Golberg's central claim was that the form, the shape, and the line of a true work of art revealed a totality, a universal truth that transcended the specificity of the subject, the personality of the artist, and therefore the differentiation suggested by history and individuality.[44] "There are indelible truths," he claimed, that can be discerned from art works of "significance" that can be applied to all periods of history and thought and "sentiment." The same "ideal values" emerge from the art of the Middle Ages and the twentieth century.[45] In Golberg's view, truth in life could be broken down into the dynamic between two linear vectors. The vertical was the spirit, and the horizontal the material. The interaction between these two became the arena for the expression of the human will; the tendency to the spiritual always assumes a right angle, and the circular expressed the brutal and the material.[46]

Boulanger's conception of the unity of form and line in music and its recurrent appearance in history suggest the influence of Golberg and Apollinaire. Either by reading them or through the popularization of their views among Boulanger's contemporaries such as Koechlin and Darius Milhaud, for whom Apollinaire was a central figure, she found a confirmation of art's role in establishing the timeless metaphysical values. Perhaps most important to her was Golberg's use of moral equivalents to characterize linear aesthetic values.[47] Golberg and Apollinaire challenged the cult of individualism, the priority of the subjective, the relativism of historicism and therefore the excesses of Romanticism. Contemporary art emerged as the medium for revealing overarching moral and absolute metaphysical truths to the modern world.

The need to locate and defend absolute values intensified after the war. Julien Benda's *La trahison des clercs* (*The Treason of the Intellectuals*), appeared in 1927 and became one of the most widely read books of its time. It created a sensation as powerful as Renan's *Life of Jesus*. Benda's argument did not emerge, however, from aesthetic concerns or religion, but rather from a secular critique of the conceits of the leading artists and thinkers of the day. He accused the intellectual, artistic, and mandarin class of modern times of becoming mere clerks who abandoned their sacred duty to uphold absolute truths regarding life, in epistemology, ethics, and aesthetics. Some version of Benda's polemic certainly came to Boulanger's attention.[48]

Benda accused the nineteenth century, Renan's generation, of propagating a false realism based on the study of history, empiricism, and materialism.[49] His critique extended to Bergson. Bergson's theory of intuition, duration, and a creative dynamism fostered individuality and change that were, for Benda, direct attacks on the existence of universal truths. Bergson's way of thinking supported the false idea that "every doctrine which honors Man in the universal, in what is common to all men, is an insult to the artist."[50] Bergson reduced God and truth to patterns of incessant change and novelty.[51] Benda aligned himself with Boulanger's critique of modernist art that defied tradition. The artist's goal had become mere individuality so that the artist might, in his own era, "set himself up as an exceptional being."[52]

Benda believed that there were rational and objective criteria that upheld "the cult of humanity in its universal aspect" underlying true art. He attacked manifestations of Romanticism and modernism, from Victor Hugo to Gabriele D'Annunzio, that "permit a tone of calm inhumanity," preaching the idea that truth evolves over time and is subject to history.[53] Truth had become "circumstantial," Benda argued. The dominant voices among contemporary intellectuals, particularly Bergson, "proclaim the decadence of that form of mind which, from Plato to Kant, hallows existence as conceived beyond change." Bergson failed to honor the "moral supremacy" of the spiritual and the "feeling of the universal."[54] The postwar era had become an age of "intellectual and moral darkness" sustained by "wild beasts," subservient technocrats masquerading as thinkers and artists. Orpheus, Benda observed, might have been able to charm these beasts. Instead, he concluded sarcastically, "One could have hoped that Orpheus himself would not become a wild beast."[55]

### Faith and the Role of the Artist

A comparable explicit dissatisfaction with Bergson that made its way directly to Boulanger was, like Benda's, located in Bergson's failure to adequately assert and defend universals in epistemology, ethics, and aesthetics. Jacques Maritain (1882–1973), whose writings from the 1920s had a direct influence on Stravinsky and his circle, including Boulanger, published his first book, *La philosophie Bergsonienne*, a critique of Bergson, in 1913.[56] The core of Maritain's argument (anticipating Benda by fifteen years) was that what Bergson achieved in his discussion of duration, intuition, and creative evolution merely extended a line of thought derived from Kant:

intellectual rationalism based on empiricism and rules of human reason.[57] Bergson failed to acknowledge the "irreducible metaphysical value of the act of being." The proof of the existence of the spiritual, and of an epistemological dualism, rested in separating the "what" of existence, what it was and could be, from the "that" of existence. Being—the act "to be"— represented the full measure of existence and was the consequence of the intuition of the metaphysical. This "last" step, which reveal that "God is subsisting Truth," a belief reminiscent of Pascal's faith, Maritain observed, Bergson could not take.[58]

For Maritain, a revival and modern extension of the philosophy of St. Thomas Aquinas could realize fully the "intention" implied by Bergson— the establishment of a contemporary philosophy of ontology. A theory of being could effectively "recall that there are criteria of truth independent of the inner movement of a thought in the process of formation."[59] Bergson's reliance on duration and dynamism thus had to be supplanted by Thomistic stasis. As Maritain argued in 1929 in the second edition of *La philosophie Bergsonienne,* a "modernist crisis" made his philosophical and theological critique of Bergson, the last apostle of a secular, relativist approach to truth and meaning, indispensable.[60]

Boulanger's relentless defense of Stravinsky and those French composers she favored—including Francis Poulenc, Fauré, and Jean Françaix— drew from this sense of crisis. Maritain offered a modern epistemological justification of absolutist aesthetics. Golberg had located form, particularly the presence of a "grand line," as the means and evidence. The mastery of objective form in music was deemed essential in the struggle against a severe moral and cultural uncertainty. When Boulanger lent her voice on behalf of composers she admired but did not quite revere—Albert Roussel, for example—she praised not any particular style—harmonic system or pitch organization—but what, in 1929, she called Roussel's resolute independence, an unimpeachable distinctiveness that displayed consistency and a sense of disciplined order and unity within each work of music.[61]

Maritain provided a comprehensive theological and philosophical basis for Boulanger's postwar absorption of absolutist aesthetic justifications, drawn from Golberg and Apollinaire, for judging the music of her time. Maritain strengthened her attachment to universal formal criteria that could link art to morality and truth.[62] In her 1920 review of Willem Mengelberg's legendary Amsterdam celebration of Gustav Mahler, Boulanger concluded that for all of Mahler's many virtues as a composer, he was not a "genius of a universal nature." Mahler failed to rise above his historical context and write music that "raises itself above all distinctions and imposes itself on everyone, imperiously." Mahler's architecture and his aesthetic were too subjective and personal, and legitimately "contrary to the French mind." Mahler lacked moderation, a sense of harmonic form, and failed to subordinate feeling to a proper sense of order. He asserted a "neo-Romanticism" and the "predominance of the I" that Latin cultures were seeking to escape.[63]

Boulanger leveled much the same criticism at Richard Strauss in 1927, when *Der Rosenkavalier* returned to Paris.[64] The work, despite its "irresistible momentum," was full of "exaggerations." It lacked balance and unity. Only when discussing the very end of the third act, when the music "becomes concerned only with itself," does she desist from qualifying a compliment with a criticism. For all of Strauss's unrivaled skill as a composer, Boulanger concluded, "He lacks moderation, his style is composite, his melodies are facile and banal, but he has the prodigious power to create life, and he therefore raises himself above any aesthetic debates. His genius subdues them." Boulanger openly doubted that Strauss would continue to captivate and mesmerize the contemporary public using tricks—personality, effect, and eclecticism—not truths. Strauss, in her view, not only lacked a sense of formal balance and a respect for universal aesthetic values but the necessary conviction that music had an obligation to defend, through aesthetic means, a genuine moral order amid Maritain's "modernist crisis." After all, as Boulanger observed in 1919, "The role of the artist is to shed light on the Beauty that resides in everything, and the role of the audience is to try to perceive that Beauty gives meaning even to the most despondent life." The proper vehicle in music was "the work of art complete in itself."[65]

Gabriel Fauré became Boulanger's model for how aesthetic ideals could be realized by contemporary composers. In a 1922 essay on religious music she located the "splendor" of Fauré's music in his capacity to create a "balance between feeling and reason." His greatest and most lasting works have all been "tempered by the well-judged and incomparable sense of order." He achieved this with "simplicity" and "without affectation and never with brutality." Boulanger found virtues of "eternal durations," "gravity stripped of all disruption" in Fauré. She was grateful that much of his music seemed "too peaceful" to be "mixed with the agitations of modern life." A sense of "purity" in the beauty and form emerges because a "line goes from the first to the last measure, without a single weakness." The hectic machine-like pace and instability of modern life was at odds with her aesthetic.

The contrast between Fauré, Mahler, and Strauss defined Boulanger's ambitions as teacher, advocate, organizer, and performer in interwar France. The music she taught and performed were reflections of a belief system that countered the "agitations" of life and culture—Maritain's "modernist crisis." Boulanger's interwar convictions had sources beyond Maritain's early work. Her ideas were indebted to three French contributions on the link between art and modernity: Jean Cocteau's 1918 pamphlet *Le coq et l'arlequin*, Paul Valéry's dialogue *Eupalinos ou l'architecte* from 1921, and Maritain's 1922 augmented and expanded collection of essays titled *Antimoderne*.

Cocteau defined the end of the long nineteenth century. He attacked Romanticism and all that smacked of the bourgeois, including Baudelaire and Wagner. The new was hailed for its lack of popularity with the inherited audience, whose addiction to an undisciplined past was stultifying. Formal clarity was prized, making Bach, although German, preferable to Beethoven, and even Strauss superior to Puccini.[66] Nonetheless, Cocteau's plea against eclecticism and long-windedness was pointedly chauvinist; skill in using "boredom as a useful drug for the stupefaction of the faithful" was German. France, although a "monarchy of intellectuals," was more hospitable to young artists on account of the opposition of "the masses to the elite," the audience of the past.[67] Cocteau, for all his personal sympathy for Stravinsky (as opposed to Schoenberg, a "blackboard musician"), focused on Satie in his search, for "the music I want . . . must be French, of France." Satie, unlike Debussy, had not traveled from the "German frying pan into the Russian fire." Satie "teaches what, in our age is the greatest audacity, simplicity." The Impressionists, by contrast, "feared bareness, emptiness, and silence."[68]

The affirmative and comfortable "warm bath" of Wagnerism, the allure of "caressing strings," and the lavish theatricality of the Russian ballet and opera Diaghilev had brought to France before 1914 did not represent Cocteau's primary fears, for the victory over them seemed assured. Rather it was "machinery and American buildings."[69] Cocteau observed that they "resemble Greek art insofar as their utility endows them with an aridity and grandeur devoid of any superfluidity. But they are not art." A surface modernity located in style that highlighted the material technology of modern times but failed to be truly art was, for Cocteau as for Boulanger, the real danger. Genuine aesthetic modernism had to seize "the spirit of the age" and extract from its "aridity" an "antidote" to the belief that art that was useless, powerless, and a mere distraction. Art had to reclaim its power, and its utility.[70] Cocteau echoed Golberg and Maritain by claiming that true modern art's greatest ally was a tradition of invariant truth that "appears at every epoch under a different disguise," wearing masks that conceals it from the public. Nonetheless, new art had to be modern, since "reality alone motivates the important work of art." Art should not be "derived" from art alone, making the mask of modernity essential.

That mask was the simplicity of Satie's music.[71] Satie was tradition's true appearance in modern times.[72] It revealed the clarity and transparency of form, and the purity of expression Boulanger located in Fauré. It was new but eschewed the surface complexity of modernity, the industrial, and the mechanical. Using Satie, Cocteau called for a national spiritual renewal, a reassertion of a French classicism that was universally valid.[73] Ingres was the model, not Delacroix. Aestheticism and theatricality, even in Stravinsky, led to music that one listened to "with one's face in one's hands."[74]

The claim that the spiritual truth in works of art and music might appear out of touch with surface hallmarks of the modern age—skyscrapers, airplanes, electric lights, automobiles, standardized mass industrial production—and instead celebrate the simplicity of the classical as the mask of tradition in modernity was the line of argument that Paul Valéry, Boulanger's close friend and advisor, took up in 1921. In *Eupalinos*, his Socratic dialogue, Valéry sought to upend Bergson's emphasis on the dynamism of life, and on change and movement as emblematic of human action and progress.[75]

Valéry extended, in a systematic manner, Cocteau's essential insight: modernity requires the assertion and reassertion of clear, simple, timeless, stationary, permanent truths that manifest themselves in art. But Valéry underscored that the role art needed to play was to reestablish community and relationships between people, counteracting the radical individualization in society, and the isolation that the war and modern life had bequeathed. The two art forms that could frame human life with eternal unchanging values that linked beauty and truth and goodness—in the tradition of Plato—and shaped a community were public arts: architecture and music. Valéry did not construe their parallel essences on the formal similarities that German idealist philosophers identified. He associated their formal similarities with the larger public function and meaning music and architecture possessed. In architectural spaces, as with music played and heard, the dependence on formal unity, order, harmony, simplicity, and purity not imitative of nature was shared. On account of this common public nature, the immortality of the individual soul, and the metaphysical realm of ideas—spiritual truths—became collective as well as individual experiences. The great building became the site for the recognition of a shared humanity, just as the public concert, the opera, and collective music making at home all inspired encounters with empathy, harmony, and wisdom.

The virtue of the formal language of musical structures as well as of classical architectural beauty lies in their common artificiality. Valéry distinguished sound, a feature of music, from the "noise" of nature.[76] In architecture, design transformed natural materials and created spaces not found in nature. Permanence, solidity, and duration in architecture and music derived from their unique dependence on the human imagination. Valéry countered Bergson's stress on the dynamism of temporal change. In music and architecture, the immanent capacity to generate a "complete work of art" was permanent and immune to "the movement of nature" and therefore biological and historical time.[77] Boulanger, following Valéry, believed music and architecture to be singular in essence but dual in substance, combining intellect and intuition amid an overall metaphysical unity. For Valéry, they were "singular existences, true creatures of man, partaking of sight and of touch—or else hearing—but also of reason, number, and language."

Therefore, through architecture and music, despite the ravages of history, contact could be restored with Maritain's permanent essence of being. Valéry shared the conviction that the search for immortal truths demanded abandoning theatricality and the spectacular, placing constraints on a narcissistic sense of individualism and machine-like efficiency and utility. The task of the two arts was to reconstitute communities with a shared sense of the sanctity of the spiritual dimension of existence, and therefore immortal truths.

What was required in modernity were buildings that Valéry described as "singing" and "speaking" and music that invoked, by its formal logic, beauty with a lasting structural clarity created in the human soul. This audible beauty derived from self-referential relationships and contrasts, the use of sound and silence, and patterns and combinations of rhythm and lines. The crisis and agitation of the times required the normative aesthetic defiance of the priority of history as either progressive or evolutionary.

Music and architecture were privileged as vehicles of the timeless attributes of truth, beauty, and goodness because they "are then two arts which enclose man in man; or, rather, which enclose being in their work, and the soul in their acts and in the production of their acts." A "totality" emerges from art—"artificial" truths—cast externally ("in space") and into our consciousness ("our knowledge") that confirms our shared "essential" humanity. "By means of two arts," with stone (architecture) and air (music)—Valéry's images of space and time—humanity "wraps itself up" in "inner laws and will." Music defies mortality and the decay of all material substances; it acts as a form of "resistance" on behalf of the essential beauty, goodness, and immortality of the human soul.[78] Music's character is neither instrumental nor utilitarian. Its subject is being—existence—defined by its evocation of the relationship between one human and another, and therefore the communal presence and public power of being.

Valéry's defense of the inherent artificial but logical coherence of formal musical elements and values justified Boulanger's encouragement of a neoclassicism that was not ironic or uniform. New music that used the elements of music differently—such as the music of Karol Szymanowski, Alban Berg, and Béla Bartók—but along immortal and truthful lines, could embrace expression and feeling by strengthening the consciousness of being in the world. Beauty in music could be based on any kind of sound, rhythm, duration, and sonority, emancipating the "modern" in music from the necessity to be progressive or novel. It was the logic of construction and form and the authenticity of intuition that gave voice to the permanent criteria of beauty and greatness.

Valéry sought to defend the immortality of the soul and offer an idealized purpose for music: a role in overcoming pessimism and despair, byproducts of the war, the influenza pandemic of 1918, and the ensuing disorienting politics, dislocation, and poverty. What was still lacking for Boulanger was an overarching contemporary metaphysical theology. She found it in Maritain, whose first foray into aesthetics dates from the early 1920s. The revival of Thomism after the Great War sought to fill a perceived vacuum of values and collapse of certainty. Even experimental science seemed to lose its claim to objectivity with the advent of post-Newtonian physics. No anchor seemed left for rebuilding communities on a shared ethical basis. Only historically contingent values, such as nationalism and class consciousness, prevailed. Within a confused and contradictory moment in history, a hierarchy of absolute values was missing that could counteract economically and politically divisive ideologies fragmenting individuals and nations. These included anti-clerical politics and a philosophical discourse that denigrated the claims of religion.

The reinvention and restoration of Thomism sought to counter modernity with stabilizing absolute truths. Maritain's strategy resembled that of Cocteau and Valéry.[79] Maritain sought the "ultramodern" that reached beyond the corrosive aspects of the modern human condition and its value-vacuum. He contested a valid surface coherence within the contemporary conditions of life. Thomism offered "universal" validity, a contrast to the "narrowness" in vision of the present moment, and a corrective to the "errors" of the age that only favored the "moment." Thomism represented the "eternal." In philosophy and in art, eternal truths were never modern, but neither pointedly anti-modern. They were ultra-modern by virtue of a Thomist disregard for the truth of the transitory within history. The ultra-modern sought to draw out those truths hidden under the masks of contemporaneity. Maritain formulated a criterion of the new that bypassed the evolution of style. The task was not to "destroy" the new and contemporary but "to conquer it and transform it."[80]

This intellectual discourse helped justify Boulanger's catholicity in judgment regarding the sonorities and materials her students chose. She wished them to trust intuition to express their singularity. But she imposed strict criteria of craftsmanship and in the judgment of form, consistently looking for a linear organizing frame—a line—in which details could fit over the duration of a work of music. After the late 1920s, Boulanger became especially sympathetic to works with explicit religious intentions—Stravinsky's 1930 *Symphony of Psalms*, his *Mass* from the 1940s, and the 1955 *Canticum Sacrum*, and Poulenc's religious works, such as his 1936 Stravinskian *Litanies à la Vierge noire*. In these works the symmetry between aesthetic and moral ideals appeared easier to establish. Music, properly realized, seemed privileged to communicate a form of love and human empathy derived from the singular presence of God.

Maritain's evocation of a modernist crisis of values, visible and audible in the divergent and seemingly chaotic character of modern culture, was widely shared beyond France. In Italy, in Germany, and throughout the nations that once made up the Habsburg monarchy—all centers of musical culture—the loss of a spiritual center and of shared values that extended beyond money and power and the material realm was deeply felt. Two extremes—a decadent secular egotism and spirit of competitive individualism and the rise of mass anonymity and conformism—had come to define modern life. Fascism and nationalism exploited the perceived absence of shared spiritual values by appealing to the ideal of community. Their version of universality was at odds, however, with the Christian traditions of genuine religious faith to which Boulanger clung.

Boulanger understood the international scope of the crisis of belief and therefore expanded her effort to place music at the core of cultural renewal beyond France. She focused on America, as her tireless efforts on behalf of Franco-American cultural collaborations during the war and after indicate. Her ambition was not merely to gain American financial support for postwar French culture. Music, a spiritual guide to negotiating the extreme paradoxes, disappointments, and contradictions of modern life, was especially relevant for the Americans, who represented for most Europeans a frightening vision of the future: a calculating modern world dominated by high finance, massive factories, and a culture of individualism and possessiveness seemingly without transcendent meaning and community.

Maritain's search for a theological justification of absolute values in art was not confined to France or Catholicism. Martin Buber's *I and Thou*, a text with an almost musical structure (as one scholar has described it), was a philosophical meditation that appeared two years after Valéry's *Eupalinos*. The genesis of Buber's thoughts paralleled the evolution of Maritain's ideas. Buber (1878–1965), the eminent German-Jewish philosopher, began what became one of the most influential works of theology of the twentieth century in 1916. He finished a draft in 1919 and the final version in 1922. Buber's train of thought and views on the role of the aesthetic in the crisis in values of the 1920s reveal a historically revealing parallelism to his French contemporaries.[81]

Buber proposed a fundamental dualism in the existential condition of all humans similar to Pascal's separation of human reason from faith in God. Buber pursued Bergson's suggestion of a distinction between intellect and intuition (shared by Boulanger) and time and space, as well as Maritain's focus on ontology. Buber's contrast was between two ways of being. The self, the "I"—the consciousness of each individual—was (as for Valéry) inevitably and fundamentally relational in character. There were two fundamental patterns: I-It, and I-Thou. The former was the I in the world engaged by the senses, the isolated "world as experience." The I-Thou, in contrast, created relationships, all conceptual, in three directions: with nature, with other humans, and with spiritual entities. It is this third aspect of I-Thou that realizes "creating, thinking, and acting."[82]

The I-Thou demands the experience of other human beings; it demands a psychic acceptance of the necessity of reciprocity, the recognition that the I-Thou is sacred and timeless and transcends experience and the external world. It brings the individual into a permanent spiritual relation with truth. Without the I-Thou consciousness, individuality, even human love and identity—all aspects of the "tempests of causality" and part of the experience of sense perception and human logic—will remain trapped in the I-It, a tragically fragmentary expression of the gift of life. Empirical experience, Buber argued, "is remoteness from Thou." The "I-It" encompasses a limited sense of time and space. The I-Thou is beyond it and, in a manner reminiscent of Pascal, does not "cohere" with it. Buber did not argue for some form of other-worldly asceticism, a despising of the mortal and the body. Without I-It "a human being cannot live. But whoever lives only with that is not human."[83]

Buber arrived at a conclusion about art similar to Valéry. The "eternal origin of art" is that "a human being confronts a form that wants to become a work through him. Not a figment of his soul but something that appears to the soul and demands a soul's creative power. What is required is a deed that a man does with his whole being if he commits it and speaks with his being the basic word to the form that appears, then the creative power is released and the work comes into being." A work of art's power, given its form-giving essence, is to propel the individual trapped in purely an I-It existence to experience the I-Thou by art's capacity to create an "event of relation." The power of the work of art resides in itself, in its form. Architecture and music are fundamentally relational and imply the existence of I-Thou in a way that transcends nature and language and reveals the spiritual presence and ultimately the divine through its purity of form.[84]

The arts forge human relationships beyond the reach of language, thereby giving music, in Buber's scheme, a priority similar to that assigned by Valéry. Buber's aim was to generate a basis of belief in the universal, timeless presence of God, one that "erupts" in all of the differentiated historical eras of the past. The eruption requires the "lifting up" of the I-It and I-Thou into "divine form." That sharing in the eruption would create community since the presence of God through the aesthetic becomes located in "a mixture of the divine and the human," sharpening the consciousness of relationships and reciprocities. The "spirit" that can unite humankind, Buber concludes, "answers by beholding, a form-giving beholding." That form has an aesthetic character and "is a mixture of Thou and It." The task for the contemporary moment was the creation, in part through the aesthetic realm, of forms that suggest the presence of divine truth and goodness, thereby "renewing" the presence of humanity within the world.[85]

Buber, like Maritain, probed the pure experience of being. He described an inner spiritual transformation germane to modernity that offered resistance to materialism, despair, isolation, and skepticism, forging a basis for the reformation of community Valéry sought through music and architecture. The criterion of form—an aesthetic category—led to normative notions of existential truth. The case of Buber reveals how widespread and current Boulanger's interwar obsession with finding a comprehensive justification for art in modernity was.

But the European discourse about the need for a stabilizing and universal set of norms in the interwar period had little impact. Maritain may have provided Boulanger and her circle a theoretical justification for new music (especially after 1927, when Maritain retracted his diatribe against the Stravinsky of Le sacre) and for avoiding either an overt association with political radicalism of the sort endorsed by Hanns Eisler and Kurt Weill, or a radical break with the surfaces of cultural continuity (evidenced in Boulanger's consistent skepticism of Schoenberg and her affinity for Hindemith). But the aesthetic modernism Maritain preached, and Boulanger and Stravinsky practiced in the 1930s and early 1940s, for all its claims to being "ultra-modern" and not reactionary or restorative, found itself uncannily consistent—as in the cases of Boulanger's friends, the Italians Alfredo Casella, Francisco Malipiero, and above all, D'Annunzio—with the conservative, anti-democratic politics of the right.[86] This could not be said (Schoenberg's and Berg's quite reactionary political views aside) of Ernst Krenek, K. A. Hartmann, Eisler, and Weill, despite their disparate appropriations of classical practices and tradition in the writing of new music.

As the interwar years came to a close, the cultural milieu, and indeed the audience for music, remained what it had been before 1914: a mirror of hierarchy, biased toward those privileged by birth and wealth. High-art musical culture was still dominated by the aristocracy and the highly educated bourgeoisie. The realities of fragile democracies, rising Fascism, and Communism in Russia dwarfed the impact of aesthetic speculation. The Princesse de Polignac, a key figure in Boulanger's life in the 1930s, was an exemplar of how persistent the continuities in patronage, amateur participation, and the sources of commissions for new music were. Married into aristocracy and the heiress of a major industrial fortune, at once French and American, for all her enthusiasm for new music, for all her eccentricities and admirably unabashed lesbianism, she, like Boulanger, remained staunchly conservative in her views outside of art.[87]

Only in the Soviet Union, and later the Fascist regimes in Italy and Germany that went far beyond traditions of state subsidy of the arts under monarchical rule in the French Republic and in the Weimar period, was the domination of musical culture by elites of class and status along a pattern set in the *ancien régime* challenged. The middle classes that formed music's public in the nineteenth century still adapted to and imitated aristocratic habits and tastes. Fascism and Communism broke this structure as the state assumed a more comprehensive and, ironically, admiring attitude to the great traditions of classical music and explicitly appropriated a high-art musical culture on behalf of ideological uniformity and control over the mass of the population.[88]

The ethical, aesthetic, and political traditionalism shared by Boulanger, Stravinsky, and indeed the circle around Polignac, was suspicious of socialism, radical mass democracy, the anti-clericalism that characterized the Spanish Republic—and increasingly nostalgic for prewar social structure and order. This political conservatism veered, at times uncomfortably, as in the cases of Boulanger and Stravinsky, in the direction of authoritarianism, and an exclusionary nationalist sentiment (evident already in Cocteau in 1918) that encompassed anti-Semitism.[89]

This political conservatism fit well with a modernism often realized with humor and subtle irony, along classical ideals, replete with austere restraints, norms, and formal coherences, and even a Thomist revival with notions of God and the immortality of the soul in mind. It even permitted a proud, if hypocritical, anti-materialism, and a contempt for the reputed pragmatic and plain realism of America. Given the collaboration with the Nazi occupation by Alfred Cortot (whom Boulanger worked with and admired as a musician) and her close colleague Jean Françaix, the collaborationist Parisian musical salons (including that of Marie-Blanche de Polignac), and the vigorous participation in musical life under the occupation by many in Boulanger's circle (with the notable exceptions of Poulenc, Georges Auric, and Koechlin), Boulanger's emigration to America in 1940 was fortuitous. She was spared the danger of working with the Germans during the war and returned to France with an unimpeachable background for her post-1945 career.[90]

### World War II, the Atomic Age, and the Cold War

The second devastating historical rupture that Nadia Boulanger experienced was the Second World War. Not only was she displaced and forced to spend years, unhappily and unsettled, in America—despite steady employment at Boston's Francophile Longy School in Cambridge, at which many pro-Boulanger Harvard students, including Carter, Harold Shapero, and Leonard Bernstein had studied.[91] But she would return, as quickly as she could, to a France ravaged by war, severely divided, and compromised by a complex history of collaboration with genocide and crimes against humanity, and of resistance.

What could the role of music be, in the culture and consciousness of France, in 1946? Boulanger, writing in October of that year to introduce the new concert season, called on great living artists to equal those who were dead and asked audiences to grant contemporary composers the same respect. But she cautioned living composers against the use of convenient shortcuts, including eclecticism and a facile novelty, at the expense of structure, clarity, and order. She warned against the incorporation of artificial markers of fashionable contemporaneity unrelated to music's norms. Boulanger admonished composers to unite "instinct and intelligence" and "feeling and form," a necessary synthesis "to give birth to a viable form."[92] She held fast to the principle of an inherent dualism—comparable to that of mind and body—in musical beauty. The material and metaphysical could be balanced and brought together in a single coherent work of art.

But Boulanger's most significant message to audiences, performers, and composers after 1945 was that in a less than "utopian world," music's role was not to give in to the world of "sensation" and materiality and just mirror, as a form of entertainment, the defining character of contemporary history. The role of music was to "speak to that part of ourselves" that honors the "joys of the soul," the immortal and immutable part of human nature. Boulanger proclaimed:

> Perhaps we can, right now, take up again the torch that, in great times, illuminated the world in an enduring manner. These dreams of glory surmounting so much misery; this pride and this confidence, when everything is crumbling around us; these memories of greatness, when we see nothing but distress and we tremble at the future, can seem like a childish game. In truth it is too easy to despair, to give up. Certainly, our anguish is the result of great misfortune, but to my knowledge, the greatest advances of the spirit have never been stopped by misfortune. We all have, on our lips, the names of men whose efforts give humanity—today just as much as yesterday—its greatest dignity. It is believing in them and living in their shadow as well as in their light that we can find once again that which we believe we have lost.[93]

A more succinct confession of Boulanger's most cherished convictions would be hard to find. Music sheds light on all that transcends suffering. It lends dignity to human life as a glorious and profound expression of its soul and spirit. Music's spiritual function depends on formal virtues that have remained stable throughout the past and retain their validity in the present and future. The task of the contemporary composer was to lend distinctive expression to, rather than invent or discover, absolute values of beauty, truth, and goodness that had been lost in the misery and distress of the war, and "illuminate" the present world through art with the very same torch of aesthetic greatness present throughout history.

Although timeless greatness was defined by Boulanger in terms of formal and logical requirements for a work, its content needed to come from the composer's individual intuition about the nature of the misery and distress of the times. Composers faced a devastated landscape, a society consumed by a sense of loss, anguish, and misfortune and fear of the future. Boulanger's return to Paris from America led her to revisit the modernist crisis that had concerned her and her contemporaries in the 1920s.

In a Paris lecture on Fauré in the late 1940s Boulanger addressed a public still struggling economically and politically. It was dominated in its musical life by followers of Olivier Messiaen and Pierre Boulez.[94]

Boulanger, despite a religious sensibility shared with Messiaen (but without its mystical element) and affinities as organists and critics (for example, a shared admiration for Dukas), kept her distance.[95] Her position was "delicate," as her colleague Doda Conrad observed, wavering between hostility and cordiality.[96] As for Boulez, in the late 1940s and early 1950s the influence of Webern and Cage on the French composer was too strong for Boulanger.[97] Caught in these circumstances, Boulanger observed:

> We know ourselves to be witness to a crisis that seems to us like no other—to us, everything seems, everything is perhaps, in doubt. We believe that never before have the most contradictory principles battled one another with such violence. Unintentionally, tirelessly, we seek the causes of these crises that oppose, and have always opposed, skepticism and faith, opportunism and conscience, facility and rigor, violence and truth, and today, quantity and quality. We are troubled, and we are quick to conclude that we are in decline. . . . However, we also see the permanence of values that I would willingly describe as moral and spiritual in nature, indestructible values, and I have chosen as the center of this talk an artist who never put them in doubt.[98]

Boulanger's sense of "decline" was fueled by the specter of new music's displacement from the center of public culture and society, strengthened by a new vital popular music. Access to it was more compatible with mass transmission than were the traditions of classical concert music and opera. The desire on the part of a new generation of composers to break with history and distance themselves from the past prior to 1945 was far stronger than its counterpart in 1918. The enemy included the neoclassicism of the interwar years, not only the more regressive aesthetic ideologies linked to Fascism and Stalinism. Boulanger nonetheless remained resolute in her interwar construct of music's character, role, and mission. She believed music could be a bulwark against radicalism and commercialism, the unique threats she termed opportunism, skepticism, violence, quantity, and facility.

At the same time Boulanger realized why 1945 was different from 1918. As she put it, there was, in 1946, "a crisis," particularly of a "doubt . . . that seems to us like no other." This perception was shared by Maritain, who offered a revision and extension of his response to the "modernist crisis" of the early 1920s. In *The Person and the Common Good*, a volume that appeared in 1946 based on lectures given between 1939 and 1945, Maritain recast his interwar diagnosis and analysis as the need to find a path between the "errors of individualism" of the nineteenth century (whose logical end point would be anarchy) and the "totalitarian or excessively communal" reaction that had so far dominated twentieth-century history—fascism and communism (whose shared instrument was dictatorship). Maritain was in search of a third way, free from the twin extreme poles of egoism and mass conformity. His revised Thomistic solution sought the cultivation of "personality," an ideal type of the human character distinct from the ideal type of "individuality."[99]

Personality is the "subsistence of the spiritual soul." Individuality, in contrast, is confined to materiality, in which love atrophies, sense perception is heightened, and "man recoils into a vacuum veiled in frivolity." Worse, action driven by individuality is evil. Maritain's distinction between personality and individuality was reminiscent of Buber's dualistic distinction of I-Thou and I-It. "Personality" required a self-consciousness of being, an interiority to self that contained a "generosity and expansiveness" and a recognition of the relational spiritual nature of our being, and therefore a Rousseau-like sense of unity and solidarity with the rest of humankind.[100]

The empathy of personality then leads to contact with others, the making of art, and a "dialogue in which souls really communicate." The key consequence is that within communication, each person finds a "spiritual homeland": the whole universe of absolute values and the divine, the source of "those indefectible goods which are as pathways to the absolute Whole which transcends the world." Personality is linked by a movement to "the supreme center" of the absolute and the whole.[101]

Boulanger's post-1945 views mirror Maritain's claim (again echoing Buber) that "our art is but the servant and cooperator of this interior principle. The whole truth function of this art is to prune and to trim— operations in which both the individual and the person are interested—in such wise that, within the intimacy of the human being, the gravity of individuality diminishes and that of true personality and its generosity increases. Such an art, to be sure, is difficult."[102]

Maritain's sense of wholeness, disciplined restraint, accessibility, and spiritual connection to the "education and progress" of human beings all matched Boulanger's objectives for new music and reinforced her postwar ambitions as a teacher. Music became, once again, a potential antidote, a tool in the spiritual renewal of individuals and communities; the aesthetic, defined in absolute terms that gave coherence, balance, and continuity in form within musical time, could serve the cause of building communities in which the good was sustained by beauty against the threats of anarchy and despotism.

## Contemporary Parallels Beyond Catholicism

Boulanger's framing of her belief in the power of music after the second rupture in history she had witnessed, an unprecedented moment of hopelessness, placed her in alignment with the leading thinkers of the age. Her instinct corresponded not only to Maritain's verdict about what had been at stake in the war and what needed to be done in its wake. Writing in 1943 in the midst of the war, Paul Tillich (1886–1965), a leading Protestant theologian and Christian Socialist who fled from Germany to America, defined the cultural moment of modernity in terms similar to Boulanger. For Tillich, the postwar crisis stemmed from the "conformism" at the core of democracy and the "breakdown of harmonism" that had led to the rise of totalitarianism. Before 1939, Tillich argued, culture failed to "create common symbols of an ultimate, uniting and obligatory character," even though for most of the nineteenth century "the law of harmony seemed to overcome the dangers of a radical cultural liberalism."[103]

Tillich, without any suggestion of Maritain's Thomist epistemology or Boulanger's formalist ideas of unity, used a metaphor of music, harmony, to define the need for shared, unifying, universal coherences—a basis for cultural certainty—that could counteract both numbing conformism and a competing tolerance of radical individualism. Tillich's challenge was Boulanger's fierce "battle" of competing and contradictory values. Tillich, like Boulanger, warned of "a complete cultural disintegration" in the mood of the times, particularly among the young. He suggested that there were four feelings abroad in the postwar world that called out for "a sufficient amount of certain truths to guide the life of society": fear, uncertainty, loneliness, and meaninglessness.[104]

For Tillich, art could offer a sense of meaning that would support Maritain's ideal of personality and transcend modernity's materiality and style. Art possessed "import" (*Gehalt*) in its forms that offered the individual contact with the divine, the holy, and the sacred, and therefore the essence of being, divine and human.[105] What distinguished the crisis of the post-1945 world from the crisis of the interwar years was a pervasive internalized sense of powerlessness, passivity, isolation, and emptiness that no conventional political or religious ideology could reach. Art, with its capacity to get beyond the surface of a meaning tied to external reality, could achieve a deeper realism and expand the sense of being and meaning that revealed, to individuals, a deeper historical continuity between past and present.

Boulanger shared Tillich's suspicion that in the existential crisis of the atomic age and the Cold War, new art had a particular role to play, first in underscoring a common thread in history and therefore a sense of a shared humanity. In her remarks for a 1936 BBC broadcast, Boulanger had spoken of "a certain character or human type [that] continually reappears throughout the ages different in clothing, different in manner, different in language, but expressing a same thought, a same aspiration, a same emotion." The connection between Poulenc and the thirteenth century was not a "revival of an old form, but as a new form of an old spirit." Boulanger concluded: "The past lights the present but also the present the past, and creates new links between them."[106] Music offered access to Tillich's need for modes of communication that could bind humanity together and dispel the sense of isolation, loneliness, meaninglessness, and fear. "Music can save us," Boulanger declared in 1938, by returning us, through music's forms, "to the real spiritual values, without which nothing is worthwhile,"[107]

Like Tillich, Boulanger also feared the rise of crass conformism.[108] In her notes to the lecture on Fauré from the 1940s, she stressed the need for "sensitivity" and "taste," virtues cultivated by music, to make the "ear, the mind, the soul . . . disposed for Beauty . . . to what in us seeks to be elevated." Echoing Maritain, Boulanger assigned to music the task of counteracting mass culture, "a type of anonymity that is most destructive (annihilating?) for one's personality." The "game" of imitation and conformity in modern culture and life led, in Boulanger's view, to the brutal slaughter of civilians during the war: the devaluation and interchangeability of human life, of anyone being "able to take the place of another."

"Art," she concluded, "lends itself poorly to this type of conformism." Music has a special role since "when we are brought together, it is each and everyone's reaction that counts . . . the intelligent, profound response of one single listener is better than the submission of a filled room. Faced with such submission, the artist is in danger . . . he would forget that his real role is one in which everyone is committed . . . the composer on composing, the performer on transmitting, the audience on listening, and everyone seeking one shared goal: the work."[109] Like Maritain, Boulanger feared the allure of giving in to the "extreme," a modern music seeking mere individuality to fight modern mass conformism, and not cultivating "personality." Like Tillich, she sensed the divine not in the artist but in the formal properties and autonomy of the work of art. Its unity, line, and coherence can transmit, in its reception, the timelessness and permanence that undermine the discontinuities and leveling circumstances of contemporary life.

In her Fauré lecture Boulanger quoted a fragment from the notebooks of Valéry that gave expression to her theological conviction about the centrality of music in the postwar era, and the link between music and faith. "One thing alone in this world can count for a soul that is not base," Valéry wrote. "It is to convince oneself that one is not alone, and that one can truly exchange what one has that is most precious with the most precious in someone else. That same feeling is that which is at the root of faith—for faith consists of the assurance that one has of an intimate but infinite being, and of an exchange with him of undefinable presents and thoughts. *One feels him, therefore he exists.* Everything else has no value in comparison with this."[110] Not only the work of music and its evocation of continuity between past and present of the certainty of truths about beauty, order, and goodness, but music's collective, public function as a common experience counted. Through music, an "exchange"—Tillich's ideal of communication—takes place with others to form an experience that could counteract Tillich's four terrifying feelings of the postwar era.[111]

This outlook remained with Boulanger as her fame and reputation spread in the 1950s and 1960s in America, England, and behind the Iron Curtain, particularly in Poland.[112] In France she hewed to a *via media* to the end, distant from the extremes of individuality she associated with Boulez (despite her close scrutiny of his music and admiration of his talent), even though, ironically, he came to share with her many convictions about unity and structure in musical form.[113]

Boulanger's focus on the permanent formalist qualities of the work of art that cut through the differentiated stylistic history of music, and the work of art's capacity to resist the ravages and ruptures of history to assert a stability and constancy of meaning—a focus particularly present in the final decades of her teaching—bears a resemblance to ideas put forth by two significant social philosophers, Hannah Arendt and Herbert Marcuse. Their lives overlapped with Boulanger although she had with them, as with Buber and Tillich, no personal contact. But like Buber and Tillich, the arguments of Arendt and Marcuse became components of the broad intellectual horizon of her students and audience during the last quarter-century of her life.

Hannah Arendt (1906–1975) was motivated, particularly in her writings on the human condition in 1958 after Sputnik, by the question of "human capacities that grow out of the human condition and are permanent." How would it be possible for humanity to sustain the human, politically, in the context of "the modern world in which we live today" which "was born with the first atomic explosions"? How, through "an understanding of the nature of society" could humanity repair and protect the permanent virtues of the human condition from being "overcome by the advent of a new and yet unknown age."[114]

For Arendt, the human condition was marked by three activities: labor, work, and action. Arendt's foregrounding of action was rooted in her allegiance to speech, and therefore thinking, in language. This was essential to politics and the task of repair and protection. But in her consideration of work poetry, and by extension music, assumed a distinct prestige, for it counteracted the dehumanizing aspects of labor and a purely utilitarian and distinctly modern definition of the human purpose in terms of wage labor and material acquisition. These characteristics were exacerbated in modernity by the impermanence of the economic order, and the prominence of technological change, including scientific progress. Work in the form of art, however, provided the human experience objects that had no utility, no exchange value, and were unique and defied "equalization," particularly through the instrument of money. Even if one bought two paintings for the same price, they would still not become equalized, just as two performances of the same musical work were never equal.[115]

The "outstanding permanence of works of art" was most notable in poetry and music, the arts least dependent on physical materiality—art forms closely aligned to acquisition by memory, and therefore "durable" beyond any physical presence. They fostered remembrance and recollection, habits of mind that for Arendt were links to the human "desire for imperishability." Music defies the weight and significance of each individual by expressing the potential of an "inner" idea and mental image evocative of a metaphysical "life in its non-biological sense." Art suggests "objective standards of the world," a sense of the permanent and sacred character of the human that "can be neither the driving necessity of biological life and labor nor the utilitarian instrumentalism of fabrication and usage."[116]

Despite a wide gulf between them in political convictions and instincts, both Arendt and Boulanger shared a belief in the necessity of resistance, particularly to the weight of history and the pressures of rational utility and utilitarian value in a mass society. This inspired them to focus on the power of art to combat contemporary threats to a debased conception of humanity, and to foster a shared belief in the uniqueness of individuals, the creative power of personality, as well as in the necessity and potential of the human community and its conduct of politics.[117]

The focus on the power of resistance of art to conformity and standardization in values and mores shared by Boulanger and Arendt found an unlikely ally in Herbert Marcuse, who was eight years older than Arendt and a bit more than a decade younger than Boulanger. Marcuse's writings, notably *One-Dimensional Man*, published first in 1964, were familiar, directly or through the attention given to them in the mass media, to most of Boulanger's students in the last decade of her professional life.

Marcuse's ambition was to show that "human life is worth living" and "can be and ought to be made worth living" and to locate the means that "offer the greatest chance of an optimal development" of "individual needs and faculties with a minimum of toil and misery."[118] Marcuse's analysis pursued the line advanced by Buber, Maritain, and Valéry in the 1920s. The primacy of materialism, and an individuality that was purely instrumental in modern history, led to the suppression of an I-Thou relationship and a sense of community. This led to conformism, utility, and standardization in human consciousness, features that Marcuse brought into high relief. In contemporary society even art had become "an omnipresent ingredient of the administered society." Art, however, retained the potential of autonomy through its "powerless" and "illusory" use of "various forms of masks and silence."[119]

The terrifying reality Marcuse described in 1964 was a contemporary world of "smooth, reasonable, democratic unfreedom" in the advanced societies of Europe and North America, created by "technical progress," one that suppressed individuality, mechanized life, and curtailed freedom. Marcuse's aim was to expose the disappearance of autonomy and independence of thought, key's to Maritain's notion of "personality." Advanced industrial society successfully promotes "deceptive liberties" and the disfigurement of freedom as a free press that practices self-censorship and sells "freedom between brands and gadgets, making apparent freedom an instrument of domination. The individual is consumed and controlled by a new technological reality."[120]

That new reality represents a monopoly of a functional, empirically based control of all human activity, creating a "one-dimensional" reality that successfully renders religion and overtly spiritual movements and religious practice mere "ceremonial" parts of an all-pervasive consumerism, a "practical behaviorism." Domination and voluntary conformity and uniformity were achieved in the post–World War II economic boom under the "guise of affluence and liberty." This was sustained by "technological rationality." An "advanced technological society" succeeded in robbing the aesthetic of its power of resistance so valued by Arendt and Boulanger. The gap of refusal and resistance between art and society was closed in the postwar world. Art's historic "alienation" and its surface of rebellion even in the garb of the radical avant-garde (as Boulanger suspected) were appropriated as "commercials." If contemporary art had been stripped of its contradictions and its transcendent truth-telling function, so too were its "classics." For Marcuse both new music and that of Bach were fundamentally altered, robbed of whatever aspect of "the transcending truths" of art, the "the aesthetics of life and thought," they once contained.[121]

Marcuse understood that the values prized by Boulanger, particularly the conceit regarding the persistence of absolute invariant criteria of beauty and greatness, although possibly inherent in a work of art, had come to life in history as a privilege of "the few wealthy and educated" who flourished in a politically repressive society. The paradox, for Marcuse, of the democratization of education and communication in the twentieth century, in which Boulanger pioneered, was that great art became integrated as "cogs in a culture-machine which remakes their content." An initial "remoteness" in the aesthetic, an antagonism, contradiction, and estrangement that demonstrated the truth of all great art, old and new, was "flattened" out and the "intent and function" of the classics and the new transformed into affirmative parts of the aesthetics of "democratic domination."

"High culture," Boulanger's main concern, is liquidated in contemporary society as a "byproduct" of technological progress and the "conquest of scarcity." For Marcuse, a superficial progressive attack on high culture by disenfranchised groups, ostensibly evidence of dissent, justified by high art's history and chronological complicity with political oppression and economic injustice, becomes, itself a symptom and product of domination.[122] Art is an acceptable and affirmative form of negation that coheres with and sustains the reductive conformism controlled by concentrated power in economics and politics. The dismissal of high-culture traditions in favor of a commercial popular culture is itself based on access to comfort, and a pervasive self-delusion and redefinition of freedom and autonomy in life, work, politics, and culture.[123]

In this way technological progress invades all the secrets and longings of the individual. Individuality, any inner resistance to the one-dimensionality of contemporary life becomes impossible, since the "solitude" that could sustain the individual "against and beyond" society in the sense of authentic freedom of thought and action (a positive alternative to Tillich's loneliness), has been eliminated by rational technical and administrative means.[124]

For all of Marcuse's pessimism, at the end of *One-Dimensional Man*, he claims that "the aesthetic dimension still retains a freedom of expression."[125] Marcuse, like Arendt, Tillich, and Boulanger, never lost the belief that the great high-art tradition in painting, literature, and music (Marcuse was pointedly reticent about music, citing his ignorance, and quite consciously deferential to the near monopoly on the analysis of music jealously guarded by his colleague Adorno) precisely on account of their origins in past societies defined by economic and political injustice and tyranny. Art from that tradition contained an impregnable and eloquent resistance. The aesthetic communicated human truths and transcendent values. Marcuse shared Boulanger's faith in the ethical integrity of high art of beauty and greatness located in the work of art.

Marcuse came from a markedly different world than Boulanger, but they were aligned in the conviction that within contemporary life, amid a "modernist crisis," the aesthetic realm, art, past and present, had a role to play. The two ruptures in history over the more than ninety years between Boulanger's birth and death were so startling and threatening to her generation that it was possible, by the mid-1970s, for a conservative French Catholic with sympathies for monarchs and aristocrats and the culture of pre-revolutionary France and a German-Jewish émigré Marxist philosopher, who became a symbol for the radical revolutionaries of the 1960s, to find common ground in aesthetics.

In 1977, Marcuse published a slender volume, *The Aesthetic Dimension: Toward a Critique of Marxist Aesthetics*. He opened it with views directly reminiscent of Boulanger's defense of great music:

> I see the political potential of art in art itself. In the aesthetic form as such. Furthermore, I argue that by virtue of its aesthetic form, art is largely autonomous vis-à-vis the given social relations. In its autonomy art both protests these relations and at the same time transcends them. Thereby art subverts the dominant consciousness, the ordinary experience. . . . I term those works "authentic" or "great" which fulfill aesthetic criteria previously defined as constituent of "authentic" and "great" art. In defense, I would say that throughout the long history of art, and in spite of changes in taste, there is a standard which remains constant. This standard not only allows us to distinguish between "high" and "trivial" literature, opera and operetta, comedy and slapstick, but between good and bad art within these genres.[126]

Marcuse's affection for art, however, differed in that his defense of the aesthetic rested on art's inherent protest against oppressive social relations. Marcuse restricted the modifier "authentic" exclusively to art that was revolutionary and subversive of established reality through its power to communicate the possibility of genuine human freedom.[127] Boulanger's belief in absolute criteria of value in music and its "means" was detached from any ambition for social change. If anything, she welcomed art as affirmative of parallel stable hierarchies of status and power in politics and society. Yet they both assumed the validity of a timeless

standard of authenticity, beauty, and greatness located in formal characteristics that transcended the history of style. That standard justified a
distinction between high art and trivial art and commercial mass culture.
For Boulanger, as well as for Marcuse, Arendt, and Tillich, the aesthetic
dimension seemed crucial in the second half of the twentieth century in
the struggle for meaning, dignity, and freedom.

Boulanger's teaching, her work as performer, and her passionate
advocacy of certain composers of her lifetime, including Fauré, Françaix,
Markevitch, Poulenc, and above all, Lili Boulanger[128] and Stravinsky,
as well as her idolization of a particular past, including Monteverdi,
Palestrina, J. S. Bach, and Beethoven, were motivated, particularly after
World War I, by a fierce religious faith. Humanity and therefore truth,
a proper awe and belief in God and the soul were all in peril in contemporary life. Great and beautiful music, realized with consummate
craftsmanship and formal mastery, when shared with one's fellow citizens,
could retard the onslaught of an all-encompassing inhumanity, banality,
and ugliness in life. Boulanger was among the most influential apostles of
a set of beliefs rooted in religion that claimed for music in the great high-
art tradition, new and old, a universal ethical significance and character
that could be applied to contemporary life. Is it too much to hope that
in the twenty-first century, a thread of continuity from Boulanger can be
woven in defense of the past, present, and future practice of the traditions of music she cherished?

# NOTES

I would like to thank Byron Adams, Christopher Gibbs, and Irene Zedlacher for their advice and assistance. Jeanice Brooks was generous in guiding me to the scholarly literature and providing me with materials as yet unpublished. Karen Zorn was kind enough to give me access to the Boulanger materials in the archives of the Longy School of Music.

1. See the 1982 biography by Leonie Rosenstiel, *Nadia Boulanger: A Life in Music* (New York: W. W. Norton, 1982).

2. First and foremost are Jeanice Brooks, *The Musical Work of Nadia Boulanger: Performing Past and Future Between the War* (Cambridge: Cambridge University Press, 2013); see also Kimberly A. Francis, *Teaching Stravinsky: Nadia Boulanger and the Consecration of a Modernist Icon* (New York: Oxford University Press, 2015); and her edited volume, *Nadia Boulanger and the Stravinskys: A Selected Correspondence* (Rochester, NY: University of Rochester Press, 2018); as well as Jérome Spycket, *Nadia Boulanger*, trans. M. M. Shriver (Stuyvesant, NY: Pendragon Press, 1992); and Spycket's *A la recherche de Lili Boulanger* (Paris: Fayard, 2004). See the essays in Alexandra Laederich, *Nadia Boulanger et Lili Boulanger: Témoignages et études* (Lyon: Symétrie, 2007). The vast array of books on Boulanger also includes Alan Kendall, *The Tender Tyrant: Nadia Boulanger, A Life Devoted to Music* (London: Macdonald and Jane's, 1976); and Caroline Potter, *Nadia and Lili Boulanger* (London: Routledge, 2006); as well as reminiscences by Doda Conrad (see below); and Bruno Monsaingeon, *Mademoiselle: Conversations with Nadia Boulanger*, trans. Robyn Marsack (Manchester, UK: Carcanet, 1985). Recent literature on Lili Boulanger has also been helpful, including Fiorella Sassanelli, *Lili Boulanger: Frammenti ritrovati di una vita interrotta* (Barletta: Cafagna, 2018).

3. For background and context, the best sources are Jane F. Fulcher, *The Nation's Image* (Cambridge: Cambridge University Press, 1987); *The Composer as Intellectual: Music and Ideology in France* (New York: Oxford University Press, 2005); and *French Cultural Politics and Music: From the Dreyfus Affair to the First World War* (New York: Oxford University Press, 1999); Barbara L. Kelly, *Music and Ultra-Modernism in France: A Fragile Consensus, 1913–1939* (Cambridge: Boydell & Brewer, 2013); and Jann Pasler's magisterial *Composing the Citizen: Music as Public Utility in Third Republic France* (Berkeley: University of California Press, 2009).

4. On Boulanger's attitude to Wagner, see Doda Conrad, *Dodascalies: Ma chronique du XXe siècle* (Arles: Actes Sud, 1997), 143.

5. See Kenneth E. Silver, *Esprit de Corps: The Art of the Parisian Avant-Garde and the First World War, 1914–1925* (Princeton: Princeton University Press, 1989).

6. See Boulanger's view of the modern and Stravinsky (she mentions the Octet) in her 1925 *Lectures on Modern Music*, Rice Institute Pamphlet 13/2 (Houston: Rice, 1926), 113, and 178–95. On the Octet, see also her "Concerts Koussevitzky," *Monde musical* 34/21–22 (November 1923): 365 and 367.

7. Jeanice Brooks and Kimberly A. Francis, eds., *Nadia Boulanger: Thoughts on Music* (Rochester, NY: University of Rochester Press, forthcoming), 144. Hereafter NBTM. The pagination is from a typescript kindly sent to me, along with the French original texts (where appropriate), by Jeanice Brooks.

8. See the 1927 article on the "return" to Bach by Charles Koechlin, "Le 'Retour à Bach,'" in *Ecrits*, vol. 1: *Esthetique et langue musicale* (Sprimont, Belgium: Mardaga, 2006), 241–55.

9. Karin von Maur, ed., *Vom Klang der Bilder: Die Musik in der Kunst des 20. Jahrhunderts* (Munich: Prestel, 1985), 100–107, 332–33, 358, 368.

10. Brooks, *The Musical Work of Nadia Boulanger*, 154, 188.

11. The sources for Boulanger's writings are her published Rice Institute Lectures from January 1925: Nadia Boulanger, *Lectures on Modern Music* (1926), and NBTM.

12. NBTM, 120–23.

13. Ibid., 142.

14. Ibid., 136–37.

15. Ibid., 144 and 150.

16. Hofmannsthal was writing in response to the opening address at the centenary celebration of Mozart in Salzburg in 1899 by the celebration's organizer, the Viennese writer and critic Robert Hirschfeld, who would become an outspoken critic of Gustav Mahler. Hofmannsthal underscored Mozart as a counterweight to the conceits of modern culture. Mozart revealed the permanence of the essence of music in form in contrast to the contemporary tide of enthusiasm for change and innovation. Writing as "Loris," Hugo von Hofmannsthal, "Die Mozart-Zentenarfeier in Salzburg," in *Prosa* 1 (Frankfurt: S. Fischer, 1950), 45.

17. Richard Strauss, *Ariadne auf Naxos: Studien-Partitur* (Vienna: Richard Strauss Verlag 1996), 80–87 (rehearsal nos. 112– 17).

18. See the elegant and concise description of her studied conservatism and sense of order in her appearance, habits, tastes, and beliefs in the memoires of Igor Markevitch, who observed that nothing could be less "bohemian" than Boulanger. Markevitch, *Etre et avoir été: Memoires* (Paris: Editions Gallimard, 1980), 132–36.

19. See Rosenstiel, *Nadia Boulanger*, 271–72, and 298. Lennox Berkeley also admired the Princess of Polignac. Writing to Boulanger after Polignac's death, she was described as "the perfect patron." Sylvia Kahan, *Music's Modern Muse: A Life of Winnaretta Singer, Princesse de Polignac* (Rochester, NY: University of Rochester Press, 2003), 367.

20. Elliott Carter, *Collected Essays and Lectures, 1937–1995*, ed. Jonathan W. Bernard (Rochester, NY: University of Rochester Press, 1997), 282.

21. Rosenstiel, *Nadia Boulanger*, 356.

22. John Haynes Holmes, "Introduction," in Ernest Renan, *The Life of Jesus* (New York: Random House, 1927), 22–23.

23. Albert Schweitzer, *The Quest of the Historical Jesus*, trans. W. Montgomery (London: Adam and Charles Black, 1910), 180, 182, 188, 191–92.

24. See Renan, *The Life of Jesus*, 121–23, 381–92.

25. See the introduction and excellent selection of writings in M. F. N. Giglioli, ed. and trans., *Ernest Renan: What Is a Nation and Other Political Writings* (New York: Columbia University Press, 2018).

26. Pascal figures in the correspondence between Boulanger and her close friend Jean Roger-Ducasse (1873–1954). See *Lettres à Nadia Boulanger*, edited by Jacques Depaulis (Sprimont, Belgium: Mardaga, 1999), 48, 66, and 157. The Pascal edition used here is the translation by J. M. Cohen: Blaise Pascal, *The Pensées* (Baltimore: Penguin, 1961). The numbering lists page and paragraph, e.g., 126:364. The French edition used is Pascal, *Oeuvres complètes II,* ed. Michel Le Guern (Paris: Gallimard, 2000). The same numbering system applies.

27. Pascal, *The Pensées*, 37:31.

28. Ibid., 44–45:73–75 and 126:364.

29. Ibid., 258:745 and 746.

30. Ibid., 82:196.

31. Ibid., 82:199.

32. The English versions of Bergson are taken from Keith Ansell Pearson and John O. Maoilearca, eds., *Bergson: Key Writings* (London: Bloomsbury Academic, 2002). The French original texts are in Henri Bergson, *Oeuvres* (Paris: Presses Universitaires de France, 1970).

33. Pearson and Maoilearca, *Bergson: Key Writings*, 181.

34. Ibid., 251. Bergson used the explicit example of listening to a melody.

35. See the excellent discussion in Benedict Taylor, *The Melody of Time: Music and Temporality in the Romantic Era* (New York and London: Oxford University Press, 2015), 73–75. As Taylor rightly observes, there is a close resemblance between Bergson's ideas and those of Edmund Husserl (1859–1938), to the German contemporary philosopher, whose 1928 *Vorlesungen zur Phänomenologie des inneren Zeitbewusstseins* (Lectures on the Phenomenologie of the Inner Consciousness of Time) (Tübingen: Max Niemeyer, 1928/2000) included an explicit discussion of the perception of melody to make the case of the blurring of sharp distinctions between past and present, and the suspension of clock time perception within the experience of the musical form. See Husserl, *Vorlesungen*, 397–400.

36. Pearson and Maoilearca, *Bergson: Key Writings*, 218–19.

37. Ibid., 207–12.

38. Copland refers to Boulanger's use of the phrase "la grande ligne"; see Aaron Copland and Vivian Perlis, *Copland: 1900 Through 1942* (New York: St. Martin's, 1984), 67. Carter describes her preference for "linear beauties"; *Carter: Collected Essays*, 283. Boulanger herself used the phrase often. See NBMT, on Berlioz (330), Fauré (527), Mozart (420), in her tribute to Auguste Chapuis (388), on Honegger (375), and in a 1919 review (151–52).

39. Pearson and Maoilearca, *Bergson: Key Writings*, 97.

40. See the reaction to this controversy over time and space on the part of the composer Charles Koechlin (1867–1950), an older friend and colleague of Boulanger's, and an avid student of philosophy, published in 1926, "Le Temps et la Musique," in *Ecrits*, 1:225–40.

41. Pearson and Maoilearca, *Bergson: Key Writings*, 115.

42. The outstanding analysis of the debate over time between Bergson and Einstein is Jimena Canales, *The Physicist and the Philosopher: Einstein, Bergson, and the Debate that Changed Our Understanding of Time* (Princeton: Princeton University Press, 2015).

43. See Part 3 and 7 in Guillaume Apollinaire, *Méditations esthétiques: Les peintres cubistes* (Paris: Eugene Figuiere, 1913), 15–17 and 22–27.

44. Mecislas Golberg, *La morale des lignes* (Paris: Editions Allia, 2017), 83–84. Golberg used drawings by André Rouveyre, a friend of Apollinaire, as exemplary.

45. Ibid., 70, also 28. On Apollinaire's status, see Darius Milhaud, *My Happy Life: An Autobiography* (London: Marion Boyars, 1995), 82.

46. Golberg, *La morale des lignes*, 51–59.

47. For Golberg on Bergson, see ibid., 114–16.

48. Benda was an accomplished amateur pianist. His tastes were conventional and oddly Romantic—Beethoven, Chopin, and Wagner. He was skeptical of Debussy and Ravel. See the analysis of Benda's life, thought, and influence in Pascal Engel, *Les lois de l'Esprit: Julien Benda ou la raison* (Paris: Ithaque, 2012), 23.

49. Julien Benda, *The Treason of the Intellectuals*, trans. Richard Aldington (London and New York: Routledge, 2007/2017), 56–66, 80, and 89–92. I am using the edition with introduction by Roger Kimball.

50. Ibid., 90, 141.

51. Ibid., 71–76.

52. Ibid., 42–43.

53. Ibid., 49.

54. Ibid., 138, also 127–30.

55. Ibid., 138–39.

56. For a fine and parallel analysis of Maritain's influence within music, relationship with Stravinsky, and his aesthetic ideas, placed in the context of a close analysis of the genesis and first performance in 1934 of Stravinsky's theatrical extravaganza *Perséphone*, on which the composer worked with André Gide and Ida Rubinstein, a work particularly close to Nadia

Boulanger's heart, see the discussion in Tamara Levitz, *Modern Mysteries: Persephone* (New York: Oxford University Press, 2012), 93–94, 147–52, and 471–73. For an amplification of this discussion of Maritain, Boulanger, and music, see Kelly, *Music and Ultra-Modernism in France*, 195–214. Maritain's most celebrated work on art is *Art and Scholasticism* (Tacoma, WA: Cluny Media, 2016). This is a reprint of the 1932 English text that contains Maritain's revised and positive reassessment of Stravinsky from 1927, although later in the 1930s he would, as Levitz has observed, retreat from what he regarded as Stravinsky's overly material definition of form, made at the expense of its spiritual character.

57. The edition of Maritain's work on Bergson used here is Jacques Maritain, *Bergsonian Philosophy and Thomism* (Notre Dame, IN: University of Notre Dame Press, 2007), 27–28.

58. Ibid., 87, 113–14, 181–82.

59. Ibid., 15.

60. Ibid., 16.

61. Nadia Boulanger, "L'oeuvre théâtrale d'Albert Roussel," in *Albert Roussel: Hommage à Roussel,* a special volume of *La Revue musicale* (April 1929), 104–12.

62. On the Boulanger-Maritain relationship, see Markevitch, *Etre et avoir été*, 224–25.

63. Boulanger, (Le Jubilé de W. Mengelberg," *Monde musical* 31/11–12 (June 1920): 182–83. Mengelberg, a fierce advocate of Mahler's music, was a friend of Boulanger's. It is important to note, however, that Aaron Copland writes: "I discovered Mahler through Mademoiselle." They "pored over" *Das Lied von der Erde* in 1922, particularly the orchestration. Copland and Perlis, *Copland: 1900 Through 1942*, 65.

64. NBTM, 262–27.

65. NBTM, 129.

66. Jean Cocteau, *Le coq et l'arlequin: Notes autour de la musique* (reprint of the 19 March 1918 Paris pamphlet), 16, 21–25, 43.

67. Ibid., 11–12, 21–25.

68. Ibid., 52.

69. Ibid., 35–36.

70. Ibid., 50–51.

71. Ibid., 26–31.

72. On Boulanger's skepticism about Satie's "vulgarity," see NBTM, 257; and Kendall, *The Tender Tyrant*, 30.

73. On Cocteau and Satie, see Caroline Potter, *Erik Satie: A Parisian Composer and His World* (Woodbridge, UK: The Boydell Press, 2016), 79–86.

74. Cocteau, *Le coq et l'arlequin*, 35, 44, 55.

75. The English version and page references below are from Paul Valéry, *Dialogues*, trans. William McCausland Stewart (New York: Pantheon, 1956). The French text, second-page references, are from Paul Valery, *Eupalinos, L'ame et la danse: Dialogue de l'arbre* (Paris: Gallimard, 1945). Boulanger praises the work in a 1926 lecture. NBTM, 448.

76. Valéry, *Dialogues*, 100 (49).

77. Ibid., 129 (82).

78. Ibid., 96 (44) and 150 (106).

79. On Maritain and Cocteau, see Stephen Schloesser, "Maritain on Music: His Debt to Cocteau," in *Beauty, Art, and the Polis*, ed. Alice Ramos (Washington, D.C.: Catholic University of America Press, 2000), 176–89.

80. Jacques Maritain, *Antimoderne* (Paris: Editions de la Revue des Jeunes, 1922), 14–16, 25–26.

81. The citations in English for the Buber text are modified by me from Walter Kaufmann's translation and the edition Martin Buber, *I and Thou: A New Translation with a Prologue "I and Thou" and Notes by Walter Kaufmann* (New York: Charles Scribner's Sons, 1970). The German text used is Martin Buber, *Ich und Du*, 11th ed. (Heidelberg: Lambert Schneider, 1983).

82. Buber, *I and Thou*, 53–54, 84–85.
83. Ibid., 148–50.
84. Ibid., 166–67.
85. Ibid. See Paul Mendes-Flohr, *Martin Buber: A Life of Faith and Dissent* (New Haven: Yale University Press, 2019), 140–44.
86. On Malipiero and Boulanger, see Brooks, *The Musical Work*, 136. On Casella and Boulanger, see Kendall, *The Tender Tyrant*, 51.
87. See Kahan, *Music's Modern Muse*. On Polignac and Boulanger, see Conrad, *Dodascalies*, 144–49.
88. The position taken by Koechlin in 1938 was that artists needed to "aid" and "guide the people" along the path of the great high-art traditions, so that the masses become the true "guardians" and "creators" in the future. Koechlin, "La musique et le people," in *Ecrits*, vol. 2: *Musique et société* (Wavre, Belgium: Mardaga, 2009), 395–96.
89. Although one ought not make too much of associations, Boulanger was a friend and colleague of Olga Rudge, the American violinist, and of her lover, Ezra Pound. Rudge was a leader in the Vivaldi revival of the 1920s and an admirer of Mussolini's. She and Boulanger performed together at the Polignac salon and Pound and Boulanger dined together in 1939 with Harvard University's president. See Anne Conover, *Olga Rudge and Ezra Pound* (New Haven: Yale University Press, 2001), 136. See also Elliott Carter's account of Boulanger's response to the political and social crises of the 1930s in *Carter: Collected Essays*, 286–87, and Fulcher, *The Composer as Intellectual*, 116–17.
90. Karin le Bail, *La musique au pas: Etre musicien sous l'occupation* (Paris: CNRS Editions, 2016), 15–16, 70, 73, 213–16.
91. See the Longy School Nadia Boulanger archives that contain extensive evidence of Boulanger's complaints and frustrations during her years there, particularly about salary, duties, and deadlines. During the war years, however, Longy was hard pressed to meet its commitments. Particularly revealing is a letter exchange between Melville Smith, the director of Longy, and a Boulanger pupil, and Aaron Copland. Copland uncharacteristically exhibited frustration with Boulanger's demands and bluntly refused to help Smith, despite his sympathies for Smith's difficulties in dealing with Boulanger. Letters dated 23 and 28 March 1942, Longy Boulanger File 4.
92. NBTM, 314
93. NBTM, 314–15.
94. See Koechlin's diagnosis from 1949 of the musical scene and the options facing musical culture in Paris in "Art et liberté (Pour la tour d'avoir)." It is sympathetic to Boulanger's reliance on models of great art in her search for an affirmative modernist path that avoided a restorative reactionary conservatism as well as a sharp and ideologically rigid aesthetic radicalism. In *Ecrits*, 2:403–16.
95. See Jean Boivin, "Convictions religieuses et modernité musicale au Quebec: L'example de Nadia Boulanger et Olivier Messiaen, pedagogues et transmetteurs de renouveau musical," an indirect but suggestive final essay in the last section on Messiaen in the excellent collection *Musique, art et religion dans l'entre-deux-guerres*, ed. Sylvain Caron and Michel Duchesneau (Lyon: Symétrie, 2009), 443–69.
96. Doda Conrad, *Grandeur et mystère d'un mythe: 44 ans d'amitié avec Nadia Boulanger* (Paris: Editions Buchet/Chastel, 1995), 186–87.
97. For a helpful perspective on the postwar years in Paris with respect to Boulez, and indirectly on the context of Boulanger's activities, see the fine introduction to the English translation of the correspondence between John Cage and Boulez edited by Jean-Jacques Nattiez, *The Boulez–Cage Correspondence* (Cambridge: Cambridge University Press, 1993). Boulanger, however, respected Boulez, and studied his works. And she also took a careful look at the music of Webern. See also Kimberly Francis's article in this volume, "Boulanger and Atonality: A Reconsideration."

98. NBTM, 521–22.

99. Jacques Maritain, *The Person and the Common Good* (Notre Dame, IN: University Press of Notre Dame 1966), 31–46.

100. Ibid., 41.

101. Ibid., 46.

102. Ibid.

103. Paul Tillich, *The Protestant Era* (Chicago: University of Chicago Press, 1948), 244; on the postwar historical context see Mendes-Flohr, *Martin Buber*, 209.

104. Tillich, *The Protestant Era*, 245–47.

105. John Luther Adams, "Tillich's Concept of the Protestant Era," in ibid., 298–99.

106. NBTM, 540–42.

107. Ibid., 435 and 554n107.

108. Ibid., 535. See also Boulanger's notes "On Hearing" from the 1940s.

109. Ibid., 521–22.

110. Ibid., 529.

111. For Boulanger, Schoenberg was not an option. His music "forbid" an escape from rigid formalism; it was sterile and without emotion. See her review from 21 January 1947, in NBTM, 341–42. See also Barrett Ashley Johnson, *Training the Composer: A Comparative Study Between the Pedagogical Methodologies of Arnold Schoenberg and Nadia Boulanger* (Newcastle on Tyne: Cambridge Scholars Publishing, 2010). Boulanger was, in contrast, an admirer of Hindemith's textbooks, his exacting standards, and his approach to the training of composers.

112. See the list of postwar students in Kendall, *The Tender Tyrant*, 73; and on the Polish connection, see Andrea F. Bohlman and J. Mackenzie Pierce, "Friend and Force: Nadia Boulanger's Presence in Polish Musical Culture," in this volume, 229–53. See also Rosenstiel, *Nadia Boulanger*, 368–69.

113. See the 1994–95 discussion, "The Work: Whole or Fragment," on Pierre Boulez's ideas of fragment and form in the superb English-language edition of the Collège de France lectures, edited and translated by Jonathan Dunsby, Jonathan Goldman, and Arnold Whittall, *Pierre Boulez, Music Lessons* (Chicago: University of Chicago Press, 2019), 592–631.

114. Hannah Arendt, *The Human Condition* (Chicago and London: University of Chicago Press, 1958), 6.

115. Ibid., 167.

116. Ibid., 173–74.

117. Ibid., 247, 257, 324–25.

118. Herbert Marcuse, *One-Dimensional Man* (Boston: Beacon Press, 1964), xlii–xliii.

119. Ibid., 238–39.

120. Ibid., 56–64.

121. Ibid., 64–66.

122. See the comparable anxiety expressed by Boulanger in 1946, NBTM, 315.

123. Marcuse, *One-Dimensional Man*, 56–65, 76–77.

124. Ibid., 71.

125. Ibid., 247.

126. Herbert Marcuse, *The Aesthetic Dimension: Toward a Critique of Marxist Aesthetics* (Boston: Beacon Press, 1979), x.

127. Ibid., xi–xii.

128. On the reception of Lili Boulanger and Nadia's role, see Leslie Thayer Piper, "Musical Canonicity or Spiritual Canonization: The Persistence of Lili Boulanger's 'Unforgettable Image' and Its Implications for Reception," in *Das Andere: Eine Spurensuche in der Musikgeschichte des 19. und 20. Jahrhunderts*, ed. Annette Kreutziger-Herr (Frankfurt: Peter Lang, 1998), 321–33.

# Index

Note: page numbers followed by "n" indicate chapter endnotes.
Page numbers in italics refer to figures, captions, tables, and musical excerpts.
Throughout the index, NB refers to Nadia Boulanger.

# Notes on the Contributors

**Andrea F. Bohlman** is associate professor of music at the University of North Carolina at Chapel Hill, where she studies the political stakes of music making and sound in the twentieth and twenty-first centuries. Her monograph *Musical Solidarities: Political Action and Music in Late Twentieth-Century Poland* (Oxford University Press, 2020) grows out of a decade of research on the work of sound and music in the opposition to state socialism in Poland. She has received prizes and fellowships from the American Council of Learned Societies, the American Musicological Society, the Max Planck Institute for the History of Science, and the National Endowment for the Humanities. She coedited a special issue of *Twentieth-Century Music* with Peter McMurray devoted to tape and tape recording. In 2017, she received the Alfred Einstein Award of the American Musicological Society for her article "Solidarity, Song, and the Sound Document" (*Journal of Musicology*, 2016).

**Leon Botstein** is president and Leon Levy Professor in the Arts of Bard College and chancellor of the Open Society University Network (OSUN), as well as author of several books, and editor of *The Compleat Brahms* (Norton, 1999) and *The Musical Quarterly*. The music director of the American Symphony Orchestra and The Orchestra Now and conductor laureate of the Jerusalem Symphony Orchestra, he has recorded works by, among others, Szymanowski, Hartmann, Bruch, Dukas, Foulds, Toch, Dohnányi, Bruckner, Chausson, Richard Strauss, Mendelssohn, Popov, Shostakovich, and Liszt.

**Jeanice Brooks** is professor of music at the University of Southampton (UK). She is the author of *Courtly Song in Sixteenth-Century France* (University of Chicago Press, 2000) and *The Musical Work of Nadia Boulanger: Performing Past and Future Between the Wars* (Cambridge University Press, 2013), and co-editor of *Nadia Boulanger: Thoughts on Music* (University of Rochester Press, 2020). She also publishes on music in eighteenth-century Britain, and directs both the Austen Family Music Books project and the international Sound Heritage network devoted to research and interpretation of music in historic houses.

**Marie Duchêne-Thégarid** is a historian of music and lecturer in literature and musicology. Her doctoral thesis, *Élèves musiciens étrangers à Paris pendant l'entre-deux-guerres*, is a study of foreign musicians in Paris between the world wars. The author of articles about musical life in France during the first half of the twentieth century and of a monograph on the Geneva International Music Competition, she is particularly interested in the history of musical pedagogy and its cultural stakes within international cultural relations. She has also coordinated the development of the *Histoire de l'enseignement public de la musique en France au xix⁵ siècle*, a database of students of the Paris Conservatoire in the nineteenth century, a project of the French national agency for research (ANR).

**Annegret Fauser** is Cary C. Boshamer Distinguished Professor of Music at the University of North Carolina in Chapel Hill. Her research focuses on music of the nineteenth and twentieth centuries, especially that of France and the United States. She is the author of *Musical Encounters at the 1889 Paris World's Fair* (Boydell & Brewer, 2005), *Sounds of War: Music in the United States during World War II* (Oxford University Press, 2013), *The Politics of Musical Identity* (Routledge, 2015), and *Aaron Copland's "Appalachian Spring"* (Oxford University Press, 2017). Together with her co-editor, Michael A. Figueroa, she is in the process of publishing the volume *Performing Commemoration: Musical Reenactment and the Politics of Trauma* (University of Michigan Press, 2020).

**Kimberly Francis** is an associate professor of music at the University of Guelph, Canada. She is the author of *Teaching Stravinsky: Nadia Boulanger and the Consecration of a Modernist Icon* (Oxford University Press, 2015); the editor of *Nadia Boulanger and the Stravinskys: A Selected Correspondence* (University of Rochester Press, 2018); and co-editor of *Nadia Boulanger: Thoughts on Music* (University of Rochester Press, 2020). She currently serves as coeditor-in-chief for the Grove Music Online revision project on women, gender, and sexuality.

**Alexandra Laederich** is the executive director of the Centre international Nadia et Lili Boulanger. She holds a PhD in musicology and her publications on French music of the twentieth century include *Nadia Boulanger et Lili Boulanger, Témoignages et études* (editor, Symétrie, 2007); *Regards sur Debussy* (coedited with Myriam Chimènes, Fayard, 2013); *Créer, jouer, transmettre la musique de la IIIᵉ République à nos jours* (coedited with Anne Piéjus, Centre de documentation Claude Debussy, 2019).

**Anna Lehmann (translator)** has translated selected songs from Patrick Modiano's *Fonds de tiroir* for *Harper's Magazine*. Her translation of Yvan Pommaux's *All of Us* for The New York Review Children's Collection is short-listed in two categories for the 2020 Prix Albertine Jeunesse. Her translations of essays for *Nadia Boulanger and Her World* are her first contributions to the Bard Music Festival book series.

**Charlotte Mandell (translator)** is a literary translator who has translated over 40 books, including *Compass* by Mathias Enard, which was short-listed for the Man Booker International Prize in 2017 and which received the National Translation Award from the American Literary Translators Association in 2018. She is currently working on a new translation of the classic novel *Monsieur Teste* by Paul Valéry for NYRB Classics and on a book of previously unpublished short stories by Marcel Proust for Oneworld called *The Mysterious Correspondent and Other Stories*. Her translation of the first book of automatic writing, *The Magnetic Fields* by André Breton and Philippe Soupault, is forthcoming from NYRB Poets.

**Gayle Murchison** is associate professor of music at the College of William and Mary. She is the author of *The American Musical Stravinsky: The Style and Aesthetic of Copland's New American Music, the Early Works, 1921–1938* (University of Michigan Press, 2012), and has research interests in Afro-European studies and the music of social and cultural movements (such as the Harlem Renaissance and civil rights movements). She has published on William Grant Still, Mary Lou Williams, and the music of Zap Mama, and is currently editor of *Black Music Research Journal*.

**J. Mackenzie Pierce** is a former fellow at the United States Holocaust Memorial Museum in Washington D.C. and at the Polin Museum of the History of Polish Jews in Warsaw. His articles appear in *19th-Century Music*, *The Journal of Musicology,* and *The Cambridge Companion to Music and Fascism*, and his research has been supported through fellowships from the Kościuszko Foundation and the Beinecke Foundation. He holds a PhD in musicology from Cornell University.

**Cédric Segond-Genovesi** teaches musicology at the Sorbonne, and music pedagogy at the Université Paris-Saclay, where he directs the Centre de formation de musiciens intervenants (CFMI) for the training of preschool and primary school music educators. His research and publications concern the analysis and interpretation of music in France during the nineteenth and twentieth centuries, particularly in relation to the work of Nadia Boulanger. He has edited several books for Aedam Musicae, including the memoirs of the composer Alexandre Tansman (2013).

**Miranda Stewart (translator)**, a former academic, is currently a professional translator and interpreter. She holds degrees from Heriot-Watt University (BA Hons) in Interpreting and Translating, as well as a PhD in linguistics; she also holds a degree from Tours University (M-ès-L). Her research interests include interactional pragmatics, sociolinguistics, and translation theory. She now lectures mainly on translation, most recently at Sichuan University Chengdu (China).

*Aaron Copland and His World*
edited by Carol J. Oja and Judith Tick (2005)

*Franz Liszt and His World*
edited by Christopher H. Gibbs and Dana Gooley (2006)

*Edward Elgar and His World*
edited by Byron Adams (2007)

*Sergey Prokofiev and His World*
edited by Simon Morrison (2008)

*Brahms and His World* (revised edition)
edited by Walter Frisch and Kevin C. Karnes (2009)

*Richard Wagner and His World*
edited by Thomas S. Grey (2009)

*Alban Berg and His World*
edited by Christopher Hailey (2010)

*Jean Sibelius and His World*
edited by Daniel M. Grimley (2011)

*Camille Saint-Saëns and His World*
edited by Jann Pasler (2012)

*Stravinsky and His World*
edited by Tamara Levitz (2013)

*Franz Schubert and His World*
edited by Christopher H. Gibbs and Morten Solvik (2014)

*Carlos Chávez and His World*
edited by Leonora Saavedra (2015)

*Giacomo Puccini and His World*
edited by Arman Schwartz and Emanuele Senici (2016)

*Chopin and His World*
edited by Jonathan D. Bellman and Halina Goldberg (2017)

*Rimsky-Korsakov and His World*
edited by Marina Frolova-Walker (2018)

*Korngold and His World*
edited by Daniel Goldmark and Kevin C. Karnes (2019)